GREATER LONDON

its growth and development

through two thousand years

Greater London

ITS GROWTH AND DEVELOPMENT
THROUGH TWO THOUSAND YEARS

Christopher Trent

WITH 118 PHOTOGRAPHS BY THE
AUTHOR AND 26 PRINTS

 PHOENIX HOUSE LONDON

26475

Preface

I T H A S taken the leisure time of five years to compile this history of
Greater London from the earliest times to the present day, the first
synoptic history, I believe, that has been attempted of this highly
complex area of towns and villages which have become absorbed in one
of the greatest 'conurbations' in the world. I do not regard the time as
wasted. I have enjoyed every moment of it myself and hope that some
of the pleasure which I have taken in doing the work will communicate
itself to readers of the book.

I have approached the work from two standpoints. One has been
observation and study of the incredible number of links with the past
which Greater London still possesses. I have visited every building and
historic site which has been mentioned in the text and have, indeed,
photographed most of them. The other is study of local collections, old
prints, old books and much other fascinating material available in the
libraries of the metropolitan boroughs and of the local authorities
outside the old County of London.

I have received generous help, and in many cases offers of help which
even in five years I did not have the time to accept, from virtually every
librarian in the area and very many town clerks and other local officers.
I have had correspondence, invariably helpful, with almost two hundred librarians and local government officers in all. I should like to
mention every one of them, because all have contributed something to
my understanding of local history and, therefore, to the writing of this
book. I am sure they will realize that it is impossible to name them
all but I owe very special thanks to the following, who have drawn
my attention to various facets of the story which otherwise might
easily have escaped me. I acknowledge with special gratitude the help
given by:

Mr J. Thirsk, the Acton Borough Librarian, who lent me Baker's
Acton and gave me much helpful information.

Mr W. G. Fairchild, the Barking Borough Librarian, who lent me *The
Book of Barking*, published by the Barking Borough Council in 1931,
and *The History of Barking Abbey* by Loftus and Chettle.

Mr J. F. Mason, the Barnet Area Librarian of the Hertfordshire County Council, who prepared for me a most helpful bibliography of the district.

Mr J. W. Wilson, the Beckenham Borough Librarian, who lent me Borrowman's *Beckenham Past and Present* and notes prepared by Mr H. R. Copeland entitled 'From Village to Borough'.

Mr W. J. Hill, the Beddington and Wallington Borough Librarian, who made available to me a number of local publications written by himself for particular occasions, especially the brochure for the 1945 Civic Week.

Mr Lionel Kaye, Town Clerk of Bromley, who gave me information about the Roman temple at Warbank, Bromley Palace and several other matters.

Mr A. H. Watkins, the Bromley Borough Librarian, who lent me E. L. S. Horsburgh's excellent book on the history of the town.

The Headmaster of the Chingford County High School, who provided me with an admirable history prepared by members of the High School.

Mr T. E. Callander, the Croydon Borough Chief Librarian, who lent me a copy of Anderson's *Short Chronicle concerning the Parish of Croydon*.

Mr J. G. O'Leary, Dagenham Borough Librarian, who drew my attention to his admirable *Book of Dagenham*, one of the finest of all local histories.

Miss G. Johnson, the Chief Librarian, Dulwich Library, who lent me Blanch's *Ye Parish of Camerwell*.

Dr F. A. Toufar, the Ealing Borough Reference Librarian, who, apart from giving me most valuable advice, drew my attention to the Elizabethan census of Ealing and made this available to me, together with other source material.

Mr Gilbert Berry, the Erith Borough Librarian and Curator of the Borough Museum, who gave me much assistance, and one of whose colleagues showed me round the many interesting exhibits in the museum and gave me a vivid and scholarly commentary on them.

Mr W. S. Stevenson, the Hornsey Borough Librarian, who lent me Lloyd's *History of Highgate* and Howitt's *The Northern Heights of London*.

Mr C. A. Elliott, the Islington Borough Librarian, who lent me out-of-print copies of the official guide containing invaluable material about the history of the borough written by himself.

Mr F. J. Owen, the Kingston-upon-Thames Borough Librarian, who gave me most helpful assistance on the sources for the crowning of kings on the Coronation Stone, and on the reasons for coronations taking place at Kingston rather than at Winchester or London.

Mr F. C. Stevenson, the Leyton Borough Librarian, who provided most helpful information about the old houses still surviving in the borough.

Mr Evelyn Jowett, the Merton and Morden Borough Librarian, who drew my attention to the scholarly *History of Merton and Morden*, published by the Council.

Mr E. J. Adsett, the Mitcham Borough Librarian, who generously supplied me with a typescript copy of historical notes prepared by himself and published in the 1951 Festival brochure.

Mr F. N. McDonald, the Paddington Borough Librarian, who lent me Robins's *Paddington, Past and Present* and some out-of-print editions of the Chamber of Commerce Guide, and also supplied valuable information about the Tyburn Stone.

Mr G. H. Humby, the Librarian at the Romford Branch of the Essex County Library, who lent me Terry's *Memories of Old Romford* and made available to me the local history collection at the library.

Mr A. W. McClellan, the Director of Libraries and Museum for the Borough of Tottenham, who was instrumental in supplying me with a great deal of source material relating to the borough in general and Bruce Castle in particular.

Mr J. T. Gillett, the Willesden Borough Librarian, who lent me a copy of Potter's *Story of Willesden*, a most valuable work, and drew my attention to the Wood Manuscript Collection.

Mr C. H. Turner, the Woolwich Borough Librarian, and Curator of the Museum and Art Gallery, who lent me a copy of Gregory's *Story of Royal Eltham* and several brochures dealing with the palace and with the ancient history of Woolwich and, above all, supported my idea that the original purpose of Eltham Palace was for use as a hunting centre.

The foregoing list includes only a few of the many to whom I owe grateful thanks in compiling this book. Without their help it could scarcely have been written, certainly not with as much detail as I have been able to include.

CHRISTOPHER TRENT.

LONDON,
   March 1965.

Contents

Illustrations

PLATES

IN TEXT

Endpapers: London figures from the album of a tourist, Tobias Oelhafen von Schoellenbach, drawn in the last years of James I's reign. *By permission of the Trustees of the British Museum.*

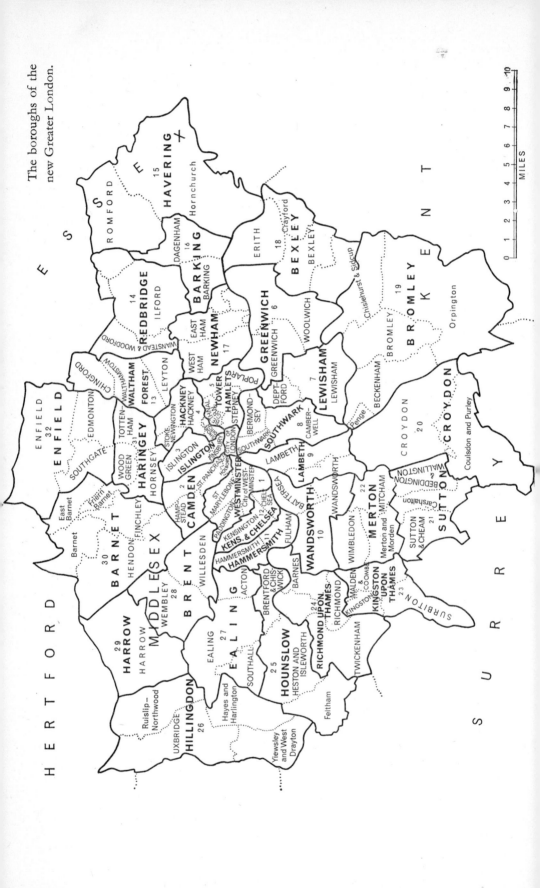

The boroughs of the new Greater London.

Introduction

In the spring of 1965 an event took place which directly or indirectly affects the lives of more than eight million people. Greater London came into existence as an administrative area, presided over by the Greater London Council, which was elected in 1964. It supplants the London County Council and the Middlesex County Council, as well as some of the local authorities on the outer fringe which fell within the counties of Surrey, Kent, Essex and Hertfordshire. It comprises thirty-two boroughs, all newly constituted and all except one materially larger than any of the old local government areas.

Every one of the thirty-two new boroughs is potentially an education unit, though it is bound to be some time before the London County Council system of unified control will be supplanted in the central areas. But the Greater London Council is the overall planning authority for the whole area of 616 square miles. It owes its existence to the recommendations of the Royal Commission on Local Government in Greater London, which reported in 1960, and is designed as a means of ensuring greater efficiency in local government over an area which amazingly includes nearly one-sixth of the total population of Great Britain, one of the largest and most populous conurbations (as the planners insist on calling them) in the world.

Harrow, officially Greater London Borough No. 29, is the only one of the previously existing local government areas which has remained virtually unchanged. Many have disappeared entirely from the map by being merged with their neighbours, even such famous places as Twickenham, which is now part of the borough of Richmond upon Thames, and Uxbridge, which has become part of the borough of Hillingdon.

A number of new names have made their appearance on the map. The borough of Camden, for instance, represents the merging of Hampstead, Holborn and St Pancras; the borough of Tower Hamlets, a particularly happy choice of a name, includes Bethnal Green, Poplar and Stepney, which were, in fact, once all hamlets administered from the Tower of London. Waltham Forest includes Chingford, Leyton

B

and Walthamstow. Redbridge is a combination of part of the urban district of Chigwell, part of Dagenham and the boroughs of Ilford, Wanstead and Woodford. Havering, another happy choice of a name, includes the borough of Romford and the urban district of Hornchurch, both part of the medieval Royal Liberty of Havering. Newham represents the administrative districts of West Ham and East Ham, together with part of Barking, Brent includes the old boroughs of Wembley and Willesden, and Haringey those of Hornsey, Tottenham and Wood Green.

This represents a major revolution, though one doubts whether people who have lived in Twickenham all their lives will now regard themselves as living in Richmond upon Thames, any more than people who lived in Eltham regarded themselves as Londoners when the metropolitan borough of Woolwich was created in 1899. Nor can one imagine Orpington people regarding themselves as Londoners rather than Kentish Men.

The revolution is all the greater because so many of the local government divisions which have been merged in these new boroughs have a continuous history of more than a thousand years. Many examples could be quoted but among them Bexley and Croydon are outstanding. Croydon is, indeed, an interesting example of the conservatism of administrative boundaries through a period of a thousand years. One thinks of it in the Middle Ages chiefly as the country home of the Archbishops of Canterbury, in contrast with modern Croydon, which is an immense industrial and commercial town and a London dormitory suburb. One might think that there was no possible link between the two. Yet Croydon in 1964 was virtually identical with the Croydon mentioned in a ninth-century charter. The parish of Croydon has always included all, or almost all, of the 12,000 acres which comprised the county borough of Croydon before it became part of Greater London.

One hamlet was detached from the parish in 1883, when the town was incorporated as a borough, and Addington, originally a parish in the rural district of Godstone, was added in 1928. But Addington is the only addition made to Croydon at least since the Norman Conquest. All the surrounding places which one tends to think of as separate towns, such as Norbury, Thornton Heath, Shirley, Norwood, Selhurst, Addiscombe, Waddon and Woodside, are hamlets or manors which fell within the mother parish of Croydon. Now Croydon, the Greater London borough, not only includes all those places but also the former independent urban district of Coulsdon and Purley, while its near neighbour Bromley, another ancient and historic parish, has been increased by the addition of Beckenham, Penge, Orpington and part of the local government district of Chislehurst and Sidcup. Many people with a feeling for local history regret this and many similar changes, but facts are facts, not proposals to be argued, and Greater London as an administrative unit is a reality.

In the following chapters the story of this vast administrative area of

616 square miles is told. And a very fascinating story it is, extending over two thousand years. It begins at a time when the Greater London area was thinly peopled, with only a few settlements, far more thinly peopled than the downlands of Sussex and Kent, and at a time when what we now know as the City of London was utterly deserted. It is a story of people, the people who have made Greater London, rather than of places, a commentary on constantly changing ways of living. Building, of course, has a place in it, but buildings are described only as a link between the present day and the people who built them and lived in them. So Victorian suburbs reflect the Victorian way of life, Hampton Court Palace the spirit of the wealthy in the sixteenth and seventeenth centuries. The squares of Bloomsbury help to fill in the detail of life in the then new Georgian suburbs.

It is the story, too, of why the people built their homes farther and farther from the commercial and administrative centre of the growing city. The towns and villages of the Greater London area fall naturally into the narrative as originally independent communities which became more and more closely linked with the metropolis until they were finally submerged, often after a period of individual expansion. The boundary between one community and another became no more than a line on a map, a line incidentally which for many has been obliterated with the formation of the Greater London boroughs.

The history of London as a town did not really begin until after the Claudian invasion of A.D. 43 and the foundation of Londinium only a few years afterwards. Londinium, the largest town in Roman Britain, was a centre of communications, a necessary link in the military and commercial traffic which flowed between the Channel ports and the northern limits of the Province. The Greater London area was traversed by a number of Roman roads, including the Watling Street, which connected the Channel ports with London, and London with north-west England, the Ermine Street, which started from London and continued to York and the northern frontier of the Province, and the Stane Street, which was the link between London and one of the most progressive centres of Romano-British culture at Chichester. Inevitably, therefore, a number of Roman settlements arose in the Greater London area, which became far more densely populated than it had ever been before.

Then came the fall of the outer Roman Empire and with it the decline of Londinium and the decay of many of these settlements, followed by the gradual recolonization of the area by Saxon invaders and the resurgence of London as the principal town of the kingdom of the East Saxons, and later as an independent community with unparalleled authority.

The bishopric of London covered almost the whole of what is now Greater London. Westminster Abbey was refounded and became one of the most important monastic foundations in the country. Kingston had a very special place in this period, too. By the time Norman William won the right of succession to the throne from Saxon Harold, the City of London had achieved the position which it was destined to hold for many centuries, of being a power in the land without the support of which a king could not rule, while Westminster had already achieved its own niche in history as the home of the kings and queens and an important ecclesiastical centre. From that time Greater London's history was divided into two parts, the development of two separate estates, the commercial and the administrative. To a remarkable extent these two estates have survived as separate entities and have remained true to their sites, with the City of London the commercial centre, remaining aloof from the administration of the rest of the London area, with special privileges and independent, if not of the Crown, at least of the government of London as a whole.

Westminster, too, has always remained the home of the royal family, whether the actual royal home has been the Abbey of Westminster, as in the case of Edward the Confessor, the Palace of Whitehall, St James's Palace or Buckingham Palace, while Parliament has also been closely associated with the royal palaces, retaining its conservatism of site right down to the present day with the modern Houses of Parliament only a few minutes' drive from Buckingham Palace.

In the period from A.D. 1000 to 1500 many of the towns and villages which are now integrated in Greater London—places such as Southwark, Barnet, Croydon, Twickenham, Kingston and Mitcham—developed a flourishing life of their own; the small farming communities within easy reach of the metropolis became linked with it because they could find a market for their produce in London. Before 1500, too, the first positive suburbs of London had been built outside the walls or across the river, the embryonic settlements which became Islington, Lambeth, Battersea and Chelsea. Although these were all independent of London they depended on it for their livelihood and many of the City's crafts were established in them.

In the sixteenth and seventeenth centuries the horizon of London expanded, with the river remaining the chief artery of commerce and almost the only means of travel. The building of Wolsey's Hampton Court Palace and the development of the palaces of Greenwich and Richmond were real landmarks in the story of London because they implanted the idea that wealthy or noble families whose main work was in London and Westminster could combine this work with a house and estate which was within easy reach of the twin cities by river.

The Great Fire of 1666 was another landmark in London's development because it gave a spur to its expansion outside the walls of the city, and accelerated even though it did not truly initiate the outward movement which has continued from then with very few breaks to the present day. Some small schemes of town planning had been carried out before, such as Inigo Jones's Covent Garden, Lincoln's Inn Fields and one or two other sites in Bloomsbury. But the aftermath of the Great Fire was a vast increase in land speculation and building both for the wealthy and the middle class, so that during the last decades of the seventeenth century and the first half of the eighteenth century almost the whole of the West End took shape, as well as most of Bloomsbury. By the time of John Nash at the beginning of the nineteenth century the cities of London and Westminster, and the greater part of the West End as far as Regent's Park and the Edgware Road, as well as large areas to the east of the Tower, were covered in bricks and stucco.

There was a parallel but less massive expansion in the still independent towns and villages of Greater London, including 'Royal' Kensington, which grew with remarkable speed from the time William III made Nottingham House a royal palace. There are still many Georgian houses in places such as Mitcham and Bromley, although these were still linked only by economic ties with the metropolis. Places like Richmond were becoming fashionable and in the heyday of the coaching era travel became possible for the ever-increasing number of middle-class people instead of being the prerogative of the wealthy.

The building of the railways was the next great landmark in Greater London's story. They changed the picture completely and made it possible for the clerk or craftsman to emulate the example of his employer and find a home for himself outside the confines of the still crowded city, travelling to his work by train every day. While the wealthy merchants were still building homes close to the country stations and travelled daily into London by first class, their assistants were beginning to rent small houses built by speculative builders and travelled third class by the same trains. The inevitable result was that many of the formerly independent suburbs were submerged. By the end of the nineteenth century the whole of the area of what became the County of London was so densely populated that local government became a major problem, partly resolved by the Act which created the County of London in 1888.

The creation of a County of London could not stop the outward expansion. Almost before the metropolitan boroughs were delineated ten years later, suburban London had spread far beyond them. Travel by car was added to travel by rail. Expansion was once more accelerated, and as arterial roads took the place of railways for the carriage of many kinds of goods, industry also spread out into the more distant suburbs. Finally, with the dispersal of population from central London, a continuing process since the beginning of the nineteenth century but vastly increased by the destruction of buildings in the war of 1939–45, the area administered by the London County Council no longer represented in any way the limits of the new Greater London. Since the London County Council was formed central London's population has decreased by 25 per cent, while that of outer London has increased by 500 per cent.

That is the background of the formation of this new administrative colossus, which includes not only the territory of the old London County Council and the whole of Middlesex, apart from a fragment which has been transferred to Surrey, but also sizable and densely populated areas of what were formerly Kent, Surrey, Essex and Hertfordshire.

1. The Birth of a City

WE KNOW man of the Old Stone Age by the weapons and implements which he fashioned, mainly from flint, and in the later stages of his development by traces of his skill in the arts and crafts preserved in caves. It is almost certain that man in the sense of a being fairly described as *homo sapiens* was living a nomadic, precarious existence half a million years ago. By contrast with this vast period of time the story of London, that is, of what is now the City of London, comprehends barely two thousand years and in that comparatively short period there are gaps in our knowledge.

Settled life in Britain began little more than four thousand years ago, when the people of the New Stone Age migrated from the Continent and established an advanced culture in southern and south-eastern England about 2300 B.C. They were followed by other peoples whose power was based on knowledge of previously untried raw materials. The weapons of New Stone Age men were of stone or wood, occasionally of bone or antler. Great as was their skill in fashioning these materials into efficient weapons, they were no match for a people armed with bronze spears and swords. So the Bronze Age inevitably succeeded the New Stone Age and this in turn was superseded by an Iron Age in which most of the weapons of war and the implements of daily life were fashioned from iron.

During the latter part of the Early Iron Age recorded history and prehistory meet on common ground. The expansion of the Roman Empire towards northern Europe was the spur which drove the Belgic people to explore the still thinly peopled country of southern and eastern England. The first migrations of the Early Iron Age people are dated to the beginning of the fifth century B.C. The invasions of the Belgae, a people of mixed Germanic and Celtic origin, did not begin until the first century B.C., only two or three decades before Julius Caesar carried out his first reconnaissance in force of Britain from his base in Gaul.

No evidence suggests that the area which became the Roman town of Londinium and the modern City of London had a settled population

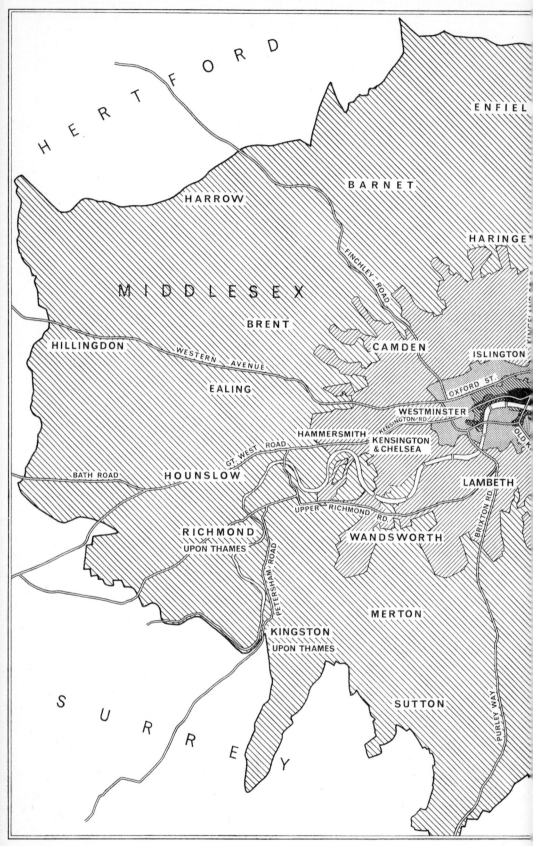

The growth of London through the centuries.

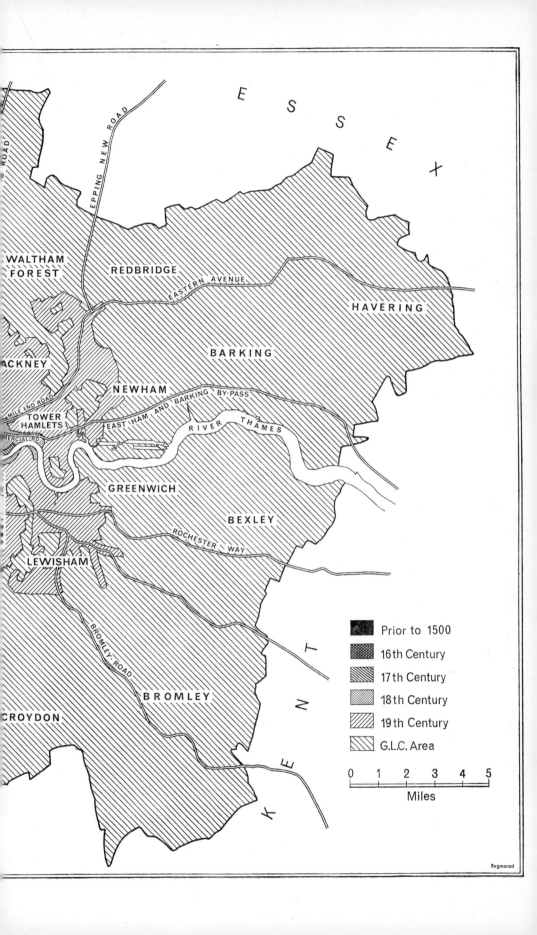

E   S   S   E   X

EPPING NEW ROAD

WALTHAM
FOREST

REDBRIDGE

EASTERN   AVENUE

HAVERING

HACKNEY

BARKING

NEWHAM

MILE END ROAD

TOWER
HAMLETS

EAST HAM AND BARKING BY-PASS

COMMERCIAL RD.

RIVER   THAMES

GREENWICH

BEXLEY

LEWISHAM

ROCHESTER   WAY

BROMLEY ROAD

K   E   N   T

BROMLEY

CROYDON

	Prior to 1500
	16th Century
	17th Century
	18th Century
	19th Century
	G.L.C. Area

0   1   2   3   4   5
Miles

Regmarad

before Caesar's expeditions in 55 and 54 B.C. It is most likely that no colony existed between the Fleet River and Aldgate before the beginning of the Christian era. To all intents and purposes London was founded by the Romans and the modern city is directly descended from the Roman town.

In the Greater London area, however, a number of settlements had been made before that time, though few of importance. The reason for this can be found in the geology of the London Basin. This is an integral part of the massive formation of chalk which dominates the landscapes in the greater part of southern England, from Dorset to Kent, and from Sussex northward to the East Anglian Heights, and even farther north to Lincolnshire and East Yorkshire. When the chalk was uplifted from the sea bed in which it was laid down it emerged in a series of ridges and troughs, synclines and anticlines in the terms of modern geology. One of the ridges rose like a dome above what is now the Weald of Surrey and Sussex (the dome has since been completely eroded away), then dipped down under the London Basin, rising again on the farther side to the north.

Vestigial remains of this great chalk formation appear in the downs of Sussex, Surrey and Kent, and in the Chiltern Hills. The London Basin stretches in effect from the escarpment of the North Downs towards the escarpment of the Chiltern Hills and their easterly extension. In this trough later sediments have been deposited and these now rather than the original chalk are the dominant factors in the landscape. The River Thames runs from west to east through its centre and in the course of its evolution has deposited considerable quantities of gravel, and in more recent geological time, valuable deposits of loam near its course when it has been in flood.

Almost all the rest of the Greater London area is covered in thick deposits of London Clay, the soil derived from which is peculiarly glutinous and presented uncommonly severe difficulties to primitive cultivators. Indeed it still gives great difficulty, unless fortified with fertilizers or with an admixture of sand, to millions of enthusiastic gardeners who are called on to turn a fragment of heavy clay field into a haven of beauty and colour.

To these factors must be added the certain knowledge that for long periods prior to the Christian era southern England had a wetter climate than it has today. The result was the formation of a dense cover of vegetation which ultimately clogged the natural watercourses of the rivers. Thus came into existence the great forests of Essex and Middlesex, in which the oak predominated and multiplied by natural regeneration. Still more important, an undergrowth mainly of brambles and thorn of great density made movement across these forest tracts wellnigh impossible until the land had been cleared and forest trails not only blazed across it but continuously maintained.

This, then, was unsuitable terrain for primitive man, whereas the chalk downs were ideal because of their absence of undergrowth and the porosity of the soils based on the chalk. The gravels were almost equally suitable, though the gravel lands were peopled generally later than the chalk. But the areas in which the London Clay predominated remained uninhabited until Roman times. To complete the picture we must remember that the lower Thames was bordered by an area of marshland of varying width. The same would be true today if it were not for the embankments, the first of which were built under the supervision of Roman engineers. The marshes were much less extensive above the site of London than below it. So even when groups of people began to desert the chalk highlands for the richer but more difficult soils of the valleys, they naturally settled on the alluvial land higher upstream. The area of Greater London held out no inducement except where the subsoil was composed of gravels, particularly in the extensive gravel beds which reach in an arc from Richmond and Wimbledon across South London to Blackheath and Charlton, and to a lesser extent the gravels on either side of the Lea Valley.

The geography of southern England has changed so much since Palaeolithic man first set foot in it that it is impossible to relate finds of Palaeolithic implements to inhabitation in the country as we know it today. After all, England was part of the continent of Europe at least until ten thousand years ago, when there was not only a land bridge linking south-east England with north-west France but the bed of the North Sea was exposed and there were ways across the marshland which was later engulfed by the sea (the rise in the level of the sea was caused by the release of water which had been locked up for thousands of years in the polar ice caps as climatic conditions improved). However, it is of interest that even in the centre of London Palaeolithic implements have been discovered during excavations for laying the foundations of modern buildings. Piccadilly, Whitehall and Millbank have all yielded their treasures, and, further afield, Battersea and Hackney. Several have been found during archaeological exploration of Wimbledon Common. In Acton not only individual weapons have been identified but a workshop floor on which the weapons were manufactured. This has been dated to the period known as Mousterian, perhaps 100,000 years ago, when most of the weapons and implements were made from flakes struck off flint cores rather than from the cores themselves.

When we come to the Neolithic period we are approaching much nearer to the realities of our own times, for then, only about four thousand years ago, the geography of the district was not so very different from what it is today apart, of course, from the immense visual changes which have taken place through the clearing of the forests and the working of the land. As Neolithic culture was centred on the chalk downlands, it is natural to find the most significant signs of Neolithic occupation in the area around Keston and Hayes, which

adjoins the chalk country and where a fine ridge of sandy or gravelly
countryside reaches up towards the foothills of the downs.

That is the background of the 'hut circles' on Hayes Common which
have been identified with probability, if not certainty, as depressions
which formed the foundations of the huts of wattle and daub in which
New Stone Age man lived. There is no doubt that the workshop floor
discovered in the same district dates from the period. A number of
Neolithic implements have been found also at Carshalton and in the
Coulsdon Common area in association with occupation sites similar to
those in the Hayes-Keston area. A find of special interest at Kenley was
that of a stone axe which (from the nature of the stone) must have been
fabricated in Devonshire. Limited commerce was carried on by the
trade routes which were established about 2000 B.C. across the uplands
of southern England.

Excavation in Toot Wood at Beckenham brought to light weapons
of similar date. Others have been discovered in almost every district
which was free of thick undergrowth. Some areas, such as Wimbledon
Common, appear to have attracted the peoples of every age. This is one
of the few places within Greater London where an occupation site of
the earlier Mesolithic Age has been discovered.

The succeeding Bronze Age has left no visible trace of permanent or
semi-permanent inhabitation like the hut circles of Hayes, but many
articles of bronze have been found, either by systematic excavation or
accidentally when industrial excavation has been taking place. Some of
the most important of the discoveries relating to the Bronze Age have
been 'hoards', a family's collection of weapons, implements or utensils,
buried, perhaps, to prevent their being stolen by a raider, or left in a
safe place during an absence that was meant to be temporary. Some may
have been the stock of a fmaily which was wiped out by illness or the
attack of a neighbouring tribe.

The possession of such bronze hoards presupposes at least a semi-
permanent bivouac, even as an interval in a nomadic life. This thought
is underlined by the number of founders' hoards which have also been
identified, that is, the working materials of a family or group engaged
in manufacturing objects from bronze, presumably for sale as well as
for their own use. Founders' hoards have come to light in a remarkable
diversity of places, on the high ground of Kensington, for instance, and
near Dagenham and Romford. A site near Bexleyheath revealed not
only a bronze founder's hoard and another hoard of Neolithic axes, but
a gold hoard also dating from the late Bronze Age, a quite remarkable
series of discoveries within a small area. In Surrey, founders' hoards
from Beddington and Croydon are of exceptional interest, as also is an
Essex example found at Bromley-by-Bow.

The West Wickham-Hayes-Keston area of Kent has been as prolific
of Bronze Age discoveries as of Neolithic ones, with one certain and
one probable founder's hoard and a number of bronze weapons in

various styles of workmanship, suggesting inhabitation over a long period. Hundreds or thousands of links with the more distant past of the London Basin must have been lost or destroyed in the centuries of urban expansion, before archaeology had become a branch of scientific inquiry, before the value or meaning of objects found during excavation could be appreciated by anyone working on the spot. That is true to a lesser extent of the remains of that part of the Early Iron Age culture which immediately preceded the development of a Roman-type civilization in Britain. However, the Early Iron Age is different from all that had gone before in the story of Greater London, if only because it is the first age with which there are still clearly visible links at surface level. Everyone who has walked across Wimbledon Common must know Caesar's Camp, where the earthworks surrounding an oval enclosure are still well marked.

The earthworks have no connection with Caesar or his legionaries; the very name is a relatively modern one, invented when it was the custom to ascribe anything unexplainable either to the devil or to Caesar. The 'camp' has been excavated and has proved beyond doubt to be an Iron Age entrenchment, probably of the third century B.C., well before the Belgic invaders had overrun south-eastern England. It is a defensive earthwork which makes use of the natural slope of the land. Its purpose was to provide a refuge for the people of the settlement and their cattle in case of attack, well placed strategically as a look-out and well placed, too, in relation to a supply of fresh water, which was an essential prerequisite for any ancient settlement. Here a spring known as Caesar's Well has been harnessed to a modern drinking fountain. It must have been equally effective just over two thousand years ago.

Loughton Camp, just outside the boundaries of Greater London, though its entrenchments are obscured by the trees of Epping Forest, is of a similar type and there is clear evidence of other Iron Age settlements near Walthamstow and at Keston, where there was a fort which made even more use of the natural slope than Wimbledon's camp, though smaller than the latter and possibly only intended as a cattle enclosure.

If these are rather meagre survivals from a period only a few centuries before the Roman occupation, many parts of the London area have revealed unmistakable proof of habitation during the Iron Age in the form of pottery fragments and a very large number of battered iron weapons and utensils. The pottery is the most interesting group of Iron Age objects, because its existence virtually proves local inhabitation during this period. Its absence on Cornhill and Ludgate Hill is equally strong evidence that London's gravel hills were not inhabited at the time. Finds have been most frequent once again in the country of the gravel beds and on the fringe of the downland country, often only just below the present ground level. In the immediate neighbourhood of Orpington, for instance, fragments of Iron Age ware characteristic of the first waves of invasion in the fourth and third centuries and of the

Belgic invasions in the first century B.C. have been found on several sites, while on others Belgic and Roman pottery have been found together, and Belgic pottery on the site of Roman houses of which the foundations were traceable, illustrating vividly the easy transition from the British world of the Belgic peoples to the world of the Roman Province. During the last century B.C. and the first half of the first century A.D., before Britain had been annexed to Rome, the links between the two countries grew closer. Trade routes were opened up which might well have brought Roman-type pottery to the Belgic people of Britain.

Lambeth is the nearest place to the city at which Iron Age pottery has been identified positively, but even this find may be misleading because it is likely that the fragments were deposited there by the river in spate. There is no doubt, however, about the finds at Enfield or Stanmore, where there seems to have been a Belgic settlement, or for that matter at Addington and Chingford and the high ground to the north of Ilford, and at several places on the southern outskirts of London, such as Beddington.

Caesar's expeditions to Britain made little impact on the London region. He is known to have crossed the Thames and fought successful engagements against the Belgic people, but his own account gives no substantial clue to the point at which he crossed the river or the route which he followed across the clay lands. By then the Belgic people had spread their influence over the greater part of south-eastern England and had made a beginning at least in the long-drawn-out process of clearing the forests of Middlesex, Hertfordshire and Essex, though it was nearly fifteen hundred years before the process could be said to be complete.

Caesar's expeditions achieved one important object. They brought home to the Belgic people that they were still not out of range of Roman arms by virtue of having crossed the Channel. As the next hundred years passed without incident many of their leaders must have thought that the danger was a remote one. In this period they were joined by many other groups of refugees from the Roman Government of Gaul, and a number of towns rather than small settlements were founded, including Colchester, Silchester and Chichester, but still the site of London remained undeveloped and the Greater London area only thinly peopled. Trade with the Roman world was increasing and many of the British chieftains were in alliance with Rome.

When the Imperial Government found an opportunity to carry out Caesar's plan for the annexation of Britain, a plan which had been pigeon-holed for a century, it made no mistake. A sizable army landed in Kent and encountered little organized opposition, then, with the Emperor Claudius at its head, marched on to complete the conquest of the south-east and celebrate its victory by marching in triumph into the Belgic town of Colchester.

That was in A.D. 43. Within ten years at the most a Roman town had sprung up on the slopes of Cornhill and traffic from the Continent was passing through it on its way to East Anglia and to the defensive positions which had been built against the potential enemies of Rome in the north and west. So began the history of London as a town. It owed its origin to its position at the lowest point at which the Thames could be forded or bridged. No crossing for heavy traffic could be made lower downstream because there was no place at which there was dry land and a good surface on both banks of the river. Here the gravel slopes of Cornhill and Ludgate Hill were matched by the gravel banks of Southwark, so that it was an ideal point at which not only to ford the river but to bridge it with as little delay as possible.

The defence of the Roman world was based on rapid transport of men and materials, its cardinal feature the remarkably fine road system surveyed with consummate skill and completed by the Roman legionaries with the help of the local people. Because of its position at the point where the river was bridged, London was destined to become the most important commercial centre of the Province of Britain, with roads converging on it from the south, and in particular from the continental crossing points, and radiating from it to the outposts of empire in the west country and the north. Roman London enjoyed more than three centuries of mainly peaceful development, becoming one of the largest of the Roman towns outside Italy, and one of the most prosperous in the whole empire.

Many of the outstanding events in its history are known. The first, a far from peaceful one, occurred within a few years of its foundation, in A.D. 61, when the revolt of the Iceni from East Anglia, led by their Queen Boudicca, threatened the security of the whole province. The Roman legions were stationed near the northern and western frontiers, for it was believed that all the south and east had been pacified and that the British leaders accepted the terms on which they had been admitted as members of the Roman Empire.

Consequently the Iceni had the field to themselves for a time. They sacked the recently built Roman town on the site of Colchester, then marched on unchecked to London, where in the absence of any prepared opposition they set fire to the wooden buildings and drove out the inhabitants. London was apparently utterly destroyed, as witness the charred timbers which have been discovered just below the level of the later Roman town, fifteen to twenty feet below the present street level, which has been constantly raised as one town has been built on the foundations of another.

This was a major disaster, the results of which were felt for years afterwards. Units of the Roman army moving with incredible speed arrived in time to quell the rebellion before much further damage had been done, but the Imperial Government determined that the events of A.D. 61 must never be repeated. The Governor was instructed to ensure that in future all town buildings should be in part at least of stone, and that every important town should be defended with walls and forts.

London was rebuilt. This time it was built in more permanent materials than wood, and as a planned town rather than as a makeshift collection of public buildings, warehouses and homes, as it had been before. Building at first was confined to Cornhill but by the second century the expansion of London had begun, an outward spread which has had several setbacks, notably after the end of the Roman period, but has otherwise progressed steadily and inexorably to the present day.

Workshops and the more elaborate public buildings which were part and parcel of every Roman town began to appear, until the whole area from Aldgate to Ludgate, from the Thames to the northern boundary by Cripplegate and Bishopsgate, was filled. The centre of the town, with the basilica and other public buildings, including the baths, was situated between Leadenhall Street and Fenchurch Street. The inner part of the city was laid out on the traditional Roman rectangular plan. Away from the centre the Roman plan was not followed so exactly. A compromise was reached between the irregular layout of British settlements and the arrangement of Roman towns, giving a system of town planning which is rightly described as truly Romano-British.

The completion of the walls as demanded by the Roman Government was delayed, but a good start had been made by the beginning of the second century and the defensive system was more or less complete within fifty years. The first stage was a rampart defence with a fort and military base near Cripplegate. Then a wall was built on all sides of the town except by the river, though in the end a wall was built also along the bank. The course of the wall was from a point between Tower bridge and the White Tower north-westward to Aldgate and Bishopsgate, then westward to Cripplegate, southward to Aldersgate and Newgate, whence it continued parallel with the Fleet River, then a broad if sluggish waterway, to a point very near where now is the end of Blackfriars bridge.

Inside this walled enclosure the people lived in an atmosphere of security as members of a close community, amply protected so long as the walls were patrolled. Londinium may never have achieved the elegance of some Roman provincial towns but enough has been found of the foundations of the people's homes to show that they had a standard of living far higher, a culture far more advanced, than those of any people in Britain before them. By the third century Londinium was more than the commercial centre of the Province. It had become its administrative capital as surely as York was its military capital.

The official religion of Roman London was the Roman Pantheism. Some of its finest buildings were temples to the Roman gods. After A.D. 313, when Constantine (the Great) recognized Christianity,

Christian churches must have been added to the temple buildings, or
the statues of the pagan gods of Rome may have been overthrown and
the worship of Christ carried on in the temples.

No Christian church dating from Roman times has been identified,
though the complete foundations of a temple to the cult of Mithras, a
Persian cult which was spread by Roman legionaries throughout the
empire, was found when the ground on which Bucklersbury House
stands was being excavated. This was one of the great archaeological
discoveries of post-war redevelopment. The foundations and ground
plan of the temple have been relaid in the forecourt of Bucklersbury
House as a permanent memorial to the London of nearly two thousand
years ago. Among the several sculptured figures found in association
with the temple were a remarkable head of Mithras and another of
Serapis, the Graeco-Egyptian god of the underworld, statues of
exceptionally fine workmanship which it is believed were carved in
Italy and brought to Britain. The statues appear to have been buried
under the floor of the temple at some time before it ceased to be used.
As Mithraism supplanted the official Roman religion in many parts of
the empire, it is conceivable that this one sacred building was used first
for the worship of Roman gods, then in the service of the cult of
Mithras, and finally as a cell of Christianity. The sequence is no more
than conjectural. But it is at least a possibility.

In A.D. 287 Carausius, commander of the forces defending Britain by
land and sea, effected a successful and bloodless revolution, declaring
himself emperor with the support of the legions stationed in Britain and
of the *classis britannica* (British Fleet), the purpose of which was to keep
the Channel free from pirates and protect the trade routes between
Britain and the Continent. The Imperial Government was fully occupied
at the time in defending its frontiers nearer home. It had no alternative
to accepting the *fait accompli* and leaving Carausius undisturbed.
Archaeological research has disclosed at least one facet of his term as
self-appointed emperor in the extraordinarily large number of coins
which were minted in London during his 'reign'. After about six years
of peaceful rule Carausius was murdered by Allectus, who in turn
declared himself emperor. Soon, however, the central government
equipped an expedition for the reconquest of the province and
Allectus was defeated and killed in battle.

The growing weakness of the central government had been exposed,
however. It could only be a matter of time before the protection of
Roman troops was withdrawn from this, one of the most distant of the
provinces. For a brief time there was peace. The Emperor Constantine
personally supervised the strengthening of Britain's frontier defences
and the defences of its most important towns. More up-to-date bastions
were added to the walls of London and the line of Hadrian's Wall
was re-established as an effective northern frontier. Yet within fifty
years London's long-established prosperity began to decline, partly

C

because of a diminution in the trade between Britain and the Roman world.

It is difficult to pinpoint the exact course of this decline. Barbarian pressure on the empire's frontiers ultimately made it impossible to maintain the British Fleet, and the Channel became a happy hunting-ground for pirates sailing from north Germany and Denmark. A decline in the standard of living on the Continent also caused a contraction of trade. One sign of the depression is the small number of coins found in London minted after the beginning of the fourth century compared with those of the second and third centuries. Many of the wealthier people emigrated from London to the west country, which continued to enjoy local prosperity. Some of the less well-to-do moved out of the city and joined the village communities of south-east England, which were still very much as they had been before the Romans came to Britain, though they, too, had enjoyed some additional prosperity from the nearness of London, which supplied a ready market for their agricultural surpluses.

By the third quarter of the fourth century many of London's fine houses had become dilapidated. Those that were damaged by accidental fire were not rebuilt. The withdrawal of the Roman legions by the Emperor Honorius in 410 was the beginning of the end. Britain was clearly in no position to defend itself against the raids of the Picts on the northern frontier and of Saxon pirates on the south and east. With no trade to support its economy London by then was a dead city, though probably a few groups of people continued to live inside its walls and there is no evidence that it ever suffered a frontal attack. The Anglo-Saxon invaders may have by-passed it as they sailed up the river to find lodgments more suited to the needs of a wholly rural people which had no experience of town life and certainly no desire to live in towns.

During the whole of the long period of Romano-British prosperity London was linked closely with the surrounding countryside, more closely probably than for a thousand years afterwards. The Roman road system was the foundation on which this interdependence was built. As we have seen, London owed its existence to its position at the lowest point downstream at which the river could be forded. In the years of wealth a great weight of merchandise was carried over London bridge, not only from the Channel ports but from the iron-mining district of the Sussex Weald and from the highly developed agricultural country which surrounded the Roman town at Chichester (Noviomagus). London was the clearing-house. From it the merchandise was carried along the roads leading to the east, north and west. No other crossing of the Thames had comparable importance in Roman times although, according to some accounts, a road was constructed to by-pass the city and ford the river near Westminster.

It has puzzled many people that the Romans found Southwark a suitable bridgehead, since the level at which Roman remains are found is well below high tide level and there can have been no embankments prior to those built by the Romans. The answer to this problem is simple, though not at first glance obvious. The Roman level, it is true, has been depressed slightly by the weight of building above it, but that is only part of the answer. The more important fact is that the last two thousand years have been a period of submergence, i.e. a period in which the level of the sea has risen relative to that of the land, owing to the release of still more of the melting polar ice cap to swell the oceans. Today, were it not for man-made embankments, hundreds of square miles of land bordering the Thames and its estuary would be inundated, as was shown by the disaster in 1928 when a high tide surmounted the embankments at Pimlico and flooded the lower storeys of houses, causing considerable loss of life. In Roman times the gravel beds of Southwark were comfortably above high-water level. Moreover it is likely that the river was shallower, its flow more sluggish, with more silting up of the channel, and that the limit of the tide was well below its present limit at Teddington. In all probability when the Romans founded London the tide scarcely reached as far upstream as that. The fording of the river would not then be interrupted at any time of the day, and this may well have been an additional reason for choosing the position for the river crossing.

The general course of the main Roman roads radiating from London is well known, but their detail is still obscure and likely to continue so, since they have disappeared in most of the Greater London area through subsequent building. The main roads approaching London Bridge from the south were Stane Street and Watling Street, which had a common course for the last few miles. Stane Street was the direct way from Chichester and the port at Portchester. Watling Street was the main artery of commerce with the Continent by way of Rochester and Canterbury and the Channel ports, especially Richborough, which became the most important of the Romano-British ports on the southeast coast. A number of lesser roads, many of them following the course of earlier trackways, served the Romano-British settlements and the villa estates, often founded by wealthy people who had served in an administrative capacity in London.

The course of the highway to the south was in alignment with Borough High Street and the Old Kent Road. Watling Street then diverted to the east, passing over the high ground above Greenwich and thence continuing in an almost straight line to the ford over the Medway at Rochester. The course of Stane Street was south-westward in a fairly straight line to the neighbourhood of Epsom Downs, where its course was preserved in a medieval trackway which has become a modern bridle path.

The important road to Colchester left the city at Aldgate, following roughly the line of Mile End Road to Stratford and Ilford. The main road to the north, Ermine Street, started at Bishopsgate and pursued a course well to the west of the Lea valley through Edmonton and Enfield towards Royston, from which it continued to Lincoln and York, with many branches to the outlying parts of the northern province. Finally, the main road to the west left London at Newgate and ran parallel with Oxford Street, at the end of which it divided, one branch going on to Shepherd's Bush and the Goldhawk Road to the crossing of the river at Staines (Pontes), then continuing to Silchester and Exeter, the other branch, the northern part of Watling Street (A5), turning north-westward up the Edgware Road to St Albans (Verulamium).

These roads had metalled surfaces, were carried on causeways over marshy or soft ground and were drained by ditches, remarkably efficient and long-lasting examples of the science of road construction, as is known from fragments of Roman roads which have been excavated, such as that on Blackstone Edge, where the metalled surface was still more or less intact. Nothing comparable with this fragment has been discovered in the London area, but near Edmonton, where the general course of Ermine Street is fairly well defined, excavation has revealed what is assumed to be the 'agger' (embankment) of the original Roman road.

The course of Watling Street beyond the crossing of the Ravensbourne by Deptford was apparently along the ridge which is now Greenwich Park rather than directly across Blackheath, as many have supposed. In this district the road has been identified not by any remains of a metalled surface, but by the characteristic hollow made by a much-used road over relatively soft ground. As late as the eighteenth century, before proper care was given to the maintenance of the roads, many of the main coaching roads were 'hollow' ways, so depressed that only the top of a coach could be seen by an observer in neighbouring fields. It is reasonable to suppose, therefore, that Roman roads which must have carried heavy traffic would have become depressed after centuries of use, however good their foundations, especially if, like the Roman roads in Britain, they continued to be used when labour was no longer available to keep them in a state of good repair. The course of Stane Street has been positively identified in Clapham and at Merton, where Roman finds have been so numerous that it is generally thought to be the site of a posting station on the main road.

Inevitably the principal centres of Romano-British activity were adjacent to this network of main roads. A map showing Roman discoveries reveals a major concentration wherever the roads crossed open country with gravel subsoil, as in the Greenwich-Blackheath area, in the north of London towards Clapton and Edmonton, and to the west of London in the Notting Hill area. Secondary concentrations occur near the course of the road to Colchester, and in the open country to the north of it around Leyton and Wanstead, which were probably linked with Ermine Street by a secondary road.

Traces of this first major development of the Greater London area are of three main kinds—the foundations of buildings, fragments of pottery and burial places. The foundations of buildings are always direct evidence of Roman influence, since the Celtic people, who continued to form the bulk of the population outside the cities, lived in rude huts very much in the way in which their ancestors had lived. Southwark was a considerable bridgehead settlement, with a number of residences facing the river and others on either side of the road leading to the south. One Roman villa is believed to have stood on the site of the present St Saviour's Cathedral. The areas of Holborn and Westminster were also developed to a minor extent. The British Museum in its Roman collection has numerous fragments from Roman buildings in Holborn and also evidence of inhumations and cremations. There were burials during Roman times, too, near Westminster Abbey, but no evidence of any major settlement in what was then an island in the marsh. There were certainly sizable settlements at Charlton and Eltham in association with Watling Street, to the north of London at Kingsbury and Edmonton, to the east at Wanstead, where there was probably a large villa, and at Rainham and Romford, and to the south near Hayes and Orpington.

Owing to the rise in the level of the Thames, it has been possible to find definite evidence of the continuance of the British way of life under Roman government in the shape of the remains of circular huts of wattle which have come to light on the foreshore of the river, well below high-water mark but in positions which must have been on dry land at the time. In several places these huts of wattle, which presumably had clay infillings, are found in association with Roman pottery of the second or third century A.D., particularly at Brentford. In some places, too, aerial survey has shown Romano-British field systems, as on Farthing Down near Coulsdon. These small, square fields were characteristic of pre-Roman agriculture but yielded abundant evidence that the people who worked them lived at a time when Roman coinage was current and Roman pottery was in use.

Stanmore, where Watling Street crossed the edge of a wide expanse of heathland, part of which is preserved in the Stanmore Commons, is one of the most interesting of Roman sites in Greater London. Here, as in Greenwich, the course of the Roman road has been inferred from a 'hollow way' and evidence has been found that a posting station on the road to the north-west was situated here. The posting station has been identified with Sulloniacae, a stopping-place for travellers to St Albans and beyond during the greater part of the lifetime of the Roman Province. As well as a posting station Sulloniacae was a small industrial centre manufacturing pottery for sale to the people of neighbouring districts. The discovery of much imported red Samian ware has obscured the fact that a great deal of pottery was also manufactured on a commercial scale in Britain itself for local use. Excavation at Joyden's Wood near Bexley brought to light a pottery kiln which was almost certainly in continuous production from the second to the fourth century. There were probably other commercial pottery kilns at Chadwell to the north of Dagenham, and at Potter's Bar, while at Peckham some evidence has been found to support the suggestion that a glass factory was situated there in the third century.

By imperial command the townspeople were buried outside the walls. The rule was strictly observed in Rome itself, where a long line of tombs greeted travellers along the Appian Way. In Roman London the rule was frequently disregarded but a large cemetery existed to the east of the city between the Roman road in alignment with Mile End Road and the Thames. Another cemetery has been discovered near West Wickham in Kent, which suggests that here, too, there was a sizable community.

In the fifth century, when the people of the countryside were in daily fear of attack from marauding Saxons, many buried hoards of coins and other valuables to save them from the invaders but never returned to collect them. Such hoards dated with certainty to the fifth century have been found at Bermondsey, Grove Park and Camberwell. An earlier hoard of the third century was found near St Mary Cray.

On the very edge of the new Greater London, just inside the parish of Keston, a Roman site of special interest has been excavated and has been maintained as a monument by the local council. The remains, which are situated in Lower Warbank Field, are of a burial ground (one circular and one rectangular tomb have been identified) and of buildings which are locally believed to have been a temple, though the evidence is inconclusive. Fragments of pottery, tiles and the number of coins found in the vicinity are evidence of a settlement here which was more Roman than British, probably a Roman villa.

As we build up this outline picture of the Greater London area as it was in Roman times, we are bound to be struck by the inescapable fact that little can be seen above ground. Most of the evidence is in the museums. There is, however, one rather exciting way in which anyone who is interested but has no special knowledge can infer with reasonable certainty the existence of Roman villas or Romano-British settlements. All over the empire Roman builders used thin red bricks, Roman tiles as they are generally called. These appear as courses in the masonry of all Roman buildings, such as the lower part of the ancient walls of London and the walls of Verulamium. Medieval church builders were often hard put to find suitable material. Often they used the ruins of Romano-British buildings as quarries. The consequence is that the fabric of almost every church in close proximity to a Roman settlement contains a number of these thin red bricks. They are often still present in the lower part of the tower even when the church has been enlarged or remodelled several times since the Middle Ages. It is reasonable to assume that if Roman bricks are found a Romano-British settlement existed near by.

These bricks can be found in scores of churches in the Greater London area, in the tiny parish church of Keston itself, for example, as one would expect. But they are equally obvious in the churches of St Paul's Cray and Old Kingsbury, and in those of North Ockendon, Chadwell and Ruislip. Roman material is most often evident in medieval churches built where there was no local building material. So nearly one-third of all the ancient churches in that part of south-west Essex now included in the Greater London area have what are apparently Roman bricks in their fabric.

2. The Dark Ages

THE two centuries which followed the collapse of the Roman Province of Britain were a dark age in every sense of the term, dark because it is unillumined by any reliable contemporary record, and dark because the picture presented by archaeological research is an uncommonly gloomy one. It is known that before the Emperor Honorius withdrew his support from Britain groups of Saxons had already settled near the coast of south-east England.

The *Anglo-Saxon Chronicle*, written hundreds of years later and preserving only oral tradition, represents the Romano-British people fighting pitched battles with the Anglo-Saxon invaders. It is unlikely that the *Chronicle* is accurate in any of its statements relating to the fifth century. Some of the Forts of the Saxon Shore, the strong fortresses built in the last phase of Roman government in Britain to protect the harbours of the south-east coast, do appear to have been defended; in some cases their defenders were slain in hand-to-hand fighting. No evidence points to similar battles for the towns or for the rural settlements. The towns by then were almost deserted. Famine and pestilence must have taken their toll, apart from the tendency for the townspeople to migrate into the countryside when the towns no longer held out the possibility of useful work or a reasonable standard of living. It is much more likely that the warlike tribes from Denmark and Germany carried out their occupation, which was spread over more than a century, piecemeal, descending on the scattered villages of the Romano-British people, long accustomed to the ways of peace, either enslaving them or driving them away. Christianity was driven from the land and the pagan Saxon gods held sway.

Yet to the Saxon invaders Greater London owes the foundation of almost all the settlements which later became the nuclei of its administrative divisions. The Saxons avoided, like all their predecessors, the heaviest clay lands, but they were almost as well equipped as the Romans to clear undergrowth, and they preferred to establish village communities, as indeed the *Anglo-Saxon Chronicle* states, by river and seashore.

The gravel terrace by the valley of the River Wandle was one of the first areas to be colonized. Tooting is a very old name, probably dating from the fifth century. Once the first permanent settlements were made they multiplied with extraordinary rapidity, so that by the eighth century the majority of the towns and villages from which Greater London has emerged were well established.

The Anglo-Saxons came mainly in small groups, often it is believed in units of a single family. They were of several racial stocks, including Jutes who settled in Kent and were the first to form a coherent kingdom, although embryo kingdoms or subkingdoms were soon founded in other parts of the country. North-west Kent, however, was largely colonized by Saxons, as were Surrey and Middlesex, and most of Essex, though the existence of Jutish cemeteries at Rainham shows that some lodgments of Jutes were made on the Essex shores of the estuary. Essex takes its name, however, from the kingdom of the East Saxons, as Middlesex does from the kingdom of the Middle Saxons. At the end of the sixth century both Essex and Middlesex and the subkingdom of Surrey gave allegiance to Kent.

By this time London was beginning to assume once more an important place in the developing economy. It owed this change of fortune to the factor to which it had owed its foundation by the Romans—its position at a convenient crossing place of the Thames. The stages by which it regained its national position are as obscure as any other part of the early Anglo-Saxon story. But its genuine importance by 597 is attested by the fact that the Pope when he dispatched St Augustine to convert the English at the invitation of Ethelbert, King of Kent, suggested that St Augustine might make London the centre of the revitalized Church. It was the accident of the warm reception given to St Augustine in Kent that persuaded him to make Canterbury his headquarters.

While St Augustine stayed in Canterbury, however, one of his fellow missionaries, St Mellitus, was charged with the conversion of the East Saxons and almost certainly chose London as the centre of his missionary journeys, possibly founding the first church in the city dedicated to St Paul on or near the site of the medieval and modern St Paul's Cathedral. So London became the see of a bishopric which included Middlesex and Essex as well as London, as it continued to do until comparatively recent times. Another see was established at Rochester to look after the spiritual welfare of the people who dwelt south of the Thames from the Medway to beyond the western boundary of Greater London.

The history of this period is given in outline in the *Ecclesiastical History* of St Bede the Venerable, the first credible historian of England and one whose record has largely withstood the test of archaeological research. The conversion of the East Saxons proved less easy than that of the Kentish people, while the work of the Christian missionaries based on London was made no easier by the turmoil in which the early Saxon kingdoms were involved during the seventh and eighth centuries. First the power of Kent waned and that of Mercia grew. Soon Essex and Middlesex accepted the King of Mercia as their overlord. Then conflict developed between Mercia and Wessex, ending with the acceptance of the King of Wessex as overlord of all the Anglo-Saxon kingdoms.

By the beginning of the ninth century London was once more playing a vital part in the nation's economy. Most of the area within the Roman walls was again occupied. Trade and manufacturing industry developed apace and the city for many generations was virtually independent of the Saxon kingdoms, whether Mercia or Wessex was in the ascendant. The pattern for the future had been set.

During most of this period there was a bishop of London appointed directly by the Archbishop of Canterbury and indirectly by the Pope. The Saxon communities of Kent, of Mercia, of Essex, of Middlesex and of Surrey had all been converted. Each community erected its wooden cross at which to pay homage to the Christian God, and later a church of timber, not one of which has survived in Greater London. The conflict between the rulers of the Saxon kingdoms did not greatly affect the people living in the few towns and the numerous villages, in which agriculture was the one and only industry.

Monasticism was introduced to many parts of England during this eventful period, monasteries serving as centres of godliness and culture and typifying the Christian way of life. Bede himself was a monk. The monastic houses became the principal and for some time the only centres of learning among the still primitive people of the Saxon settlements.

Barking Abbey was by far the oldest and for much of its history one of the most important religious foundations in the Greater London area. Nothing has survived from the Saxon Abbey, the gatehouse and a few fragments from the later medieval buildings. But excavation in 1910 showed conclusively that it was one of the largest of the abbeys and priories not only in Greater London but in the whole of England. In its early days it must have exercised a great influence on the people living in the communities of Essex near the banks of the Thames.

The researches of Colonel E. A. Loftus made it possible to piece together the outline of its early history with far more certainty than that of many similar foundations. During the reign of the Essex King Sebbi two abbeys were founded by Erkenwald (or Erconwald), who was later canonized. One was the abbey of Chertsey, of which he was the first abbot, the other the abbey of Barking, of which his sister Ethelburga was the first abbess. The date of the foundation of Barking is still a matter of conjecture but the Chertsey Register, a later medieval manuscript, may well be right in placing it in the year 666. Erkenwald was appointed Bishop of London in 675 and retired about 692 to Barking Abbey, where he died, though he was buried in St Paul's Cathedral.

During the first two centuries of its existence Barking Abbey was a community of nuns and monks but, like the rather similar abbey of Whitby in Yorkshire, was always ruled over by an abbess. When it was refounded towards the end of the Anglo-Saxon period under the rule of St Benedict it was, like Romsey, wholly a nunnery. The abbey was always wealthy, drawing its revenue from numerous manors which were granted to it. Only a few years after it was founded it received the manors of Rainham and Dagenham. By the time of the Norman Conquest it included in its estates much of Ingatestone and Great Warley, as well as Rainham, Dagenham and Barking itself, and it had a footing even in London in the parish of All Hallows by the Tower, which became known as All Hallows, Barking.

Stow, the earliest of the historians of London, says that he saw St Erkenwald's tomb and that of King Sebbi side by side in old St Paul's, while the actual charter by which the abbey was granted the usage of land in Rainham and Dagenham in 692 is still in existence and dated.

Nothing is known of the history of the abbey after that until Danish invaders in 870 set fire to it and either murdered or carried away the nuns. The second abbey on the site under the regime of St Benedict was endowed in the reign of King Edgar about 996. The first abbess of the new foundation was Wulfilda, a nun of Wilton who was appointed to her office by the Bishop of Winchester with the approval of Archbishop Dunstan of Canterbury, who was himself one of the chief spirits in the spread of the new monasticism of the tenth and eleventh centuries.

From that time Barking Abbey had a stong link with the Crown both before and after the Norman Conquest. It is significant that William of Normandy, after defeating the Saxon forces at Battle and being crowned in the newly completed abbey church of Westminster on Christmas Day 1066, thereupon, as far as is known, travelled to Barking Abbey and used that as his headquarters while his camp just outside the city of London (where the Tower of London now is) was being fortified and a permanent castle built. King William's stay at the abbey is in part a matter of legend. It is, however, documented fact that the King confirmed the abbey's land holdings almost immediately and allowed the Anglo-Saxon abbess to remain in office, although later abbesses were appointed from the Norman ruling class.

Westminster Abbey was founded later than Barking and in its early days did not have so much influence. The tradition that it was founded by St Mellitus in the first half of the seventh century has no evidence to support it, but it is certain that there was a community of Benedictine monks very nearly on the site of today's Abbey by the middle of the eighth century. It was called the West Minster apparently from its position to the west of London.

There may have been other monastic foundations in London in this early period of Anglo-Saxon Christianity but none that played an important role in the life of the people. By the eighth century a new danger was threatening London and all the Anglo-Saxon communities within easy reach of the Thames or of the coast; that, of course, included all the communities within the Greater London area. This was a case of history repeating itself to an extraordinary degree. Just as the Britons of the Roman Province had lived for generations in terror of attack by bands of pagan warriors descending upon them from across the sea, so the Anglo-Saxons in their turn must have been in perpetual dread of attack from the well-armed pagan peoples of Scandinavia.

Two peoples were concerned, one derived from Scandinavia, the other from Denmark and adjoining parts of Germany. The Scandinavians, or 'Norsemen', were pre-eminently sailors, who attacked and plundered the countryside near the coast and navigable waterways, then withdrew, carrying their booty with them. The majority of their attacks were carried out on the north country. The Danes, though they too were excellent sailors, did not often risk the long voyages which the Norsemen were accustomed to make (one group of Norsemen colonized Greenland, others many parts of Ireland, the north of England and north Scotland). The Danes most often sailed across the Channel at its narrowest point and made landfall on the coast of Kent or Sussex, or sailed round the Foreland and up the estuary of the Thames.

These latter were the people with whom London and south-east England were concerned. As was the case four hundred years before, the invaders were pagan, the defenders Christian; the invaders warlike and skilled in the ways of war, the defenders accustomed only to the ways of peace and devoted to their agriculture. And this was as true of London itself as of the surrounding countryside, the people of London playing their part in agriculture by cultivating the land outside the mouldering Roman walls of the city.

Well before the eighth century Christianity had become well established in Britain. It had become a real power in the Anglo-Saxon kingdom, in which the position of the Pope as Supreme Head of the Church was universally recognized. So the war against the Danes was a holy war waged with all the authority of the Church and with the full strength of the Anglo-Saxon leaders, who were united by this one tie even when they found it impossible to present a united political front.

At first the Danes came to England only for plunder, but by the beginning of the ninth century they had started to settle. They overran East Anglia and a good deal of Kent, then penetrated westward into Mercia and Wessex. Often groups came from Denmark and north Germany in the late spring when they had sown the crops in their native fields, lived off the land in England during the summer, and returned home in time for harvest. The position of many of the Anglo-Saxon communities was unenviable. Though the attacks on them are mostly unrecorded, peaceful existence was rare over considerable periods.

The raiders did untold damage and caused untold loss of life. The abbeys of Barking and Westminster were sacked; London itself was attacked in 839, when many of its citizens were killed, many of its homes damaged or burnt to the ground. At that time there was still no central government, no one who could organize the call-up and training of an adequate militia, no navy to repel the invaders before they landed. If one did not know the subsequent course of history, one would think that the ultimate conquest of the whole of Anglo-Saxon England was predestined.

The clergy repeatedly called for unified defence. Many of them were active in sustaining the morale of the defenders when their city was attacked, and it was due to their influence that the kings of Wessex, which so far was relatively unscathed by attack, were recognized as kings of all England. By the time of the sack of London Egbert had received tokens of loyalty from the chieftains of East Anglia, Essex and Kent, and had forced the submission of Mercia. By the time Alfred became King in 871 he was sovereign of a genuinely united England. But it was an England now threatened by complete Danish control. Although London itself was not occupied, its trade was severely damaged and many of the villages in the Greater London area had Danish overlords. So it was with a special feeling of gratitude that the burgesses of London received news of the Treaty of Wedmore concluded between Alfred and the leader of the Danes after an army trained by the English king in the west country had fought and defeated an organized Danish army.

The Treaty of Wedmore envisaged the partition of England between the Danes and the Saxons. Commonly it is said that the part ceded to the Danes, and now known to historians as the Danelaw, was that part of England which lies to the east and north of Watling Street. That is accurate so far as the midlands and north country are concerned, but was not true of the London area, where the effective boundary was the River Lea and the estuary of the Thames. So Tottenham and Enfield remained under Saxon government, while places like Barking and Dagenham were ceded to the invaders.

London remained stoutly English, as did all the settlements of the Middle Saxons (Middlesex) and of the country south of the Thames. As a condition of occupying eastern England the Danes agreed to accept Christianity, another way in effect of saying that they promised religious toleration. So Christianity was not driven from the land, and in many of the erstwhile Saxon settlements Saxon and Dane worked on the land side by side without apparent signs of conflict. It was an uneasy peace, however, and a short-lived one, though it gave London a breathing space and allowed it to recover much of its lost prestige and re-establish the internal trade routes.

In 894 the Saxons not only defeated a Danish force in pitched battle but immobilized their ships. The Danes had sailed up the Lea and

anchored off Tottenham opposite the point where Bruce Castle now
stands. Thereupon a Saxon task force energetically cut a new and
deeper channel across the marshland bordering the course of the Lea
so that the Danish ships were left high and dry and the invaders could
be dispatched at leisure. It has been said that confirmation of this has
been provided by the discovery of the remains of a Danish ship in the
Tottenham marshes, but this most likely represents a ship burial, a
common enough form of burial for chieftains, especially those slain in
battle.

Under the aegis of King Alfred, London's walls were rebuilt and
new defences added. An effective militia was recruited to man the
walls and to act as a striking force in case of further trouble. Alfred
died in 901 and left behind him a country at peace and the embryo of
constitutional government. In the fifty years following his death the
Danelaw was reoccupied and foreign influence removed from the
land, though thousands of the Danish and Norse invaders remained
and were integrated with the English people. Alfred's capital had been
Winchester, which was still the capital at the time of the Norman
occupation in 1066, but London became during the tenth century
undisputedly the most important city in the land as well as the
wealthiest.

In this century Kingston assumed and retained a singular importance.
It was probably the most important settlement in the subkingdom of
Surrey. Early manuscripts refer to it as a renowned place and it was
pre-eminently a 'King's Town' until the time of King John, who
made it over to the freemen. There was a palace or royal residence
here from the seventh century, and in 838 Kingston was the meeting
place for the Great Ecclesiastical Council which resulted in the lasting
partnership of the Wessex (English) throne and the Archbishops of
Canterbury, with the blessing of the Pope. That might explain why
coronations were solemnized here rather than in Winchester, the
administrative capital of Wessex. Also, since the Thames could be
forded here, Kingston was a convenient meeting place for the people of
Wessex and Mercia (including, most importantly, those of London).

Whatever the precise reason, it seems certain, as the *Anglo-Saxon
Chronicle* asserts, that Kingston was the scene of the coronation of
several of the Saxon kings in the tenth century. The kings took their
vows and received the ceremonial sceptre on the sacred stone, which is
now placed, rather sadly surrounded by an ornate cage, outside the
modern Guildhall and directly opposite another ancient survival in
Kingston, the later medieval Clattern bridge. The kings believed to
have been crowned on it include Edward the Elder, Alfred's immediate
successor, Athelstan, Edmund, Edred, Edwy, Edward the Martyr and
Ethelred II, between them spanning almost the whole of the tenth
century. The earliest written record of the stone appears in a topographical work by John Speed published in 1627. This records that the

stone was set in a Saxon chapel adjoining the parish church, where it remained until the chapel collapsed in 1730.

The tradition of the use of the stone for the coronation of Saxon kings is a strong one but it is no more than a tradition, though one in accordance with the age-old custom of placing newly elected kings on a sacred stone. There is no real reason to reject John Speed's statement: 'At Kingston stood the chair of majesty whereon Athelstan, Edwin and Ethelred sate at their Coronations.' The stone itself is a slab of sandstone derived from the Reading beds. It has been suggested that it is a glacier-borne boulder. Equally it might have been one of the stones of a prehistoric sacred monument.

Chelsea is another place which achieved unexpected though brief renown even earlier than Kingston. When Offa was King of Mercia and Mercia had obtained the token allegiance of the East Saxons, several synods were held at Chelsea between 787 and 793. At one of these representatives of Pope Adrian I were present to discuss the administration of the Church in England, and in particular the desire of King Offa to establish an archbishopric in Mercia to rank equally with the sees of York and Canterbury. Lichfield was chosen as the archiepiscopal see and continued to administer the Church in Mercia independently until after King Offa's death. Further synods were held here until Danish pirates laid waste the Thames-side parishes and Chelsea, together with its neighbour Fulham, entered a new dark age. It is as difficult to understand the eminence of Chelsea in the time of Mercia's dominance as it is to understand that of Kingston when Wessex became the leading state in England, although it was a place obviously convenient to London and well served for transport by the Thames. By the time of Domesday Survey, however, it was no more than a riverside hamlet with a population well under one hundred.

The peace of the countryside was shattered once again in 980, when the Danish attacks recommenced. For some years the Danish leaders were literally bribed to leave England in peace, a special tax called Danegeld being raised for the purpose of paying them. But the threat was ever present and London alone among English towns was considered secure against attack. When war blazed out again in 1010 King Ethelred took refuge in it. This time, however, the Danes were intent on conquest and had an adequate navy and army to achieve it. In 1013 even London was compelled to submit to the Danish King Sweyn, and Ethelred fled to Normandy, leaving Sweyn as undisputed king of the country as well as of his native Denmark.

Sweyn's son Canute had to fight to retain England. London declared its independence and after Ethelred's death named his son Edmund as king. The tradition is that Edmund collected an army from London and defeated the Danes under Canute at Brentford, and subsequently met there to sign a treaty partitioning the kingdom after a brief period of dual kingship, whence the proverbial 'Two Kings of Brentford'. As the poet Cowper has it in *The Task*: 'United yet divided, twain at once, so sit two Kings of Brentford on one throne.' Cowper was comparing the kings' uneasy position with that provided by the newfangled settee or sofa! The difficulties of dividing and ruling, however, were solved by the murder of Edmund and the collapse of further resistance to Canute only a few weeks afterwards.

Now that Edmund was dead London accepted Canute, but was strong enough to make an independent treaty with the new king, to accept him willingly rather than surrender to him. Its strength had been undermined by the wars but it remained virtually an independent community governed by its own laws for the following five hundred years irrespective of what king was nominally on the throne.

Denmark by the eleventh century was a Christian country and Canute contributed vastly in money, men and material to heal the scars of war. The churches which had been destroyed during the war were rebuilt. Abbeys such as those of Barking entered on a new life of prosperity and useful service. When the Danish dynasty ended in 1042, Edward, the son of Ethelred, and known as the Confessor because of his piety, restored the Saxon line by agreement with the Danes and was duly elected by the Saxon Witan, or council of wise men, which was dominated by the leaders of London. Material and cultural progress was resumed and was scarcely interrupted by the accession twenty-four years later of a Norman king.

In spite of the very great advances made in the last four hundred years of the Anglo-Saxon period and the dominant position which London occupied for much of that time, there is extraordinarily little left above ground to serve as links with the period. Unlike the Romans, the Saxons were until the tenth century builders in wood, and not a single early Saxon church has survived in the whole of Greater London, nor is there a single one intact of the stone churches which began to replace the wooden buildings late in the period. All have been rebuilt subsequently. Many of the churches in the district listed in Domesday were probably of timber. Here and there Saxon work is identified in the fabric of more recent churches. At Cheam what may have been the fabric of a Saxon church has been built into a memorial chapel, and for the expert rather than the layman signs of Saxon workmanship are evident in a number of other places, such as the old parish church at Kingsbury, where a quantity of Roman material is built into the fabric. The eighteenth-century antiquarian Stukeley deduced that the church was built inside a Roman fort or encampment (a deduction for which there is no solid evidence). For the rest, there is only Kingston's coronation stone and the lineal earthwork in the Harrow district known as Grim's Dyke, which may have served as a boundary of Offa's kingdom.

The Strand at Temple Bar, from an oil painting by John Collet, 1760–70. Sir Christopher Wren's Temple Bar, erected in 1672, which marked the dividing line between the jurisdiction of the City and of Westminster, remained in position until 1878. Ten years later it was rebuilt as an entrance to the Theobalds Park estate near Enfield. The vehicle under the arch is a carriage built by Francis Moore, with wheels more than seven feet high. It is believed that Hansom based the first cab to bear his name on this design.

Perry's Dockyard, Blackwall, in 1801.

Blackwall and the Isle of Dogs have been centres of maritime activity since the East India Company made its headquarters at Blackwall early in the seventeenth century. This interesting print of Perry's Dockyard was executed two years after government sanction had been given for the building of enclosed docks at the Isle of Dogs.

The Tower and the Pool of London, from an engraving in the British Museum by W. Daniels, 1805.

This print gives some idea of the difficulty which ships had in unloading at the authorized wharves in the Pool. Commonly the ships anchored in midstream and discharged their cargoes by tender. Instances are recorded of ships standing a month in the Pool before their cargoes were unloaded. This overcrowding led to the Act of 1799 which authorized the building of alternative docks and wharves for discharging cargo lower downstream and was the beginning of the intricate system of the present-day London Docks.

[3]

Archway Road, from a print of 1813.

The construction of the Archway Road was one of the first by-pass schemes to be carried out in Britain. Its purpose was to make unnecessary the ascent of Highgate Hill, the entrance to which is on the left, and so provide an easier route to the north. The turnpike gate is in the centre, while in the background is the old Highgate Archway, which was replaced in 1900.

Samuel Whitbread's Brewery in Chiswell Street, Finsbury, from a painting by D. Wolstenholme Jnr, 1820. Samuel Whitbread established his first brewhouse in Finsbury in 1742 and purchased the site of the premises pictured above in 1750. A modern brewery has replaced the eighteenth-century buildings.

The Red Lion at Kilburn, from a contemporary print, at the end of the
eighteenth century.
This print is an apt commentary on the fact that Willesden, which includes
Kilburn, in spite of its proximity to London, was a village surrounded by
countryside until the building of the railways. Its population in 1801 was a
mere 751. It grew by 1871 to 16,000 and by 1939 to 209,000, its peak.

High Road, Kilburn, in 1886.
This contemporary photograph shows the development of the area after the
beginning of the railway age. Beyond the row of Victorian houses and shops,
however, there are trees and green fields.

[6]

Angel Inn, Islington.
The Angel was formerly a coaching inn built in the seventeenth century as a stopping place for travellers from the north who preferred to stay the night rather than take the risk of being robbed by City thieves. The galleried courtyard is shown on page 128.

Crayford High Street in 1832.
This contemporary print shows Crayford when it was still a prosperous little township having little or no connection with London, and its prosperity was founded on its craft industries, especially the production of printed fabrics, an industry established more than three hundred years ago.

The Old Market House, Brentford.
This reproduction from a lithograph by G. F. Bragg dated 1849 shows the
market house, which was built during the reign of Charles II, just one year
before it was demolished. A charter for a weekly market and annual fair was
granted to the Priory of St Helen's in 1307. The market rights were held by the
Hawley family from the time of the dissolution of the monasteries, but these
rights were finally bought by the Middlesex County Council in 1891 and the
market continued to be held in the open square until 1932.

3. Life in Medieval London

THE change of government in the eleventh century made extraordinarily little difference to the growth of London. The reign of Edward the Confessor did, however, lay the foundations of a duality of power, that of London itself, and that of Westminster, which persisted in modified form throughout the Middle Ages and on into more recent times. The City of London was, as for many centuries, the centre of trade and commerce and controlled the finance which was essential to the well-being and sometimes to the very existence of the kings, but Westminster became the home of the sovereigns and the centre of the administration of justice and of law-giving.

Since the destruction of the West Minster by the Danes life among the marshes to the west of London had been dormant. It remained for Edward, the most godly and the most unworldly of all English sovereigns, to rebuild the Abbey on the island in the marshes and to build the palace which became the principal seat of the kings. Edward spent the last few years of his life in virtual seclusion, watching his brain-child come to life, the great new abbey with its noble church and elaborate conventual buildings, and the palace which was built under the shadow of the church and virtually formed part of the monastic foundation.

Edward endowed the Abbey lavishly. Among the manors which he made over to it was that of Hyde, especially important because it had within it a source of fresh water, an absolute essential for new communities since, even in the eleventh century, the Thames was contaminated by the sewage of London. The water was conveyed to the Abbey by conduit from a spot at the lower end of the Serpentine, now marked by an inscribed memorial stone erected in 1870 on the site of the conduit house. When the manor of Hyde reverted to the Crown in 1536 on the dissolution of the Abbey of Westminster the spring was preserved as a head of water and is mentioned in a charter of Queen Elizabeth in 1560. The conduit house was not removed until 1868, when the spring had been cut off by drainage.

Edward had spent much of his early life in exile in Normandy, so it was not surprising that he had developed a genuine admiration for the skill of Norman master masons and for the cultural life in Normandy that was far in advance of what had been achieved in England. He turned to his old friends at the Norman court to supply craftsmen and masons. The abbey church of Westminster, which was consecrated the day before King Edward died, was a Norman church rather than an Anglo-Saxon one.

Before he retired from an active part in the government of the realm, King Edward had installed Normans in the highest offices of State and Church. It is significant that a Norman became Bishop of London and so far as the records show was well received by the people of London. The opposition of the Earl of Wessex and other Saxon landlords and chieftains to the growing Norman influence was not necessarily matched by active opposition on the part of the merchants and crafts-men of London. It is more likely that their policy was determined by a desire for internal peace so that the trade and commerce on which they depended could continue to expand without interruption. They welcomed the trade routes opened up between England and Normandy.

When Edward died, however, the Witan elected Harold rather than William of Normandy to be king, and this could not have happened without the acquiescence of the London burghers. William of Nor-mandy invaded England to claim what he regarded as his rightful inheritance, with the all-important support of the Church. The cardinal mistake of those, including Harold, who had successfully defied King Edward's authority, was to appoint a Saxon prelate to the See of Canterbury against the will of the Pope. So although when Harold rode south after dealing successfully with the threat to his sovereignty in the north country, he augmented his forces with drafts from the City of London before riding on to do battle with William, when he had been slain on the field of Senlac the leaders of London were only lukewarm in their support for a possible Saxon successor.

William rode north from Sussex to Southwark, confidently expecting to be welcomed in the City. The welcome was not forthcoming, and rather than attempt to make an onslaught on London Bridge, still the only crossing of the Thames, he retired from Southwark to cross the river higher upstream and approach London from the west. The people of London realized that there was little future in continuing to support Edgar Atheling, the Saxon elected by the meeting of the Witan in London on Harold's death, and shortly William was acknow-ledged as king.

It is quite untrue, as so many historians have said, that London fought for Edgar Atheling against the conqueror. It would have been impossible for William with the small force at his disposal to take London by storm. The walls had been in good repair since the time of King Canute and were well manned. Without the support of London neither William nor any other king could have had real authority.

More accurately, London people had seen the light. They had come to the conclusion that in the circumstances the best interests of their city and of the country at large would be served by accepting William as king. In reaching this decision they had been influenced, no doubt, by the Bishop of London, as the people in the countryside were influenced by their priests, most of whose sympathies were with the Norman, whom they saw as a man of God whose faith had been vindicated by his victory over Harold.

William was crowned in the Abbey of Westminster only ten weeks after his victory at Senlac. He was the first of a long line of English kings to be crowned in Westminster. The ceremony was attended by many of the leaders of London. As a condition of accepting the new king the burgesses of London exacted a promise of a charter giving them an equal or greater degree of self-government than they had had in the days of King Edward. The promise was fulfilled. London's first formal charter addressed to the Bishop and all the burgesses of London, whether Norman or English, was published in 1068, or soon after-wards. Its first clause restates emphatically the continuance of all the laws and customs that existed 'in King Edward's day'. The charter, which can still be seen in the Guildhall archives, is written in Anglo-Saxon, the greatest possible compliment to the people of London. It was followed by many other charters given by later kings, illuminating the vital though sometimes troubled relationship between the city burgesses and the royal family through the ages.

There was no need for the leaders of London life to crave a return to the days of Good King Edward. They demanded (and obtained) much more. It was left to the others—the less fortunately placed in the English realm—to yearn for the imagined happiness of life under the last of the Saxon kings.

London was not included in the inventory of land and possessions ordered by King William and known as the Domesday Survey, of which there are many photographic copies derived from prints made in Victorian times by the photographers of the Royal Artillery as part of the function of the Ordnance Survey. The parishes adjoining the City, however, do appear in Domesday, and the picture presented of con-temporary Southwark, Lambeth and Holborn has made it possible to build up a panorama of the environs of the City in the eleventh century.

One of William's first acts after his coronation was to begin the building of a powerful fortress, which was nominally for the defence of London but which also served as a means of holding London people in check. This was the fortress which we know as the White Tower of the Tower of London. It was situated just within the Roman walls where they abutted on the river, but additions made to it in the later Middle Ages resulted in the castle being astride the line of the walls. The City never had jurisdiction over it, for it was a royal castle governed for the king by its constable, who also had authority over the neighbouring parishes to the east, the Tower Hamlets, which today are represented by the populous residential and industrial areas of the East End.

The Tower was built very near the camp which William had pitched while he negotiated with the burgesses. The work of converting the camp into one of the strongest fortresses in England took longer than expected, but within ten years of his accession William could feel secure behind the outer wall and the still uncompleted keep if ever he had need to take up a defensive position. In fact the need never arose, and the fortress, which stands today much as it was in the eleventh century apart from the insertion of larger window openings in the seventeenth century, was completed in the early years of the reign of Williams's successor, William Rufus. The fortress was known as the White Tower for the simple reason that it was customarily white-washed throughout the Middle Ages.

In the eleventh and twelfth centuries the castle was simply the White Tower with an outer defensive wall. On two occasions in the twelfth century it played an important part in London's history. When Stephen and Matilda were fighting for the crown, the Earl of Essex was Constable. To ensure his continued support he was given control of the City by Matilda. It was an unheard-of happening and the Earl was unable to assert his authority. Soon he was Stephen's prisoner and the Tower was returned to the Crown by way of ransom. Stephen cele-brated the occasion by restoring all London's rights.

When William Longchamp, Regent while Richard I was engaged in the crusades, made the Tower his headquarters he provoked the citizens of London into revolt. They supported John, another son of Henry II, later to become king, and the London militia was led by John himself when it besieged the Regent and compelled him to surrender the Tower. The tables were turned a few years later when John, having achieved his ambition of becoming king, found his erstwhile allies in London among the forefront of those who demanded the signing of the Magna Carta and faced the ignominy of the Tower being seized as a guarantee that the bill of rights would be signed. The Mayor of London was one of the signatories to the charter.

Apart from its interest as an example of Norman military building, the White Tower, now degraded into a museum of European arms and armour, is notable for the earliest and the most beautiful example of Romanesque architecture in London in its Norman chapel, which has been restored but not materially changed in appearance since the eleventh century. It is characteristic of the Norman builders that they should reserve their finest craftsmanship for the chapel, for all the most beautiful buildings in the new London which was taking shape under the aegis of Norman master masons were churches. Few have survived fire and expansion, but the church of St Bartholomew the Great in Smithfield gives a very good idea of the kind of church the Normans and their immediate successors built in London, some as the chapels of

monastic foundations, others as parish churches. Before the dissolution
of the monasteries in the sixteenth century there were more than a
hundred churches in London, mostly small, but some, like St Paul's
Cathedral, magnificent buildings comparable with any in the Middle
Ages.

The present church of St Bartholomew the Great is the choir of the
church which served the Augustinian priory and hospital of St
Bartholomew founded by Rahere in 1123. Rahere was a nobleman and a
courtier of Henry I. The priory and hospital were built to fulfil a vow
which he made when he recovered from an illness in Rome. Its sur-
passing interest derives from the fact that it was the first of many
London institutions endowed by wealthy people and designed to
relieve the sufferings of the sick and maimed. It has come down in
history as a hospital rather than a religious foundation. That is because
its medieval repute was so high that King Henry VIII allowed it to
continue its work after the Dissolution and actually increased its endowments, so that he was in effect a second founder of what became one of
the largest and most famous of London's voluntary hospitals.

It is difficult to think of the Middle Ages as a time when men gave
much thought to charity. It was a period in which right and might were
all too often equated, but in a crowded community like London considerable efforts were made to help those who could not fend for themselves. At first charity was mainly under the aegis of the Church, in
later days under the equally powerful aegis of the guilds. Most of the
religious foundations in the City cared for those who sought refuge
within their cloisters, while St Bartholomew's Hospital was the first
of a number of foundations designed especially for this purpose. Many
of these have come down to us only as names, like Spitalfields. The
priory of St Mary Spital was founded before the end of the twelfth
century in an area which later became well known as the district of the
silk weavers, many of whom were Huguenot refugees. The Elsing
Spital Priory was founded in Cripplegate in the fourteenth century. Its
charter placed on it the duty of caring for a hundred blind people.
Probably far more than a hundred blind men and women found shelter
within its gates.

The Temple Church is one of the oldest monastic churches still
forming a part of the modern London scene. Its nucleus is a round
church, by far the most elaborate and most interesting of the four
remaining in England. After savage bomb damage, it has been well
restored. Its original style was that of the Transitional phase of architecture, when Gothic forms were being superimposed on the traditional Romanesque style. The chancel, or Oblong, was added about
sixty years after its foundation in 1185 and shows the Early English
style of Gothic well developed.

The church in the twelfth century was the chapel of the Order of
Knights Templars. When that Order was dissolved in the fourteenth

century because of lack of support and suspicion of corruption, the church and its surroundings were granted to the Knights Hospitallers of St John, who in turn leased it in order to increase their revenue to the Guild of Legal Experts, who were beginning to take the place of the clergy as advocates in the courts.

The Temple became an Inn of Court and the Temple Church the chapel of the lawyers. Its special place in London life was recognized in Tudor times when, like Westminster Abbey, it was made a Royal Peculiar, i.e. a church outside the ecclesiastical jurisdiction of the bishops.

In London, or rather just outside the walls of London, Clerkenwell was chosen as the site of the great priory of the Order of St John of Jerusalem, which was founded early in the twelfth century. In the following three hundred years Clerkenwell Priory became one of the most important and effective of the religious houses in and around London. The original Priory was several times rebuilt but all the conventual buildings as well as the church have disappeared except for the crypt of the present church of St John. The Priory gatehouse, however, which was built in 1504, remains one of London's outstanding landmarks, and by a strange conservatism of site after many vicissitudes, including use as the editorial office of the *Gentleman's Magazine* in the eighteenth century and as a tavern and the headquarters of the Urban Literary Club in the nineteenth century, has been taken over by the Most Venerable Order of St John of Jerusalem, a British Order of Chivalry incorporated by charter of Queen Victoria. This Order has much the same purpose of tending the sick and the wounded as that of the original Knights Hospitallers, though it owes no allegiance to the religious ideals of the medieval body.

The name Clerkenwell is derived from the Clerks' Well, which according to Stow was near the west end of Clerkenwell church and was so named because the Ancient Company of Parish Clerks used to meet here. Near by, on the site of the church of St James, was the nunnery of St Mary, which was founded even earlier than the priory of St John and continued in active service until the Dissolution in 1539. Like many of the religious houses, it was dedicated to the rule of St Benedict.

The monastic house which achieved the greatest fame in the later Middle Ages was a Carthusian monastery known to us simply as the Charterhouse. This was founded towards the end of the fourteenth century and is properly described as the Priory of the Salutation of the Mother of God. It was built on part of Smithfield (the Smooth Field), always an open space in medieval London, under which it is said fifty thousand victims of the Black Death were buried. After the Dissolution Sir Edward North built a home on the site of the cloister, using much of the medieval masonry, but in 1611 the ideals of the original Charterhouse were revived when through the munificence of a London

merchant it was refounded as the Hospital of King James in Charterhouse, to include a free school, the forerunner of today's Charterhouse
School, and an asylum for eighty poor men. Pensioners are still housed
there and the school is still used for educational purposes. When the
original Charterhouse was removed to Godalming the buildings were
taken over by the Merchant Taylors' School, and since this in turn
removed to Moor Park they have been used as St Bartholomew's
Hospital medical school.

The orders of preaching friars were well represented. Most of them
had London establishments from the thirteenth until the sixteenth
century. The Priory of the White Friars was one of the largest and one
that has made its greatest mark on the City's history. This Carmelite
House was founded about 1240. Though it is perpetuated only in the
name of Whitefriars Street, the privilege of sanctuary attached to
the sacred ground of the monastery was allowed to continue after the
Dissolution until the end of the seventeenth century. By then the right
of sanctuary had been abused by criminals and debtors and the riff-raff
of London's squalor. As 'Alsatia' it had become a dark precinct into
which no law-abiding citizen dared enter. It was a no man's land
poised on the razor edge which separated the jurisdiction of the City
from that of the county. The abolition by law of the right of sanctuary
was long overdue.

The Augustinian or Austin Friars are also remembered chiefly by a
name on the map, Austin Friars by Throgmorton Street. In this case,
however, a fragment of the Priory survives in spirit (though unhappily
not in stone owing to the bombardments of 1940 and 1941) in the
Dutch church rebuilt from the ruins of the nave of the thirteenth-
century Augustinian priory church. The Priory after the Dissolution
was given to Protestant refugees from the Continent and by custom
became the exclusive preserve of people who had emigrated from
Holland.

The Order of Black Friars, the Dominican, has given its name to
a district as well as to the bridge over the Thames adjacent to the point
where the Fleet River flows into the parent river (by way of a sewer in
modern times). The Dominican friary won international fame when
Henry VIII chose it as the scene for the ultimate triumph of his campaign to secure a divorce from Catherine of Aragon. King Henry at
this time was in residence in nearby Bridewell House, a small Norman
castle-palace known to have been used as an occasional residence by
sovereigns from Norman times, though never having the dignity of
Westminster or even of the White Tower. King Henry had it rebuilt,
but after his time it was never used as a royal residence and was granted
by Edward VI to the City Corporation. It was ultimately used as the
infamous Bridewell prison.

Of the monastery of the Grey Friars not even a name survives as a
reminder. The site of the church of the Grey Friars was used for

building Wren's Christ Church and the site of their conventual buildings is occupied by the General Post Office.

Of the parish churches which served the 107 parishes into which the City of London was divided, eighty-six were destroyed in the Great Fire of 1666 and only fifty-one of those destroyed were rebuilt. By a process of attrition the number had been reduced to forty-seven by 1939. Of these eighteen were damaged beyond repair during the bombing of the Second World War. That is a sad tale of a dwindling architectural heritage spread over five hundred years. But it is perhaps more remarkable that there are some medieval churches still in existence. Several of these contain real gems of Gothic architecture. St Andrew Undershaft in Leadenhall Street represents the period just before the Reformation. St Ethelburga's, Bishopsgate, the smallest of the city churches (dedicated to the Ethelburga who was the first abbess of Barking and sister of Erkenwald, Bishop of London), represents the early part of the fifteenth century, St Helen's, Bishopsgate, is typical of the thirteenth and fourteenth centuries (this church also served a priory of Benedictine nuns), St Sepulchre Without Newgate in Holborn, as its name suggests just outside the medieval walls, is a rare anomaly, a Gothic church rebuilt by Wren, a Renaissance architect, but still Gothic in character.

Another remarkable restoration, but one carried out in our own time, is that of All Hallows, Barking by the Tower, a handsome medieval church believed to be of Anglo-Saxon foundation but predominantly Gothic. It was burnt to a shell during the wartime raids and has been rebuilt as a peacetime memorial and has resumed the position it has held since 1922 as Guild Church of Toc H. One part of the church which escaped destruction during the war was the brick tower, added during the Commonwealth, the only example of Cromwellian architecture in London, and incidentally the tower where Samuel Pepys took his stand to watch the progress of the first Great Fire. St Giles's, Cripplegate, almost as severely damaged as All Hallows, and mainly dating from the sixteenth century, is also being restored in close harmony with its original appearance.

Secular building proceeded faster in London, too, than in any other part of the country. The houses of the merchants were more and more sumptuous, taking up more and more space, so that all except the wealthy were herded together in almost unbelievable conditions of overcrowding. There was a greater gap in the fourteenth and fifteenth centuries in London between the haves and the have-nots than there has ever been in any English city at any time in history. In spite of energetic measures taken by the Lord Mayor and the aldermen (and by the sovereign) to prevent it, there was a steady drift from country to town, and far more people were crowded together within the walls of the City than could be accommodated. Many of these were without possessions and without special skills, and were destined to add to the always large number of beggars and petty thieves who contrived to make a living from the charitable or unwary. Congestion ultimately became so great that London perforce began to expand.

The Palace of the Savoy was built in the thirteenth century (the present Chapel of the Savoy dates from a rebuilding early in the nineteenth century). York Place, the town residence of the Archbishops of York down to the time of Cardinal Wolsey, when it was used as the nucleus of the Palace of Whitehall, was another palace on the north bank. On the other side of the river the Palace of the Archbishops of Canterbury at Lambeth was an imposing group of buildings which originated in the time of Archbishop Langton about 1220 and was elaborated and enlarged by many of his successors.

Other great residences followed though it was not until the sixteenth century that the line of houses or palaces along the Strand which were such a feature of London in Pepys's time was completed. The Bishops of Ely had a palace outside the city walls from the thirteenth century. Substantial ruins of this Gothic mansion remained in the eighteenth century, and even today the oratory of the bishops built in 1290 remains as the church of St Etheldreda in Ely Place.

The expansion of trade and the increasingly conservative government of the City are represented by the foundation and development of the craft guilds. These had overriding authority over all the members of the trades they represented. They determined the quality of the work, the training and terms to be offered to apprentices. They also had substantial funds which many diverted to the education of the children of members, help for the widows of deceased members and other charitable purposes. In later times all became primarily charitable foundations. Many of them remain so to this day, when their members are drawn from all walks of life rather than from the narrow circle of the craft or trade from which they originated.

Sir Richard Whittington is one of the most famous characters of the City of London in the last decade of the fourteenth century and the first two decades of the fifteenth. He was certainly one of the wealthiest merchants of the time. Although his work has become legendary there is no reason to doubt that he was directly responsible for the building or rebuilding of the Guildhall or that he gave munificent endowments to St Bartholomew's Hospital. In tradition and incidentally in pantomime he is associated with Highgate and with various interpretations of the age-old theme of local boy makes good. The most popular form of the tradition is that Dick Whittington, accompanied by his cat, was walking away from London and near the foot of Highgate Hill sat down to rest. While sitting there he heard the peal of Bow Bells, which suggested the jingle 'Turn again, Whittington, thrice Lord Mayor of London'.

The Whittington Stone near the foot of Highgate Hill commemorates this legendary event, with an inscription enumerating the three occasions on which Sir Richard Whittington was Lord Mayor—1397, 1406 and 1420. This stone is said to be on the site of at least two previous ones, of which there are records, and the legend is obviously an old one, though there is no known special connection between Whittington and Highgate. However, a more solid memorial to his fame (apart from the hospital named after him just beyond the stone) was the group of almshouses which were erected early in the nineteenth century to house a priest and twenty-four almspeople—single women over the age of fifty-five.

The Saddlers and the Bakers are historically the two earliest livery companies (as the craft guilds came to be known). Both were incorporated by the first decade of the fourteenth century. The Mercers is the company which takes civic precedence although it was not incorporated until 1393. Because these companies virtually controlled the trade of the City, the craft guilds or livery companies also controlled the government of London, the Lord Mayor and aldermen invariably being drawn from their ranks.

Contemporary accounts suggest that the City companies discharged their responsibilities with skill and restraint, although there are a hundred and one examples to show that there was often hard feeling between the labouring and even the apprentice class and the masters. The City government then was strong but it was threatened once, in 1381, when Wat Tyler, the leader of the Peasants' Revolt, assembled his ill-armed force on Blackheath, then marched on London, setting fire to the Palace of the Archbishop of Canterbury in Lambeth and the Palace of the Savoy and, wonder of wonders, entering the gates of the City, thrown open for him and his followers by traitors within, and finding a great deal of support among the apprentices. It is almost incredible, though true, that Tyler's men were admitted to the Tower, where Archbishop Simon Sudbury was murdered.

One section of the London community took the law into its own hands and seized the opportunity to redress its wrongs, looting the houses of the wealthy and killing hundreds of foreign workers, who had brought their skilled crafts to enhance London's trade. The situation was saved by young King Richard II, who courageously faced the rebels at Mile End and promised them redress of their grievances. Most of the rebels dispersed because they regarded the King as their friend, but Wat Tyler himself was struck down by Sir William Walworth, the Lord Mayor of London, at Smithfield. After that the harshest punishment was meted out to those who had dared to defy the City fathers' authority.

Seventy years later events came near to repeating themselves. In 1450 another revolutionary army laid siege to London. Again it was drawn mostly from Kent. Again it was mustered on Blackheath, but this time its leader was Jack Cade, an *émigré* Irishman rather than a native of Kent like Wat Tyler. Twenty thousand men, according to one account, poured into the City, demanding a repeal of the Statute of Labourers, and burning the fine homes of London merchants. Once more, as in the case of the rebellion led by Wat Tyler, Jack Cade's force dispersed on a royal promise, which remained unfulfilled, that they would be pardoned and their grievances redressed; though the death of Jack Cade of wounds received at the hands of the Sheriff of Kent was a more dignified affair than the murder of Wat Tyler by Sir William Walworth.

The Guildhall was built between 1410 and 1440. It was an emblem of the wealth and power of London as much as a building of utility. The great hall, which is the oldest civic building in London, shows (in spite of its several restorations) that money was no object when it was being built, and that as much care was lavished on it as on the City churches. Only the crypt, the porch and the walls of the splendid hall, more than 150 feet long, are medieval.

The building of the Guildhall, together with the embellishment of the medieval St Paul's Cathedral, were matched outside the City walls by the rebuilding of Westminster Abbey and the enlargement and re-designing of the Tower. By the fifteenth century the Tower was a very different place indeed from the simple fortress which had been London's chief bastion in the twelfth century. It well deserved its official title, 'His Majesty's Royal Palace of the Tower of London', for it was transformed into a concentric castle during the thirteenth century, most of the work being financed and supervised by Henry III. The Traitors' Gate, which was the fortified water-gatehouse, dates from this period, as also do the outer walls and many of their defences.

Westminster Abbey was rebuilt about the same time on a scale far grander than that envisaged by Edward the Confessor. The new church built in honour of St Edward the Confessor was consecrated in 1269. Further changes were made later. The nave was rebuilt once more in the fourteenth and fifteenth centuries and the Lady Chapel was dis-mantled in 1503 and replaced by Henry VII's Chapel, the most perfect example in Britain of the consummate elegance of the latest period of Gothic building.

The royal palace of Westminster was not neglected. Edward the Confessor's modest residence was rebuilt in the reign of William Rufus about 1097. Westminster Hall survives from this rebuilding, although only the lower stages of the walls can be dated with certainty to the original eleventh-century structure. The palace became something more than a royal residence in the later Middle Ages. The King's Court, the supreme legal tribunal in the country, sat in Westminster Hall from the thirteenth century.

This picture of peaceful development and expansion was threatened seriously only once by Wat Tyler's rebellion, but there were many set-backs in the orderly advance of London. The strong feeling against foreign elements in the City's economy, which as we have seen found full expression at the time of Wat Tyler's incursion, had already caused acute embarrassment in the thirteenth century, when it led to the expulsion of the Jews in 1290. This precipitate action created a temporary financial crisis, but the place of the Jews was gradually taken by Italian financiers, after whom Lombard Street, still one of the City's banking centres, is named.

The Black Death in 1348 caused fantastic loss of life, especially among the poorer classes. Many of the more wealthy fled the City and escaped the worst ravages of the plague. The immediate consequence was a shortage of labour and a demand for higher wages, but the City guilds surmounted the economic obstacles and emerged as wealthy as ever by the end of the century.

While the vast majority of the people lived within the limits of the old city and trade of every kind was their chief preoccupation, the market and fair days were the red-letter days in their calendar. St Bartholomew's Fair, the most significant of all the fairs, was held in Smithfield every year in the third week of August at the feast of St Bartholomew from 1133 until 1840.

Around the walls there was a kind of no man's land which was within the jurisdiction of the City authorities, extending as far as the bars which were set up on the principal routes out of town at the beginning of the thirteenth century or earlier, partly to mark the boundaries of the City authority, and partly to facilitate the collection of tolls. Temple Bar was one, Holborn Bar another. Small communities grew up in the vicinity of these bars and spread westward along the main roads. Holborn was quite a considerable place before Tudor times, including Gray's Inn and Staple Inn, and a number of other inns between what is now Theobald's Road and Fleet Street. By the end of the fifteenth century it had virtually become a part of London, though not, of course, under its jurisdiction. The main factor in this development was undoubtedly the growth of the Inns of Court.

Farther west the parish of St Giles was also expanding. There the Hospital of St Giles for lepers had been founded in 1117. It became comparatively wealthy through bequests, and sheltered many of the great number of lepers in London. As leprosy became less common it extended its charity to the old and infirm. It was in decline when Henry VIII dissolved the foundation and the lepers' church became the parish church of St Giles-in-the-Fields.

During the fourteenth and fifteenth centuries the village near the Hospital of St Giles grew, an early comentator mentioning its rural aspect and congratulating the village on the excellence of its gardens and orchards. To the north of London Finsbury was slower to develop, chiefly because the area of Moorfields was undrained marsh. Fitzstephen, a chronicler of the twelfth century, referred to play upon the ice by the youth of London when the fen was frozen over. From the beginning of the fifteenth century, however, when a causeway was built across Moorfields, development began to take place, but Clerkenwell remained the effective limit of the urban area in this direction and Finsbury was best known for its fields, which were set aside for the practice of archery because they were unsuitable for cultivation.

The story of the medieval suburbs to the east of London is inseparable from that of the Tower Hamlets. These came into existence as separate entities in the twelfth or early thirteenth century, when the Constable of the Tower became responsible for the defences of the Thames below London and of the lower part of the Lea valley. The Constable was given special powers which amounted to a delegation of the government's authority over the people living in the latter-day boroughs of Stepney, Poplar, Bethnal Green, Hackney and Shoreditch. So the Constable's authority reached from the boundaries of the City to Old Ford and Stratford and to Limehouse, Shadwell and Wapping. In effect, he was lord of a vast manor, including all these places. His unique position was perpetuated by the custom still followed at the beginning of the nineteenth century, by which the Constable of the Tower rather than the Lord-Lieutenant of Middlesex was responsible for raising the militia to defend the castle and the City.

Stepney's parish church, dedicated to St Dunstan and All Saints with St Thomas and St Faith (the patron saints of two other Stepney churches destroyed in air-raids), is evidence of its medieval growth. Originally a Saxon or early Norman foundation, it was enlarged in the thirteenth century and redesigned again two hundred years later, when it was able to accommodate several hundred worshippers. It lost its stained-glass windows during the war but remains a handsome essay in the late Gothic style. It is the centre of an almost deserted town, the busy trade of its high street which runs past it transferred to the Commercial and Mile End roads.

Across the river Southwark had become a town of first importance in its own right before the end of the Middle Ages. It was in an important strategic position as a bridgehead settlement, as it had been in Roman and Anglo-Saxon times. When a new London Bridge of stone was built, between 1176 and 1209, Southwark people were allowed to hold their market on the bridge. The priory of St Mary Overie stood north of the present St Saviour's Cathedral.

St Thomas's Hospital was another of Southwark's religious foundations dating from the early part of the thirteenth century. It was the forerunner of the modern St Thomas's Hospital by Westminster bridge, to which site it was transferred in 1871. The trade carried on by Southwark was second only to that of the City. There were workshops for making glass, for smelting iron, for making leather goods and for dozens of other manufactures. In 1295 Southwark was represented in the embryo Parliament and continued to return members to Parliament throughout the later Middle Ages, the only town in the London area to do so in the fourteenth century; Westminster was not represented until 1547. Houses and workshops stretched down the main road to the

Tabard Inn. Guest-houses and inns were numerous and Southwark
showed every sign of being prosperous. Any doubt of its importance
would be dispelled by the knowledge that the Tabard Inn, its site now
marked by a coloured mosaic design, was the place where pilgrims in
Chaucer's time gathered at the beginning of their long journey to
the shrine of St Thomas in Canterbury, himself a London man and
London's patron saint.

4. London's Countryside in the Middle Ages

THE links between the City of London and the area which is now Greater London were tenuous in the Middle Ages. They were forged to a large extent by mutual dependencies. The people of London depended on the surrounding countryside for a constant supply of food. The people of the countryside were glad to exchange their food surplus for the manufactured products of London and Southwark.

The proximity of London, the workshop of medieval England and an inexhaustible market for corn, wool and, above all, hay, inhibited the neighbouring counties from becoming industrialized. Far fewer craft industries flourished in the Home Counties than in other parts of England. There were, of course, exceptions but the vast majority of the parishes within twenty miles of London were wholly agricultural, their life revolving round work in the fields and around the weekly market in the nearest town, and the occasional fair at which the lords of the manor and the heads of the monastic houses often bought enough supplies of non-perishable goods to last a whole year.

By the fifteenth century the nuclei of almost all the towns and dormitory suburbs of Greater London had come into existence, and many of the administrative divisions of the twentieth century, most of which were based on parishes which have had a continuous history from the Middle Ages. In some cases a change of emphasis took place. What had been only a subsidiary hamlet became more important than the parent parish. Uxbridge, for instance, in the earliest records appears as a hamlet of Hillingdon parish, and it is in keeping with the historic legacy that the name of the Greater London borough has reverted to Hillingdon. Often, however, the medieval manor or parish has survived with extraordinarily little change in its boundaries.

Many are listed in the Domesday Survey, and it is possible to build up a picture of the whole area as it was in the latter part of the eleventh century. It is much more difficult to fill in any significant detail in the

41

history of the development of these early villages. That is more often than not because they had no real history apart from that consequent on the changing pattern of life over the centuries. They all shared in the economic consequences of the break-up of the feudal system. They mostly suffered from the ravages of the Black Death. Even if individual manors did not suffer casualties from this scourge they felt its economic aftermath, with the emergence of a class of landless workers who were in such short supply that the very nature of agriculture had to be changed. The arable land decreased in acreage, partly because there were not so many mouths to feed; the area under permanent pasture increased. Above all, the landless labourers, because they were indispensable to the farming community, were able to exert increasing pressure, and gradually they improved their working conditions.

This was not achieved without major unrest, in which the people of Kent played a prominent part, especially in the Peasants' Revolt led by Wat Tyler. Gradually life on the land approximated to the pattern of today. The process of change accelerated from the reign of Queen Elizabeth I onwards, when much of the land which had been cultivated on the open field system was enclosed and villages began to be built in compact groups, often round a village green.

That is the general picture. It is as true of Crayford as it is of Twickenham, of Enfield as it is of Beckenham. The background differs slightly from district to district because of local circumstances. Much of north-west Kent, for instance, was enclosed as early as the eleventh or twelfth century. Fields alternated with common land and waste, as they do today. The fields were generally much smaller than modern ones, the common land and waste land occupied a vastly greater proportion of the whole, but there was a basic similarity. In other districts, as on the northern fringe of London, enclosure did not take place on a large scale until the sixteenth century and was not completed for another two hundred years. But such differences are the exception rather than the rule and the life of the people in the several counties which make up the area did not differ except in detail.

The people of Kent, however, always enjoyed a rather greater degree of freedom than those of other counties and a class of independent yeomen farmers, midway between the great landowners and the landless labourer, was well established there much sooner than in other districts.

> A squire of Wales, a knight of Cales,
>   And a laird of the North Countrie,
> A yeoman of Kent, with half a year's rent,
>   Will buy them out all three.

That, of course, is not only a comment on the special position of Kentish yeomen but on the traditional prosperity of farming in Kent. It was due in no small measure to the greater efficiency and better land utilization where there were enclosed fields.

The Forest of Middlesex covered the greater part of the former county though, like the adjoining Forest of Essex, it was discontinuous and included a number of clearings in which the Anglo-Saxon communities had started cultivation. These communities were infrequent compared with many parts of the country and did not expand to any appreciable extent or multiply for several centuries. They were still relatively few in the tenth century.

The forest was an area of mixed woodland in which the oak predominated, and of open, partly heather-covered country, including Hampstead Heath and the Harrow Weald district. That is no doubt the reason why even as late as the sixteenth century sizable towns to the north of the Thames were few and far between and the perils from highwaymen to travellers approaching from the north correspondingly greater. There is some authority for thinking that in the twelfth century the forest approached within sight of the walls of London with a strip only a few miles wide between it and London in which cornfields and pasture land predominated.

Fitzstephen supports this picture: 'On the north are fields for pasture and open meadows. The arable lands are like the rich fields of Asia which bring plentiful corn. Beyond them an immense forest extends itself, beautiful with woods and groves.' It is a tribute to the intensive agriculture carried on in those parts of Middlesex which were free of forest that when the counties were assessed for wool tax in 1341 it was the second richest in England.

The forest was good hunting country with a plentiful supply of stags and wild boar. In that part of the forest nearest London yew trees were numerous and these were encouraged because yew wood was regarded as the best for making bows. William Maitland names 1218 as the year of the disafforestation of Middlesex but it is unlikely that the same forest laws ever applied to Middlesex as to Cornwall or Essex. Certainly the hunting was still good to the north of London in the reign of Henry VIII, when a royal proclamation called for the preservation of game for the King's use from the Palace of Westminster to Highgate, Hampstead Heath and Hornsey Park. Severe penalties were laid down for those who killed game within that area. When Princess Elizabeth was at Canonbury Tower she still found the surrounding woodlands excellent for hunting and hawking; Highgate then was a mere hamlet in the forest, a part of the village of Hornsey. It was not until the fourteenth century that the Bishop of London, the titular lord of the manor, had a road built through Highgate from London to Hornsey, and then on to Whetstone, erecting a toll-gate which became known as the Highgate. This road through the forest supplanted the older way by Crouch End, which became unusable because of the heavy clay over which it passed and the consequently deep ruts made by vehicles.

In many instances it is impossible to fill in more detail in the medieval picture because the records on which local history might be based are

E

lost. There are happily exceptions, however, Some medieval manors were granted to bishops. Though the actual grant was usually made to an individual bishop, in practice the grant was carried on from bishop to bishop through the centuries, and an association between the bishopric and individual manors was maintained for well over a thousand years. It is much easier to trace the records of an institution such as a bishopric than those of a lay manor. Kent again is the county in which the largest number of manors, including Bromley and Bexley, came under episcopal control at an early date.

Bromley is typical. Its history can be reconstructed in much greater detail than that of most parishes. Its story begins with the granting of the manor to the Bishop of Rochester but the date when that grant was made is not known. All that is certain is that the relationship was well established by the tenth century in the time of King Edgar, who confirmed the terms of a grant of land to St Andrew's Priory, Rochester, that is, the cathedral priory. This charter actually exists in the British Museum and defines the area of land concerned as extending in one direction to the boundaries of Chislehurst, in another to those of Keston, in another to those of Wickham, and finally to the boundaries of Mottingham. The precise, though not the approximate, date of even this charter is questioned. The charter itself was dated the 955th year from the incarnation of Jesus Christ and A.D. 955 is often quoted as its true date. This cannot be precisely accurate, however, since Edgar did not succeed to the throne until 959 and Dunstan, who is a signatory to the charter as Archbishop of Canterbury, also did not take office until 959. A.D. 960, therefore, is a more probable date.

The next hundred years, as we have seen, were a troubled time in the whole of eastern England and not least in that part of Kent which has been absorbed in Greater London. Many of the manors were ravaged by Danish incursions. The massacre of Danish settlers on St Brice's Day in A.D. 1002 at the tragic command of King Ethelred was the signal for another more disastrous series of Danish invasions, which culminated in the siege of Canterbury, in which thousands of the citizens were killed before the city surrendered.

It was against this historic background that the manor of Bromley was wrested from the monks of Rochester, probably at the instance of King Ethelred, who presented it to one of his ministers about 990. The monks and Bishop of Rochester were in no position to resist. In all probability their priory and cathedral had been left in ruins, and it is not surprising that the King believed that the property would serve a more useful purpose for the Crown than for the Church. However, Ethelred was compelled by the increasing pressure of the Church to restore the land to Rochester in 998.

From that time there is no record of Bromley being anything but a manor of Rochester, although soon after the turn of the millennium the Danes boldly sailed up the Medway and captured Rochester. This made little difference, however, to Bromley. It only meant that the manor's tithes which found their way to Rochester were seized by the Danes, while with the accession of Sweyn the profits of the whole country were attributable to the Danes. The position was restored when under Sweyn's son and successor, Canute, much of the damage which had been done to England's religious foundations was repaired. The ecclesiastical life of Rochester began again.

After the Norman occupation William appointed his kinsman, Odo, Bishop of Bayeux, Earl of Kent. For a few years Odo appropriated many of the estates belonging to the See of Rochester, including Bromley, possibly because the bishopric of Rochester was vacant or disputed. By 1077, when Lanfranc had been installed as Archbishop of Canterbury and had appointed Gundulf as Bishop of Rochester, the Earl of Kent had no hope of maintaining his hold on the estates of the Church, since it was with the help of the Church that William had succeeded to the throne of England. At the urgent request of Lanfranc, William convened a county meeting near Maidstone (on Penenden Heath according to some accounts), presided over by the Bishop of Constance. The result of the conference was that the Earl of Kent was compelled to return unequivocally all the possessions of the sees of Canterbury and Rochester which he had appropriated.

Almost immediately after this further confirmation of the grant of Bromley and other Kentish manors to the See of Rochester the Domesday Survey was held and the only effective medieval land registry compiled. There the manor is described specifically as the land of the Bishop of Rochester, and we learn from it that part of the estate was cultivated by the Bishop personally, that there was a water-mill in operation, and that the manor included a considerable acreage of oak woodland which provided acorns for swine to feed on in the autumn.

The total extent was between 4,000 and 5,000 acres, approximately the same as the nineteenth-century parish of Bromley and about two-thirds that of the twentieth-century borough. One-tenth of the area fell within the lord's demesne, that is, the area worked directly by or rather on behalf of the bishop, about one-half consisted of waste land, woodland and common land, and the remainder was cultivated by tenants tied to the land virtually as serfs and giving service to the bishop or his bailiff in lieu of rent. The population was approximately 250.

The Domesday Survey does not mention a church but this is not sufficient evidence that one did not exist. A church was certainly in existence in the twelfth century, when payment was being made to the bishop for consecrated oil used for baptism. There is no clue in Domesday either to the nature of the bishop's residence or palace, as it has become known. We can be sure, however, that a residence existed and that the bishop resided in it occasionally, as he did by convention in the residences attached to other Kentish manors which belonged to the see, whether or not the bailiff or manager was in permanent residence.

By the end of the twelfth century the episcopal manor house was in ruins. Bishop Glanvill reconstructed it in a style suitable for a bishop's residence, but it is still not known what sort of a house it was. By the early part of the sixteenth century it had once more fallen into disrepair and had to be rebuilt for a second time.

Through the efforts of this same Bishop Glanvill, Bromley became a market town in 1205, when King John made a proclamation to the Sheriff of Kent, granting the right to hold a market at Bromley every Tuesday throughout the year. By that time, too, part of the manor had been subleased and the first of the free Kentish families who contributed so much to the development of Bromley and neighbouring settlements were already in residence. These manorial tenants are properly described as holding their land in fief by knight service to the bishop. By then also the rector of Bromley had attained what were virtually the rights of a lord of the manor and several rectors held manorial courts, although this right was questioned by a number of bishops.

Records show that towards the end of the thirteenth century the Gilbertian situation arose of tenants being compelled to pay fines for petty breaches of regulations both to the rector and to the bishop. The matter was only resolved when the King called on the bishop to prove his rights to levy fines and taxes in the whole of the manor of Bromley. The bishop was able to justify his claims on the ground of immemorial rights and by implication the claims of the rector were disallowed.

The manorial rights of the rectors of Bromley, so far as they existed at all, arose solely from custom and were never formally recognized. They continued to be exercised until 1536, when the rectory reverted to the see by royal decree. That meant to all intents and purposes that the priest in charge of Bromley was no longer a rector but a cleric appointed by and responsible to the bishops. The manorial revenues which had been enjoyed by the rectors for so long were now diverted to the bishop's treasury and the bishop was required only to pay the curate in charge a reasonable stipend. Future curates in charge, or vicars as they came to be known, in spite of protests, were grossly underpaid because the finances of the See of Rochester were always more precariously balanced than those of some other sees.

However, there is no doubt that the rectors of Bromley were personages of real importance. One of them, Richard de Wendover, was appointed Bishop of Rochester in 1235. He was elected by the monks of the cathedral priory of St Andrew, an election which needed to be ratified by the Pope, who withheld his approval for three years, during which the see was vacant, on the ground that Richard de Wendover was not a sufficiently learned cleric to administer the see. But in 1238 the Pope's approval was given and Richard was consecrated.

In 1477, when the Tuesday market had been held for over 250 years, a new charter was obtained from the Crown the effect of which was to change the market day from Tuesday to Thursday and to authorize the holding of two annual fairs, one on 3 February, the other on 25 July. So Bromley became established as a highly important trading centre and probably one of the richest sources of income for the lord of the manor in north-west Kent. In practice the bishops leased the rights to hold the weekly market and the two annual fairs, which were of real commercial importance so long as the wool boom continued. This part of Kent was well suited to pasturing sheep and there was always a ready market for the fleeces. Later the commercial significance of the fairs declined and they became local holidays, attracting entertainers of one sort and another whose organized merry-making was of a far less respectable nature than that associated with a twentieth-century fairground.

The fairs as well as the weekly markets were held in the market-place, the booths and tents for the fairs being pitched round the market-house. The traditional market has lived on but both fairs were suppressed in 1865, when a new town hall was built to take the place of the old timber market-house.

Although it was an important place by the end of the fifteenth century, it would be wrong to think of Bromley as a large one by any modern standard. Life was still centred on the parish church, the bishop's demesne and the market-place, and a few scattered hamlets near the chief tenants' farmhouses at Sundridge, Bickley and Widmore. But the total population was not more than seven hundred, a population which had not varied much since the end of the thirteenth century. Although in this respect records are lacking, it is probable that the population was greatly reduced by the Black Death and that recovery was slow, as in the recorded instances of neighbouring townships. It is likely also that after the rebellion of Wat Tyler some of the landless workers migrated from Bromley, while the growing city of London was near enough to attract young men who were dissatisfied with conditions on the farms. The drift from country to town was as much a feature of the later Middle Ages as it was of any period in history, with the one exception of the massive migration at the time of the Industrial Revolution.

Other manors had a bewildering succession of lords and no settled policy of development such as was possible when the lord of the manor was a bishop or the dean and chapter of a cathedral, or if it was a royal manor. The manor of Edmonton, for instance, together with Enfield, was probably granted by King Offa to the Abbey of St Albans. If so, it was most likely sold by the Abbey, for it was in the possession of Asgar the Dane, Master of the Horse under Edward the Confessor, about the middle of the eleventh century, an interesting commentary on the degree of integration between English and Danes which had been achieved by King Canute and his successors, even in an area like Edmonton which was outside, though only just outside, the Danelaw.

By the time of the Domesday Survey the manor, together with that of Enfield and over a hundred other lordships, had been granted by William of Normandy to Geoffrey de Mandeville, who took the title Earl of Essex, as Odo, Bishop of Bayeux and half-brother of William, took the title in similar circumstances of Earl of Kent.

Nothing further is known of Asgar or his descendants, but the assumption is that Asgar's family was degraded like that of most of the Saxon thanes, though they may well still have held land from de Mandeville. Between the end of the eleventh century and the end of the fifteenth the manor passed through a number of families by marriage or purchase, no one family standing out as responsible for any major development or improvement of the manor. In 1480 it was held by Sir Richard Carleton, a friend of Richard III, who was charged with high treason within a year of the accession of Henry VII, and the manor, as always on such occasions, was escheated to the Crown, i.e. was confiscated by the King, and remained vested in the Crown. It formed part of Queen Henrietta Maria's settlement, was seized and sold by the Parliamentarians in 1650, but reverted to the Crown at the Restoration.

A few places stand out in sharp contrast with the gradual and often uneventful development of the manors in the Home Counties. Croydon established itself at a very early date as a place of special importance in the same way as Bromley, the town growing up round an episcopal residence, in this case that of the Archbishop of Canterbury. Just as Lambeth Palace was regarded as the town house of the archbishops, so Croydon Palace came to be regarded as their principal country residence, although the palace did not achieve its greatest fame until Tudor times.

The manor formed part of the endowment of the archbishops from Anglo-Saxon times and the old manor house was rebuilt in the fourteenth century to make it a suitable country home for the archbishop, who at that time ranked second only to the sovereign in importance. The palace was enlarged again by Archbishop Stafford in 1450 and subsequent years. The present Gothic porch belongs to the fourteenth-century rebuilding, the banqueting hall to Archbishop Stafford's enlargement. The parish church and the archbishop's palace formed the nucleus of the medieval town, but by the fifteenth century building had taken place up the hill towards the High Street and the name Old Town to describe the part of Croydon centred on the church is found in a document of 1437.

Fulham, where the manor had been in the possession of the See of London since Saxon times, became ultimately the official residence of the Bishops of London, though here the medieval settlement did not approach the size of Bromley or Croydon.

Hornsey is one of the many manors to the north of London which were in the possession of the See of London from the time of the Conquest or earlier. Its name appears to be an alternative to Haringey, adopted as the name of the Greater London borough. It was a vast manor and parish, which included what is now Highgate and a great stretch of densely wooded countryside to the north, as well as the hamlets of Muswell Hill, Crouch End and Stroud Green.

The Bishops of London had a hunting-lodge on the manorial land believed to have been on the site of the present Highgate golf-course. It has been suggested that Hornsey's parish church of St Mary was rebuilt about 1500 with stone taken from the fabric of the bishop's lodge. The tower, the only surviving fragment of the medieval church, is the oldest building in Hornsey, standing rather incongruously beside the modern parish church, which was built in 1889 close to the site of its three predecessors.

The historic site of which most is known in the Middle Ages, however, is Hornsey or Haringey Park, which was a clearing in the hunting forest. It was here that an important group of nobles, including the Duke of Gloucester and the Earl of Arundel, staged a demonstration against the dictatorial government of Richard II and, in particular, his confidence in the Earls of Oxford and Suffolk. The King appears to have been alarmed at this demonstration and acceded to most of their demands, including the banishment of the Earl of Oxford. Fifty years later Hornsey Park again comes into the annals of romantic history as the place where Thomas Southwell was accused of having said masses in the lodge over instruments used for devising necromantic means of destroying the person of King Henry VI. This emerged in the trial of the Duchess of Gloucester, in 1441, for practising sorcery against the King's life. Southwell was condemned to be hanged, drawn and quartered at Tyburn but died in prison before the sentence was carried out. The Duchess was condemned to perpetual penance but her case aroused a great deal of sympathy among nobles dissatisfied with the King's management of State affairs.

Yet another incident in the medieval story of Hornsey was the meeting in 1483 between Richard of Gloucester and the Lord Mayor and Corporation of London, who were said to be arrayed in scarlet and attended by five hundred citizens who joined the royal procession. The Duke of Gloucester had with him on this occasion the boy king, Edward V, whom he had virtually kidnapped at Stony Stratford and was conducting to London with a strong force of cavalry. King Edward rode at the head of the procession from Hornsey through Highgate and was welcomed on his way by thousands of loyal citizens who lined the route where it approached the walls of London. Seven weeks later he had disappeared, together with his brother, the Duke of York, and was never seen again. By then the crown had been offered to and accepted by the Duke of Gloucester, who became Richard III.

Kingston, which had enjoyed such fame as the coronation place of several of the Saxon kings in the tenth century, retained its royal associations until the fourteenth century. A major event in the

thirteenth century was the meeting here between Louis, the son of the
French King, and the English barons to negotiate a settlement after
Louis had accepted the barons' invitation to help them dethrone King
John, but the King had died before the dilemma could be resolved.
The treaty resulted in the accession of Henry III.

That perhaps explains why Kingston was one of Henry's favourite
towns and one, incidentally, where the barons who were the King's
enemies rallied their forces before the battle of Lewes in 1264. Still
more significantly, on the death of Edward III in 1377, emissaries of
London came to Kingston to do homage to Richard II. During the
fourteenth century the town achieved its greatest prestige and customarily returned two members to Parliament.

The foundation of St Mary Magdalene was endowed early in the
fourteenth century by Edward Lovekyn, by whose name it is still
known. Edward Lovekyn was Bailiff of Kingston; John Lovekyn, his
heir, was four times Lord Mayor of London and still further endowed
the foundation, thus forging a permanent link between the people of
Kingston and the burgesses of the City. The link was made still
stronger when Sir William Walworth, who was apprenticed to John
Lovekyn, and, as recorded in the previous chapter, was Lord Mayor at
the time of Wat Tyler's rebellion, bequeathed still more to Lovekyn's
foundation. From what was originally a chantry chapel there developed
the free grammar school founded in the reign of Queen Elizabeth I.
The chapel, which has been beautifully restored, was used as the main
classrooms until a modern school-house was built in the nineteenth
century.

Havering is a name which appears frequently in the medieval annals
of the country to the east and north-east of London. This, too, has been
adopted as the name of a Greater London borough. It was used in the
Middle Ages to describe an area which included Hornchurch, and
which became the Royal Liberty of Havering. In Hornchurch during
the Norman period was the only church within the whole of the district,
which also included Romford, originally a hamlet of Hornchurch.
There are references to a Saxon palace at Havering and this may have
been near the present village of Havering atte Bower, where there was
certainly a royal lodge in Tudor times, but evidence of its precise
position is lacking. In all probability, like Eltham, it was originally a
hunting-lodge conveniently situated for use as a base by royal parties
for hunting in the Forest of Essex, of which a fragment survives in the
nearby Hainault Forest. Whatever the exact situation of the palace, it
was responsible for giving Hornchurch and the surrounding villages
and hamlets special privileges within the Royal Liberty, in which there
were seventeen manors, nine of them in Hornchurch.

Some mystery also surrounds the priory or hospital of Hornchurch.
It is called Cornutum (horned) in a charter of Henry III, and is known
to have been an alien priory administered by the monks of St Bernard.

It was confiscated by the Crown during the reign of Richard II, in common with most of the alien priories of Britain. The church of the Horned Monastery is now the parish church of Hornchurch, famous for its emblem of a bull's head and horns at the east end of the chancel. A prosaic but quite possible explanation is that the name and the emblem are both related to the tanning trade, which was established here by the twelfth century and remained the staple trade of the district for many hundreds of years. The market at Romford, which was chartered in 1247, gave the tanners of Hornchurch an outlet for their goods on the main medieval highway.

In many of the ancient parishes which make up the Greater London of today the church is the only link with the Middle Ages, as indeed is the case at Hornchurch. Many reflect in their size or elaboration the agricultural prosperity of the district. Two of the most interesting in Kent and Surrey respectively are Crayford and Carshalton. Both, like most medieval churches, are exceptionally well sited. Crayford church stands on a hill dominating the modern industrial town as surely as it dominated the high street of the medieval village. Dedicated to St Paulinus, it is of Norman foundation, and Norman workmanship can be traced in the walls of the present nave. Most of the church, however, including the noble tower, represents a complete rebuilding in the fifteenth century. Its fabric is of Kentish ragstone and locally quarried flint from the chalk downs. A special feature of the interior is the division of the nave into two parts, with the arcade between them. The fine south doorway is a tribute to the thirteenth century and was doubtless a later embellishment of the Norman church.

The parish church of Carshalton, dedicated to All Saints, is also built partly of locally quarried flint and stone and retains the characteristic workmanship of many periods of English church building. The lady chapel, which was the chancel of the medieval church, is in the style of the thirteenth century, its timber roof dating from a hundred years later. The south aisle is in the Early English style of the thirteenth century but the effect of the fine medieval craftsmanship is lessened by the late nineteenth-century rebuilding, which though it left these parts intact degraded the chancel to a lady chapel and substituted a new chancel and nave. That is true of all too many churches in Greater London, but Carshalton church has a special place in many people's affections, if only because it is situated beside the ponds which mark the headwaters of the Wandle, while the park lands and gardens on the farther side of the water preserve remarkably the spirit of an ancient village, in spite of the busy main road which separates the churchyard from the ponds.

A few, but only a few, of the medieval settlements retain fragments of pre-Reformation houses but these are not nearly so numerous as medieval churches. Orpington Priory is outstanding as an example of a medieval rectory (the name Priory is misleading). Parts of the present building may well be of the thirteenth century. It is surely one of the very earliest of homes still standing in the parishes of Greater London. The 'Ancient House' opposite the church in Walthamstow village, an extremely handsome timbered building rather marred by neo-Georgian shop fronts, is also pre-Reformation in origin and has been well restored.

Even the parishes nearer the City developed only slowly between the eleventh and the sixteenth centuries. Islington, for instance, remained a village, its most notable building the Hospice of St Anthony, which from the fifteenth century onwards cared for the needs of lepers and to some extent supplanted the earlier lazar-house at St Giles. It has been suggested that the original of the Whittington Stone was a landmark set up to catch the eye of passing travellers and remind them to drop money into St Anthony's alms box.

St Pancras and St Marylebone, too, were quiet villages which, like all the other settlements of the Greater London area, had no link with London except in the exchange of goods. Both were watered by one of London's now hidden rivers. The Fleet divided the parish of St Pancras into two almost equal parts with the Old Church close to its banks. The Tyburn watered the fields of St Marylebone, dividing to flow into the Thames by two separate streams, containing within them the island in the marshes on which the first Westminster Abbey had been built. Paddington was even smaller, a tiny village centred on the parish church of St Mary on Paddington Green and scarcely expanding at all until after the sixteenth century.

Although most of the markets and fairs in the rural districts were parochial affairs, some had a much wider fame. One or two of them, though scarcely rivalling St Bartholomew's Fair, enhanced their prestige as time went on and became of national or international significance. Barnet Fair is one of these which has survived with vigour the perils of the nineteenth century, when so many fairs were degraded. Indeed it absorbed what was left of Bartholomew Fair when that was removed from Smithfield. Its first charter was granted by Henry II, and it is still held in the first week of September.

Uxbridge and Pinner Fairs are others which proudly boast a vigorous existence from the Middle Ages to the present day, though of a very different kind from that of Barnet. Others equally well known, like that of Mitcham, are of more recent origin. Held on the Three Kings Piece on three days of August, it may have been chartered by Queen Elizabeth I when she visited Mitcham in 1598. If so, the charter has disappeared. Even if the original purpose of the annual fair is lost except in the case of Barnet, the weekly street markets or markets held in the market square, as at Kingston and Romford, are a vivid reminder of those far-away times.

The importance of the monastic foundations was, as we have seen, very great in the daily life of the City. It was almost as great in parts of the countryside, though some of the monastic foundations were so small that they can have made little material difference to the life of the neighbouring settlements except as a possible refuge in sickness or extreme adversity.

Bermondsey grew up around its monastery as surely as Westminster developed around its abbey. Bermondsey was a dependent priory of the Abbey of Cluny. Founded soon after the Norman occupation it was heavily endowed by offerings and bequests from kings as well as noblemen and became one of the most powerful outside London. Early in the fifteenth century it achieved the status of an abbey in its own right; it was chartered by Henry VI with the agreement of the Pope and the Abbot of Cluny.

It was an occasional royal residence as well as a monastery. More precisely, a royal house was attached to it. The widows of two English kings, Henry V and Edward IV, took up residence there after the sovereign's death. The link between the great monasteries and the royal house was always a close one, and it was at Bermondsey that Henry II held a vital meeting of clergy and barons in 1154, the meeting which some historians regard as the first assembly of an English parliament, although the constitution of the meeting was more like that of the Anglo-Saxon Witan.

There is no doubt now that Barking Abbey was the most important, powerful and the wealthiest nunnery in Britain, and continued to be so for more than three hundred years. Among its nominated abbesses in the twelfth century were Matilda (or Maud), the wife of Henry I, Matilda, the wife of King Stephen, Mary, the sister of Thomas Becket, and Maud, the daughter of Henry II. It must be remembered that in this period the Abbess of Barking held the rank of a baron with all the privileges and obligations associated with the title except that of following the king into battle, and that the actual day-to-day management of the Abbey was in the hands of the prioress, nominally second in command.

When abbesses came to be elected in the thirteenth century, yet another member of the royal family was appointed to the office, Maud, the daughter of King John, who was Abbess for five years. There is further evidence of the close connection between the Abbey and the sovereign about this time in the rights which the Abbey enjoyed in the Forest of Hainault and in the numerous gifts which are recorded as being given to the Abbey from the king's demesne at Havering.

A new abbey church was built in the twelfth century, enlarged in the thirteenth century and was little altered afterwards except for the addition of one or more towers. Excavation of the foundations has shown conclusively that the abbey church was by far the largest nunnery church in the country, 337 feet long and 100 feet wide at the transepts, 80 feet longer than the corresponding Benedictine nunnery church of Romsey. The surviving so-called 'Curfew Tower' was the

gatehouse of the Abbey, built in the fourteenth century and reconstructed in 1460. There is a twelfth-century stone rood in the chapel
over the gateway, and this rood was an object of medieval pilgrimage.
The adjoining parish church of St Margaret was not part of the Abbey
but co-existed with it. Built about 1215, it was enlarged in the fourteenth century and again in the fifteenth.

The latter part of the fourteenth century was a time of disaster for the
Abbey, just when its revenues were increasing as Barking itself grew
and its market became more important. The disaster took the form of
serious flooding, first noted in 1377 and repeated in later years, resulting
in the devastation of much of the Abbey's possessions along the
Thames. This, following close on the heels of the Black Death in 1349,
undermined the Abbey's very existence. The dikes along the Thames
had fallen into disrepair, possibly because of the shortage of labour
after the Black Death. Alternatively they may have become inadequate
through a slight fall in the level of the land or a rise in the level of the
river about that time. There are records of extensive flooding in other
parts of the country during the latter part of the fourteenth century.

The expense of rebuilding dikes and keeping them in repair reduced
the Abbey to comparative penury, so much so that successive abbesses
were excused many of their customary dues and obtained some additions to their revenues. It is recorded in one of the still extant State
papers that, in recognition of the great losses suffered by the Abbey
through the inundation of the marsh lands of Dagenham and Rainham
and Barking, Henry IV in 1409 remitted for ten years payments customarily made by the Abbess to the royal exchequer. It also acknow-
ledges the expenses to the Abbey of repairing the river defences.

The heyday of Barking was over but the Abbey continued to rank as
a major one until its dissolution, and there are no records of wild
accusations of immorality or incompetence being levelled against its
abbesses like those made against the abbots and abbesses of many of the
great monasteries early in the sixteenth century. It was not included in
the list of smaller monasteries which were surrendered to Henry VIII
by Act of Parliament in 1536, but three years later the Abbess was one
of the prelates asked to sign away their monasteries voluntarily in order
to avoid enforcement by Act of Parliament.

The Abbess, Dorothy Barley, agreed and gave the deed of surrender
to the Royal Commissioners on 14th November. Two years later, it is
said, the Abbey buildings were unrecognizable. The King was planning
enlargement of his manor house at Dartford and of the palace at
Greenwich. Here was a fine supply of stone which could be carried by
barge to Dartford and Greenwich cheaply and quickly. By the end of the
century only shapeless fragments remained except for the great tower of
the church, which was still standing in the last decades of the nineteenth
century, and the gatehouse, which has survived to the present day.

What Barking Abbey was to the Essex bank of the Thames estuary,

Lesnes was to the south or Kent bank. It was an Augustinian abbey
(not priory as many have supposed) founded by Richard de Lucy in
1178, under the name of the Abbey of St Mary and St Thomas the
Martyr for Canons Regular of the Order. The circumstances surrounding its foundation are interesting in themselves, more particularly
because they serve as a link between Lesnes and Thomas Becket,
Thomas of London. De Lucy was an associate of Becket both when he
was Chancellor and when he had become Archbishop of Canterbury.
When the dispute arose between Becket and the King on the always
vexed matter of royal prerogatives de Lucy remained loyal to the King
and was twice excommunicated by Becket for his continued loyalty. It is
suggested that the Abbey was founded by him as a form of penance
just eight years after Thomas was murdered within the precincts of
Canterbury Cathedral, and that he dedicated it to St Thomas as some
recompense for having deserted his holy friend. A year after the
foundation of the Abbey Richard resigned his office of Justiciar and
became a member of his own Abbey, where he died three months after
he took up residence, and was buried in the chapter house.

Lesnes was not destined to have an ordinary history at any stage. The
second Abbot, whose coffin slab was also found in the chapter house,
accepted the reformed and sterner rule of Arrouaise, an abbey in the
Arras diocese of France which rebelled against the growing laxness of
the Augustinian Order in the same way as the Abbey of Cîteaux, the
forerunner of the Cistercian Order, rebelled against the laxity of the
Benedictine rule. This reformed Order of Arrouaise included in all
about thirty houses on the Continent and nine or possibly ten in
England, including Carlisle and Dorchester as well as Lesnes.

By the thirteenth century the long struggle between the Canons of
Lesnes and the forces of nature as represented by the tideway of the
Thames had begun, and they continued until the Dissolution. Just as
the Abbey of Barking provided most of the finance necessary to keep
the river defences in order on the north bank, so the Abbot of Lesnes
made himself responsible for a long stretch of the river between Erith
and Woolwich. Between 1230 and 1240 the river wall was breached on
several occasions and disastrous floods followed, and it was 'at the
request of the whole countryside', according to a medieval document,
that the Abbot undertook the future direction of the work. Thereafter
it was always the repair of the river wall that bulked largest in the
secular activities of the Abbey.

According to Lambarde, the Abbot in 1279 recouped some of the
Abbey's expenditure by enclosing part of the marshland of Plumstead.
It is likely that the Canons played a large part in the reclamation of an
area which was extremely fertile by Tudor times. In 1330 the Abbey
received the benefits of the living of Aveley 'to offset the expenses of
repairing the dikes and of entertainment through being close to a main
road'.

Lesnes was certainly close enough to the main road from London to Canterbury to receive many distinguished pilgrims to the shrine of St Thomas, including Edward I. Entertaining royalty was a very expensive matter. There is every reason to think that this dual and inescapable expenditure proved a continuing drain on the resources of the Abbey, for by 1383 we find that a will drawn by a fishmonger, or more strictly a fish merchant, of the name of William de Kelleshall is dated and signed as 'at my mansion house within the Abbey of Lesnes'. It was commonplace in the fifteenth century for monastic houses to draw rent from secular tenants of dwelling-places within the precincts but this is one of the earliest recorded instances in all Britain.

Ten of the first nineteen monastic houses to be suppressed were Augustinian abbeys or priories, and Lesnes was one of them. The Abbot formally handed over the keys of the Abbey to Cardinal Wolsey's agent on 18 February 1525. That was the end of three and a half centuries of corporate endeavour, but by the sixteenth century Lesnes was but a shadow of its former self and work was no doubt found for the resident Canons, who unlike the majority of monks were ordained and whose primary purpose was to spread the gospel in the spirit of St Augustine.

The tragedy was that although work might be found for the Canons, the extensive monastic buildings were allowed to decay. How extensive they were can be inferred from the partial reconstruction which has been made by members of the Woolwich Archaeological Society in co-operation with Christ's Hospital, the owners of the land. The reconstruction also gives a slight idea of the magnificence of the church and of some of the conventual buildings. Glazed and painted tiles comparable with those at Strata Florida in Wales, and of which the most perfect example is the tiled floor of the chapter house of Westminster Abbey, were found during excavation. There are fragments also in the museum of the Purbeck marble which was brought by sea to give added lustre to the pillars of the church. The site of the Abbey was sold again and again and more than once was dug over for building materials, until in the seventeenth century the small part of the walls that had survived was made good and the land bequeathed to Christ's Hospital.

A well known but far less important nunnery than Barking was the Priory of Kilburn. This had no existence before the Norman occupation and was serving no useful purpose at all by the time it was suppressed by the commissioners of Henry VIII. However, it was undoubtedly the first settlement on the site of modern Kilburn and gave its name to the district. It was situated on the Hampstead side of the Kilburn High Street only a short distance from the modern highway. Not a trace of it has survived, but an etching of about 1722 shows that some of the Priory building had been converted into a substantial private house which was then still in good repair.

The origins of this Priory are rather obscure. A tradition is that it was a hermit's cell or hut before it could be dignified with the name of priory. This is unlikely. There is, however, evidence that the land on which it stood was made over to the Abbey of Westminster by one Godwin, the legendary hermit, early in the twelfth century and that, with the consent of the Bishop of London, a priory was established here by the Abbey for three nuns and a chaplain. The three ladies in question are said to have been maids of honour to Matilda, Henry I's wife, who was certainly a most religious person and may have inspired in her young friends a desire to devote their lives to religion. She is also known to have had especially good relations with the Abbot of Westminster. She was the same Matilda who was nominated Abbess of Barking.

Godwin was the first warden, and successive wardens or chaplains were appointed by the Abbot of Westminster, who made over further property from time to time to the Priory in consideration of the nuns saying prayers for the souls of the abbots and brethren of Westminster. Later the Priory acquired further manors in Knightsbridge and also in Surrey and Kent. In the thirteenth century the control passed from the Abbot of Westminster to the Bishop of London and the number of nuns increased as the needs for a larger priory to accommodate pilgrims to the shrine of Our Lady of Wilsdon increased. This shrine was situated in the parish church of St Mary and at the time when the pilgrimage was most popular attracted visitors from London and many places farther afield. But it had no accommodation of its own and was in a singularly isolated position, surrounded by dense woodlands and uninhabited common and waste land. The calls which were thus made on the Priory of Kilburn were too great for it to sustain. In spite of its considerable endowment it was reduced by 1377 to great distress and called for an inquiry by the Bishop of London, who deplored the conditions of poverty remarked upon by travellers to the shrine. By the Dissolution the commissioners' inventory shows that it was in possession of forty acres of cultivated land in Willesden, apart from its other endowments. Nevertheless it was suppressed by the Act of 1536, which applied to monastic houses with a yearly value of less than £200. The priory lands were transferred by the King to the Knights Hospitallers of St John of Jerusalem, and when that Order was also dissolved, only a few years later, to the Earl of Sussex. The estate was later divided and by the eighteenth century only the abbey farm (the priory, like so many others, had been elevated in the imagination of its owners to the status of abbey) remained as a reminder of its four hundred years of service.

The history of Acton Priory is even more obscure than that of Kilburn. Virtually nothing definite is known about it, though the mansion that was built on its site after the Dissolution has bulked large in Acton's history. Traditionally the Priory is known as Berrymead, or

Berrymeade, Priory, but it is quite likely that this name became attached to it only after it had ceased to be a monastery. One local historian says that the Priory contained upwards of forty nuns, a most unlikely statement or, if true, one that suggests that Acton Priory must have been a much more important establishment than the dearth of records suggests. It is not even certain that it was a nunnery. It is known, however, that after the Dissolution it was granted, along with the manor of Acton, which had been held by the Dean and Chapter of St Paul's, to Lord Russell, first Earl of Bedford. Following the custom of the times, the fabric of the Priory was used in the building of a mansion, which has been remodelled on several occasions since then, though the house of today almost miraculously retains traces of the old mansion, including, it is said, a secret panel in the drawing-room giving access to one of the small hideaways which were often built into houses of the sixteenth and seventeenth centuries.

Many famous people lived in Berrymead Priory, including the Dukes of Kingston. Edward Lytton Bulwer (Bulwer Lytton), afterwards Lord Lytton, was one of the last of its distinguished residents before it was converted into a club and in the 1960's a social centre for the employees of an adjoining bakery. It stands today in the cramped surroundings of Salisbury Street, dwarfed by the municipal offices, but little more than fifty years ago, in 1912, it was still a gracious residence in a noble park. 'The entrance to it', says W. King Baker, writing in 1912, 'is on the north side of High Street, and there still stands the Gothic doorway with its overgrowth of ivy. One of the things that must be regretted in the modern history of Acton has been the loss to the town of the beautiful estate once surrounding this beautiful old mansion.'

Nineteenth-century prints show that it was a magnificent house, forming with its park an architectural landscape of a more pleasing kind than most of the Victorian era. It had an ornamental lake, which has now totally disappeared, and a good deal of mature timber, with well-tended gardens and many evergreen bushes. There is a great deal to be said for Baker's thought, 'if it had been realized what a great advantage to the town it would have been to have had these beautiful well-wooded grounds for a central park directly adjoining the site upon which the municipal buildings have now been erected, doubtless the small difference which stood between the old local board and the owners would not have been allowed to prevent the purchase from being completed'. Needless to say, the park has been obliterated by new building, and Baker's lament pinpoints a classic example of what might have been if modern ideas of town planning had come into their own fifty years before they did.

Syon Abbey at Isleworth was a far more important foundation than Acton and more is known about it. It was a nunnery founded in 1414 by Henry V and was granted a part of a royal park, presumably Twickenham Park, which lay on the Middlesex bank downstream from

Kingsbury Old Church. Part of the fabric of this ancient church is composed of bricks taken from the remains of Roman buildings. Kingsbury is situated close to the line of Roman Watling Street, a fact which explains the abundance of Roman material available to the medieval builders. The church, which is dedicated to St Andrew, is an Anglo-Saxon foundation, several times enlarged and restored towards the end of the nineteenth century.

Grim's Dyke (*top*).
This earthwork,
consisting of a well-
marked ditch and bank,
is the most arresting of
the surviving earthworks
in Greater London.
Situated to the north of
Harrow Weald, it was
most probably
constructed as a
boundary defence of an
early Anglo-Saxon
kingdom.

The Tabard Inn (*left*).
According to Chaucer,
pilgrims to the shrine of
St Thomas at
Canterbury assembled at
the Tabard Inn. Its site,
now occupied by a
public library, is
commemorated by this
modern mosaic depicting
Chaucer and the pilgrims
at the 'Prize Feast'.

...es from a Pier of Old London ...ge (*right*). These stones, which ...e taken from one of the piers of ...London Bridge when it was ...olished in 1832, are in the ...chyard of St Magnus the Martyr. ...approach to Old London Bridge ...through the churchyard and ...er the church tower.

...ew City Landmark (*below*). ...ing the wholesale reconstruction ...e area to the north of London ...., made necessary by enemy ...bardment, this fragment of the ...ieval church of St Alphage was ...ilt stone by stone. The ultra- ...ern block of steel, glass and ...rete in the background is named ...the church St Alphage House.

The Cross Keys, Dagenham (*top*). While modern Dagenham has grown into one of the most populous of twentieth-century communities, the old village has survived almost intact, including the inn, which faces the parish church across the road and dates from the sixteenth and seventeenth centuries. Renovation has not obscured the signs of its early origin.

The Whittington Stone (*left*). This stone commemorates Sir Richard Whittington, one of the most famous citizens of London in the fourteenth and fifteenth centuries, three times Lord Mayor, in 1397, 1406 and 1420. In tradition this same Richard is identified with the legendary Dick Whittington and the stone is said to be on the site of the one on which Whittington sat and heard the peal of Bow Bells, suggesting to him the words 'Turn again, Whittington'.

Enfield Market Place. The octagonal market house or 'cross' was built in the classical style between 1820 and 1830 and has since been restored. The embattled tower in the background is that of the parish church of St Andrew, which dates from the fourteenth century.

The Great Barn of Ruislip (*below*). This barn is part of the Ruislip Manor Farm estate. The Manor Farm, which dates from the end of the sixteenth century, together with the Great Barn and another more modern barn, was presented to the local government authority in 1932 by King's College, Cambridge, which has been lord of the manor since 1441 when Henry VI founded King's College.

The Horns of Hornchurch (*left*). The head of a horned bull takes the place of a cross at the east end of the church of St Andrew, Hornchurch. The head is of stone, the horns of copper. It may be linked with the name of the town (there is some evidence under a charter of Henry III for a 'monasterium cornutum' here, i.e. horned monastery, the priory or hospital which was a dependency of the Hospice of St Bernard). Another explanation is that the bull's head is linked with the tanning industry, which was a staple industry in the later Middle Ages.

Walthamstow Village (*below*). Walthamstow, like Dagenham, has retained many of the old buildings which won it the reputation as late as the nineteenth century of being a place of singular beauty. One of the oldest domestic buildings, not only in Walthamstow but in all Greater London, is pictured here, the Ancient House, formerly known as the White House, which may well have been built before the end of the fifteenth century, although only the upper storey retains some early workmanship. Opposite is the parish church of St Mary.

Orpington Priory. The priory at Orpington was never a priory in the
sense of being a community of monks but is the comparatively modern
name by which this handsome flint-built residence is universally known. It
is, in fact, one of the few pre-Reformation clergy houses which have
survived in Britain and, like the Ancient House at Walthamstow, ranks as
one of the domestic buildings of most ancient foundation in Greater
London. The roof is modern but careful restoration has preserved the
spirit, if not entirely the appearance, of the medieval house.

The Moat of Ruislip ' Priory '. This still well-filled moat surrounds the site which is now occupied by Ruislip Manor Farm. Although the Manor Farm, more accurately the Manor House, was not built until some time after the Reformation, it is almost certain that it is on the site of the residence of the Prior of Ruislip, who was responsible for supervising the English estates of the Benedictine Abbey of Bec in Normandy. Known as a priory by reason of the prior's title, it was, however, never a monastic community but the home only of the prior, a strictly administrative officer, and his servants.

the present approach to Richmond bridge. When more land farther upstream was granted to it, the Abbey was removed to approximately the site of the present Syon House. The community consisted by statute of sixty nuns, seventeen monks and eight laymen to help in running the estate. There was little or no contact between the nuns and the monks, who lived in separate cloisters, except in church. Even then the monks' choir was at the west end of the church, the nuns' at the east end.

The nunnery was dissolved in 1539 and within a century the abbey buildings had disappeared. They must have been considerable to accommodate so many residents. There is some evidence that the Abbey had been built at a high price, even for those days, and the buildings were in good enough repair at the Dissolution to serve as the home of Queen Katherine Howard in 1541 and 1542. We know, too, that the Duke of Somerset used much of the material to build his mansion on the site when he was granted the land. But all signs of the monastic buildings and of the church have vanished, a significant fact, since the mansion has an almost continuous history of occupation from its completion soon after the grant to the Duke in 1547. However, those are the facts. Syon was one of the most famous abbeys of the Greater London area but left behind it no more traces than Acton. Nor is there any evidence that the brethren and sisters of the Abbey ever wielded any influence on the people of the surrounding countryside. They seem to have lived a life of complete seclusion, their Abbess concerned wholly with the saving of the souls of those committed to her care. Syon was certainly no Barking.

Merton Priory was one of the more powerful of the monastic houses round London and one which played a large part in the social development of Merton and Morden, though a succession of priors failed to find favour with the local people and were often accused of being bad landlords and of treating the free labourers as serfs. In this they were often only carrying out the letter of the law, which sought to prevent labourers moving from place to place to make better bargains with other landlords when labour was scarce.

Merton was one of the three largest priories of Augustinian Canons in Britain. It was founded about 1120, when a Norman knight to whom Henry I had granted the manor of Merton invited the Prior of Huntingdon Priory to found a cell in Merton. This Norman landowner, known to history only as Gilbert, had been Sheriff both of Surrey and of Huntingdon. By the thirteenth century the Prior had control of more than two hundred manors spread over sixteen counties, most of them bequeathed by wealthy people who had had some service from the Priory.

The management of such large estates taxed the priors, and as in the case of many other monastic houses, poor management resulted in inferior husbandry and a diminution of the revenues, when one would

Bow Bridge in 1818.

have expected them to increase. Before the Dissolution the number of Canons Regular resident had shrunk to a mere dozen and the work of charity and education for which the house had been famous had almost ceased. It had become a very different priory from that in which the Statutes of Merton were promulgated when Henry III, who had a permanent lodging in the Priory, held a council there in 1236.

For the people of Merton and neighbouring manors, the Dissolution meant only a change from a clerical to a secular landlord. Probably few regretted the fabric of the Priory being torn down to help build the great Tudor palace of Nonesuch. Originally the Priory buildings adjoined the present parish church but soon it was transferred to a new site by the banks of the Wandle, where excavations in 1914 and since have revealed the whole ground plan of the church and Priory buildings. A surviving fragment of the twelfth-century gatehouse was removed and re-erected in the churchyard of the parish church between the west end of the church and the vicarage.

Walter de Merton, one-time Chancellor of England and the founder of the college of Oxford University which bears his name, was one of the Priory's most distinguished benefactors. He advanced education on a local as well as a national scale when he gave land at neighbouring Malden for the foundation of a religious college for twenty 'Scholars of Merton'. The foundation was later transferred to Oxford.

Stratford (West Ham) was another flourishing community of the Middle Ages which virtually owed its existence to a monastic house. Here the first stage was the building of a bridge and causeway over the marshes, the very first Bow bridge, which remained, as it is today, an important link on the main road from London to the east. The Cistercian Abbey of Langthorne was built at the end of the causeway, a convenient stopping place for royal parties on the way to Havering. It was responsible for an enormous amount of good work in the four centuries of its existence in reclaiming the marshes for pasture land and for the development of the wool trade. Towards the end of its long and useful life it helped in organizing the labour needed to transform the pastures into arable fields in which to grow corn, of which the people of London were sometimes woefully short.

Probably not all the religious houses in the Greater London area are recorded. Many abbeys and priories in all parts of the country are no more than names, known through the accident of the preservation of a royal charter or some other document relating to their building or administration. But there are two others which had at least some local if not national importance. One is Bentley Priory, founded in the neighbourhood of Harrow close to the manor house of Headstone, which was used as an occasional residence of the Archbishops of Canterbury (though not on the same scale as Croydon Palace). According to tradition Archbishop Thomas Becket stayed at this manor during part of the time that he was banished from court.

The other is the foundation of St Mary and St Thomas at Ilford, a medieval hospital and lazar-house founded in the twelfth century by an abbess of Barking Abbey. This foundation has been passed down through the ages, even after the Dissolution, when it has been in turn the responsibility of the Church and of various lay masters and still does service as an almshouse.

Ruislip stands out in the story of the Middle Ages as a place which became famous as the headquarters in England of a foreign religious foundation, the Abbey of Bec in Normandy. As the society of the eleventh and twelfth centuries was strictly an Anglo-Norman one and the two countries were regarded as one, it was natural that many of the English foundations should be cells of French monasteries, to which a large part of their revenue found its way, thus giving rise to the intense popular feeling against alien priories when Normandy was no longer united with England and especially when England was at war with France.

It is usual to refer to Ruislip Priory but there was never a priory at Ruislip in the ordinary sense of the term. Rather the 'priory' was the residence of the English administrator of the extensive possessions of the Abbey of Bec, an administrator who had the rank of prior. Confusion is made worse confounded by the fact that in the eleventh century the Abbot of Bec maintained two priors in England for the management of the Bec estates, the Prior of Ruislip and the Prior of Ogbourne. When a change was made and the administration vested in the hands of one prior, this official continued to be known as the Prior of Ogbourne (the senior prior) although his headquarters were at Ruislip. The estates, like those of the few remaining alien priories in general, were confiscated by the Crown during the fifteenth century, although at intervals during the Hundred Years War the Crown had held the estates in trust for the Abbey (the Church was regarded as being above war, as it is today above party politics).

Other French abbeys apart from Bec were granted manors in the Greater London area in Norman times. So Harmondsworth was a manor of the Abbey of Rouen and owes its wonderful medieval tithe barn, said to be the largest in Britain, to this period of its development, while Lewisham and Greenwich were manors of St Peter's at Ghent at least until 1400.

Medieval wars and rumours of war made even less impact on the people of the countryside than they did on the people of London. Many of the ordinary husbandmen may never have heard of the Hundred Years War. Politics, whether national or international, fell far beyond their horizon, even when the serfs had become free labourers and the land was being worked in part by increasingly prosperous small farmers paying rent for their land instead of giving service to the lord of the manor.

The rebellions led by Wat Tyler and Jack Cade did, however, make more impact, if only because they were the outcome of genuine discontent with the existing order of things and particularly with the continued effort of successive governments to tie the people to the land of their birth, to prevent the drift from country to town, and to depress the standard of living at a time when without legislation the labourer could have made almost any terms he chose with the landlords. Both rebellions found most support in Kent, and both Wat Tyler and Jack Cade drew their forces chiefly from the countryside to the south of the Thames. Many recruits, for Jack Cade at least, came from Surrey. The names, for instance, of several men of Carshalton who were pardoned for their part in the rebellion are recorded. And that is true of several other parishes. The area to the north of London, however, had cause to remember Wat Tyler's attack on London, for one of the leader's lieutenants, Jack Straw by name, led a party of the insurgents to Highgate and Hornsey, being welcomed everywhere he went. On the way he sacked the manor house of Highbury, known as Highbury Castle, since when the area rather than any particular house or inn has come to be known as Jack Straw's Castle, though a well-known inn near Hampstead's Whitestone Pond also perpetuates the name.

The Wars of the Roses were a matter of much less concern to the average man. The wars were clashes between rival parties of noblemen and rival claimants to the throne. Just as the burgesses of London were prepared to accept any contestant who held out the prospect of a firm government, so the country landlords were anxious only for an end to the hostilities, which could bring none of them any good and might conceivably harm their trade. Barnet, or rather the part of Enfield Chace which lay immediately to the north of the town, was the site of the pitched battle which proved to be the beginning of the end. It was on Easter morning, 1471, that the bloodiest of all the battles between the Yorkists and the Lancastrians was fought and ended in the death of Warwick the Kingmaker and the decisive victory of the Yorkists. Hadley High Stone marks the spot where Warwick is supposed to have fallen. It was erected some distance away in 1740 but removed to its present position, at the junction of the Great North Road and the old road to St Albans, to agree with the findings of more recent research on the actual site of the battle.

5. The Sixteenth Century in Town and Country

In the years between 1485, when Henry of Richmond was welcomed by the City of London as King Henry VII, to 1603, when Queen Elizabeth I ended her long and prosperous reign, a bloodless revolution took place, one of several which changed the English way of life between the fifteenth and the twentieth centuries. This was a real social revolution which affected the lives of almost everyone and paved the way for a rapid advance towards the ideas and social organization of the seventeenth and eighteenth centuries. It is an over-simplification to say that these changes were the results of the Reformation and the Renaissance. Rather the Reformation, the divorce of England from religious traditionalism, and the Renaissance, the spread of classical knowledge to a wider circle of students, were symbols of the changes. They were closely interrelated; both sprang inevitably from new attitudes to the place of the individual in society and the inviolability of privilege.

London and the rural districts around it felt the effects of this revolution more violently than most parts of England. That was to be expected, seeing that London was the hub of the English world, as it was later destined to become the centre of an Empire and a Commonwealth, the first faltering steps to which were taken towards the end of the sixteenth century. At the least it amounted to an acceleration of all the changes which had been taking place since the thirteenth century, the gradual improvement in the status of the labourer, the increase in the wealth of the landed proprietors and of the merchants and manufacturers of London and other towns, the improvement in the methods of land utilization. At the most, it amounted to an uncommonly sweeping change in the way of life of all except the poorest in town and country, an equally swift transition from a policy of *laissez-faire* to one of organized activity directed more than ever before to the specific objects of personal and national aggrandizement. It was, in effect, the beginning of a commercial age, of an expanding economy, increasingly based on overseas trade, the benefits of which were bound sooner or later to be felt by every estate in the realm. The idea of loyalty to sovereign and country began to take the place of unquestioning service, while devotion to the Church as the spring of all worth-while action was supplanted by the idea of a wider ethic in which the Reformed Church played a part, though scarcely a dominant one.

The break with Rome was accompanied by the dissolution of the monasteries but both were symbols of the same phase of transition in thought. One important consequence was that whereas in the Middle Ages a high proportion of the nation's wealth (and this is especially true of London) was diverted to building churches and endowing church charities, from the sixteenth century onwards church foundations were more neglected and a greater part of the national wealth was poured into the building of palaces and mansions, and of better homes for less wealthy people.

After the Reformation there were no more chantry chapels, very few new churches except when places of worship were required to serve new centres of population or when a church had been destroyed by storm or fire and was rebuilt. Some churches in the countryside were deserted, so little used that they were allowed to decay and were ultimately desecrated, becoming barns or parish halls, or merely serving as quarries for building material.

The monastic buildings suffered worst. Scarcely one was left intact but the conventual buildings of the monks or nuns served their new owners well when they came to build a new house on the monastic site. In the City of London the end of the monastic way of life provided some much-needed space in which to erect secular buildings. Partly because of this the sixteenth century in the City was a period which above all others except those immediately following the Great Fire and since the Second World War is seen pre-eminently as one of building activity.

Stow, writing at the end of the century, might have been describing the London scene of the nineteen-sixties when he complained bitterly of the congestion in the streets and of the constant destruction of old buildings and the erection of new ones. To him in the last fifty years of the century London was in a permanent state of being rebuilt. And so it must have seemed, though there was almost as much rebuilding in the first half of the century, when Sir Edward North raised a magnificent mansion (see page 32) on the site of the Charterhouse, which he had been granted at the Dissolution. It was in North's house that Queen Elizabeth I stayed before her coronation, and from which she left to embark at the Tower on a barge which carried her to Westminster for the ceremony.

Sir Thomas Gresham's Royal Exchange must have involved a devastating amount of initial demolition. Though no trace of it remains, exact reconstructions have been possible from contemporary records.

These show that it was the most opulent commercial building which had ever been erected in London and bore comparison with the buildings of two centuries later in its size and in the lavish way in which it was fitted out and decorated regardless of expense. The 23rd of January 1571 was a proud day for Sir Thomas, as well as a momentous one for the City, when the Queen paid an official visit and declared the Exchange open. The Royal Exchange was the symbol of London's commercial growth and marked the transfer of Europe's financial centre from the Continent to England. Almost the whole of the Cheapside area was rebuilt, its workshops extended, its wares, manufactured for sale at home and abroad, of vastly greater value than ever before.

London had ranked for long as one of the busiest ports in western Europe. Now the port redoubled its activity. New warehouses were built on the Surrey bank; servicing British and foreign ships became an industry in itself, while the handling of the exports and imports gave employment to hundreds of men. Wool, hides, leather and saddlery were among the chief exports; wines, silks, spices and dried fruits among the most important imports. To an increasing extent manufactured goods were also being imported—tableware of all kinds, including the finest glassware from Italy. Though none of these old warehouses is intact, the restored Anchor Inn in Southwark close by the site of the Clink jail started in life as an Elizabethan warehouse and still bears ample evidence of its origin.

Henry VIII and Queen Elizabeth as well as the City fathers realized that a home-based industry was preferable to dependence on imports. Italian craftsmen, therefore, were encouraged to settle in London, bringing with them many skilled crafts, especially in the making of fine glassware. For a time the old indignation against foreign workers that had had such tragic effects at the time of Wat Tyler flared up again, but soon the Italian craftsmen, like the Huguenots and other Protestant refugees, were accepted as good employers of labour and a worthwhile addition to the population of London.

This transition was all the easier because the City's religious establishments had given employment to a number who were thrown temporarily out of work at the Dissolution. Expansion of home manufacturing gave fresh hope to these unfortunates. There was little comfort for the out of work in the sixteenth century, especially in a town like London, which with its suburbs in the reign of Elizabeth approached a population of 300,000. Food supply was a problem, particularly as far as transport and distribution were concerned, even for those who had the money with which to buy it. For families who had no breadwinner life became desperate and many must have died of starvation. The alternative was vagrancy or seeking a living by begging or by robbery in the streets. The penalty for being caught (and hundreds were caught every year) was to be hanged even for a first offence. Many executions were held at Tyburn, where the Bayswater Road,

Oxford Street and Edgware Road join today. In 1571 Tyburn tree was erected, a permanent triangular gallows which remained a dominant feature of the scene for the next two hundred years.

Though there was no mercy for the petty criminal, the mere fact that more money was circulating made life easier for many who might otherwise have been tempted to make a living on the wrong side of the law. London was indeed humming with activity. St Bartholomew's Fair attracted buyers from all over the civilized world. The cattle and horse market at Smithfield was the most important of its kind in Britain. In the first decades of the sixteenth century printing works had been established in the City, producing even finer work than that which had been coming from the printing press of William Caxton since the first workshop had opened in Westminster in 1476. Starting with Caxton's printing shop, trade had stormed even the stronghold of Royal Westminster, as evidenced by the recent discovery through excavation on the Treasury site in Downing Street of a cobbler's workshop dated to the reign of Henry VIII. The find revealed evidence of other finely wrought leather work, such as scabbard sheaths for daggers and swords. The workshop was doubtless linked in some way with the needs of the Palace. The incorporation by charter of the East India Company in the year 1600 was a milestone in the establishment of a network of trade routes with London at the apex of the network.

Trade was the keynote of expansion also in many of the small but growing towns around London. The first market-house in Uxbridge was only one of many built during the century, when the church porch, the traditional place for the market, became too small for business to be transacted there. Trade in any case had been divorced from the shadow of the Church. However, it was further evidence of the natural conservatism of English people that in cases where the market had already been removed from the precincts of the church and a cross set up to mark its new home, the market-house was generally built around the cross, even though its religious significance was half forgotten.

The wind of change was blowing through Royal Westminster as vigorously as through the City. The building of the new Palace of Whitehall is described in Chapter 7. That was only one of many developments which resulted in Westminster becoming a more gracious and architecturally distinguished place. Henry VII's Chapel, the crowning pride of the Tudors, designed as a shrine for Henry VI, was completed in the reign of Henry VIII, in 1519. As Washington Irving aptly expressed it: 'The eye is astonished by the pomp of architecture and the elaborate beauty of sculptured detail.' The fan tracery of the vault alone must rank as the supreme example of late Gothic architecture.

This chapel set the tone for the rebuilding of the settlement which had grown up in the shadow of the Abbey and of the Palace of Westminster. The mean hovels which had become an eyesore were swept away and a new Westminster was built in the Tudor style. The houses, however, were still mainly of timber or timber-framed and peculiarly vulnerable to fire.

That was equally true of many of the new houses being built in the City. One of them which survived the Great Fire was over the entrance porch of St Bartholomew the Great; some time later it was covered in tiles and its real nature only revealed by the blast of a Zeppelin bomb in the First World War. It re-creates vividly the appearance of the typical small merchants' houses at the end of the century, as Staple Inn in Holborn does the image of the more elaborate buildings of the time. However, brick and stone were also being used on an increasing scale. The elaboration of City men's homes is quite staggering. One rather earlier than the sixteenth century has been preserved, the hall of Sir John Crosby's mansion, which was demolished in 1910 but was re-erected in Chelsea under the expert eye of Walter Godfrey.

Not only London and Westminster but many other parts of the Greater London area shared in the excitement of some of the great events of the sixteenth century. Before the century started a rabble of Cornish rebels had been defeated, in 1497, at the crossing of the Ravensbourne in Deptford. Their leader, Lord Audley, paid the ultimate penalty at the scaffold on Tower Hill the very next day. The citizens of London who walked across London Bridge, by now a completely built-up area, had the opportunity of reflecting on the fate of traitors when they saw the heads of those who had been executed displayed in prominent positions on the bridge approach.

The reign of Queen Mary was especially momentous. The succession of a Roman Catholic queen to the throne did not, perhaps, unduly disturb the City merchants. The prospect of a Spanish consort did not move them to the anger that it inspired in many parts of the country. They accepted Mary in the same way as they had accepted Henry VII and as later they welcomed Elizabeth. They acquiesced in the separation of the Church of England from the Church of Rome. They acquiesced, most of them, in the restoration of the Papacy by Mary. Only when these things threatened the peace of the country and the freedom of communication with the Continent were they moved to action.

They could not, however, overlook the armed risings against the Queen, and especially the rising which, like those of Wat Tyler and Jack Cade, originated in Kent, and this time was led by a Kentish gentleman, Sir Thomas Wyatt. At first all went well with the Wyatt rebels, who assembled in the traditional style on Blackheath and marched directly on London. But Wyatt's force was unable to overcome the defences of London Bridge and retired badly mauled. Sir Thomas marched over rough tracks upstream through Lambeth and Battersea and then across country to Kingston, where at last he won a crossing of the river. Even there he had to fight for it. The people of Kingston, loyal to the Queen, destroyed one of the piers of the bridge

and did what they could to impede Sir Thomas's progress. They were
rewarded for their good work with a charter for a fair, the proceeds of
which were allocated to keeping the bridge in repair. Tired and dis-
pirited, the rebels reached the outskirts of London, but there was no
fight left in them. They were scattered and Sir Thomas was seized and
executed.

On 30 November 1554 there occurred one of the most colourful and
astonishing sights which London had ever witnessed, a full muster of
the Lords and Commons walking in procession to Whitehall and there
kneeling before Cardinal Pole and receiving from him absolution for
the realm from its sins of heresy and schism. The Cardinal had arrived
in England a week earlier and after staying the night at Gravesend had
sailed upriver to Westminster in the elaborate splendour of a Cardinal
Prince.

> Our silver cross sparkled before the prow.
>   The ripples twinkled at their diamond-dance.
> The boats that followed were as glowing gay
>   As regal gardens.
>   Tennyson, 'Queen Mary.'

There was a far darker side to the picture. Queen Mary showed no
mercy for those who for reasons of conscience refused to accept once
more the Roman Catholic faith. It was not only churchmen like
Cranmer who suffered. The scourge fell equally on the men in the
street: 'The persecution had sunk now from bishops and priests to the
people itself. The sufferers were sent in batches to the flames. In a single
day thirteen victims, including two women, were burnt at Stratford le
Bow.' In these pregnant words Green summed up the horrific picture
of this phase of Mary's reign. 'Four people', we are told, 'were burnt
together in one fire.' They were ordinary citizens who had gathered at
the Saracen's Head, one of the many inns just outside the walls of
London, to carry on their devotions according to the Protestant
routine. In Smithfield many Londoners were burnt at the stake. Three
were burnt in Uxbridge.

The story was the same in almost every town round London. Many
must have heaved a sigh of genuine relief when Elizabeth succeeded to
the throne. Certainly Londoners turned out in their thousands to cheer
her on her way to her coronation at Westminster. Even when the
novelty had worn off she was received with equal fervour by the people
of Greenwich and Deptford when she went to Greenwich in 1588 to
review the citizen army mustered to protect London if attacked by the
Spaniards. She was a welcome visitor to the City on numerous occasions when she attended major functions there such as the opening of
the Royal Exchange.

The influence which Mary had exerted on the development of
London and its social life left no trace. Naturally this was especially

true of Westminster, where Queen Mary had re-established the Abbey
of St Peter and expelled the one and only Bishop of Westminster, who
had been confirmed in office by Henry VIII. Under Queen Elizabeth the
Abbey was once more dissolved. The abbey church was made a Royal
Peculiar and the buildings of the abbey given for the foundation of
Westminster School, where today the abbey refectory serves as the
school hall and the monks' dormitory is the Great School Room.

One consequence of the Reformation was the final absorption of
most of Southwark in the City territory. In effect the City bought
Southwark. It happened like this. Much of medieval Southwark was in
the possession of the monastic houses of St Mary Overie and of Bermondsey, while other land had been granted to the Archbishops of
Canterbury. On the Dissolution all this land passed to the Crown: the
church of St Mary Overie, renamed St Saviour's, became the parish
church (which in 1905 was raised to cathedral status), and ten years later,
after protracted negotiation between the City and the Protector
Somerset, almost all of Southwark was handed over in 1550 to the City
on payment of approximately £1,000. Only the Liberties of the Clink
and the Paris Garden and a small area, including Suffolk Place, which
was Crown property, remained outside the control of the City. From
this time onwards the City and Southwark were one and Southwark as
the Ward of Bridge Without achieved a still greater prosperity, with
many of the City industries gradually being transferred to the south
bank of the Thames. Stones were set up to define the limits of the
City's jurisdiction, and renewed periodically. One, of the early nineteenth century, still stands by the railing of the cathedral garden.

The exclusion of the Clink and Paris Garden Liberties had a further
unexpected result. The reign of Elizabeth witnessed the flowering of
English drama, which reached its highest expression in the works of
William Shakespeare. But the City fathers, already looking forward to
the Puritanism of the Commonwealth, disapproved of the theatre on
principle, maintaining that the performances were an excuse for
riotous gatherings of vagabonds and prostitutes. That is why the Globe
and other famous theatres of Elizabethan and Jacobean times were
situated in the Clink Liberty or in Paris Garden.

Feeling ran high between the City and the court, which in the person
of Elizabeth and later of James I was whole-heartedly in favour of the
new form of artistic expression. On one occasion the City petitioned the
Crown to prohibit the performance of plays in the Liberties adjoining
City property. Happily the petition was disregarded. But it is easy to see
the trend of opinion which gradually hardened until the City was in the
forefront of opposition to Charles I in all his policies. A trial of strength
between the Crown and the people who financed the Crown was
predestined.

In this period there were four theatres on the Surrey side of the river,
three in the Clink Liberty. These were the Rose, built in 1587, where

Marlowe was first performed and Edward Alleyn was one of the actors; the Globe, opened in 1599, where many of Shakespeare's plays were first performed; the Hope, opened in 1613; and in Paris Garden the Swan, opened in 1596. The very first theatre designed for stage plays was in Shoreditch. It was opened to the public by James Burbage in 1577 and was known as the Theater; within a year the Curtain was opened near by. James Burbage's son, Richard, was also associated with the theatre established in the refectory of the former Blackfriars monastery but he had almost insuperable difficulty with the City authorities.

Well before the end of the Elizabethan era London was beginning to spread more rapidly to the west. There was a continuous line of houses along Holborn as far as St Giles. The first dwelling-places were built in Drury Lane. Houses were being built, too, on and near the sites of the religious houses of Clerkenwell, where a pest-house for the care of sufferers from the plague was opened in 1590 and continued to treat sufferers until 1736, a grim reminder that this scourge was with the people of London for hundreds of years, not merely in the two years in which it decimated the population before the Great Fire. There was major rebuilding, too, at the Inns of Court, especially at Lincoln's Inn, where the Tudor gatehouse still stands (it was completed in 1518) and the Hall, built a few years earlier, is still in a remarkably good state of preservation, and at Gray's Inn, where the Elizabethan Hall was virtually destroyed by enemy action but has since been restored and its stained-glass windows replaced.

Although major building in Bloomsbury was deferred until the next century, the grant to John Russell, first Earl of Bedford, of an estate which had previously been Church property—the 'Convent' or Covent Garden—was a forewarning of the drastic changes which overtook this part of London within a century and a half.

Commerce expanded downriver from the Tower and a rash of warehouses appeared by the river's bank in what is now Stepney. The defences of the river were strengthened here, as they were along most of the course of the Thames as far upstream as Battersea, where the Marsh Wall was completed in 1560 and resulted in a large additional acreage of land being available for grazing. Deptford and Woolwich came to life when naval dockyards were established there, and hundreds of houses were built before the end of the century for the dockyard workers.

In the open countryside the disappearance of the abbeys and priories was felt more than in central London. It is often said that the monastic houses had outlived their usefulness by the time of the Dissolution, but the good and often indispensable work for which the abbot or abbess was directly responsible is often overlooked. By the time of Henry VIII admittedly education in its widest sense had spread beyond the confines of the cloister and, as events after the Dissolution proved, education could by then be better organized than it had been under the rule of the heads of the monastic houses. Similarly, the monasteries had doubtless outgrown their usefulness as centres for dispensing charity to the sick and aged. They were steeped in an unyielding tradition and refused to keep abreast of changing attitudes. They were no longer required, either, to give shelter to wayfarers. The idea of secular inns was well established by the sixteenth century.

All that is true, but it is equally true that despite their alleged extravagance and their retention against all persuasion of a baronial atmosphere hundreds of years out of date, the abbots and abbesses were still important landlords, many of them excellent ones who carried out what we should today regard as public work, the maintenance of roads and bridges and the like, far better than their successors, even if the latter proved more ready to develop agriculture on more scientific lines.

Nowhere is this shown better than in the case of Barking Abbey. The river had robbed the Abbey of much of its wealth but the Abbey still made good the damage at its own expense. When the Abbey endowments passed to the Crown or a nominee of the sovereign the responsibilities undertaken by the Abbey were sadly neglected. Already by 1565 the road from Dagenham to Rainham, where there was a ferry to the Kent shore, was said to be impassable because the bridge over the River Beam had decayed. The matter was brought before the quarter sessions almost every year between 1565 and 1608. One year it was reported that citizens had been drowned while trying to cross the river. By 1583 the bridge had entirely disappeared. Petition after petition was addressed to Queen Elizabeth, imploring her to have the bridge repaired (for this was now royal land and had not been granted to any other landlord). But nothing was done and in 1608 the quarter session court, despairing of success of further approaches to the sovereign, ordered the parish authorities of Hornchurch and Dagenham to repair the bridge at their own expense. So essential work which had been carried out for many centuries by the Abbey was through default of the sovereign transferred to local authorities, which had to raise the money from the citizens at large.

The sixteenth century was in many diverse ways a century of progress, but in no way so conspicuously as in its growing consciousness of the need to relieve the plight of unfortunate citizens, especially the old and the infirm. It was a century of charities comparable in number and value with those of the two following centuries. Doubtless the dissolution of the monasteries brought home to people the need to care for their less fortunate fellows, though suffering was accepted as part and parcel of living and it was destined to be a long time before any really effective action was taken at national level. However, the monastic houses had been by tradition retreats for the aged and hospitals for the sick (however poorly they maintained the tradition), and when the monasteries ceased to exist something had to be put in their place.

Some charities were founded at the instance of the sovereign from funds made available by the Dissolution, others were established by noblemen either out of genuine sympathy or because they felt that the mantle of the abbots had fallen on them in every sense of the word, especially when they leased a monastic house from the Crown and built themselves a fine modern mansion from the fabric. So long is it since the earliest charities were founded that it has often proved impossible to distribute them in modern times in accordance with the original intention of the founder. In such cases they were incorporated in the Charity Commissioners' Scheme of 1857—the year which in a very special sense stands for the fusion of the original ideas of charity with the modern concept of public welfare.

The records of the towns and villages which have become part of Greater London reveal a great many of these 'difficult' charities, for instance, the bequest by a Mrs Leonard of Barking in 1556 of sufficient money to provide one good load of charcoal for the poor of the parish of Barking before Christmas, while the Nutbrowne bequest of the same parish provided for the revenue from the rectory of Ash in Kent, amounting to an annual sum of £6 13s. 4d., to be used for the distribution of bread among the poor of the parish—all except 13s. 4d., which was to be given to the vicar of Barking on condition that he preached a special sermon. When this charity came to the notice of the Charity Commissioners in 1857 it was found that no vicar had preached such a sermon within living memory, nor had received the 13s. 4d.!

A little later Sir James Cambel bequeathed the very large sum of £100 to be spent on acquiring land, the yearly profit from which should be used 'for the better maintenance and relief of the poor of the parish'. Land was duly acquired and the annual rent of 45s. was distributed at the Feast of St Michael under the south porch of the parish church for many years. Other bequests left various sums of money to be distributed as alms, one in the case of Barking providing for the annual distribution of a florin each to twenty-seven poor fishermen or their dependants. The difficulty of deciding the recipients of this charity after the fishing port ceased to exist is obvious, not to mention the earlier difficulty of selecting the twenty-seven most worthy applicants out of the total of those engaged in the fishing industry (about 1,500 were actively employed in 1851).

The Dissolution and the complete embargo which it placed on any form of monastic life provided in many cases the spur for an outstanding act of charity. The history of Highgate Hermitage is a case in point. When one speaks of a hermitage in this context, one is speaking only of a home for some deserving person, with perhaps a tiny chapel attached. The idea of the solitary hermit was never one which found favour in England and residents in the Highgate Hermitage were very likely gatekeepers of the bishop's park, their hermitage in effect the park lodge. However, the Hermitage counted as a religious foundation and was within the gift of the Bishop of London. It was dedicated to St Michael, essentially a Norman saint, giving point to the legend that the hermitage was established when the Anglo-Norman Bishops of London resided at Highgate. At the time of the Dissolution the hermitage was forfeited to the Crown as a religious foundation, and the property vested in Sir Roger Cholmeley. Sir Roger, who was Lord Chief Baron of the Exchequer and afterwards Lord Chief Justice of the King's Bench, erected at his own expense in 1562 on the site of the hermitage a free grammar school, which was confirmed by letters patent by Queen Elizabeth. To this building the Bishop of London added a chapel in 1565 and made over endowments additional to the very substantial endowments made by Sir Roger for the maintenance and running of the school. Its income grew steadily from less than £20 in 1600 to more than £750 in 1818, and the school ultimately became one of the select group of English public schools. Its revenue when public schools as such were instituted in 1830 was small compared with that of a Winchester or Eton, but it was approximately the same, about £1,000 per annum, as that of Harrow, which had been founded about the same time as Highgate.

Harrow was founded by a private benefactor, John Lyon, to whom the Queen granted a charter in 1572 to establish a free grammar school. Thereafter the endowments of this famous school were built up gradually by private benefactions. 'Our house was built in lowly ways', as the Harrow School song has it. It was a private benefactor, too, who founded the Hampton Grammar School in 1556. The grammar school at Barnet, where part of the Elizabethan Hall survives, was founded in 1573 by the Queen herself, who conveyed the school-house and the land it stood on to 'Twenty-four discreet honest men', the governors of the school. Many other schools were founded, either by the Queen or by Edward VI before her, through their ministers, such as Christ's Hospital in 1552 on the site of the Grey Friars.

It had been most definitely a part of public policy in the time of Henry VIII to divert a part at least of the revenues obtained by the Crown from the monastic houses to further education. It is astonishing how many of our public schools and grammar schools were established in that period, one demonstrable fact at least to relieve the picture of insensate greed which many writers paint of Henry VIII. It was bluff King Hal himself who granted the manor of Wembley, previously the property of the Priory of Kilburn, in 1535 to the Page family, two of whom became governors of Harrow School and used the revenues derived from Henry's grant to increase the endowments of Harrow. It is only fair, however, to bear in mind that Dean Colet founded St Paul's School in 1509—well before the Dissolution.

No single man exemplified the policy in the latter part of the century better than Archbishop Whitgift, who was at once the greatest of the post-Reformation Archbishops of Canterbury and a great benefactor of Croydon, where he frequently entertained Queen Elizabeth. Archbishop Whitgift's foundation combined the aims of charity and education. The Whitgift Hospital of the Holy Trinity, completed in 1599, was an almshouse for the aged and infirm and a place of free instruction for the children of the parish of Croydon. The latter developed into the Whitgift School and the Trinity School.

The Whitgift Hospital is one of many sixteenth-century buildings of unusual beauty and interest which have survived the ravages of nearly four hundred years within a few miles of London's centre. Eastbury by Barking is one of the most perfect examples of a manor house built in the middle of the century. It consists of a rectangular block with projecting wings, its hall distinguished by a splendid long gallery, with a Tudor fireplace still intact and much of the original walled garden.

The Old House at Homerton (Hackney) is built to a rather similar plan. It was the home of Thomas Sutton, who purchased the Charterhouse site in the City and endowed the first Charterhouse School.

Selsdon Park is a much larger but much more altered version of an Elizabethan gentleman's estate, while at Chingford is Queen Elizabeth's Hunting Lodge (the Queen was a great huntress, whose favourite bases for the hunt were Chingford and Enfield); within a mile there was another handsome Elizabethan mansion known as Pimp Hall, where the most interesting surviving fragment is the vast dovecot, a very important adjunct of country houses of the sixteenth century when pigeons provided a source of fresh meat during the winter months to vary the rather dreary diet of salted meat and game. Upminster Hall (now a golf house) and Southall Manor are two other Elizabethan mansions which have been restored and altered but have not lost their character. The seven-storey tower of Canonbury is an interesting part of the great mansion of Sir John Spencer. It is possible that the buildings adjoining it on the west are also of sixteenth-century origin.

Although no Tudor village comparable with Chiddingstone remains in the London area, something of the Tudor spirit survives in Cheam, where the Old Cottage by a rare stroke of insight was re-erected on its present site when proposals were made to demolish it during road reconstruction. The Tudor manor house or farmhouse of Whitehall near by is also remarkably intact.

The discovery of a census taken in Ealing in 1599 (the reason for the census is not known) throws a vivid light on the people who were living in the villages round London, the kind of households in which they lived and on the work of these growing communities. It is the earliest census which has so far come to light. The number enumerated is 427, including servants. Among them are the vicar, the 'doctor in physic', retired merchants, farmers, tailors, a ploughwright, a miller, a bricklayer, a carpenter, a smith and a wheelwright. Living with the bricklayer were an apprentice and a maid; the miller too had a maid; so did several of the farmers, but by far the largest household was that of

G

Edward Vaghann, Deputy Clerk of the Pipe (the annual rolls of Exchequer accounts) in the Exchequer, who had living with him and his wife a valet, a butler, a cook, a coachman, a bailiff, a gardener, three clerks, seven servants and two under-gardeners or labourers. The most interesting household of all, though, is that of Richard Hampton, who lived with his wife and only one servant. He was 'Her Majesty's mole-catcher'. Can he have been one of Greater London's first suburban commuters?

6. Times of Contrast

For London, and to a lesser extent for the towns and villages within a day's ride of it, the seventeenth century was full of incident. It was a century of chaos and change, with none of the steady progress of Tudor and Elizabethan times, yet progress was achieved and by the century's end Greater London had begun its inexorable outward pressure.

The century is remembered most easily by the Civil War, by the plague and by the Great Fire. All these catastrophes were vitally important to London but they were insignificant incidents compared with the most vital change that threatened it, expressed in a phrase as the need to expand.

The need had existed for generations. To some slight degree expansion had become a reality before the death of Queen Elizabeth, expansion, that is, beyond the traditional corset of the City walls and the adjoining Liberties. Gradually Westminster was becoming joined to the City but the juncture was one of big houses, of the homes of churchmen and noblemen. No real effort had been made to build for the rapidly expanding middle class, though merchants had built houses on the rural outskirts of the capital. Yet by the end of the seventeenth century the picture had changed completely. A great deal of what we call the West End was planned, a small proportion of it built. Most definitely the era of London as a walled city had come to an end.

The Civil War retarded expansion, the plague and the fire aggravated the need to expand, but this momentous change was predestined, quite apart from those events. It took place rather against the will of the court, which traditionally desired to keep Westminster separate from the City and to prevent building in the neighbourhood of the royal palaces, first Westminster, then Whitehall, then St James's. For a long time Parliament supported the Crown in its efforts to limit the growth of London but though the forces of traditionalism could make time stand still for a few years, it could not turn the hands of the clock backwards. Neither Crown nor Parliament was able to halt the flow of people from the country to London. They could not for ever prevent building to accommodate the newcomers. They were indeed as powerless to prevent the course of events as the planners of the twentieth century have proved to be.

As in all subsequent centuries too, since the newcomers to the metropolis were generally without means they were crowded into old decaying properties, some of them into the derelict mansions of noblemen who had long moved out of town. New homes were built for relatively wealthy people who chose to leave the overcrowded streets of the City for more comfortable and spacious surroundings. They were prompted in many cases, long before the year associated with the most horrible ravages of the plague, by the knowledge that more people were struck down by this terrifying disease, for which there was no treatment, within the City walls than in the comparatively rural surroundings to the west of Temple Bar.

The seventeenth century was also a century of revolution in taste expressed in every phase of cultural activity but most obviously in architecture. The Renaissance came to London in no uncertain fashion and, rather narrowly interpreted in the first half of the century under the guiding hand of Inigo Jones, set a pattern for the new expanding London which dominated the urban landscape for nearly two hundred years—in spite of the more adventurous ideas introduced by Sir Christopher Wren and some of his imitators.

The first signs of classical ideas derived from Italy had appeared in English building nearly a century before, when Wolsey was influencing the building of the essentially Gothic palace of Hampton Court by engaging Italian craftsmen for decorative details. The startling contrast between the old and the new, between the modified Gothic architecture which is known as the Tudor style and the fully fledged Renaissance architecture, is vividly illustrated in Hampton Court itself. Part of the Tudor palace of Wolsey is still intact and beside it are the Garden Front and Fountain Court of Wren designed to imitate the classical splendour of the Palace of Versailles. Hampton Court, together with a number of other royal palaces built or rebuilt in the sixteenth and seventeenth centuries, is described more fully in Chapter 7.

In the reign of Elizabeth I some great houses in the country had been built in the classical style, such as Hardwick Hall ('More glass than wall'). But the Queen herself is believed to have been conservative in her taste and to have deplored such newfangled essays in classicism. That may be a figment of the imagination but it is a fact that few classical buildings had appeared in London by the end of the sixteenth century. The Gothic style persisted for a decade or more of the seventeenth century, as witness the house with projecting upper storey at the Inner Temple entrance, a room on the first floor of which is popularly known as Prince Henry's Room, after Henry, the elder son of James I. The date of this house is between 1610 and 1612. It is virtually the only building of its kind dating from the early part of the seventeenth century in inner London (in contrast with the true 'Elizabethan' style of Staple Inn), though in the country round London a number of the great houses show a continuance of the Elizabethan fashion of pointed gables and irregular profiles. This tendency is particularly well seen in buildings such as Holland House in Kensington (1607), Charlton House in Kent (1612) and Boston Manor in Middlesex (1622–1623).

Whereas a Gothic building had invariably an irregular profile, the classical buildings embodying Renaissance ideas were entirely regular, their profile based on a rectangle, their façade pierced at uniform intervals by uniform windows. This is the kind of house, whether palatial mansion for the wealthy and the noble or modest dwelling-place for the merchants and other members of the middle class, which made seventeenth- and eighteenth-century London an utterly different place from the London of the Elizabethan era and continued to set a style, although in a modified form, which survived into the nineteenth century.

Many people think of the squares and streets and terraces built in this tradition as Georgian. That is because the eighteenth century was a time of even greater expansion than the seventeenth, but the tone was set in the seventeenth century and the plan of development in the West End was determined before the eighteenth century began.

Speculation in land values was no new thing. No period in our history has been completely free from inflation. Land values have constantly increased and the freehold possession of land has always been the best of all possible hedges against inflation. Land inside the city walls had become disproportionately valuable long before the seventeenth century, for the simple reason that there was competition for its use and overcrowding caused an inflationary spiral in rents. The new factor in the seventeenth century was the fashion to live at some distance from the City. Competition for the available land reached a peak after the Great Fire. That new building had to be licensed by the Privy Council was an additional factor. Speculators of 1965 know that a parcel of land with planning permission for a new house is worth far more than its face value. The landowners of 1620 knew equally well that if they had royal assent for the development of their fields as a residential area the good solid clay would turn into a gold mine overnight.

The reason why the Italianate Inigo Jones was able to exert so much influence on the shape of the new London was that he was a favourite courtier of James I, appointed to what we should call the Civil Service office of Surveyor-General. Authority was delegated to him by the Privy Council to regulate the expansion of London. He retained this position with a different title during the reign of Charles I, and was in office without a break from 1615, when he was appointed, until the outbreak of the Civil War. He was most diligent in his duties and made it a condition of a licence being granted that new building should be in

Cheapside, 1637.

a style approved by him, frequently to his own designs. It is quite in-
correct, however, to think of Jones as an architect in the modern sense
of the word. He was an artist of unusual brilliance, the designer of the
settings for the court masques, and a man quite capable of setting the
style for a building with a drawing and rough plans which the master
mason or bricklayer responsible for the job carried out in his own way
in conjunction with the master carpenter and others associated in the
building as master men. So in a sense Inigo Jones may be said to be the
inspiration of all, or almost all, houses built between 1615 and 1640 in
London and its immediate environs, yet the architect of none of them.
This is the best interpretation to put on the phrase so frequently used to
describe an individual house, 'attributed to Inigo Jones'.

When a landlord had obtained his licence he developed the property
in one of several ways. The most fashionable way was to build a house

for himself and invite friends and acquaintances to take a lease of parcels of adjoining land. Alternatively (and this later became the usual practice), he might lease a part of the estate to a speculator or a consortium of master builders, who in turn would sublet to occupiers of the houses they had built.

The vast majority of the houses were leasehold, for the compelling reason that the land on which they were built was entailed and could not be sold. At the end of a specified period, ranging on average from forty-two years in the seventeenth century to ninety-nine years in the nineteenth century, the land reverted to the estate, together with the houses built on it. In practice the leases were renewed, often on payment of a substantial 'fine'. It is on this basis that the vast fortunes of some families who had been granted land in the London district were built.

The Russell family, Earls and Dukes of Bedford, was one of the first to seize the opportunity. Some dwelling-places had already been built on the Bedford estate in Drury Lane and Long Acre, with or without requisite planning permission. The fourth Earl sought to develop the whole area included in the angle between Drury Lane and Long Acre lying behind his Strand mansion. The area was still known as the Convent Garden, i.e. part of the land which his family had been granted at the Dissolution of the Abbey of Westminster. The early seventeenth-century Covent Garden was the result. It was one of the first successful schemes of town planning in Britain, and is still discernible in the *mêlée* of the modern market and its attendant offices. The arcade on the north side suggests the Earl of Bedford's design. One house in the north-west corner, though not dating from the first laying out of the square, does give an idea of the kind of residence which was built at this time with entrances by way of the colonnade, while the church of St Paul is almost but not quite precisely as originally designed, since it was later destroyed by fire and then sedulously rebuilt brick for brick. The vast portico of the church is unchanged, a wholly Italianate conception, all the more remarkable because it represents a dummy entrance at the east end. The real entrance to the church has always been at the west end facing towards Bedford Street.

There is a story that the Earl of Bedford was a prudent if not parsimonious gentleman and demanded of Jones that the design for the church should be as inexpensive as possible—'like a barn'. Jones is said to have promised that the Earl should have the most beautiful barn in Christendom. The story is probably apocryphal, for the church was not a particularly cheap one to build and its lack of ornamentation, apart from the magnificence of the portico, is in keeping with the spirit of the Italian Renaissance.

Here, then, was set the pattern for the future expansion of London. The development did not consist merely of building a number of houses in a given acreage. Far from it. The houses must form part of a design in keeping with the taste of the times. There should be a church and also a market or later a shopping centre (the fact that Covent Garden has become a market is wholly coincidental). The central area or square, as it came to be known fifty years later, must be the centre-piece of a coherent plan with lesser streets radiating from it for the dwelling-places of people who could not afford the elaborate houses of the square itself. So each development constituted a neighbourhood in the modern sense of the term, a self-contained community.

Meanwhile a start had been made on a smaller and less ambitious scheme in Lincoln's Inn Fields, where Sir Charles Cornwallis was the landlord and had applied for a licence in 1613. Sir Charles's request was rejected but the very fact that he had made it moved the lawyers of the Society of Lincoln's Inn to petition the King to convert the fields in the same way as Moorfields into 'walks to the great pleasure and benefit of the City'. The royal response was to appoint a commission to collect the necessary finance for the project. The threat of building adjacent to Lincoln's Inn was averted and the 'walks' became the Lincoln's Inn Fields of today, while building for which a licence was given was, for more than a century, confined to the west and south sides. Apart from the interest of the development, there is additional interest in the fact that even at the beginning of the seventeenth century the people of London regarded Moorfields and Lincoln's Inn Fields as public open spaces worth every possible effort to safeguard.

Two of the mansions built on the west side have survived with little alteration, Powis House, No. 66, at the north-west corner, and Lindsey House, now divided into two, Nos. 59 and 60, a little farther to the south. The similar house next door was built nearly a century later and forms a fascinating commentary on the minor changes of style which altered the appearance even of a house which was clearly intended as a copy, though perhaps not a literal one, of Lindsey House.

These changes adjacent to Lincoln's Inn led indirectly to the develop-ment of Great Queen Street, which linked the fields with Long Acre and in which the very first house had been built in 1604. The area from Lincoln's Inn to Covent Garden, including Great Queen Street and Drury Lane, had become one of the most fashionable parts of London by the outbreak of the Civil War. The medieval church of St Giles-in-the-Fields was found to be unsafe and the opportunity to build a larger church was taken. The new church was consecrated in 1630, while the rebuilt chapel of Lincoln's Inn was completed in 1623. The latter is the exception which proves the rule that all building of the period was Italian in conception, for this chapel is a most unusual essay in the Gothic style. It, too, is attributed to Inigo Jones, though this can only mean that the Surveyor-General agreed to a reversion to type, either because he lacked the power to enforce his wishes inside the precincts of Lincoln's Inn or because he recognized that a Gothic church was indicated in this case to conform with the Gothic buildings of the Inn.

Building and rebuilding were continuing, too, in the districts where partial development had already taken place. York House in the Strand, built for George Villiers, Duke of Buckingham, favourite courtier of James I and Charles I, was a notable contribution to Greater London's beauty, and though the house itself was not destined to survive the onslaught of redevelopment, its water gate, traditionally the work of Nicholas Stone, a close associate of Inigo Jones, is a happy reminder of it in the Victoria Embankment Gardens, reflecting not only the extravagance of the Duke of Buckingham but the large area which was won from the Thames by the building of the embankment in the nineteenth century.

In the City the seventeenth century had opened auspiciously with the formal union between England and Scotland making for easier trade between the two countries, but the accession of Charles I did nothing to allay the City's misgivings about the Court and its influence on English life. More and more of the aldermen were embracing some form of Puritan doctrine. Their hopes that the new King would co-operate with them in enforcing what they regarded as a higher moral standard were disappointed. Allied with the City's conservatism, which appears in retrospect reactionary, there was liberal support for plans to modernize the City's services. Its main streets had been paved for the first time in the reign of Henry VIII, with runnels to permit sewage to escape more rapidly to the Fleet River and to the Thames. A limited amount of water was brought underground in leaden pipes from the springs of Hampstead. The admission of four-wheeled vehicles into the streets of the City doubtless helped trade but aggravated the amount of refuse for disposal as well as often blocking the highways. Some knowledgeable leaders in the City's Council foresaw both the greater incidence of the plague and the probability of a fire which would destroy the City. Their warnings were largely unheeded, partly because the expense involved in any effective action was prohibitive.

There is no doubt, however, that the threat of the plague did drive a number of the City merchants to seek homes away from their places of business. In 1615 a royal proclamation was published that all future buildings should be in brick, being, in the words of the Privy Council, 'a material far more durable from fire, beautiful and magnificent'. The county authorities of Middlesex were ordered to pave Drury Lane and the town of St Giles-in-the-Fields in 1605. Until then conditions had not changed much since the roads were so bad that 'when the King went to Parliament faggots were thrown into the ruts of King Street, Westminster, to enable the royal coach to pass along'.

Facilities for the berthing of merchant ships in the Fleet River were improved. Above all, in the first half of the seventeenth century a successful project was launched through the combined efforts of the City, the Court and an outstanding engineering genius to bring an adequate supply of fresh water to the City, an incalculable benefit and an essential service which had been neglected for far too long.

Hugh Myddelton was one of the few truly great figures of the first half of the seventeenth century. He made the greatest contribution to the welfare of London that has ever been achieved by a single man. It would have been as fitting a tribute to Myddelton as to Wren to write the epitaph 'Si monumentum requiris, circumspice', the difference being that the still eloquent monument to one man is London's great cathedral, to the other the New River. This, for the first time, brought unpolluted water to the City in unlimited quantity—and not only to the City but to the growing suburbs around its northern perimeter which, like the City itself, had so far depended on the supply of local wells, some of which showed signs of running dry, while others had become polluted. An Act of Parliament had been passed in 1571 approving a scheme to divert the River Lea to the City of London to supply drinking water, but this proposal was never acted upon.

According to Holinshed most of London's drinking water was taken from the Thames at London Bridge and fed by pipes to Leadenhall, which became a main centre of distribution in 1582. By then there were also sixteen conduits bringing water from the springs of Hampstead and Highgate. There was a great deal of congestion at the conduits. Clearly the queue habit had not been invented, for the City Corporation issued a mandate forbidding people to go to the conduits armed with clubs and staves, while a new conduit, such as that presented by William Lamb, from which is derived the name of Lamb's Conduit Street off Theobald's Road, was a great occasion. Lamb protected his conduit jealously and issued pails to women to serve the water, many making a living by selling it.

Myddelton was a native of Denbigh, North Wales, a mining engineer who had gained a reputation for the efficient way in which his Welsh copper mines were worked and had established himself as a leading goldsmith in the City of London. He was undoubtedly one of the wealthiest commoners of his time (his father had been Governor of Denbigh Castle in the reign of Elizabeth I). His plan was to harness the springs of the River Amwell where it rises near Ware in Hertfordshire and conduct the water to the metropolis by an artificial channel.

He formed a small company for this purpose and started work in 1609, with the unofficial backing of the City government. The plan was, of course, a grandiose one. It would rank as a major feat of civil engineering at the present time and rivals the epics of canal construction of the eighteenth and nineteenth centuries. It is twenty miles as the crow flies from the springs of Amwell to the City. The course chosen by Myddelton, the shortest practical course for the New River, was thirty-eight miles in length and involved the making of cuttings up to forty feet deep and the building of about two hundred bridges, some of them essential to cross valleys, others made necessary by the objection of landed proprietors whose estates lay on the route.

Some of the opposition from the landlords was not so much frivolous as unscientific. They complained that their meadows would be turned into quagmires; some thought that making a new river, which they called a ditch, would be a danger to their livestock; others again insisted that the highway would be flooded. As the work proceeded, however, opposition died down and unreasonable fears were allayed by the obvious interest which was taken in the progress of the work by the King when staying at Theobald's Park.

Myddelton's greatest achievement was his victory over the porosity of the ground through which the cuttings were made. He might so easily have found himself in the same position as the nineteenth-century builders of the Cong Canal designed to link Lough Mask and Lough Corrib by a navigable channel, who after five years' labour involving several hundred workmen found themselves with an admirable canal the only drawback of which was that the porous underlying rock bed allowed the water to filter through it so that the canal was emptied in a very short time. Myddelton's problem was not quite so acute as that facing the English contractors in Ireland in 1854, but they at least had the benefit of nearly 250 years of additional experience behind them. Myddelton's solution was literally a solution—of clay and other materials—which provided a sufficiently non-porous bed. The aqueducts were wooden, which was the reason why one part of the river where it flowed between Highbury and Hornsey was called the Boarded River. This sector was rebuilt in 1776 and an earthen embankment substituted, the river channel being lined here, too, with a clay solution. The architecture of the New River aroused the enthusiasm of at least one distinguished critic, Sir Christopher Wren, who referred to it as 'this noble aqueduct'.

One might have foreseen the next stage of the epic endeavour. The cost proved far higher than estimated, about half a million pounds. By 1611, when Myddelton's need became urgent, the City merchant bankers were unwilling to take further part in the scheme, a fact which is regarded by most historians as an act of extreme ingratitude in view of the vast benefits likely to accrue when the scheme was completed. However, James I stepped into the breach and with conspicuous fairness advanced half the total cost of the scheme in exchange for half the shares of the company.

Accordingly the work was completed on 29 September 1613, on the very day when Myddelton's brother, Sir Thomas, was elected Lord Mayor of London. The stream flowed into an enormous reservoir prepared for it at Pentonville near Sadler's Wells. Myddelton was knighted and later created a baronet for this and other great engineering feats but he earned his living to the end of his days as an engineer. All his capital had been invested in the New River Company and apathy in making use of the water now available in unlimited quantity was so great that in twenty years the company paid only one dividend. So James I failed to reap the reward of his forward thinking. The royal

An artist's impression of the scene at Bush Hill, near Edmonton, showing one of the timber troughs which gave the New River the name of Boarded River.

half share was returned to Sir Hugh by King Charles I for a fixed interest of £500 a year, but the full reward for this unorthodox and ambitious venture did not come for nearly two hundred years, when the shares were worth more than three times their original value after having fallen to almost nothing.

By then the New River Company had carried out many improvements and augmented the supply of water from the River Lea, installed purification plant and brought the piping system up to date. The people of London were extraordinarily suspicious of piped water from the beginning but by the nineteenth century the Corporation of London was still showing practical tokens of its gratitude by paying gratuities to impoverished descendants of the Myddelton family. Later in the nineteenth century the New River Company purchased the High-gate and Hampstead Ponds Company and the Artesian Well Company, and so monopolized the water supply of nearly all north London. It is intriguing to read that in the 1870's complaints were being received from the public that this monopolistic company was 'inclined to exercise its power somewhat despotically'. The same complaint is heard not infrequently since water supply has become a public undertaking!

A contemporary writer gives a vivid description of the opening ceremony in 1613. A troop of labourers, it seems, carrying spades, shovels, pickaxes 'and such like instruments of labourers' employment' marched round the reservoir and presented themselves 'before the mound where the Lord Mayor, Aldermen and a worthy company beside stood to behold them'. Then the foreman delivered a speech in verse and 'at these words the floodgates flew open, the stream ran gallantly into the cistern, drums and trumpets sounding in triumphal manner'.

The New River was a modern conception in every sense of the term, its completion a notable triumph, but bringing unlimited water to London was one thing, distributing it another. For two hundred years until 1816 it was distributed throughout the City by elm pipes, which had to be renewed frequently, at the rate of five thousand to eight thousand a year. Unfortunately the elm trees are fast disappearing from London's countryside but most of the older trees which have survived show mute evidence of this in their lopped branches. The only power to pump the water through the pipes was provided by windmills with a two-horse mill to supplement the usual power when there was no wind. In the eighteenth century the New River Company undertook to provide water at a height of six feet above the pipes. If this was not sufficient for consumers they installed forcing pumps.

The beginning of the nineteenth century was a time of severe competition and the New River Company substituted iron pipes for elm ones, in spite of a great outcry that the use of iron pipes would induce cancer. The change-over received full government backing inspired by a desire for a greater use of iron owing to a prevailing depression in the industry. That was the background of the New River Company's gaining control of the London Bridge Company when the bridge was demolished in 1832. By that time the New River was estimated to be providing nine thousand million gallons of water annually.

The end of the story is the unveiling of a memorial to Sir Hugh Myddelton at Islington Green by Mr Gladstone in 1862. By then the Metropolitan Water Board had taken over the function of the New River Company. Their headquarters are in Rosebery Avenue on the site of the original 'Water House' at New River head. The New River itself, cut back at its London end to the pumping station in Green Lanes, Stoke Newington, where it is diverted into the two adjoining reservoirs, still supplies an important part of London's water, while its course through Islington is perpetuated in the New River Walk, an uncommonly pleasant local amenity.

The expansion of London, though not its trade, was retarded by the outbreak of the Civil War. In its dispute with the Crown, Parliament had the solid support of the City. As London disposed of more than half of the total national product, the eventual end of the war was predetermined, though few, even of the most extreme opponents of the Crown, could have foreseen that their determination to limit the authority of the sovereign, especially in financial matters, would end in the execution of the King on a scaffold erected outside the banqueting hall of the Palace of Whitehall, in which he had taken so much pride.

Until the very last days of the war many of the more moderate Parliamentarians still hoped for a compromise which would leave Parliament in full control of the country's finance but would permit the King to continue as titular head of state. During 1645 a meeting was arranged between commissioners of King Charles and representatives of Parliament at Uxbridge. The Duke of Richmond was the leader of the royal deputation. Other members were the Earl of Southampton and Lord Clarendon. The Earl of Northumberland headed the Parliamentary deputation. The conference lasted more than three weeks, during which the Royalist commissioners found accommodation at the Crown, the Parliamentarians at the George. Meetings were held at the Treaty House, still standing, which Clarendon himself described as 'a good house at the end of the town'.

Unhappily no basis for agreement was reached, the King refusing to abandon what had become the main plank of his policy, the retention of episcopalian government within the Church. Just as a little more boldness on Prince Rupert's part might have ended the war almost before it began, so the slightest concession on the King's part at this turn of events might have ended the war and saved his life.

Like the Wars of the Roses, the Civil War consisted of a number of isolated engagements between the Royalist army and detachments of the military forces raised by the Parliamentary leaders. Few of the engagements were near enough to London to cause the City any great concern. The rule was 'business as usual' except early in the war, in 1642, when the battle of Brentford brought hostilities to the threshold of the City.

While the Civil War itself did not make a great impact on London, the London authorities in co-operation with Parliamentary labour gangs had made elaborate preparations to defend the City against Royalist attack. The passive works of defence were begun in 1643 and included a wall and ditch encircling the City and Westminster on the north, linking a number of batteries and redoubts, one of which was in St Giles, another near the site of Bloomsbury Square, another near Islington Green.

Acton as well as Brentford suffered from the engagement of 1642. When the Royalists had seized Brentford they advanced towards London and a pitched battle was fought on 12 November. The exact site of the engagement is in doubt. A contemporary account refers to it as taking place at Acton. Almost certainly, however, the fight was joined at Turnham Green or the adjoining Acton Green. Certainly, too, before the battle the Parliamentary forces concentrated in and around Acton and used the village as their operational headquarters. On the morning of the battle, when news of Prince Rupert's approach was received, they marched towards Acton Green under the Earl of Essex, Captain-General of the Parliamentary forces, and stood their ground, barring the way to London.

It has been argued that the King missed a golden opportunity of taking London by surprise. Evelyn in his diary says: '12th November was the battle of Brentford, surprisingly fought and to the great consternation of the City had His Majesty, as it was believed he would, pursued his advantage.' Evelyn arrived with his detachment at the crucial moment but took no part in the battle, which was virtually over before he arrived and, as he says, he was 'not permitted to stay longer by reason of the army's marching to Gloucester, which would have left both me and my brothers exposed to ruin without any advantage to His Majesty'.

The battle itself was rather indecisive. The initiative was taken by the Earl of Essex, who was gaining an advantage when the Parliamentarians ran out of ammunition. On the very point of retreat Colonel Hampden, according to one account, arrived with more ammunition and 'then we gained our battle with little loss'. The Royalists' version of the battle is not recorded. What really happened is probably that Prince Rupert saw that an easy victory was not possible, did not think of the possibility of taking London by storm in the event of success, and withdrew before he had suffered severe losses, thinking discretion the better part of valour at this early stage of the war.

In spite of Evelyn's loyal conviction to the contrary, the Royalists may have been well advised to retire because, although London must have been unprepared for an attack, Parliament had been raising troops for about six months and Essex had already garrisoned a number of towns from Northampton to Worcester. Almost certainly he had trained, or partly trained, bands in reserve for the defence of London. Yet looking back on those stirring events of more than three hundred years ago it is evident that the King's only hope of victory, and that a very slender one, was a swift and unexpected defeat of the opposition and a surprise attack on London. The tragedy from his point of view was that he was just not strong enough to achieve the break-through and lacked the resources in terms of money, men and materials to build up an army which could hope to be a match for Parliament backed by all the resources of the City and of the chief towns in the provinces.

One factor unknown to the Royalists was the reaction of the merchants of London. The King and Prince Rupert could not have guessed, for instance, that the idea of peace was being canvassed among some of the influential leaders in the City following the indecisive battle of Edgehill. With the Royalist troops advancing so rapidly towards London there was a real fear that a break-through might be possible and that next day they would find their princely possessions or their lives endangered. Some of the aldermen were thinking that since Parliament had shown that it really intended defiance and was prepared to take up arms in defence of what it conceived to be its rights, the King would be in a much better humour to parley with the more moderate Parliamentarians backed by the wealth and influence of the City. History must reserve its judgment and can only speculate on what might have been. If Essex had listened to Colonel Hampden's advice to send a detachment of troops from Turnham Green through Acton and along the high road through Ealing to outflank the Royalist army and take it in the rear, and if Prince Rupert's striking force had

been destroyed by this manœuvre, the King might not have felt strong
enough to prolong the struggle.

After the battle the Parliamentary force retired to Acton and quartered itself there. 'Almost every house in the village', says the Rev.
Prebendary Harvey, 'was now filled with soldiers. Even the rector was
turned out of house and home to make room for Colonel Urry, who
had command of the force stationed in the village.' The rector of Acton
was a Dr Daniel Featley, who was for many years rector of Lambeth
and Archbishop's chaplain. Coming to Acton in 1627, he had won a
golden reputation for himself by 1642. Then the soldiers not only took
possession of the rectory but emptied its cellars, burnt his corn stacks
and destroyed his stables. The porch of the parish church was broken
down, the font was defaced, the windows smashed and the rood
screen mutilated beyond repair. All the furniture of the church was
carried into the High Street to make a bonfire.

The Puritans seem to have had a special dislike of this rector of
Acton, for a party of soldiers was dispatched to pursue him to Lambeth,
where he had escaped after leaving his Acton home. Once more he
escaped, leaving the church at Lambeth by a side door while service
was in progress on hearing that the soldiers were approaching to take
him prisoner. Despite his fine reputation and apparent willingness to
accept the Puritan regime, he refused to sign the Covenant, which in
effect declared it was lawful to take up arms against the King. His case
was brought before the House of Commons, which solemnly declared
him to be a traitor, sequestrated his living at Acton and his rectorship at
Lambeth, and placed him in close arrest in a house in Aldersgate Street.
He found the rigours of confinement too great for him, and though he
was removed to other accommodation in Chelsea, where conditions of
imprisonment were better, he died in April 1645 and was buried in the
chancel of Lambeth church.

As the war drew to its close the centre of interest changed from the
west of London to the south-east. Throughout the war Kent had been
loyal to the King. It remained so even when the King's army had been
virtually driven from the field and the victory of the Parliamentarians
was assured. Canterbury was the centre of actual resistance to the prevailing government by local committees which had been established
by the Long Parliament, but support for any movement against this
government was assured in every parish. Kent, like Norfolk, has held a
reputation through the centuries for independence. Had not the Men of
Kent won special privileges from William of Normandy? Had not
Kent been in the forefront of the struggle against oppression in the
Middle Ages? Was not Blackheath the rallying ground for those who
were prepared to risk their lives in the defence of their rights? Towards
the end of the war manifestoes were being passed from hand to hand
declaring that every Royalist had been forced out of business by the
local committees and that only adherents of Cromwell had any prospect

taple Inn, High Holborn. Founded probably in the fourteenth century
a hostel for wool staplers, the inn soon became an inn of chancery and
mained so until 1884. The original hostel was completely rebuilt during
e reign of Elizabeth I, the period from which this fine façade dates. It
as been restored several times, on the last occasion in 1950, when damage
used by a flying bomb six years earlier was made good.

Barnet Grammar School. It was in 1573, the date on this gateway of the hall of the old grammar school, that Queen Elizabeth I founded the grammar school at Barnet by letters patent, but it was not until 1587 that the buildings were completed and handed over to the 'twenty-four discreet honest men' who became the governors of the school. The school remained in its original home until 1932, when new buildings were erected near by under the auspices of the Hertfordshire County Council.

Elizabethan House in Smithfield. The damage done by a bomb dropped from a zeppelin during the war of 1914–18 brought to light this fine Elizabethan house built over the medieval entrance gate of St Bartholomew the Great, Smithfield. Previously the timbering was covered in tiles of much more recent date. The medieval archway was originally an entrance to the nave of the priory church of St Bartholomew, founded early in the twelfth century.

Highgate School (*facing*). Founded by Sir Roger Cholmeley in 1576, Highgate School became one of the most important English public schools. All its old buildings were demolished in the nineteenth century and rebuilt, as this photograph shows, in an unusually restrained style for the period, between 1865 and 1868.

Hornchurch Chaplaincy (*above*). William of Wykeham presented the living of Hornchuch to New College, Oxford, which claimed episcopal rights until 1903. So the incumbent of Hornchurch was neither a rector nor a vicar but came to be known as the Chaplain and Vicar Temporal. His home from the earliest days has been on the site of this ancient house, still known as the Chaplaincy, but named Wykeham Lodge.

Tudor House in Cheam. Cheam is unusually rich in weather-boarded houses dating from the sixteenth and seventeenth centuries. Whitehall, shown here, is one of the oldest and is almost certainly of Tudor foundation. According to unconfirmed tradition the house was used as a Treasury building during the Great Plague of 1665–6, when many government departments were evacuated.

Almshouses at Harefield. This picturesque group of early seventeenth-century almshouses built round three sides of a shallow quadrangle were the gift of a Countess of Derby. They are situated on Church Hill only a short distance from the parish church, in which there is an uncommonly fine monument to Alice, Countess of Derby.

Trinity Hospital, Greenwich. Here
by the banks of the Thames at
Greenwich the ultra-modern
overshadows the ancient but fails to
dominate it. In the background are
the stacks of a modern power-station,
in the foreground the buildings of
Trinity Hospital, otherwise known
as Norfolk College, which was
founded in 1613 by Henry Howard,
Earl of Northampton, whose arms
are on the side of the tower facing
the river, and who is buried in the
chapel of the hospital.

Chelsea Hospital. Chelsea Hospital
was built between 1682 and 1692,
and is one of the most outstanding
domestic buildings designed by Sir
Christopher Wren. It was the brain-
child of Sir Stephen Fox, aided and
abetted by Charles II, who laid the
foundation stone. The guns and
cannon-balls in the foreground are a
permanent reminder of the purpose
of the hospital to serve as a place of
retirement for elderly or disabled
soldiers. It still fulfils this purpose
and houses nearly five hundred
pensioners.

Canonbury through Four Hundred Years (*below*). The building of Canonbury Square, as it appears today, began soon after 1800 and was completed by 1826. Some of the later houses of this development are shown in the foreground. Canonbury Tower in the background, a red-brick tower sixty-six feet high, formed part of a sixteenth-century house belonging to the Priory of St Bartholomew. Since it has been remodelled its lower storey has been put to use as a repertory theatre.

Highgate Village (*facing*). A few, but only a very few, of the village suburbs of the seventeenth and eighteenth centuries have retained their character. In some cases, such as that of Dulwich, this has been achieved by the deliberate action of estate trustees, in others, such as Highgate, it has been due more to the enthusiasm and village consciousness of the people living there. Pond Square, pictured here, shaded by fine trees and surrounded by graceful dwelling-places, of which some are eighteenth century, is the very centre of Highgate Village. The building of the Archway Road early in the nineteenth century contributed to the seclusion of Highgate, previously on the Great North Road.

Sir Hugh Myddelton (*right*). One of the greatest benefactors of seventeenth-century London, Hugh Myddelton, a Denbighshire man and an engineer of imagination and determination, was knighted and later created a baronet for his work in pioneering the New River. In spite of limited assistance from the City companies and the positive support of James I and Charles I, Sir Hugh failed to reap any financial reward from his courageous plan and died in 1631 still dependent on his profession for a living. This statue on Islington Green by John Thomas was unveiled by Mr Gladstone on 2 August 1862.

Lincoln's Inn (*below*). The foundation of this Inn of Court may have been in the fourteenth century, though records prove its existence only from the early part of the following century. The Old Hall, left, is the earliest surviving building, pre-dating the end of the fifteenth century, with the south bay added in 1642. The chapel, right background, is one of the few essays in Gothic architecture by Inigo Jones, designed to conform with the existing buildings of the Inn and completed in 1623.

The New River at Cheshunt. Sir Hugh Myddelton's New River, designed to bring abundant drinking water to the people of London, had its origin in springs near Amwell. From there it flowed by a course roughly parallel with that of the Lea through the Hertfordshire countryside into Middlesex and the outskirts of London. Today, more than 350 years after the engineering of what Sir Christopher Wren called 'this noble aqueduct', the New River continues to serve its purpose, flowing through the unspoilt country of Hertfordshire, as here near Cheshunt.

The End of the Course. When it was opened in 1613 the New River flowed into a vast reservoir at Pentonville, not far from the site of Sadler's Wells. Today, under the auspices of the Metropolitan Water Board, its course has been cut short by several miles so that it ends at the pumping station in Green Lanes, Stoke Newington. Two reservoirs have been constructed here, known as the East Reservoir and the West Reservoir. In this photograph the New River on the left and the East Reservoir on the right are pictured from Lordship Road, less than half a mile from the terminal at Green Lanes.

of fair dealing. The Long Parliament 'has filled the kingdom with serpents, bloodthirsty soldiers, extortionate committees, and the rogues and scum of the kingdom have been sent to torment and vex the people, to rob them, and to eat the bread out of their mouths'.

Sir Thomas Walsingham, the Lord High Steward of the manor of Eltham, was one of the original members of the Committee of Kent which was constituted in 1643. He did what he could to mitigate the severity of Parliament's instructions but he was not helped by the temper of the Kentish people, whose slogan was 'For God, King Charles and Kent'. Soon the Committee of Kent was calling on Parliament to supply troops to maintain order. The people's immediate reply was the Petition of Kent, signed by twenty thousand knights, clergy and commoners of the county. It was proposed that a delegation should take it to Parliament, marching from Rochester on 29 May, the birthday of the Prince of Wales, by way of Blackheath to Westminster. The petition called in no uncertain terms for the end of war between King and Parliament and the immediate disbanding of the Parliamentary army. There was little secrecy about the proceedings and Parliament had good warning of the march, doubly alarming news because it was reported that many of the officers of the fleet which was anchored in the Downs had come ashore to join in the demonstrations.

Parliament's reaction was 'to leave the whole business to the General', that is, General Fairfax, who was Commander-in-Chief in succession to the Earl of Essex (the latter had died at Eltham in 1645). Fairfax marched at the head of a force of seven thousand to Blackheath. Some of his officers found quarters for themselves in Eltham and Greenwich, most of the men camped in the fields surrounding Eltham Palace. The marchers were intercepted on Blackheath ten thousand strong but poorly armed, if they had arms at all, and no match for General Fairfax and his trained bands. Their leaders talked with the General, who refused to allow them to send ten of their number to present the petition to Parliament. Both sides grew impatient. It was a position when the death roll might have been heavy, but the General's horse formed into battle line, advanced on the crowds, and began to force them back. Disorder or panic followed. There was no pitched battle. Only three hundred cavalry were necessary to round up the laggards and drive before them most of the ten thousand back towards Rochester.

Within a few months the King was captured and by the end of January 1649 he had been tried and executed. But though the Kentish rebellion had been easily quelled and the King executed, the tale of wanton damage and senseless vandalism which is the unhappiest feature of these years was far from over. The parts of Kent which were close to London suffered worse than most districts, perhaps because the people of Kent had been designated as a potential danger to the Commonwealth.

H

On the outer fringes of the London area Kingston saw as much of the Civil War as any place. At one time it was a Royalist stronghold and was occupied successively by Royalist and Parliamentary troops. Then in July 1648 it witnessed the very last engagement of the war, when Lord Villiers met his death in a skirmish with a detachment of Parliamentarian troops which had pursued him from Reigate.

The years following the King's execution were quiet and prosperous. Foreign countries soon overcame their scruples in carrying on commerce with a nation which had executed its King. The City maypole was torn down, the theatres of the Paris Garden and the Clink Liberty and Shoreditch were closed. Even stronger action than hitherto was taken to drive prostitutes from the City, but otherwise little occurred to mark the transition from Kingdom to Commonwealth. A few, like the Earl of Southampton, the son of Shakespeare's patron, had cause to bless the Commonwealth leaders, for an application to demolish his town mansion near Holborn and redevelop the estate, which had been refused by the Privy Council in 1636, was granted by Cromwell's Government in 1652. This was the only major development scheme approved before the Restoration. The name Southampton Buildings has been passed down to the present as a reminder that, Civil War or no Civil War, there were still hundreds of Londoners who sought accommodation outside the limits of the City.

But by 1659, with Oliver Cromwell dead, the majority of people, including the leaders of the City, were ready for the monarchy to be restored. There was little opposition to General Monk when he took the law into his own hands and marched at the head of his troops down the North Road through Barnet and on to London in a determined and ultimately successful effort to resolve what he regarded as an intolerable period of indecision. Pepys, like thousands of other Londoners, was nonplussed by the turn of events, at how General Monk 'had pulled down the most part of the gates and chains that he could pull down and was now gone back to Whitehall. The City look mighty blank and cannot tell what in the world to do.' He was quick as a good Royalist to see on the next day, 11 February (1660) that 'it was very strange how the countenance of men in the Hall [Westminster Hall] was all changed with joy'. The preliminaries were quickly over and when Charles arrived from Holland a truly royal welcome awaited him. It seemed as though the whole of London was in the streets to cheer him as he drove to Westminster, his way, as Evelyn says, strewn with flowers. It was as though a new era had begun. Even the most dour of London business men felt that they had had enough of a republican government and looked forward with confidence to a golden age.

In many ways the promise was fulfilled. The restrictions of the Commonwealth were removed. The King at first dealt wisely with the aldermen of London and made no demands which could not be met without prejudice to the welfare of the people. The golden image had already become slightly tarnished when first the year of the plague and then the year of the fire interrupted London's development but brought the people of London temporarily far closer to their King, the King far closer to the people, than was ever possible again.

In both calamities—and they were real calamities, not events magnified by historians—the King did far more than was required of him. For the four days of the Great Fire he and his brother, the Duke of York, were in the City encouraging the Lord Mayor and the people and doing all that they could by mobilizing the resources of the Palace to save life and property. In the year of the plague, though the King could take no active part to alleviate the suffering, he made large donations to help the widows and children of those who had died.

In the hot summer of 1665 the plague spread far beyond the confines of London. Many rural parishes like that of Paddington were badly affected. According to the parish registers of St James's, Sussex Gardens, the plague appeared in the village towards the end of June and was carried there by Londoners who had been employed to pick peas. Out of sixty-eight deaths recorded between June 1665 and June 1666, thirty-six were from the plague and that out of a population which was not likely to have been more than a few hundred.

The first outbreak in epidemic form was not in the City itself but in Long Acre, and the parish of St Giles was the worst affected of any parish, whether in or outside London. According to one account the death roll between May and August of 1665 was proportionately three times as great in St Giles as in the City. As Sir Thomas Payton wrote: 'That one parish has done us all this mischief.' The records, incomplete as they are known to be, show more than three thousand plague deaths during 1665 in the parishes of St Giles and St Andrew, Holborn. In one month, July, nearly fourteen hundred bodies were buried in pits dug within the parish of St Giles, an almost incredible total (yet one which cannot be doubted) having regard to the relatively small area which had decayed into overcrowded slum property.

Many contemporary observers regarded both the plague and the fire as symbols of the wrath of God directed at the profligacy of the Court, a fact which shows that though the Restoration was welcomed vociferously, there were still many who looked back with regret to the Commonwealth days of Puritanism.

The fire, though it destroyed more than half the City, did at least mitigate the plague. There is no possible doubt about the connection between the two. The plague is known to have been transmitted by fleas carried by rats. The fire not only destroyed thousands of rats but, more important, destroyed their habitat. It also relieved the overcrowding which, though it had not caused the disease, as many believed, had contributed to its rapid and uncontrollable spread.

It is difficult to visualize the scenes of confusion which followed the four days' fire. Hundreds certainly lost their lives, tens of thousands lost their homes. Many of the well-to-do had friends or relatives to whom they could go for shelter. The labourers generally had no one to whom to turn for assistance. So they camped out in the fields of Finsbury and Clerkenwell, and out towards Tyburn, wherever in fact they could find a field in which to rest. It is a picture of human deprivation about which contemporary writers said little, partly because the suffering and the want and the exposure were outside their experience.

John Evelyn, however, gives a fascinating account. 'One might have seen', he says, '200,000 people of all ranks and degrees dispersed and lying by their heaps of what they could save from the fire. His Majesty and Council took all imaginable care for their relief by proclamation for the country to come in and refresh them with provisions.' Even if we allow for exaggeration in Evelyn's figure of 200,000, it is clear that vast numbers of London people made for the open country.

Within a remarkably short space of time tents, then huts, were provided to shelter the old and infirm. Later, much later, brick-built houses began to appear like a rash in the green fields, and what were intended as temporary homes became in many cases semi-permanent ones like the 'prefabs' built as emergency homes after the Second World War.

London was presented with a crisis and at the same time with an opportunity for rational reconstruction not to be repeated for nearly three hundred years. The opportunity was lost. The pressing need to rebuild overshadowed every other consideration. A mixed commission was appointed, with Sir Christopher Wren a dominant figure in its deliberations. The rebuilding of London owed a great deal to Sir Christopher, who stands in very much the same relation to the second half of the century as Inigo Jones did to the first half.

Jones had been discredited, along with many of the court favourites, after the Civil War. His ideas had died with him. Wren and his associates were imbued with the ideals of the Renaissance but their interpretation was very different from that of Jones. It is probable, too, that Wren had a more personal part in the rebuilding of London than Jones had in the earlier expansion of the metropolis. St Paul's Cathedral is a monument to his genius; the narrow and unordered streets of the City as they were rebuilt were equally a monument to the conservatism of the City aldermen who desired nothing but the resurrection of what had existed before the fire.

Although the first consideration was to rebuild the City—and to rebuild it in brick and stone so as to avoid a repetition of the fire— urban development rapidly spread outwards in every direction. The still intact rows of rather drab houses in Fournier Street and adjoining roads show the kind of new building carried out beyond the eastern confines of the City. But to the west development was much more orderly and here the speculator catering for the needs of the wealthy and urbane came into his own as never before.

Outside the Royal Exchange in the seventeenth century.

The most effective participants in this free-for-all were Lord Southampton and a commoner—an astute speculator, Nicholas Barbon. To
these two should be added the name of the first Earl of St Albans,
better known as Henry Jermyn. The Earl of Southampton followed
fairly closely in the footsteps of the fourth Earl of Bedford. He had a
start on the others because his licence, as we have seen, was granted
during the Commonwealth. He took advantage of the time available to
him by building a mansion for himself and designing a square, the
various plots surrounding which were let on building leases. John
Evelyn dined with the Earl on 9 February 1665 and noted in his diary
that he was 'building a noble square and piazza and a little town. His
own house stands too low, some noble rooms, a pretty cedar chapel, a
naked garden to the north, but good air.'

Although Evelyn may think of the Earl's home as rather outlandish
in appearance he does at least give credit for the good air. That is all
the more understandable when one realizes that if one stood in the
'naked garden' one could look to the heights of Hampstead and Highgate without any intervening obstruction. That was the beauty of
seventeenth- and eighteenth-century Bloomsbury. There was nothing

between the new houses and the open country. So must some twentieth-century immigrants to an Orpington or a Barnet or a Hornchurch feel when they look out from their gardens into open country, only to have their view enclosed by new streets and rows of houses twenty years later. However, the Earl of Southampton's conception was the first estate in London to be called formally a square. It was the beginning of Bloomsbury and the model on which all the other Bloomsbury squares were built in the course of the next century and a half.

What the Earl of Southampton did for Bloomsbury the Earl of St Albans did for the St James's district, and only a very little later. Both Bloomsbury Square and St James's Square had markets and side streets like Covent Garden. St James's Square had a church, too, St James's, Piccadilly, which was completed in 1683. In the last decades of the century many other landlords and speculators widened London's peri-meter and incidentally added their names to the map of London, among them Sir Thomas Bond, Sir Thomas Clarges and Richard Frith.

Soho Square came into existence in this period, while the area to the south of the Strand was completely reconstructed, especially Essex Street and neighbouring thoroughfares and, farther north, Red Lion Square. These last two developments were the work of Barbon, who worked with the Russell family on the development of Bedford Row, where several of the seventeenth-century houses survive. Barbon was also responsible for the development of the York House estate and the creation of Villiers Street and Buckingham Street. By the end of the century most of the wealthy people of London had found alternative accommodation, as well as a great number of the less wealthy middle class, in the streets adjoining the 'noble squares'. Only the beginning of the war with France in 1702 halted the outward expansion for a time.

The Civil War, the Commonwealth and the Restoration had many indirect consequences for some of the towns and villages near London. This was especially true of the still numerous settlements which looked to a bishop as lord of the manor. The aim of Parliament had been not simply to limit the power of the sovereign. It was equally determined to abolish the episcopacy and to rid the country of the many real and even more numerous potential abuses which had arisen from the autocratic position of the bishops. Many Parliamentarians felt that the bishops had taken on the mantle of the medieval abbots, that they diverted a great deal of the nation's wealth to their own personal use and had become as retentive of outworn tradition as the heads of the monastic houses two hundred years before. No sooner was the battle won than the first-fruits of victory were gathered. The harvest was typified by the passing into law of a bill for the abolition of the episcopacy.

Cromwell and his supporters followed closely in the footsteps of Henry VIII. Cynical historians often accuse Henry of suppressing the monasteries in order to enrich the royal treasury. The Parliamentary action in suppressing episcopacy was accompanied by an order that all episcopal estates should be sold and the profits on the sale used to augment the Government resources. No exact calculation is possible and no reliable estimate has been made of the acreage involved, but it was very considerable and in Kent probably amounted to well over ten per cent of the county. Bromley was one of the episcopal manors offered for sale and it was duly sold to one Augustine Skinner, in 1647, for £5,665 11s. 11d., equivalent to more than £100,000 at the present time. One may assume that the estate was cheap at the price, for the purchaser was one of the Commissioners appointed by Parliament to give effect to the law in Kent. He was thus in the position of being seller and purchaser at the same time.

Dr John Warner was the dispossessed Bishop of Rochester, a very stubborn as well as an uncommonly brave man. Undeterred by the thought that others, such as Archbishop Laud, who had dared to defy the Government had been beheaded, and encouraged, perhaps, by the news that the King was still parleying at Hampton Court with the Commonwealth leaders, who at this stage of negotiation were still prepared to offer some concessions, he positively refused to move from the palace of Bromley, which by then had become the principal residence of the Bishops of Rochester. In April 1648 the High Sheriff of Kent was ordered by authority of the Lords and Commons to eject him. Dr Warner remained. Mr Skinner appealed to Parliament. Another order was issued to the High Sheriff, allowing three days for the Bishop's ejection. This time Dr Warner went. But it was nearly two years since the Bromley estate had been offered for sale.

It must have been a great day for Bishop Warner when Charles II was welcomed as sovereign and the Restoration of the sovereign was closely followed by the restoration of the episcopacy and the return of the former episcopal estates to their various sees. Dr Warner was one of the eight bishops who had survived the Commonwealth and was alive to be reinstated. He immediately resumed residence in the palace, which in the meantime had been sold by Augustine Skinner to others who had carried out long-needed repairs. He lived there happily until his death in 1666 at the age of eighty-five.

In his will Dr Warner left a legacy of £8,000 for the foundation of Bromley College, which has survived with increased scope to the present day. The seventeenth century was a period in which private philanthropy assumed a greater importance than it had previously. As in the previous century there was an increasing awareness of the need to alleviate distress in all classes of the community and to improve the circumstances in which ordinary men and women were compelled by their birth to live. It is significant, at least, that in Bromley Bishop Warner's generous foundation was followed in 1716 by the establishment of a charity school entirely at the expense of private individuals and in 1732 of a workhouse built by the churchwardens on land leased to them for a nominal rent by the Bishop of Rochester.

A similar sequence can be observed in other parishes, but Bromley College was in a class by itself. Bishop Warner's will provided for a hospital or almshouse for twenty poor widows of orthodox clergymen. Preference was given to widows of clergy who had worked in the Rochester diocese but if there were not sufficient applicants from the diocese the college was to be open to the widows of clergy in any diocese. Provision was made from his estate also for pensions for the widows and a salary for a chaplain. Actually the terms of the will were that the building could be erected anywhere in the diocese, but the executors of the will decided that Bromley was the most appropriate place and the first Bromley College was completed by about 1680.

It was a most tasteful and attractive group of buildings in the classical style arranged round a quadrangle, with mock cloisters. A second quadrangle was built from the proceeds of further bequests and donations and opened in 1805, accommodating a further twenty widows. The original quadrangle was allowed to remain almost unaltered, while thirty-five years later a new endowment made possible the building of the adjoining Sheppard College, a residence for the daughters of widows who had resided with their mothers during their widowhood and were often left in financial straits and without any means of earning a living on their mothers' deaths. There was only accommodation for five daughters, who incidentally by the terms of the endowment were required to be spinsters, but the foundation proved its worth many times over, especially as its members received a pension similar to that allowed to the widows.

Morden College, Blackheath, has been called with some reason the most sumptuous almshouse in England. It was founded in 1695 'for poor honest and sober merchants who have lost their estates by accidents and perils of the sea'. It was designed in the first place for members of the East India Company, of which Sir John Morden was a prominent member, but later became a retreat for retired seafarers, whatever their connections, who had fallen upon misfortune. Appropriately the trustees of the foundation were and still are the aldermen of the City of London. Appropriately, too, the designer of the building, one of the loveliest of its kind in the London district, was Sir Christopher Wren. Another charitable foundation, but a much earlier one, of the seventeenth century in Greenwich is Trinity Hospital, formerly known as Norfolk College, founded by Henry Howard, Earl of Northampton, in 1613.

The foundation by Louis XIV of France of the Hôtel des Invalides in 1670 provided the model on which Chelsea's Royal Hospital was designed. It was entirely the idea of Charles II, who helped to finance the scheme to provide a home in pleasant surroundings for retired members of the army. Sir Christopher Wren prepared the initial designs, and the hospital (or more strictly almshouses) was completed about

1710. The buildings have been kept in wonderful repair and little altered and still accommodate nearly four hundred pensioners.

The Greater London area has innumerable examples of lesser endowments, some made in the lifetime of the benefactor, others by legacy. Sir John Wollaston's Highgate Foundation is typical. By his will dated 15 April 1658 he bequeathed the six almshouses which he had built at his own instance at Highgate to the governors of the Free School at Highgate and their successors for ever on trust, for the use of poor men and women of honest life who were inhabitants of the parish of Hornsey. He also left an annuity and about eleven acres of land to provide an annual pension of fifty shillings for each of the residents and to keep the almshouses in repair. The trust was still operative when the Charity Commissioners' investigation was carried out in the nineteenth century. By then, however, it had been added to by another philanthropic resident of Highgate, Edward Pauncefort, who not only took it on himself to rebuild the almshouses of the Wollaston bequest because they had fallen out of repair but also to build a number of additional ones and a charity school for girls. On his death in 1723 he left an ample legacy to pay a pension of £5 each year to the widows for whom his own almshouses had been built, and £10 a year for a minister for their spiritual wants (as well as to maintain the charity school and the girls elected to it). It was acts such as these which made the lives of many old people tolerable at a time when no effective national scheme had come into operation.

The only national scheme which had shown results worth mentioning was that laid down in the Poor Law Act of 1601, by which each parish was made responsible for its poor. Like so many Acts of Parliament, the Poor Law Act was observed only by a small proportion of the local authorities concerned, and the breakdown of communications consequent on the Civil War reduced the number still further. It remained for private benefactors to assure the minimum standard of living for old people and cripples. Some parishes, however, levied a poor rate, others devoted the market dues which they collected for the relief of the sick and needy. But these were the exceptions rather than the rule. It was typical of the growing social conscience of the Court that James I, who had rebuilt Theobalds (which he had exchanged with the Cecil family for Hatfield House), granted in 1619 the manorial right to hold a weekly market at Enfield to trustees for the benefit of the poor of the parish.

Widows more often than any other class benefited from private benefactions, and very comfortable quarters they were given in many cases, as we can judge from the large number of seventeenth-century almshouses which have survived and are still adequate to provide homes for those who need them. The Ravenscroft Almshouses in Barnet, originally known as the Jesus Hospital, were erected in 1679 for the maintenance of six poor women. The sponsor in this case was

James Ravenscroft, a local merchant, who endowed the almshouses in his lifetime. It is a coincidence that the John Garrett Almshouses are adjacent to Jesus Hospital. These owed their existence to the will of John Garrett, who died in 1728 and was a near-contemporary of James Ravenscroft. Garrett was even more specific than Ravenscroft and laid it down in his will that the almshouses should be for 'poor widows'. Both these foundations (and the same is true of many others in Greater London) have been increased by subsequent donations or bequests, and it is interesting to learn that the Garrett Almshouses were restored in 1902 with the help of a grant made by Jesus Hospital.

Hackney surely had in the seventeenth century as many charitable foundations as any district. The Spurstowe Almshouses were built with a bequest of a vicar of Hackney who died in 1665. They were rebuilt in 1819 from funds which had accumulated, and still seem up-to-date and admirable homes for anyone, let alone 'the local poor' for whom they were intended. The Monger Almshouses were founded in 1699 by a Hackney resident, Henry Monger, in his lifetime, while the Bishop Wood Almshouses were built in 1690 from funds provided by a trust established by Dr Wood, who had been born in Hackney in 1607. An interesting feature of this foundation is that the chapel, which seats only ten people, is the smallest church in England. In Stepney the lovely Trinity Hospital in Mile End Road was opened in 1695, founded by the Corporation of Trinity House.

Education, too, was in the mind of many thoughtful people. Almost as many charitable foundations were established as in Tudor times for the education of the sons (not the daughters) of poor people as for the sustenance of widows. The Lovekyn foundation in Kingston has already been mentioned as the forerunner of the free grammar school nominally founded by Queen Elizabeth. It is far less well known than the famous Tiffin Schools in the same town, which owe their origin to a charitable bequest made by the brothers Tiffin in 1639. The bequest was of £150 for investment for the benefit of the sons of the 'honest poor to be taught in some good school'. This bequest multiplied itself by wise investment and supplied the finance to build the school for boys by Fairfield at the end of the nineteenth century and the corresponding school for girls somewhat later.

The Alleyn foundation at Dulwich is still better known. Edward Alleyn, the actor of Elizabethan days, honoured by the court with the appointment of Keeper of the Queen's Bears, became a most successful land speculator in the early part of the seventeenth century. He purchased Dulwich manor in 1605. The value of the estate was enriched by discreet development of the property for housing, but the act by which Alleyn is chiefly remembered is the foundation of the College of God's Gift. The foundation was remarkable for remembering girls as well as boys. The original plan was for a master (warden), four fellows, six indigent brothers and six indigent sisters, together with twelve poor

scholars drawn from Camberwell and other parishes in which Alleyn
was interested. So the ideals of shelter for the poor and education were
united. A condition of the foundation was that the warden should be
an Alleyn or Allen, a tradition which was maintained for nearly 250
years. By the time the tradition was allowed to lapse the warden had
become the Master of Dulwich College.

It is difficult to imagine Dulwich Village, as it is still called, as a
hamlet in the midst of densely wooded country (even though residents
of Dulwich today are unanimous in remarking on the rural atmosphere
and the beauty of the nearby woods). In Alleyn's time Charles I was one
of many royal and noble visitors who found good hunting in the
neighbouring woods. At one time after Alleyn had purchased the
manor the yeoman huntsman in ordinary to the King issued a proclamation calling on the people of Dulwich to forbear from hunting or
molesting the King's stags with greyhounds, hounds, guns or any
other means.

Alleyn's foundation grew rapidly after his death. So did one of the
bequests he made by will, that of a small collection of paintings in the
College Hall. From this bequest, added to by many others, including
that of the Desenfans, grew Dulwich Picture Gallery, one of the
honoured art collections of Greater London.

The foundation of a parochial boys' school in 1669 in Lambeth Road
was on a very different plane from Alleyn's but just as significant. This
school was renamed after Archbishop Temple when it was rebuilt in
1902 and became after the passing of the Education Act of 1944 a
secondary school. Many other Greater London schools have their
origin in parochial schools of the seventeenth or eighteenth century.

The social pattern was changing, slowly but surely. The New River
was a symbol of the scientific and material advances which were taking
place. The crisis of the Great Fire compelled builders to devise quicker
means of raising houses. Within twenty years Clerkenwell had become
a residential area, in which the number of houses increased from four
hundred in 1661 to more than eleven hundred by the end of the
century. People, too, became more conscious of a need to escape from
the urban landscape to the green fields for fresh air and relaxation.
Pepys and Evelyn both mention on frequent occasions the habit of
Londoners to go for picnics in the open country which was, after all,
only a mile or two away. Clerkenwell was especially popular and
towards the end of the century the craze for 'taking the waters'
swelled the number of week-end visitors to an extraordinary extent.

'Merrie Islington' was famous for its inns and taverns throughout
the century. Londoners were learning how to enjoy themselves and
they chose as the place for their enjoyment hostelries in what was then
the open country, as they have done ever since.

In spite of the number of seventeenth-century houses which have
survived in and near central London, it is difficult to re-create in

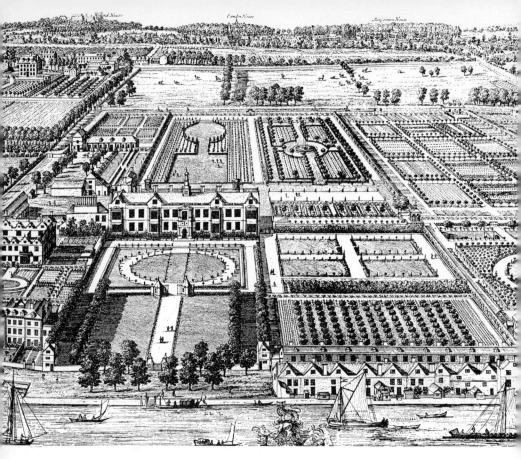

Kip's view of Chelsea, 1699, showing Beaufort House.

imagination the towns and villages further afield, partly because the settlements, even if relatively important places, were still small, partly because the houses built in the seventeenth century were mostly demolished subsequently, to be replaced by what contemporary people regarded as finer and more sumptuous accommodation. The manor house of Stoke Newington, for instance, was occupied by a John Gunston, a wealthy linen draper, after the Restoration, but in 1695 it was found to be in need of repair and was demolished. A row of houses took its place but these, too, were demolished early in the present century to make way for the new town hall. That is a sequence of events paralleled in many places on the fringe of London.

In spite of the tendency to demolish and rebuild, there are still seventeenth-century houses in Hornsey, especially in Highgate Village, and in suburbs such as Wimbledon, where the Eagle House is a perfect example of early seventeenth-century architecture, and Battersea, where the Old House was completed in 1699, and in many other places. A number of country mansions, too, such as Ham House, are part of the twentieth-century heritage. (See Chapter 9.)

The idea of industrial suburbs was still in embryo and most of the growing communities were rural in every sense of the term. Chelsea, for instance, in 1664 had 300 acres of arable fields out of a total of 630 acres. A further 128 acres consisted of pasture land and most of the rest of meadow, common land and gardens. The area occupied by houses was negligible in proportion to the whole. Kip's view of Chelsea in 1699 shows Beaufort House surrounded by great areas of open cultivated land.

Kensington was best known for its market gardens and its orchards. This and other villages in the Greater London area were increasing their repute and their profits alike by supplying cabbages as well as hay for the London market. The coaching era had started, and places like Southwark were deriving great profit from catering for coach passengers. The only district in which industry in the strict sense of the term was becoming established was the riverside area on both banks of the river. On the south bank especially Deptford and Woolwich were busy dockyard towns, while Woolwich forged its first link with the army when in 1671 the ordnance establishment was removed to the Warren, and the Woolwich marshes a few years later were chosen as the practice ground of the Master Gunners of England.

The spirit of science was in the air. The scientific approach to life had royal support. The opening of the Royal Observatory at Greenwich in 1675 was an illuminating sign of the times.

7. Palaces from the Fifteenth to the Seventeenth Century

OF ALL the places in Britain which are known as Royal, Westminster most deserves the prefix. It has been Royal Westminster since before the Norman occupation until the present day. There is a real constitutional link between Edward the Confessor's Palace of Westminster and Buckingham Palace, the residence in London of the royal family since the reign of Queen Victoria. At no time in those thousand years has Westminster been without a royal palace except during the brief period of the Commonwealth. For long periods it has had more than one. Today ambassadors are still accredited to the Court of St James's, which has held the rank of a palace since Tudor days. The Tower of London, too, is still known officially as Her Majesty's Royal Palace and Fortress, perpetuating the tradition of its special position as a Royal Liberty on the outskirts of the City of London.

Five other royal palaces in Greater London played an important part in the sovereigns' lives between the fifteenth and the seventeenth centuries; Eltham, Hampton Court, Greenwich and Richmond have retained a part at least of the buildings as they were in their heyday, but none has survived as a royal residence. Their place has been taken by Windsor. The remaining one, Havering, has disappeared entirely. The Palace of Kensington became a royal home much later than any of these. Its story belongs mostly to the eighteenth century and later. There was a palace, too, at Kew for a short time in the last decades of the eighteenth century and the early part of the nineteenth after George III had purchased it in 1781. Queen Charlotte died there in 1818. Today it is more generally known as the Dutch House.

The medieval Palace of Westminster was contemporary with Westminster Abbey as rebuilt in the reign of Edward the Confessor. In a sense the two were integral parts of a single foundation. It is probable, though not certain, that a royal palace was attached to the Abbey of

Westminster before the time of King Edward. If so, Edward was responsible for rebuilding it completely. He was certainly in residence in his palace in 1066 when the abbey church was consecrated, only a day before he died.

King Edward's palace was the nucleus around which grew the palace which was the principal home of the sovereigns until the reign of Henry VIII. Later when it had ceased to be a royal residence it was still known as the Palace of Westminster. Today, though the building which succeeded it after a fire in the nineteenth century had swept away the old palace is popularly known as the Houses of Parliament, it is still officially the Palace of Westminster, its fabric in the charge of the Hereditary Lord Great Chamberlain.

William of Normandy adopted Edward's palace but throughout his reign he was too busy pacifying the country and organizing its internal defences to pay very much attention to Westminster. He may well have visualized the Tower as the future residence of the sovereign. His successor, William II, coming to the throne at a time when most of the great castles had been planned, if not completed, carried out the first major enlargement of the palace.

Westminster Hall was his most important addition. By all accounts it was the most magnificent hall so far built in England. Happily it escaped the fire of 1834 and, apart from the crypt chapel and its cloisters and the Jewel Tower, is the only part of the medieval palace which has survived. It is not, however, precisely as William Rufus built it. Later kings, especially Richard II, enlarged and embellished it in keeping with the architectural ideas of the times. The hammer-beam roof, its most striking feature, was added during Richard's reign. Its timbers rotted but it has been reconstructed in minute detail and must look at the present time almost exactly as it did in the later Middle Ages. It is a tribute to the skill of the Norman master masons and to the strength of the materials they used that the walls are, in part, still those of the hall of William II.

The medieval sovereign was the symbol of law and justice. Westminster Hall took on added national importance as the scene of its administration. The principal court of law was convened here under the aegis of the sovereign from the middle of the thirteenth century. When the King had ceased to be the 'fount of all justice' the supreme court continued at Westminster until 1882, although in practice as the business of the court became more extensive trials were held not in the hall itself but in buildings erected on its west side. It was in Westminster Hall, for instance, that Charles I stood his trial, and that Oliver Cromwell was named Lord Protector. Here, too, at a meeting of the Grand Council, Richard II was deposed only a few years after work on the building was completed.

It was natural that the royal palace should become the meeting place of parliament. Early parliaments were specifically summoned by the

sovereign to perform the function which today would be known as that
of a consultative committee (as in theory they still are). As parliament
developed into a representative assembly which depended less and less
on the approval of the sovereign the House of Commons was given its
own meeting place in the Palace. Its first meeting in St Stephen's
Chapel, the former chapel royal, was held in 1547. It continued to meet
there until 1834.

St Stephen's Chapel had been built during the first half of the fourteenth century. It was destroyed by the fire of 1834, but St Stephen's
Hall was built on its site and its walls are said to be in exact alignment
with the walls of the former chapel. The crypt of the chapel survived
and was renamed the church of St Mary Undercroft. St Stephen's
adjoins Westminster Hall, underlining the important role which the
sovereign continued to play in government and the close relationship
between the House of Commons and the Throne until the time
of Oliver Cromwell. The site of the door through which Charles I
walked into the chapel and attempted unsuccessfully to arrest the most
unruly Members of the Commons shortly before the outbreak of the
Civil War is shown by an inscription, but the door no longer exists.
That day in 1641 was the last time that a sovereign in his official
capacity entered the House of Commons (although a break with
tradition was made when George VI visited the new chamber of the
Commons when it had been rebuilt after bomb damage).

Westminster Palace was still the principal residence of the sovereign
when Henry Tudor succeeded to the throne. During his reign it won
fresh fame for the splendour of the receptions which were held there
and which impressed foreign visitors as much as they did the noble
families of England. Most people saw it as the perfect setting for the
new king, of whom everyone hoped so much after the long period of
uncertainty and disillusion which had been the worst feature of the
Wars of the Roses.

When Henry VIII succeeded his father he made little change in the
royal routine and numerous state banquets were held in Westminster.
Then in 1512 fire badly damaged parts of the building. Although
repairs were made, Henry never seems to have settled down in Westminster again. By then he had decided that a new and more splendid
palace was essential for the dignity of the English ruling house.

Henry was a great admirer of York Place, a large and elaborate
mansion less than a quarter of a mile from the Palace. York Place was
the property of the See of York and the usual London residence of the
Archbishops of York. It had been in the possession of the see for more
than two hundred years, during which it had been repeatedly enlarged
and improved until it vied in elegance and magnificence with the royal
palace. Henry was a frequent visitor while Wolsey used it as his London
home. There is a tradition that he first met Anne Boleyn there at one of
the Cardinal's receptions. The tradition is not historically unlikely

since Anne's father, Sir Thomas Boleyn, is known to have been on terms of friendship with Wolsey.

The Cardinal's fall from royal grace took place in 1529. Within a year King Henry had deserted Westminster and taken up residence in Wolsey's old home, with plans to enlarge it still further. The episcopal land and the house had been duly voted to him by Parliament and he purchased additional land from Eton College and some private owners, creating from it an estate which included the site of the future St James's Park as well as Whitehall. He renamed Wolsey's home White-hall Palace, as Shakespeare records in *King Henry the Eighth*:

> Sir,
> You must no more call it York Place, that's past;
> For, since the cardinal fell, that title's lost;
> 'Tis now the king's, and call'd Whitehall.

From then until near the end of the seventeenth century Whitehall Palace was the principal residence of the court. The King celebrated his victory, material as well as moral, over Wolsey and his occupancy of the new palace by marrying Anne Boleyn in its chapel in 1533, following the wedding with a banquet which became a legend in the King's own lifetime—and that although Henry VIII was known through the length and breadth of the land and in a dozen European countries for the sumptuousness of his table, for his enormous appetite and for his insistence that his guests should prove their appetites to be no less than his own. Henry died in the palace in 1547 before his dream of a royal residence to excel in size and beauty the homes of all Europe's crowned heads could come true. However, several new courts had been built, and the fine new Holbein Gate gave a touch of added splendour.

Henry VIII's successors took as much pride in Whitehall as he had himself. During the reign of Queen Elizabeth further major additions were made. The most important of these (although it did not seem so very important at the time) was the building of a new banqueting hall in 1581. This was the third banqueting hall built on the same site close by the Holbein Gate and a much more elaborate one than any which had preceded it, though probably not intended as a permanent struc-ture. The hall was used for meetings of the Queen's council as well as serving its original purpose of a place of entertainment.

Both Queen Elizabeth and King James I used the banqueting house to demonstrate their sympathy with the theatre. Whitehall Palace was probably the scene of the first performance of Shakespeare's *Othello* in 1604, and Shakespeare had appeared as an actor on numerous occasions. Only a year later the King decided that the existing hall was inadequate for its purpose, though not yet thirty years old.

The new banqueting house opened in 1608 with a performance of Ben Jonson's *Maske of Beauty* in which the Queen took part. It is easy to think of James I as a rather dour Scotsman. It is evident from this single

I

fact that he was willing to fly in the face of public opinion in a way quite out of keeping with the character some historians attribute to him. At the time that Queen Anne performed in the *Maske* the Corporation of the City of London had outlawed the drama, so that plays were performed only in theatres built on land belonging to the Crown. It must have seemed a really shocking thing to the Puritan City fathers that the Queen of England should make such a spectacle of herself.

Fire, the arch-enemy of medieval buildings, struck again in 1619. Not only the banqueting house but a number of adjacent buildings were destroyed. Many Londoners saw the fire as retribution for the scandalous performances which had been given in the banqueting house. But King James was not dismayed. He regarded the fire only as a good reason for rebuilding the palace in still more magnificent style incorporating Renaissance ideas. He confided his ideas to Inigo Jones, the court Surveyor-General as well as a friend and confidant of the King.

A plan for the new palace is preserved in the library of Worcester College, Oxford. If it had been completed it would certainly have been the largest and most costly of the world's royal palaces and an extravagance greater in relation to its times than the notorious Palace of Versailles. Fate decreed otherwise. Only a modest start could be made in King James's lifetime, while the purse-strings of Charles I were far too closely controlled to allow him to proceed much further. The one part which was completed was a banqueting house to replace the one burnt to the ground in 1619. It was one of the finest buildings designed by Inigo Jones (probably with the help of John Webb, his favourite pupil). It is also the only still present reminder of the elegance and architectural excellence of the seventeenth-century palace as it was intended to be.

Whitehall, and most often the banqueting house, was the place in which many of the political decisions which altered the course of history were made. Although Charles I was tried in Westminster Hall, he was executed on a scaffold mounted outside the banqueting house. Here Parliament offered the crown to Cromwell in 1657, and it was here, too, that a few weeks later he declined the suggestion 'to assume the title of king'. Paradoxically, it was here also that the address of loyalty was presented to Charles II, and it was from the river stairs of the Palace of Whitehall that James II sailed away and thereby resigned his crown.

The last great event enacted in the Palace was the meeting of the Lords and Commons in 1689, at which the crown was offered to William, Prince of Orange, and his wife Mary. Neither Queen Mary nor the King really liked Whitehall. Both found it inconvenient and the King believed that its position by the river made it unhealthy. Some further alterations were made, however, before he finally left it and Whitehall's history as a palace came to an end. The river frontage of Queen Mary's apartments was improved and new steps constructed from the terrace to the place where the royal barge was moored (this is particularly interesting since these stairs came to light during excavation for government offices after the Second World War).

In 1698 fire took its last toll. Virtually the whole of the palace was destroyed except the banqueting house, but from the time of the fire even the banqueting house ceased to have any royal significance. William III designated it the Chapel Royal of Whitehall but it was never consecrated. In 1890 Queen Victoria agreed that it should be used as the permanent home of the Royal United Service Museum. In the future it may recapture some of the splendours of the seventeenth century as a place for special government entertainment.

With the disappearance of Whitehall the Palace of St James's became the usual London residence of the sovereign and the scene of most court functions, but from this time onwards the official residence of the king and the actual place in which he chose to reside were often different. William himself certainly preferred Kensington.

St James's was by no means a new palace. It stood on part of the land which Henry VIII acquired and made into the manor of St James. A lepers' hospital dedicated to St James the Less had once been on its site. The hospital as a religious foundation was dissolved and the King had a relatively small house built in its place between 1532 and 1540, probably as an overflow residence made necessary by the destruction of Westminster pending the completion of the Palace of Whitehall. It had continued in use often as the Queen's House and it is interesting to recall that both Charles II and James II were born here, as well as James II's daughter Mary, who became Princess of Orange and Queen of England.

The gatehouse and parts of the chapel are the most significant remains of the first palace of Henry VIII, to which a number of additions were made later. There is a persistent legend that the gatehouse and the chapel were both designed by Holbein and this may well be true. More recent parts of the palace include York House, where the Duke of Windsor lived when Prince of Wales, and Clarence House, which was built in 1825 for the Duke of Clarence, later William IV. From the end of the seventeenth century all court functions were held at St James's until 1861, when many were transferred to Buckingham Palace.

The story of the Tower of London as a royal palace is brief, though it has importance in medieval constitutional history and in the relationship between the City of London and the Crown. Doubtless Norman William planned the Tower principally as a symbol of Norman authority to check the exuberance of the people of London, but it was also (and this is often overlooked) a vital strongpoint in the defence of London against attack. In the eleventh century London was much more likely to be threatened from attackers sailing up the broad waterway of the Thames, along which there were no settlements of any size and no important defences below London, than from any other direction. So this great Norman fortress palace became a token of protection as well as a symbol of authority. It was to be expected that it would play a part in the ceremonial attached to the Crown. A part of the White Tower itself could have been used for royal apartments and probably was during the reign of William II, who is likely to have worshipped in the Norman chapel. Henry I, however, began a more elaborate royal residence situated between the White Tower and the river. Little is known of these royal apartments except that they continued in use until the seventeenth century, when they were demolished by order of Oliver Cromwell and were never rebuilt.

With the royal family firmly established in Westminster as a permanent residence, it became the custom for British sovereigns to spend the night before their coronation in the palace of the Tower and then drive through the City on their way to the coronation ceremony in Westminster Abbey, giving those who lived and worked in the City an opportunity to show their loyalty and their acceptance of the new king. Queen Elizabeth I, who after all had been a prisoner in the Tower, spent the night before her coronation at the residence of the North family and sailed upriver to the ceremony at Westminster. But such exceptions were few.

Charles II was the last king to follow precedent. He spent the night before his coronation in the Tower, receiving the next day the most tumultuous welcome in the City and along the Strand which had ever been given to a sovereign. He was also the last sovereign to sleep in the Tower, which became more and more a place of confinement for State prisoners, who all too often, as Anne Boleyn and many other famous people had done, ended their confinement by being beheaded. Lord Lovat, implicated in the Jacobean rising of 1745, was the final prisoner to be beheaded; he was executed in 1747. But the tradition of State prisoners being incarcerated in the Tower persists and several spies were imprisoned there during the two world wars of the twentieth century.

Apart from these official and ceremonial residences, and the almost equally important palaces within a day's journey of London, such as Windsor and Hampton Court, most English sovereigns also visited, chiefly for hunting, a number of houses rather farther afield. It must be remembered in this context that hunting was pre-eminently the sport of kings and the nobility from the earliest times until the seventeenth century. Some of these country houses, such as Eltham, were genuine palaces in which many kings held court. Others, such as Havering, were palaces by courtesy only, in the sense that any dwelling-place built for a sovereign's use on land that formed part of a royal manor came to be known as a palace.

Eltham has a distinguished history as an occasional royal residence spanning over three hundred years—from 1270 to 1629. Its once magnificent buildings are mostly forgotten, but the great hall survives as one of the finest examples of medieval domestic architecture.

The manor of Eltham emerges into the light of history at the time of the Domesday Survey, when it was one of the hundreds of English manors granted by William to his half-brother Odo, Bishop of Bayeux, Earl of Kent, but nothing is known about the manor house or castle of the Clare family, which held the manor in the thirteenth century, a residence in which Henry III was certainly a guest at Christmas time in 1270 and where Edward I was also in residence for a time. We know this for certain because some of Edward's charters were granted at Eltham.

It is not clear how Eltham became a royal palace. Antony Bek, Bishop of Durham, is credited with building the mansion, and recent excavation has confirmed this, at least to the extent that major additions and alterations were made about the time of Bek. In 1305 the Bishop presented the new palace to the Prince of Wales, later Edward II, but Bek continued to live in the manor house and died there in 1310. From that time onwards the palace was exclusively a home of the royal family.

Another account states that Bek bequeathed the manor on his death to Queen Isabella, wife of Edward II. Prince John, her second son, was born there in 1316. Another John, King John of France, came to Eltham forty years later as the Black Prince's prisoner. From one or other of these events the house became known as King John's Palace. It was a favourite holiday home of Edward III, in whose reign there are records of many tournaments, at one of which, according to an unsubstantiated account, the Order of the Garter was instituted. Richard II convened Parliament there on more than one occasion. For Henry IV it was a favourite Christmas-time retreat, and the present great hall was built or rebuilt during the reign of Edward IV.

In Tudor times the fame of the Palace waned as that of Greenwich waxed. Henry VIII and Elizabeth I both spent part of their childhood there, but neither used it much as a residence when they succeeded to the throne. However, it was still very much a royal residence at the beginning of the seventeenth century, even if not often used. The last record of a sovereign's visit is that of Charles I in 1629.

Eltham had virtually ceased to exist as a residence before the Restoration. During the Civil War soldiers were quartered in and near the Palace. They destroyed the fences that enclosed the park, they killed the deer, spoilt the gardens and ransacked the Palace.

Colonel Rich was instructed by General Fairfax in July of 1649 to restrain the looters and rode to Eltham at the head of a token force. But he was far too late. Irreparable damage had been done, as was confirmed by a parliamentary survey of the palace carried out in October of the same year.

Sir Thomas Walsingham kept his appointment under Cromwell as Lord High Steward of the manor and it was under his direction that four thousand of the oak trees which beautified the park were felled and the timber sent to the naval shipbuilding yard at Deptford.

Colonel Rich must have liked Eltham because in 1651 he purchased a part of the estate, though the palace was even then unfit for use as a residence. Evelyn in his diary for 1656 described the Colonel as the ruthless despoiler of the noble woods and parks of Eltham, but Evelyn was prejudiced. Rich in all probability was a man of tolerance uncommon among the military leaders of Parliament. He was rewarded for his toleration by being dismissed from his command when he became critical of Cromwell's conduct of affairs in 1655. He had been implicated in the abortive rising of the 'Fifth Monarchists' who imagined, rightly or wrongly, that Cromwell aspired to be king. They held a meeting of protest at Mile End but the meeting was broken up by the Parliamentary horse and all the leaders thrown into prison. By the time Charles II came to Eltham to survey this precious part of his birthright most of the Palace had been demolished and the material carted away for building purposes, and the great hall had been converted into a barn.

But for the fact that it was so well suited to use as a barn, even the hall might not have survived. As a barn it was used until the middle of the nineteenth century. The estate was administered as part of the Crown lands (it had remained royal property and had been let on lease), but it was not until 1931 that Mr Stephen Courtauld took over a new lease, restored the great hall, and also built the present house which, with the grounds, was ultimately acquired by the War Office. It has been used as headquarters of the Institute of Army Education and as the officers' mess of the Royal Army Educational Corps, but the remains of the Palace itself are scheduled as an ancient monument in the care of the Ministry of Works. Apart from the interest of the hall, the walls of the tiltyard recall the tournaments held by Edward II and the bridge which spans the moat dates back to a reconstruction carried out at the end of the fourteenth century, when Geoffrey Chaucer was Clerk of the Works.

Hampton Court has a very different history and a very different place in English life from Eltham. At the beginning of the sixteenth century the land on which it was built was part of the manor of Hampton, which had been granted to the Knights of St John of Jerusalem. Wolsey leased part of this manor from the prior for the very generous yearly rental of £50, part of which was to be devoted to payment for the services of a priest who would be appointed by the prior to the chapel of Wolsey's proposed house. When he took the lease Wolsey had not achieved the distinction of being appointed cardinal, but this honour was bestowed on him in the following year and seems to have been the pretext on which he embarked on one of the greatest building adventures of all time.

His avowed purpose was to build a residence suitable for a cardinal and for the undisputed and apparently unchallenged master of the English realm. Wolsey's design was for a mansion of red brick built round five courtyards. It was planned to incorporate all the newest ideas of architecture and ornament. So although in essentials the house looked back to the monastic plan of buildings ranged round cloisters or courts and was protected by a moat with drawbridge, the gatehouse and the apartments were embellished with Renaissance-type ornament, in particular the terra-cotta medallions of Roman emperors.

The gatehouse and two of the courts remain, the Green Court and the Clock Court, which takes its name from the astronomical clock decorated with Wolsey's arms. Surprisingly the clock, which was restored in 1879, is working with complete reliability.

One interesting innovation in Wolsey's palace was a constant supply of water brought by pipe from the springs of Coombe on the slopes of Kingston Hill. The place where the pipe was laid under the river was about half a mile upstream from Kingston bridge. Three of the conduits in Coombe are still in existence, the Coombe Conduit, the Ivy and the Gallow.

Wolsey did not enjoy his brain-child for long. By 1526 his prestige at court was falling and he felt it necessary to present the palace and its grounds to the King, who was said, probably with good reason, to be jealous of the opulent setting in which his Chancellor held court. As the satiric poet Skelton put it:

> The Kynge's Court
> Should have the excellence;
> But Hampton Court
> Hath the pre-emynence.

Almost immediately Hampton Court became a favourite residence of the royal family. King Henry amused himself by gilding the lily and before his death much of Wolsey's palace had been rebuilt and the great hall, one of the finest examples of Tudor architecture in Britain, had been added. King Henry also enclosed the whole of the manor of Hampton and some adjoining manors to form a chase, but after his death the fences were taken down and most of the land reverted to agriculture.

Queen Elizabeth was only occasionally in residence but she was here when she summoned a meeting of the Grand Council and took the final decision to execute Mary Queen of Scots. The hall of Hampton Court rivalled the banqueting house of Whitehall as the setting for Jacobean plays and masques. Here, as at Whitehall, the tradition persists that Shakespeare was one of the players. If he was not, certainly a number of his plays were presented. Charles I spent some of the happiest and the unhappiest days of his life in the Palace—on honeymoon with Queen Henrietta Maria and as a prisoner of the Parliamentary leaders in 1647.

When William and Mary came to the throne Hampton Court was still a Tudor palace in outward appearance, however much the state rooms had been modified. William liked Hampton Court, all the more because his doctors regarded it as a healthy place in which to live. With Kensington it became one of his two favourite residences and he made it one of Europe's most spectacular palaces.

Sir Christopher Wren was commissioned as architect-designer. The results of his work are seen in the whole of the east and south sides of the modern palace. The main Tudor court was demolished and the Fountain Court put in its place, with the principal state apartments surrounding it. The gardens were laid out afresh and Bushy Park and the Home Park designed in subordination to the palatial conception. So the chestnut avenue in Bushy Park was a ceremonial approach to the reconstructed palace. The Long Water and its avenues pointed to the new east front of the palace. The landscape gardeners of later years made important additions, among them probably Lancelot Brown (Capability), but Hampton Court as we know it is in its major features the work of Sir Christopher Wren and King William. It continued as a palace in fact as well as in name until the reign of George III, who chose Windsor as his 'country seat' and began the practice, which has continued to the present day, of using part of the Palace as grace and favour residences, particularly for the widows of court officials.

The heyday of Greenwich Palace was not so long as that of Hampton Court, but like Hampton Court it achieved its greatest fame in Tudor times. The royal manor of Greenwich dates only from the early part of the fifteenth century. Henry VI gave his former Regent Humphrey, Duke of Gloucester, the right to enclose an area surrounding the house which he had built on the site, and this house reverted to the Crown and became known as the Palace of Placentia.

It was a modest residence which was inherited by Henry VII. Here a son, Prince Arthur, was born to the Queen, formerly Elizabeth of York, and here the celebration feast to commemorate the Prince's birth was held. For several years Elizabeth was in more or less permanent residence, and started her triumphal journey to her coronation from the Palace, sailing upriver to meet the King at Tower Pier.

Henry VIII was born at Greenwich in 1491, and Prince Arthur continued in residence after he had married Catherine of Aragon, who disliked the place intensely and blamed her gastric ailments on the climate, which she found almost insupportable after the warmth of Spain. Henry VIII was even more attached to Greenwich than his father had been. He had, after all, spent a happy childhood in it. He was married to his brother's widow in the private chapel and Catherine now apparently became resigned to the Greenwich climate. They lived there together for the greater part of twenty years, during which Catherine played as big a part as Henry in raising the prestige of the English court and in entertaining foreign royalty and ambassadors. The Emperor Charles V was one distinguished visitor. It was his first meeting with Henry but he learnt the lesson which Henry tried so hard to teach him, that England would never be a party to the domination of Europe by the military force of a single power.

Anne Boleyn, like Elizabeth of York, sailed in a famous river pageant from Greenwich to the Tower Pier before driving through London to her coronation at Westminster, and it was at Greenwich once more that her daughter, the future Queen Elizabeth, was born. Henry made no effort to rebuild the Palace, though he extended it and was responsible for laying out the gardens.

Greenwich lost some of its attraction for the royal family in the following reigns though Edward VI and Queen Elizabeth held court there quite often. James I restored some of the traditions of pageantry which had originated with Henry VIII's flair for investing formal occasions with the aura of romance. Queen Anne was attached to the place and it was for her that James commissioned Inigo Jones in 1616 to build what we know today as the Queen's House. Anne died before her new house was completed and the plan for a Queen's House remained in abeyance until Charles I had it completed for Queen Henrietta Maria. Under Charles Greenwich reeovered all its lost glories. With its gardens and its ranges of buildings spanning the architectural history of England from the fifteenth to the seventeenth century, it must have presented a most impressive appearance.

Like so many other royal houses, Greenwich, or Placentia as it was still known then, was allowed to decay during the Civil War and the years of the Commonwealth. It was offered for sale by order of Parliament in 1652 but no purchaser could be found for the Palace, though some of the park land was sold. Two years later the Queen's House was converted into a country residence for Cromwell.

When Charles II came to the throne his mother took up residence again in the Queen's House, and the King, with one of those typical gestures of defiance and extravagance, decreed that the whole of the Tudor and Jacobean buildings must be swept away and a new palace built on the site in the contemporary style of architecture.

John Webb, Inigo Jones's pupil and kinsman, was the surveyor for the new palace, which was to be known as the King's House, but only the western part was completed, chiefly owing to lack of funds, before the King died. James II had no love for Greenwich, and although the Queen's House was made over to his Queen, Mary of Modena, she was seldom in residence and nothing further was done towards the rebuilding of the Palace. James is, however, credited with the suggestion that it should cease to be a royal home and be transformed into a naval hospital.

It was left to William III, however, whose heart was set on the completion of Hampton Court in the Wren style, to give reality to this suggestion by establishing by charter in 1694 the Royal Hospital of Greenwich. The charter states that the objectives of the hospital included the support of seamen incapable of further service at sea and unable to maintain themselves, the relief of widows of seamen killed on active service and the maintenance and education of their children.

The Palace was never again a royal home. What had been intended as the King's House was duly completed under the guidance of a commission, which included Sir Christopher Wren, with John Evelyn as treasurer. Vanbrugh was first secretary of the commission and later succeeded Wren as surveyor-in-chief. Evelyn records a great deal of bickering among the commission members but subscriptions towards the completion of the hospital were surprisingly generous and the first naval pensioners took up residence in 1705. It was a worthy counterpart to Chelsea Hospital which, as an army charity, served almost precisely the same function. It continued as a hospital until 1869. Four years later it became the home of the Royal Naval College, as it still is today, though the Queen's House since 1937 has been the National Maritime Museum.

The only other important Tudor palace in Greater London was Henry VII's foundation at Richmond. The manor of Sheen had been a royal manor since the thirteenth century and there had been a royal residence there since the reign of Edward I. By the time of Henry VII's accession the palace was in ruins. The King, liking its situation, rebuilt it completely and renamed it Richmond after the castle town in Yorkshire of which he was Earl.

One of the gates and some other small fragments remain of the Tudor palace in which King Henry spent much of his time and in which he died. Later sovereigns also used it as a regular place of residence, Queen Elizabeth living there during her last years. In the seventeenth century it gradually fell from grace, for no other reason probably than because it was a far less magnificent home than Hampton Court and served no real purpose in the pattern of royal residences. Like the medieval palace of Sheen, it decayed through sheer neglect. By the eighteenth century much of its fabric had become unsafe and it was demolished.

A mansion belonging to the Earl of Nottingham and named by him Nottingham House stood on the site of Kensington Palace in the latter half of the seventeenth century. This was purchased by William III, who was advised that the air of Kensington would be beneficial to his asthma and commissioned Sir Christopher Wren to enlarge and in part redesign the house. The south front and the Clock Court were two of the most notable improvements made by Wren, but they were not completed until 1697.

The fire which destroyed Whitehall Palace in the following year was added reason for the King to make Kensington his principal home in London, and it was here that he died in 1702. After that the Palace continued a royal one, though the sovereign was seldom in residence. The Orangery was designed by Wren or possibly Vanbrugh, when the Palace was occupied by Queen Anne. Still further additions were made in the reign of George I. George II lived there briefly, and was the last sovereign to do so. But we owe to Queen Caroline the laying out of Kensington Gardens as an artificial but highly effective landscape. The damming of the West Bourne to form the Long Water and the Serpentine is said to have been her idea. The trees (most of them now replaced) of the Broad Walk were planted. The Round Pond was added as a decorative feature and the gardens of the Palace itself were redesigned.

Arches of Triumph, seventeenth-century engraving by Stephen Harrison.

8. Eighteenth-century Expansion in Town and Country

THE eighteenth century was a century of consolidation in the City after the rapid expansion of its commerce and the growth in its national influence during the previous two centuries. It was equally a century of growth in the West End of London, with an upsurge in building which before 1800 had engulfed almost the whole of the area between St James's Palace and the Oxford Road, with several estates in course of development to the north of the Oxford Road.

With the rapid expansion of the villages near London into suburbs Greater London became much more than the modest overspill from the City and Westminster which it had been in the seventeenth century. Now for the first time villages situated up to five or six miles from the City began to expand apace, and before the end of the century the embryo of linear expansion which we call ribbon development could be observed.

In the latter half of the century 'improvement' was in the air—improvement of the facilities for comfortable living, improvement in lighting, in road-making, in travelling and in the architectural design of public buildings. Before the nineteenth century began towns and villages on the outer perimeter, such as Richmond and Twickenham, had begun a separate expansion almost as remarkable as that of the West End of London. They maintained their separate existence but their growth looked forward to the time when all would be joined together by continuous urban development.

In the City the most important event, and the most significant since the foundation of Gresham's Royal Exchange in the reign of Queen Elizabeth, was the development of the functions of the Bank of England. The Bank had been founded in 1694 but it was not until the eighteenth century that the full implications of this great institution were appreciated. It marked the end of one epoch and the beginning of another: the end of the epoch in which money-lending and banking had been almost synonymous, the beginning of the ordered financial structure of modern commercial practice. Jewish money-lenders, as mentioned in Chapter 3, were the first who might be called bankers in London. They were expelled and their place was taken by Italian money-lenders who carried on the Jewish tradition and served their purpose well enough. But the growth of London's trade was so rapid that there inevitably came a time when merchants could not feel that their vaults were a secure resting place for gold and bullion.

Ultimately the Royal Mint became the repository of temporarily unused capital. It had many advantages from the merchants' point of view and was regarded as a wholly safe place for deposits—safe, that is, until Charles I raided it and only returned the bullion he had 'borrowed' on condition that a permanent loan was made to him. That certainly shook confidence in the Royal Mint, and the Goldsmiths' Company became its rival in the banking business. But even the Goldsmiths' Company could not resist Charles II's requests for loans, and the Bank of England developed from small beginnings into a universal depository in which merchants were encouraged to place their capital for safe keeping—and receive interest on it. From its earliest days, too, the Bank was designed to facilitate international trade. Except that it was nationalized in 1946 the Bank of England in essentials is unchanged in constitution and functions.

The accession of George I in 1714 had vital importance for the City because from that time onwards the sovereign never again sought to interfere in its affairs, and the privileges which had been so jealously guarded for so many centuries were accepted as a matter of course. It was perhaps symbolic of the new order of things that the new St Paul's Cathedral was completed in 1710, a memorial not only to its creator, Sir Christopher Wren, but to the wealth and power of the City, a great edifice which towered above every other building and in those days could be seen from every part of the City and from most of the growing suburbs on the south as well as on the north bank of the river.

Only faltering steps were taken towards the further expansion of the West End in the first fifteen years of the century, though Marlborough House (1709–10), built for the Duke of Marlborough, was one of the finest of Sir Christopher Wren's later essays in domestic building. The boom in building which had followed the Great Fire had expended itself. Some of the more adventurous of those who contributed to late seventeenth-century expansion had been rewarded with bankruptcy, a few with the loss of considerable family fortunes. The position was analogous to that which prevailed in the nineteen-twenties, when the quick profits won by those who had been clever or fortunate enough to start early in the stupendous expansion which followed the end of the First World War encouraged a vast number of builders, many with little experience, to follow in their footsteps. The demand fully met, it only needed an economic slump for tens of thousands of houses to remain untenanted, with consequent ruin to the speculators.

At the beginning of the eighteenth century money was not nearly as plentiful as it had been twenty years before. For a time the demand for new houses for City merchants and minor members of the aristocracy had been met. The war with France was in this case the immediate cause of economic contraction and very few new schemes were initiated until after the Treaty of Utrecht in 1713. That long awaited and welcome peace was the signal for a fresh wave of urban development greater even than that of the seventeenth century.

The all too few examples of the homes of the early part of the century, as at Queen Anne's Gate, which was built in 1704, contrast most favourably with the far less exciting and more modest homes which were being raised towards the middle of the century. The attractive plan of the square as the centre of a self-contained community with a nobleman's house and a church in the square, and other large houses in keeping with its dignity, was abandoned. Noblemen were becoming less interested in their town houses than in their country estates. What was wanted most was a relatively inexpensive town house, if possible in a fashionable district within easy reach of the City and Westminster. The vast majority of the tenants or leaseholders were men who earned a living in one way or another from the commerce and industry of London town. To these were added thousands of people looking for homes without the means to build or rent a home of any but the most modest proportions. So with a few notable exceptions, such as Cavendish Square, economy of frontage became the main prerequisite of speculative building. Houses were tall and narrow, their gardens long and narrow, and for economy's sake standard designs were adopted, so that one house was precisely like its neighbour and most likely precisely like houses in streets a mile away.

Uniformity (some contemporary critics called it monotony) took the place of artistic diversification. The tendency was made all the more positive by the Government's determination to avoid a repetition of the Great Fire. External decorative woodwork of any kind was absolutely forbidden; even the woodwork of windows was recessed, so that the front door became the only part of the house which invited elaboration or ornament. Pediments disappeared, their place taken by a continuous parapet which hid the attic floor from observers at street level, while the change from casement to sash windows also made for greater uniformity. Brick was the almost universal material for building. So great was the demand for it that most of the villages on the outskirts added a brick-field to their market gardens and orchards and hay-fields. This was a development which did nothing to enhance the beauty of the countryside around London, though it added to the prosperity of many of the ancient settlements.

Hanover Square was one of the first new squares laid out after the Treaty of Utrecht. Around it many of the streets which became part of Mayfair were planned, and a completely new suburb was born rivalling the purlieus of St James's. About the same time the Burlington estate was developed in the area immediately to the north of the Earl of Burlington's Piccadilly mansion. Old and New Burlington Streets were both well lined with new homes by 1730, Sackville Street and Savile Row not much later. By comparison with many other schemes of development this was rather a higgledy-piggledy affair, but with money now flowing freely in a country which had recovered from the economic ravages of war, the houses were occupied as soon as they were built, and some good examples have survived, especially in Savile Row.

Grosvenor Square was the centre of the most ambitious of all the planned developments of this period. Its gardens were laid out by William Kent and a real but rather unsuccessful effort was made to revive the glories of the first St James's Square and of the Earl of Southampton's brilliant success at Bloomsbury Square. Grosvenor Square was for long the largest square in London, but the original scheme for palatial residences standing in their own grounds had to be abandoned because of lack of customers. Cavendish Square was also planned before 1725 and was linked with developments in Welbeck Street, Wimpole Street, Harley Street and Vere Street, where St Peter's Church was designed as the church of the new estate by James Gibbs, one of the two or three leading architect designers of the day. The church was opened for worship in 1724. Most people admired the classical idiom in which Gibbs designed it, and for a time it was one of the most fashionable churches in London, though now it has been degraded into a chapel of ease for All Souls', Langham Place. Nearer the river, in close proximity to the Palace of Westminster, Smith Square, notable for the handsome church in its centre, was begun in 1725.

Finally, Berkeley Square belongs to this period of rapid and mainly successful expansion. It had been laid out and the first houses round it built by early in the eighteenth century, but then progress lagged. England was again at war in 1741 and for the time at least the demand for West End homes had been satisfied once more. For every ten houses built between 1725 and 1745 probably not more than one was completed in the following twenty years.

It is a strange fact that in this thriving first half of the eighteenth century, when so much was built so successfully, little attention was given to the very obvious need to build new churches to minister to the vastly increased congregations. The development schemes which included a new church were the exceptions rather than the rule, and there was a good deal of justification for the view that it was an age of irreligion in which the old ideals of piety had been put to flight by the new ideals of wealth and influence.

This was a relatively new tendency. It is true that after the Reformation many churches were allowed to fall into disrepair, until the degradation of the medieval churches became a national scandal. But that was natural enough in a society which was only just beginning to grow accustomed to the idea of diverting its surplus resources to lay rather than ecclesiastical purposes. The rebuilding of churches in the City after the Fire showed without the possibility of doubt that the period of neglect and apathy was over by the second half of the seventeenth century. In the early years of the eighteenth century public indignation was expressed at the number of churches which were inadequate for their congregations or had become unsafe or dilapidated.

By 1711 the position had become so bad that Government support was forthcoming for essential church building. In that year an Act was passed levying a tax on coal, the profits of which were to be devoted to building fifty new churches in the cities of London and Westminster and in their suburbs. Why fifty, no one knows. Apparently no one knew at the time. Certainly fifty were not built in pursuance of the Act. Within a very few years new Acts were passed scaling down the amount of public funds that could be expended for the purpose, and though the coal tax remained it was diverted to purposes other than those of the Church.

One of the ecclesiastical 'improvements' sanctioned under the Act was the refurbishing of the Abbey Church of Westminster, and the addition by Hawksmoor of its two west towers. One would think that this exercise scarcely came within the real purpose of the Act, any more than the addition of towers or spires to a number of existing churches. In all only eight new churches which might conceivably be regarded as inspired by the Act were built, either in London, Westminster or its immediate suburbs, between 1711 and 1730. St Mary-le-Strand was the first. James Gibbs was chosen as architect and a very fine job he made of it. In the eighteenth century, of course, it was not on an island site as it is today. Then it was backed by thickly grouped houses and stood out above them, a genuinely artistic composition in a recently developed area.

Many critics complained that Gibbs's style was baroque. It is impossible to deny the charge, but difficult to understand why it should be a matter of criticism that an English architect should experiment in a style which brought new life to the development of the classical ideal in many parts of the Continent, and which in Gibbs was never tasteless or disharmonious. Gibbs was also the architect of St Martin-in-the-Fields, completed a few years later. The finance for rebuilding the old church of St Martin, however, was provided by the parishioners and no call was made on the coal tax fund, a rare enough event to be remarkable in the first half of the eighteenth century. Gibbs also added the steeple to St Clement Danes, so that this Wren church, one of the

The Royal Naval College, Greenwich (*above*). Designed to take the place of the medieval palace of Placentia in 1664, it was never completed as a palace and became the Royal Hospital of Greenwich in 1694. Many architects contributed to it, including Webb, Wren, Vanbrugh, Hawksmoor and Ripley. It was completed about 1752. This, the Queen Mary block, was begun by Wren and completed by Ripley.

St James's Palace (*below*). Founded by Henry VIII in 1532 on the site of a leper hospital dedicated to St James the Less, from whom it takes its name, the palace has been frequently enlarged and restored. Only the gatehouse and parts of the Chapel Royal survive from the Tudor palace. This is Friary Court, one of the several courtyards enclosed by the palace buildings.

The Great Gate of Hampton Court. The original Hampton Court Palace was built for Cardinal Wolsey between 1515 and 1520 in the Tudor Gothic style with Renaissance ornament. The Great Gate, pictured here, is part of the original Tudor palace, to which additions were made later by Sir Christopher Wren. The moat which the bridge leading from the gate crosses was excavated in 1909 and the double row of King's Beasts, a not altogether happy addition, is modern. The palace was built on land leased by Wolsey from the Priory of the Order of St John of Jerusalem.

[26]

Richmond Palace (*top*). Henry VII built himself a palace at Sheen, which he renamed Richmond after the Yorkshire town from which he derived his title Earl of Richmond. This gateway is part of Henry's original palace. Above it are the weather-worn arms of the King.

An Eighteenth-century Summer-house (*middle*). This summer-house in the grounds of Osterley was designed by Robert Adam in 1780.

In the Gardens of York House (*bottom*). Sir Ratan Tata, an Indian merchant prince, was the last tenant of York House, Twickenham, which later became the council offices of the Twickenham Borough Council. The riverside gardens in which this group of statuary is situated are open to the public. Sir Ratan was responsible for placing the statues, which are of Italian marble and were imported from Italy in 1905, in the gardens. The precise meaning of the group is doubtful, but possibly they represent the Nereides, the river nymphs.

Swakeleys, Ickenham (*top, left*). This photograph, taken across the River Pinn, widened here to form an artificial lake, shows one of the finest Jacobean mansions in Greater London, built about 1638. Pepys described it as 'the most uniform house in all that ever I saw'.

Holland House (*top, right*). Although damaged almost beyond repair by enemy bombardment, part of the exterior of Kensington's Holland House has been restored by the London County Council, but much of the interior has been converted into a dormitory annex of the King George VI Youth Hostel. Of approximately the same date as Swakeleys (the foundation stone was laid in 1607), it is in a less ornate version of the Jacobean style.

The Dutch House, Kew Gardens (*bottom, left*). Popularly known as Kew Palace, this Jacobean mansion in what came to be known as the Dutch style was completed in 1631 as a private residence. It acquired the name of palace when it was purchased by George III in 1781, and it continued to be an occasional royal residence until about 1820.

Kneller Hall (*bottom, right*). The development in architectural styles between the early part of the seventeenth century and the beginning of the eighteenth is well illustrated by Kneller Hall, Twickenham, which was built in 1709 for Sir Godfrey Kneller, official state artist from the reign of Charles II to that of George I.

[28]

Chiswick House. This Italianate house, built between 1725 and 1729 for the third Earl of Burlington on the model of an Italian villa, was not designed as a residence but as a 'temple of arts' in which the Earl could display his magnificent collection of paintings and statuary. The adjoining Jacobean mansion in which the Earl lived has disappeared, as have the wings added to the villa late in the eighteenth century by James Wyatt for the fifth Duke of Devonshire.

Boston Manor. Boston Manor, originally a Tudor mansion, was remodelled and given a 'new look' in the seventeenth century and has since been extensively restored. It was the residence of the lords of the manor of West Brentford, one of whom in the reign of Queen Elizabeth I was Robert, Earl of Leicester. It was finally purchased by the Brentford District Council in 1923.

Kenwood House. One of Greater London's best-known historic homes, Kenwood House was bequeathed by Lord Iveagh to trustees for the benefit of the public in 1925. It is on the site of an early seventeenth-century house which was purchased in 1754 by William Murray, first Earl of Mansfield, who employed Robert Adam to remodel the house. Of the south front, pictured here, the central block and the orangery, extreme left, were allowed to stay much as they had been, but Adam added the library, right, to match the orangery, and also created the fine north portico.

Gunnersbury House. The Gunnersbury Park estate was acquired from the Rothschild family in 1926 and thereafter administered jointly by the borough councils of Acton, Brentford and Chiswick, and Ealing until the formation of the Greater London boroughs. It was originally a manor of Ealing, but in 1760 the estate was purchased to serve as a residence for Princess Amelia, daughter of George II. Many of the trees which grace the park were planted in her time. After the death of the Princess in 1786 the estate was again sold and the mansion demolished. A Regency house, or to be precise two Regency houses, were built in its place. The south front of the present mansion, which was enlarged and altered during its tenure by the Rothschild family during the nineteenth century, is pictured here.

The William Morris Gallery, Walthamstow. This fine and entirely typical Georgian mansion was built in 1762. It was known then, and still is today, as the Water House and was the home of William Morris for eight years. In 1950 it became an art gallery dedicated to William Morris's work.

The Hall of Eltham Palace. The Great Hall is the sole surviving part of the medieval palace. It was built during the reign of Edward IV and retains its hammer-beam roof. After the Civil War the Hall was used as a barn and was not restored until the beginning of the present century.

Langtons, Hornchurch (*above*). An interesting story lies behind the use of this late Georgian mansion as council offices and its gardens as a public open space. In 1929, just three years after the formation of the Hornchurch Urban District, the Langtons estate was presented to the council by a Mrs Parkes on condition that the house should be preserved in its entirety and the gardens maintained in their traditional style. Both conditions have been honoured faithfully.

A Beddington Landmark. This dovecot was built early in the eighteenth century to replace a Tudor one. It was an important adjunct to the well-being of residents in Beddington Hall, the mansion of the Carews (which has now been replaced by a modern building, only the great hall having survived). Between two thousand and three thousand birds tenanted the nine hundred nests in the dovecot and provided a supply of fresh food during the winter, when most of the available meat was salted.

[32]

master's less impressive essays, would accord with the new splendour of St Mary-le-Strand.

Nicholas Hawksmoor was the principal architect of the Queen Anne churches—so called even though they were completed long after the Queen's death. In one of the happiest of all artistic collaborations in the history of architecture Hawksmoor had the help of Sir John Vanbrugh, the architect of Blenheim. Together they achieved what might have seemed impossible, a distinctive style of church building, in spite of meagre and often insufficient funds, making each church a landmark for its district and earning unstinted praise from their contemporaries as well as from posterity. In the City, St Mary Woolnoth is a fitting monument to their mutual inspiration, in the East End Christ Church, Spitalfields, St Anne's, Limehouse, and St George in the East, and in the West End St George's, Bloomsbury. All these were completed by 1730. St George's, Hanover Square, by John James, was opened in 1724, St John's, Smith Square, by Thomas Archer, in 1728, and St Paul's, Deptford, by the same architect, in 1730. There was also the fine church of St Alfege in Greenwich, which was designed by Hawksmoor, with a tower added by John James in 1730. The Gothic church of St Giles-in-the-Fields was rebuilt, and Shoreditch church, by Dance, was completed in 1735. The church of St George the Martyr in the Borough was rebuilt by John Price on the site of a Norman foundation and completed in 1736.

That is almost the whole list of churches built in the first half of the century apart from one or two in the more distant suburbs, such as St John's in Hampstead, which like St Martin-in-the-Fields was constructed from the proceeds of public subscription, and St Mary's in Rotherhithe, where a dilapidated Gothic church was replaced by a fine classical building capped by a famous spire, which is a well-known riverside landmark. It is an extraordinarily short list. For the rest, in the first half of the century at least, parishes had to be content with adding a classical aisle to the existing Gothic nave, or rebuilding and enlarging a part of the church to meet the needs of the influx of parishioners without any attempt to design a new and harmonious building.

The Peace of Paris in 1763 released another flood of new building which lasted until the beginning of the wars with France thirty years later. Builders and speculators alike started again where they had left off, but there were two differences. One was that architecture became a profession for the first time, and a very honourable one at that. The days of the artist designer who left the carrying out of his designs to the master builder, the days when anyone could call himself an architect with scarcely any training, were gone, never to return. The influence of the Adam brothers and of William Chambers was paramount in bringing about this change, which had many obvious advantages, though it was powerless to prevent the spate of drab and monotonous building which ran riot in the mid-Victorian era.

K

Robert Adam and his brother set a completely new standard of speculative building in the Adelphi. Though nothing survives of the colonnade facing the river, there are still a few houses in the near vicinity which show the family genius in building conservative yet original town houses. The Adam brothers were also responsible for most of Portland Place and Chandos Street and part of Fitzroy Square, while William Chambers was the architect of Somerset House, of the central part of Albany and of a number of houses in Portman Square.

Bedford Square was laid out in the Adam style though not by the Adam brothers themselves, as also was much of the Haymarket, where at least one Georgian shop front remains as a reminder of the grace of the eighteenth century. Even earlier shop fronts dating from about 1750 survived the destruction of the Second World War in Artillery Lane just to the east of the City. Portman Square was completed in 1768, Bedford Square six years later. The latter is the best preserved of Georgian squares and still gives a vivid impression of how it must have appeared at the end of the eighteenth century.

Two important developments which took effect shortly before the outbreak of war were in the Baker Street district and in the Sloane Square area, where one of the first of the 'New Towns', so called at the time, was begun in 1780 and virtually completed by the end of the century, making solid if slow progress through the years of war. It was the work of the distinguished architect Henry Holland, who leased part of the Cadogan estate in 1780. The first buildings were in Sloane Street, Cadogan Place and Hans Place, and the whole estate was named by him Hans Town in compliment to Sir Hans Sloane.

Londoners showed a great liking for this new conception of a self-contained community, with shops and open spaces as well as gracious houses, and there was never a dearth of prospective tenants. The new town was ultimately engulfed by the spreading tentacles of Belgravia, but in spite of much rebuilding it has kept a suspicion, if no more, of its eighteenth-century separateness.

The West End was by no means the only part of Greater London to expand rapidly during the century. Bloomsbury made steady if less spectacular progress (its extension to the north was deferred until the next century). Great James Street was built between 1720 and 1730, Great Ormond Street and John Street a little later. Queen Square was laid out in the first decades, together with streets such as Old Gloucester Street, the streets of 'little houses', which were utterly destroyed by aerial bombardment in the Second World War. On the outskirts of the City, Ely Place, a typical Georgian precinct, was laid out in 1775 by Charles Cole, Deputy Surveyor to the Crown, who also undertook a number of development schemes in a private capacity. Ely Place took its name from its position on part of the site of the Palace of the Bishops of Ely, and the private chapel of the Bishop was retained as part of the precinct. It still stands as the church of St Etheldreda, the first medieval church in London to revert to the Roman Catholic Church. The nineteen Georgian houses in the Place were the subject of a hotly contested building preservation order in 1963, when it was said with reason at the public inquiry that it represents a rare type of Georgian development and is the most perfectly preserved of Georgian precincts of similar date in the whole of England.

Other districts developed towards the end of the century include Manchester Square, Brunswick Square, Fitzroy Square and the southern end of Gower Street, which pointed a long finger into the open countryside.

Finsbury Square was laid out in 1777 to the design of George Dance. It was a very fine square indeed, which unhappily has been so much rebuilt that it is difficult to re-create it in the imagination. With its development the City Road became a partly built-up area, and from this period or slightly later must date what many regard as a traditional rhyme:

> Up and down the City Road
> In and out the Eagle,
> That's the way the money goes,
> Pop goes the weasel.

At least four inns claim the distinction of being on the site of the original Eagle.

The characteristic feature of West End development was that it took place in open fields where there had been no village before, chiefly, as we have seen, on the estates of landed proprietors, a factor which contributed largely to the homogeneous character of these western suburbs and to the close-knit pattern of the various development schemes. The existing villages around London were equally, in modern parlance, 'ripe for development', but development inevitably was piecemeal and few estates comparable with those of the West End were laid out afresh.

Camden Town and Somers Town are apparent exceptions to this general rule. In a sense they were akin to Hans Town, in that they were built as individual communities separated if only by a small strip of open country from adjoining suburbs, but designed to provide homes for less prosperous people. How popular Kentish Town became in a short time, together with the nearby area of Tottenham Court Road, is vividly illustrated by the increase in the population of St Pancras parish from six hundred to over ten thousand between 1776 and 1831. Even in the twentieth century few places have shown so rapid a rate of growth. By 1800, too, Islington, until then the playground of London, had grown into a sizable town in its own right. Its period of rapid expansion started with the laying out of Highbury between 1760 and 1790. Shoreditch became almost as popular as a suburb for City men. Hoxton Street and Hoxton Square were built early in the century, about

Hackney in 1805.

the same time as the attractive almshouses which are now the Geffrye
Museum (1715) and formed the nucleus of the new development.

Hackney was one of the most fashionable of the northern suburbs,
though inevitably its development began rather later than that of
Shoreditch or Islington. Towards the end of the century it was
described as 'a populous village inhabited by such numbers of merchants and wealthy persons that it is said there are near a hundred

gentlemen's coaches kept'. Stepney Green did not lag far behind fashionable Hackney, as witness the fine Georgian houses which face the narrow green today.

It was very pleasant and convenient for London business men to live in villages or small towns surrounded by open country (for eighteenth-century people were as keen on green fields and fresh air as those of the twentieth century), but until the very end of the period it was a way of life which had many drawbacks as well as advantages. The most serious was the risk of highway robbery—and a very real risk this was. The notorious Dick Turpin was not born until 1705 and for a long time he made his headquarters in the Hackney Marshes. Accounts exist of isolated attacks in almost every part of the outskirts of London up to 1750 and occasionally afterwards. A journey across Hampstead Heath or Hounslow Heath was genuinely perilous even in the comparative security of a stagecoach.

That is one good reason why the towns and villages beyond the outer fringe of heathland (including Putney Heath and Wimbledon Common) were slow in developing as suburbs, tending rather to grow individually as self-contained communities attracting retired people and people of leisure rather than London business men. Another reason was that they were farther from the metropolis than the distance which it was convenient to drive a carriage and pair twice a day. Until the short-haul coach became commonplace at the end of the century, a private carriage was the only effective means of 'commuting', although from the nearer villages some people still travelled on horseback or on foot, or by river from the Thames-side suburbs.

A bell was rung periodically at the Angel, Islington, to announce the departure of a convoy of foot passengers across the fields to the City. They gathered at the end of St John Street and were escorted into the precincts of the City by an armed patrol. It was usual, too, for carriages to travel in armed convoy from the region of Hyde Park Corner to Kensington, so great was the risk of attack on this stretch of then lonely road, especially after dark in winter, when it was difficult for London merchants to return to their homes before nightfall. Clapham Common had a particularly unsavoury reputation. Sir Thomas and Lady Hankey were robbed there in 1751, and a highwayman was shot point-blank by a Captain Freeman ten years later. There is even a record of a hold-up at Clapham in the first year of the nineteenth century, but that is exceptional. Generally the heyday of the highway-men ended well before the end of the century and travel became relatively safe.

The lives of highway robbers were forfeit once they had taken part in a single hold-up. It was still an era of public executions, at Newgate and Tyburn among other places. Few felt regret at the execution of hundreds of men who in the twentieth century would probably escape with three years' imprisonment. As Boswell says in his *London Journal* of

The Angel Inn, Islington.

May 1763: 'My curiosity to see the melancholy spectacle of the executions was so strong that I could not resist it, although I was sensible that I would suffer much from it.' And suffer from it he did, but 'there was a most prodigious crowd of spectators. I was most terribly shocked and thrown into a very deep melancholy.' But Boswell was unusually sensitive and far in advance of his times.

When William III commissioned Wren to restyle Nottingham House, which was renamed Kensington Palace, Kensington inevitably became prospectively a place of fashion in which, later, many distinguished men of letters and artists resided, such as John Stuart Mill, Holman Hunt, Sir John Millais and Thackeray. Sir Isaac Newton lived in a house near the modern St Mary Abbots Church at the beginning of the eighteenth century until his death in 1727. The earliest residential scheme on West End lines was the remodelling of King Square at the beginning of the century. The square was enlarged, gardens planted, fine houses built around it and it was renamed Kensington Square. By the end of the century Kensington numbered several thousand inhabitants. It developed still faster in the early part of the nineteenth century. Edwardes Square, where the charm of Regency architecture is still a notable feature of the urban scene, Brompton Square, Montpelier Square and Pelham Crescent had all been completed before the accession of Queen Victoria.

Highgate grew from the few handsome seventeenth-century residences on the hill referred to in Chapter 6 into a compact eighteenth-century township centred on Pond Square, with the accent still on gracious houses designed for residents of substance. Hampstead during

Dagenham Lake, formed by one of the breaches in the Thames, which were successfully repaired in 1715–20, remains today and is known as the Gulf.

the century became one of the most popular and one of the wealthiest of the suburbs to the north of London. There was some terrace development here but a number of the houses built were detached, standing in their own grounds. Many of them are still the homes of wealthy people, and indeed one needs to be wealthy to maintain elegant houses of this kind built nearly two hundred years ago with more regard to design than durability.

Fenton House in Hampstead Grove is one of the finest. Flask Walk and The Mount are also early, while Church Row retains dwelling-places which span the period 1730 to 1800. There are signs, too, of the speculative terrace house development in the High Street, though the effect of what must have been a peculiarly attractive composition accentuated by the steep pitch of the hill has been almost obliterated by modern shops, which replace the ground floors of the original houses.

And so one might go on indefinitely, finding at least some Georgian growth in almost every village and town. Stoke Newington High Street was a fashionable area and there were some fine new houses built as far afield as Edmonton and Enfield, Chingford and Walthamstow. Until this century the river had been the traditional means of transport for London people. It was still much more used than it is today. That explains the comparatively early and rapid growth of riverside villages both upstream and downstream and at considerably greater distances from London and Westminster than the most popular landward suburbs.

Greenwich was the doyen of these riverside villages. By the end of the century it could fairly be described as a town centred on its handsome new classical church and on the classical palace which had become the Royal Naval Hospital (the Royal Naval College of today). Many of the houses round Greenwich Park and Blackheath were imposing residences, a few of them rather out of keeping with the times in their eccentric design. The castellated mansion on Maze Hill to the east of Greenwich Park known as Vanbrugh Castle was designed by Sir John Vanbrugh as his home. It is like no other house in the Greater London area, a gesture of defiance by this great artist and dramatist.

There is nothing eccentric, however, in the Ranger's House (formerly Chesterfield House) on the other side of the park, dating from early in the century with wings of about 1750, or in the pleasant homes straggling up Crooms Hill, built between 1720 and 1760, or even in the smaller houses built about 1725 or earlier in Albury Street, which formed the boundary between the boroughs of Deptford and Greenwich. Across the heath, the Paragon, an adventurous essay in speculative building, bears the hallmark of the last decades of the century, as do a number of other houses on Blackheath Hill. But they are all distinguished and in their own way highly typical of the period.

Farther downstream, Woolwich was also becoming a town, but one based rather on industry and the needs of defence than on residential expansion. The Royal Arsenal was transferred here. The Royal Military Academy was established by Royal Warrant in 1741. The Royal Artillery barracks, surely the most handsome of all surviving eighteenth-century military buildings, were built between 1780 and 1802, with a grand sweep of frontage 1,200 feet long.

Upstream Chelsea was half suburb, half independent community, with the first houses in Cheyne Row built in the early decades of the century, and Cheyne Walk virtually complete before the outbreak of war in 1793. Pleasant riverside homes were built along the waterfront at Chiswick and Hammersmith and Strand-on-the-Green. There were many late Georgian houses round Kew Green and a most handsome group at Isleworth near the parish church which, like many others along the river, was enlarged in the eighteenth century, so that it

Green's End, Woolwich, *c.* 1790.

became a strange mixture of Gothic and Renaissance design. The parish churches of Richmond and Twickenham are two others similarly treated, but it was an almost routine procedure arising partly no doubt from a desire to retain something at least of the medieval church, but more particularly from a lack of sufficient funds to build a completely new eighteenth-century place of worship. The new Georgian brick-built naves have been described as 'red brick boxes'.

Richmond had become a place of fashion long before—almost as soon as the royal palace had been remodelled in Tudor times. By the eighteenth century the palace was dilapidated but part of its grounds was used to build grace and favour residences, especially when George III was frequently resident at Kew. The Maids of Honour Row is as fine a group of houses as any dating from the first quarter of the century. It is said to have been planned for ladies of the court who could not be accommodated at Richmond Lodge in the Old Deer Park when the Prince and Princess of Wales made it their home in the latter years of George I's reign.

There are scores of other Georgian houses round the Green and up Richmond Hill. The terrace with its wonderful view over the fields to the wide loop of the Thames by Twickenham was planned during the reign of George III, and Wick House was built about 1772 for Sir Joshua Reynolds, and most probably designed by Sir William Chambers. At the very summit of the hill by the entrance to Richmond Park the Star and Garter Home for disabled servicemen is on the site of the famous Star and Garter Hotel, the most fashionable of all the week-end resorts to which London people drove at summer week-ends, a hostelry which retained its popularity and prestige for much of the nineteenth century.

Speculative building for profit was not confined to London and its inner suburbs. It comes as something of a surprise, however, to find the speculative builder in action and with great success as far afield as Twickenham. Twickenham, of course, was known to very many people as a desirable place of residence by the beginning of the eighteenth century. It had the reputation of being the 'haunt of poets and men of letters, many of whom had made their homes on the Middlesex bank above Richmond far enough from London city to be remote and yet near enough by river, or towards the end of the century by road, to be convenient for meetings of the literary gatherings in London'. This was no doubt an attraction. It became towards the end of the century full, as some contemporary writers saw it, of dowagers and aging spinsters, a kind of Bath or Tunbridge Wells without a spa.

Brewer, in his *Beauties of England and Wales*, abandoned any effort to describe it except to say that Twickenham conveyed an impression of luxury 'which the utmost labours of the pen would vainly endeavour to impart'. This, clearly, is the kind of setting in which the speculative builder might reap a rich reward. And so it happened. Sion Road and Montpelier Row were built between 1720 and 1725. We know that the latter was built as a capitalistic venture by a Captain John Gray, and that the houses as soon as they were completed were let on lease. Although the Captain worked partly on borrowed capital and apparently recompensed the carpenters by a lease of some of the houses, he made a great success of the venture. He deserved to do so, for the houses he built, brick terrace houses of three storeys and a basement, with fine classical doorways, in the vernacular style of the early eighteenth century, make a fine architectural landscape. Their chief interest for us today, perhaps, is that many of them remain almost as they were built and, in spite of the introduction of a Victorian block, Montpelier Row as a whole has not changed its character.

The modified classical style in which London was expanding into the country is one which has satisfied the critics of almost every generation. These houses in Twickenham were admired as the very latest thing when they were built. They inspired the admiration of Cobbett a century later. Though Victorian critics turned against them, as they did against everything Georgian in the glory of their own vigorous essays in ponderous grandeur, twentieth-century critics have returned to them with as much enthusiasm as those of the eighteenth century. They must have been extremely pleasant houses in which to live, at least for the householders, and not so inconvenient as many even for the servants. The basements were well lighted and with the accent less here than in town on the conservation of space the staircases were relatively easy to climb and the ascent to the topmost of the three storeys not overmuch for the elderly to attempt.

The houses in Sion Road are smaller than those in Montpelier Row but very much in the same spirit. They were built for less distinguished residents than those who took leases of the houses in Montpelier Row, but they were just as comfortable and their workmanship was just as good. People are as happy to live in them now as they were then, even though one of their amenities has been lost for ever, the green lawns between the road and the river bank.

To what extent the people who lived in these new housing estates earned a living in London is not known for certain. Most of the residents had London connections. Many, as we have seen, were retired, but it is likely that a nucleus at least of those who made their home by the riverside had business or professional work in the metropolis and made the journey to London several times a week, if not every day. Greater London was already beginning to take a positive shape, determined still, as it had been in the sixteenth and seventeenth centuries, more by the course of the river than by any other single factor.

Twickenham has been called the supreme example of the 'classical' town. So it must have looked in the famous view from Richmond Hill in the eighteenth century, with the classical vistas of Cambridge House and Marble Hill and Orleans House, set in their ornamental parklands, filling the scene between Richmond Bridge and the Twickenham ferry with the growing classical-style town clustered around the church and York House. The only two of these mansions which survive are York House and Marble Hill, the latter only because it was purchased by the London County Council in 1902 in order to preserve the view from Richmond Hill, an imaginative achievement by a council which was only indirectly concerned and was then fully occupied with the pressing problems of organizing the essential services of the more crowded communities. The Twickenham Council made a contribution to the purchase, but improvement in the sense of widening streets and providing essential services was here, as in almost every other community on the fringes of London, a far more urgent preoccupation than preserving what was beautiful or historic for its own sake. York House, purchased by the Twickenham Council a quarter of a century later, served, appropriately, as municipal offices.

Marble Hill, though by no means the most magnificent of the mansions of Twickenham, has great historic interest. And it stands today, like Montpelier Row, very little changed in appearance or in setting. It still looks out over green fields to the broad waterway of the river, its landscape is still a wooded one, and it still gives the impression of a house that could be lived in with grace and comfort. It was built just after Montpelier Row, probably before 1730, for the Countess of Suffolk, the good friend of George II. Just as Montpelier Row represents so well the vernacular style of the period, Marble Hill recalls its more sumptuous style, with its almost perfect classical proportions, its rectangular, three-storeyed block, its Ionic portico and pediment, and the really magnificent staircase which gives access to the chief rooms of the house on the first floor overlooking the sweep of the lawns to the river.

It is tragic that all the other houses which made the riverside of Twickenham famous have disappeared. The parkland of Orleans House and Radnor House survived but the houses have vanished. The name Orleans House originated when Louis Philippe, who became King of France, resided there. Contemporary prints show it to have been a handsome rectangular block with a projecting wing and a rather ornate wall decorated at intervals with battlements continuing the line of the house along the river frontage. But even the battlements were classical in design and the composition a pleasing one, in spite of the fact that it departed considerably from the accepted classical tradition. Twickenham House, on the site of the royal manor house near Richmond Bridge, was demolished in 1887.

The smaller Georgian houses which stood in the meadows between Twickenham and Teddington suffered the same fate during the nineteenth century, while all that remains to remind us of one of the great figures of Twickenham, Alexander Pope, are the names of a house which had no link with him in his lifetime, of a road, and incongruously of a telephone exchange. But Strawberry Hill, Horace Walpole's home, is still with us, the very antithesis of the classicism of the century and in particular of Twickenham. Walpole rented an undistinguished house at Cross Deep in 1747 and renamed it Strawberry Hill, almost immediately beginning the long process of structural alteration which in the end transformed a modest classical house into a 'Gothic castle' after Walpole's own heart.

He frequently quarrelled with his designers. After all, was he not the true designer himself? Among them appear such distinguished names as Richard Bentley and Robert Adam, the former a close friend of Walpole until they had worked together for a few years on this eccentric project! And eccentric it was in an age in which the Gothic ideal had been discarded, according to most contemporary architects, for ever.

Many of its details were copied from medieval models, even down to the cloisters and angle towers, and the fan-vaulting of the gallery over the cloister. One reads with amusement that the chimney-piece in the round drawing-room was adapted from the tomb of Edward the Confessor in Westminster Abbey and 'improved' by Robert Adam, and that the circular ceiling of another room was copied from the chapter house at York. It was certainly a good £20,000 worth of romantic imagery, jeered at by some, praised beyond reason by others, in the last decades of the eighteenth century when it had finally taken shape. It can be viewed with tolerance and some admiration today as evocative of the first stage of the Gothic revival which was embraced with equal enthusiasm by Victorian builders, and as the only mansion of its kind in the whole of Greater London.

It would be too much to hope that a building of such pretensions could remain untouched for nearly two hundred years. In the latter half of the nineteenth century new wings were added, though in much the same style as the original, and part of the façade was degraded in the course of extensive rebuilding. After 1927, when it became the home of St Mary's Training College, some of the nineteenth-century work was demolished and the north front rebuilt brick for brick as Walpole designed it, while the rest of the house was carefully restored.

Something of the spirit of the place emerges from the words of an anonymous writer quoted by Fisher Murray. The author gives what he calls an account of a little kingdom on the banks of the Thames. 'The whole place is one continuous garden. Plenty and pleasure are the ideas conveyed by its fields and meadows. 'Tis governed by a king whom arts not armies recommend to the dignity. He is formally proclaimed by muse and acknowledged by the people. Their last monarch, Mr Pope, was the terror of knaves and fools and the darling of the learned and virtuous. He reigned long over them and was succeeded by their present sovereign, Mr Horace Walpole.' This percipient author rightly inferred that the 'genius of inhabitants inclined towards architecture rather than commerce. What is more remarkable, no stranger resides for a few days among them without being inspired by their rapturous affection for this earthly elysium.'

One wonders what this writer would have thought if he could have viewed the scene sixty or so years later, when we are told that the first thing which struck the traveller along the Twickenham bank of the river was 'the number of villas rising tier upon tier and standing, as it were, on tiptoe, all eyes to catch the largest possible share of the charming landscape. These are so numerous and the majority so frequently change hands that the occupiers this year are seldom the inhabitants of the next.' That, of course, is a tilt at Richmond, which by the middle of the nineteenth century had abandoned all pretensions to being a secluded resort, but it pinpoints the change that by then was beginning to dim the eighteenth-century elegance of the whole riverside from Westminster to Hampton Court.

It is strange that Twickenham, which was so significantly the home of fashion for the whole of the eighteenth century, should have had such an insignificant earlier history. It was part of the manor of Isleworth at the time of the Domesday Survey, and until the beginning of the seventeenth century was no more than a small village clustered about the church. Apart from the manorial estate near Richmond bridge and Whitton Park most of the parish even in Tudor times consisted of unenclosed fields and included the southern flank of Hounslow Heath, which was not effectively enclosed until the beginning of the nineteenth century.

After the close of its most fashionable era it continued to grow so rapidly that by 1937 it had become a borough swallowing the former parishes of Teddington and Hampton, which had developed considerably while Twickenham was still in the chrysalis stage and where Garrick had his famous villa with its Greek temple by the river designed by Robert Adam. Twickenham itself has now been submerged by the Greater London borough of Richmond upon Thames (to give it the full official designation).

Brentford was one other riverside settlement which won fame in the eighteenth century, though its story does not belong so much to the expansion of London as to the troubled history of Middlesex politics in the eighteenth century. In this century Brentford came close to justifying the claim, which has been made often, without the slightest foundation, of being the county town of Middlesex. Brentford Butts at the time was the polling place for the Middlesex parliamentary elections, and it was here that John Wilkes was elected to Parliament in 1768. He was prevented from taking his seat in Parliament, a process repeated four times before the end of 1769. 'Wilkes and Liberty' became the motto of Brentford people. The hustings were scenes of confusion and often violence, but in the end 'Wilkes and Liberty' triumphed when this stormy petrel of Middlesex was allowed to take his seat in Parliament in 1774.

It is an obvious fact, but one seldom commented upon, that nine-tenths of the vast expansion during the early part of the century took place to the north of the river. London was a city of the north bank. The only link with the south bank in the first half of the eighteenth century was London Bridge, So apart from Southwark the south side of the river was neglected, a world as distant from Chelsea or Fulham as if it had been separated by the full width of the English Channel, especially as so much of the south bank was marshy. There were great houses like the Palace of the Archbishops of Canterbury at Lambeth, a few fine residences like Old Battersea House, but nothing at all that can conceivably be called a suburb. Southwark was a close-knit community (several of the present houses on Bankside belong to this period, and Hopton's Almshouses were founded in 1752); a ribbon development extended down the main road to the south, with numerous coaching inns, of which only the George has come down to us in something approaching its original form. This main road provided a link also with Camberwell and Dulwich, the only villages to the south which showed early development. Camberwell Grove was a favourite spot for merchants' residences, their owners travelling in their carriages over London Bridge to join the thousands of carriages coming in from the north, east and west, and there sharing in the inevitable traffic blocks but delegating to their coachmen the discomfort associated with parking in the overcrowded alleys and yards.

Dulwich was a Georgian village with a character of its own, but rather on the lines of Hampstead. Its tree-planted grass verges gave it a special distinction; most of the houses secluded behind the green were ample and well built, not monotonously to one design, as in so many Greater London developments, but each one or each pair planned as a composition in its own right. They vary in date from about 1750 to the end of the century, and were mainly what were known as gentlemen's residences, but it is notable that Bell House in College Road, one of the finest of them all, was built between 1765 and 1770 for Thomas Wright, a City alderman.

The seclusion of these few villages on the Surrey bank was near its end by then. The idea of improvement, as has already been noted, was in the air. One of the greatest improvements was the linking of the north bank with the south by bridges at several places and consequently the opening up of limitless new vistas for building along the straight roads which were built at the southern approaches to the new bridges.

Westminster bridge, the very first link between the two banks except London Bridge, was opened in 1750. Opposition to the idea had been fantastic and was centred on the Thames watermen, whose livelihood was won by ferrying passengers from one bank to the other. There was a horse ferry at Westminster, another at Horseferry Road, very near the site of modern Lambeth bridge, linking the Palace of Westminster with the Palace of the Archbishops of Canterbury. The See of Canterbury held the manorial rights over the Lambeth horse ferry. The sum of £3,780 was paid in compensation to the see, and a further £3,000 to the owner of the rights of the Westminster ferry. The improvement of London certainly involved some unexpected expenses.

The success of Westminster bridge was immediate. Indeed it was not long before it had to be rebuilt to carry the great press of traffic which used it. Now bridge followed bridge. Blackfriars was opened in 1769, Battersea in 1771. The same was happening farther upstream. The first Putney bridge was completed in 1729, the first Kew bridge in 1759. The building of the last-named was particularly significant. Brentford had always been one of the most important fords over the rivers Thames and Brent but the adoption of Richmond Lodge as a favourite royal residence vastly increased the use of the ferry adjoining the ford and at the same time its importance. The account book for the horse ferry for the period 1734–7 is still in existence and shows a great number of payments made on behalf of Frederick, Prince of Wales. In this case the owner of the horse ferry obtained permission to build a toll bridge, the first of the several bridges across the river at Kew. Maintenance of the first wooden structure was more costly than the total of tolls received, and a second bridge had been opened by 1789. For a time the two bridges stood side by side, until the added hazard to river traffic compelled the demolition of the earlier one.

The effect of the bridges on the expansion of London was not, of course, immediate, but it is still possible to find a number of late Georgian houses in Kennington Park Road and in Wandsworth Road, Lambeth, which were among the first to be built along the bridge

Paddington Church in the latter half of the eighteenth century.

approach roads. But full-scale development of the area thus 'reclaimed' was deferred to Regency and early Victorian times.

Another striking improvement to Greater London was the construction of the first City by-pass road, the New Road as it was called, which also served as a by-pass for the busy Oxford Road. It linked Paddington with Islington (it included the Marylebone and Euston Roads of today) and gave direct access to Essex from the west without the need to pass through London. It was completed in 1757 and was extremely popular with the people who lived in the newly developed areas to the north of the Oxford Road. In 1798 it carried the first coach plying for hire in the London area from Paddington to Islington, as opposed to the existing multiple services of stage-coaches plying from places outside London to the metropolis.

Until the outbreak of war in 1793 the authorities of the City and Westminster vied with each other, too, in beautifying the capital and making travel easier. The walls and all the gates of London were demolished between 1760 and 1767, though Temple Bar (never, of course, an actual gate of the City) was retained as a ceremonial entrance. By then the Mansion House, by George Dance the Elder, had brought new life to City functions which until then had been held in the home of the Lord Mayor, which had been invariably within the City limits. In Westminster the screen for the Admiralty courtyard by Adam, the Horse Guards by William Kent and Somerset House by Sir William Chambers all added lustre to the scene. Wren's theatre in Drury Lane was demolished to make way for a new and more magnificent structure by Henry Holland, completed in 1794, and work on Sir Robert Smirke's Opera House, opened in 1809, was already under way at the end of the century. The roads of Westminster and the City were repaved and street lighting introduced. Proposals were made to cover in the Fleet River, the stench of which had become an offence to the whole of the City. That was only a small step in the right direction, for in Charles Dickens's time it was still reasonable to describe the Thames itself as a mighty sewer that ebbed and flowed.

The City was always conservative but generally forward-looking where commerce was concerned. The presence of the Borough Market in the Borough High Street impeded commercial traffic to an intolerable extent, so in 1756 an Act was passed transferring the market to its present site near the southern end of London Bridge.

In all this story of progress one thing was still lacking, as it had been in the first half of the century—a realistic approach to the vexed problem of building new churches. Certainly there were a few new churches in the last half of the century, but not in proportion to the growth of population. Finance was still the stumbling-block. The building of a church was an expense to be avoided if possible, unless it was the rebuilding of a church which had become derelict and dangerous. Battersea parish church and St Mary's, Lewisham, in the seventeen-seventies, and St Mary's, Paddington, in the seventeen-nineties are typical of the work being done, yet Wesley could raise the funds to build a magnificent temple in the City Road in 1777–8.

In one place at least there was a revival in religious feeling. The Clapham Sect, remembered chiefly for the active part it took in agitation against the slave trade, was primarily a group of religious people living in the old town of Clapham, and in the Georgian residences which still stand along the north side of the Common. They deplored the irreligion of the age, the decay of the churches, and gathered together for prayer meetings and brought moral pressure on the authorities to change their attitude. It was largely due to their pressure that Holy Trinity was built on the Common in the seventeen-seventies, not perhaps a particularly handsome church but a new one built in the spirit of the age and adequate in size to house its congregation in comfort.

The picture of life in London and its surroundings between 1750 and 1793 is largely one of peaceful activity. In the City and Westminster the even tenor of life was rudely interrupted in 1780 when indignation against the Acts of 1774 and 1778 reducing the penal laws against Roman Catholics came to a head in the Gordon Riots. The leader of the movement against Catholic emancipation in London was Lord George Gordon, a Member of Parliament who is said to have gathered sixty thousand followers (this may be an exaggeration) and led them into Palace Yard to the very door of the House of Commons. The situation, it is said, was saved by the courage of Colonel Gordon, a kinsman of Lord George and also a Member of the House, who threatened to

L

plunge his sword into Lord George's body if his followers crossed the threshold.

However, that did not save London from serious riots when the mob became completely out of hand and disowned even its own leader. In a week thirty-six serious fires were started, a number of Catholic chapels were sacked, and the shops of Catholic tradesmen looted. Newgate Prison was seriously damaged by fire and the prisoners released. The Bank of England was attacked. The people of London in self-protection chalked the words 'No Popery' on their doors. In the end troops were called in and the rioters defeated in a number of pitched battles, in which perhaps four hundred were killed. The incident is vividly described by Dickens in *Barnaby Rudge*.

The disturbances spread beyond the confines of London and Westminster. The rioters' anger was directed in particular at Lord Mansfield, who had shown sympathy for Presbyterians and permitted Quakers to make an affirmation instead of taking an oath in civil cases, and finally had directed a jury to bring in a verdict of 'not guilty' in a case in which a Roman Catholic priest was accused of celebrating mass. He was denounced as a Papist and a Jesuit, so it is not surprising to find that one of the first objectives of the rioters was Lord Mansfield's house in Bloomsbury Square, which was burnt to the ground with the loss of all his valuables, including one of the largest private libraries in the country. Not content with this outrage, the mob made for Lord Mansfield's Hampstead home, Kenwood House, which had been reconstructed for him by Robert Adam only twelve years before and which he had embellished with fine furniture and tapestry. Had they succeeded in their object one of Greater London's most distinguished links with the eighteenth century would have disappeared.

What precisely happened cannot be known. The tradition is that the rioters reached the Spaniard's Inn, only a short distance from the house, and by a piece of master strategy were invited in for a drink by the landlord, Giles Thomas. He gave them the freedom of the house and the cellars and meanwhile sent for a detachment of horse guards, who arrived in time to bar the way to Kenwood House and confront the now intoxicated rioters who, though they outnumbered the soldiers by twenty to one, turned and fled back towards London.

Then in 1793 England was once more at war. As had happened so many times before, progress and expansion were halted. This time the country's resources were strained as never before, though miraculously the City's commerce continued to flourish, but on a much reduced scale. The loss of the American colonies had struck them only a glancing blow, for British ships were sailing farther and farther afield and the population of Britain itself was increasing apace. The Napoleonic Wars, however, were a real threat to the economy. At one time the war appeared to be a threat to the country's very existence as an independent sovereign state. It was a gloomy ending to a century of light and colour, a halting of the steady progress in which the standard of living of most of the people had improved and the middle class had become established not only as a numerous but as a solid and dependable part of the population. It was a sign of the expanding horizons of the people at large that the first copies of *The Times* newspaper appeared in 1788 and soon found a market of thousands who were able and willing to read it.

9. Country Houses, 1600–1830

DURING the seventeenth and eighteenth centuries, when London was growing in size and importance but most of what is now Greater London was agricultural land worked by the people of still rural communities, the country mansions were an important link between the life of the rural areas and of the City and Westminster. With only brief setbacks the standard of living in the country improved in this period as it did in London itself: with increasing wealth most of the lords of the manor rebuilt their ancient manor houses in the new style of architecture which was the symbol of the new prosperity. Instead of rebuilding completely many concealed an Elizabethan façade with a brand-new Renaissance or Georgian front in order to be in the fashion. That is the reason why so many houses apparently dating from the seventeenth or eighteenth century prove on closer examination to have low timbered rooms, the ceilings supported by oaken beams which were certainly placed in position long before the exterior of the house was remodelled.

The traditional landowners were by no means the only or the most significant builders of gracious homes in the countryside during these two centuries. Frequently the lord of the manor leased or sold part of the manorial land, so that a newcomer to the district could build himself a house in the country. These newcomers were most frequently wealthy London bankers, financiers and merchants. In many cases they not only built a country home but converted the land they had leased into a park landscaped without thought of cost by the finest landscape gardeners of the time. Some purchased an old manor house, often a dilapidated one, and built their new home on its site. Whether the house was on virgin ground or on the site of an old manor house it was built often as a status symbol apart from making a fine residence for the owner's family. Wealthy men tried to surpass the elegance of their friends' homes. A number of City men donned the mantle of the country squire with surprising ease. Some who had attained the highest honour of the City of London, that of service as Lord Mayor, became the benefactors of relatively poor parishes in the Greater London area, endowing charities, subsidizing the building of schools, rebuilding the cottages on the manorial estates, contributing lavishly to funds raised for every kind of improvement.

Thus to some degree the wealth of the City was distributed throughout the country districts. During the seventeenth century only the wealthiest of London men could afford the vast expense of building a great house and laying out park lands on frequently unsuitable terrain. In the eighteenth century their number increased and there could have been few parishes which did not have a City magnate's mansion, more often two or three or four of them.

It sounds trite to say that everything has its season, from trad jazz to hooped skirts, but history exemplifies the truth of it at every turn. The town mansions of noblemen had had their day, and they had mostly ceased to be private houses before the end of the nineteenth century and were either demolished or used for some quite different purpose. Bedford House, the old Somerset House, Northumberland House and scores of others had disappeared. So it was with the country mansions of Greater London. They had their heyday in the eighteenth century. More houses, generally smaller ones, were being built in the first decades of the nineteenth century. But few survived as country residences into the second half of the twentieth century.

As London spread its tentacles in every direction following the line of the railways, the country estates lost their character of rural retreats, becoming more like green oases in a desert of red brick. The cost of maintaining them increased out of all proportion. When an owner wished to sell he found it increasingly difficult to find a buyer for the house, but if he was an intelligent business man he knew that he was sitting almost literally on a gold mine. The value of the land from which the park had been landscaped in a previous generation became worth far more than the house. A few parks were too far from a railway station to appreciate so soon but their land, too, turned to gold when a network of roads supplemented the network of railways, and buses and motor-cars carried London-working residents quickly and easily to the nearest station. Many owners inevitably sold to the developers: other houses became schools or hospitals, or even business premises.

The end of the story belongs to Chapter 14. By the end of the nineteenth century the need for open spaces in the suburbs was recognized by almost every local authority. Many of the estates were purchased by town or county councils, with or without the assistance of public subscription. The parks became public open spaces, the mansions were converted into municipal offices or libraries. In the present century the work of the local authorities has been helped by the National Trust and other interested bodies, and by the generosity of wealthy owners who have presented their houses and their land for public enjoyment.

Syon House is a happy exception, one of the few which has remained privately occupied through all these vicissitudes. It takes pride of place in what can only be a selection from the many estates in the Greater London area which it would take a whole volume to describe in detail.

This sumptuous house is situated near Isleworth, on the site of a nunnery (see page 59) dissolved in 1539. The estate was granted to the Duke of Somerset in 1547. Substantially, the central part of the mansion is the typical Tudor residence which the Duke of Somerset had built. There is Tudor brick in the angle turrets and much of the fabric was derived from the monastic buildings.

The Duke of Somerset was not long left in possession. He was beheaded for treason in 1552; his successor at Syon, the Duke of Northumberland, was beheaded on a similar charge by Queen Mary, who restored the estate to the remnants of the colony of nuns expelled at the Suppression. Parts of the conventual buildings were rebuilt. It was one of only about a dozen monastic houses which were re-formed in this reign.

Directly Queen Elizabeth I came to the throne she took the obvious course of underlining the work of her father by dissolving the new abbey. The estate was granted to the Percys, Earls of Northumberland. Additions to the house were made during the seventeenth century, when all the battlements were renewed, but nothing else was done except for adding a colonnade to the east front (possibly to the design of Inigo Jones) until the latter part of the eighteenth century, when the ubiquitous Adam brothers carried out a thorough renovation which amounted to rebuilding the interior, including the hall, in the typical Adam style. There was further restoration in the nineteenth century and the then Duke of Northumberland had the entrance gates from Northumberland House re-erected here when the latter was demolished, a still-present link with the London that has disappeared for ever.

Osterley Park, only a short distance away from Syon House, is in the same tradition, though on a smaller scale. The two are curiously similar in history. Both were Tudor mansions, both owe a great deal in their present form to the Adam brothers. The main difference is that the Adam stamp is set most strikingly on the interior of Syon House and on the exterior of Osterley, which shows far less evidence of its Tudor origin. Its link with Tudor London, however, is stronger, for this was no nobleman's mansion but the country home of Sir Thomas Gresham, prince of city financiers, who bought an earlier farmhouse on the site and converted it into a house fit for a prince. And for a queen, too, for Elizabeth I visited him at Osterley on several occasions.

The Adam work here is difficult to appreciate at first glance. It was spread over a long time, is inconsistent and derives extraordinarily little from native genius. Adam began by rebuilding the house round a courtyard, filling half of one side of the courtyard with an Ionic portico in which he consciously copied features of the Temple of the Sun at Palmyra. This may not have been an altogether happy experiment but it would be a carping critic who found fault with the state apartments, which were not only designed by Adam but furnished by him too. Many people will find themselves for once agreeing with Horace Walpole, that most critical of all critics, who referred to the tapestry room as the most superb and beautiful that could be conceived. But Horace was still Horace. After thus commending Adam by implication he complained that he had 'stuck diminutive heads in bronze not bigger than a half-crown into the chimney-piece'. It was a case of Greek meeting Greek. Adam perhaps was over-preoccupied with detail, Walpole certainly over-concerned with the criticism of detail—especially when he describes the Etruscan room, 'painted all over like Wedgwood's ware', as a tumble into bathos.

Osterley, now in the care of the National Trust and administered by the Victoria and Albert Museum, bereft of its art treasures but retaining much of its Adam furniture, is one of the places which must be seen to be understood. It has a peculiar fascination of its own as re-creating far more vividly even than Kenwood the essential excellence as well as the insignificant faults of the brotherhood of architects who influenced the landscapes of London's country as effectively as they did the urban landscape with the Adelphi.

Although Ham House, which is situated close to the banks of the Thames on the Surrey bank opposite Twickenham Ferry, has not, like Syon House, retained its tradition of private ownership to the present day, it was lived in by the same family from 1637 until 1948. In many ways it is one of the most interesting of the great houses which are open to the public. Its origin was as a comparatively small country home built in 1610. Twenty-five years later it came into the possession of the first Earl of Dysart, whose daughter Elizabeth became Countess of Dysart in her own right. Elizabeth married first Sir Lionel Tollemache and after his death John Maitland, Earl of Lauderdale, who as one of Charles II's leading ministers was rewarded with the honour of a dukedom.

The Duke and Duchess of Lauderdale were personally responsible for enlarging the house and refurnishing it with the most costly and beautiful furniture which it was possible to obtain. So although parts of the house of 1610 can still be traced, Ham House as it is today is a monument without parallel to the architecture and *décor* of the Restoration period. It was never refurnished. It passed after his mother's death to the third Earl of Dysart, her only son by her first marriage. He and his successors of the Tollemache family concentrated in the ensuing 250 years on preserving the furniture and fittings as they were in the glorious time of the Lauderdales. Amazingly the contents of the rooms today are almost exactly the same as those shown in the inventory of 1679. The Tollemache family presented the house and park to the National Trust in 1948. The furniture was purchased for the nation and as at Osterley is in the care of the Victoria and Albert

Museum, although Ham House inside and out is as unlike the popular conception of a museum as anything one could imagine.

The same Duke of Lauderdale who contributed so much to the embellishment of Ham House had his own mansion in Highgate. Unhappily Lauderdale House in what is now known as Waterlow Park is scarcely recognizable for what it once was. However, mutilated though it is by rebuilding and by fire, it still recalls something of its seventeenth-century elegance when, as persistent tradition has it, Charles II 'borrowed' it as a residence for Nell Gwyn. It was modified periodically to suit the tastes of Georgian and Victorian residents, who included Lord Westbury, the distinguished Lord Chancellor. Then in 1889 Sir Sydney Waterlow made a gift of the estate to the City of London and the City Corporation is still responsible for it. The park's name was changed to Waterlow in honour of the donor.

Charlton plays a similar role in the Kent tradition as Ham in that of Surrey. It was built about the same time as the original Ham House but was never enlarged or materially altered. Sir Thomas Vavasor, for whom the original Ham House was built, was a court official, so was Sir Adam Newton, for whom Charlton was built.

Sir Adam was tutor and secretary to the Prince of Wales, Prince Henry, elder brother of Charles I. He moved from London to the Kentish countryside about 1610. The exterior of the house and part of the interior are in an interesting Jacobean style. It is a good example of the E plan generally used for country houses of the Elizabethan period, and retained for some built in the early decades of the following century. The porch is especially fine and beautifully moulded. Many of the rooms, including the long gallery, retain their original panelling. Some of the ceilings are miracles of plaster decoration. Charlton's days of splendour are farther away in time than Ham's but it continues to do good service in the control of the local authority as a community centre.

The Eagle House at Wimbledon is a less famous mansion of the same period. It is a gabled residence of red brick, less classical in its design than Charlton, and has lost some of the character which it must have had when it was a country residence standing in park lands. It has stronger links with the City than Ham or Charlton, for it was built about 1613 for a London merchant, one Robert Bell, a member of the Girdlers' Company and a foundation member of the East India Company, the wealthiest of a long line of Bells who had their roots in Wimbledon. Restored late in the nineteenth century, its garden front is little changed in appearance. As at Charlton several of the wonderfully fashioned plaster ceilings of the Jacobean period have survived.

Robert Bell set a fashion followed by other prosperous City men who built homes for themselves in the sheltered valley of the Wandle or between the river's course and the Wimbledon heathlands. Claremont House also dates from the seventeenth century, and there are several others which were built in that century, though altered beyond recognition.

Wimbledon House was occupied successively by the Earl of Bristol (who commissioned John Evelyn to lay out the garden afresh but the latter found the task difficult: 'It is a delicious place for prospect but the soil is cold and weeping clay'), by the Duke of Leeds, one of Charles II's chief ministers, and was purchased by Sir Theodore Janssen, a director of the South Sea Company, in 1712. Sir Theodore, not content with the house that had sheltered such distinguished noblemen, demolished it and built a larger mansion. Then the South Sea Bubble burst and Sir Theodore was required by Parliament to pay more than £200,000 towards the losses incurred by his company. He took the only course open to him. He sold the manor of Wimbledon— to Sarah, Duchess of Marlborough, surely the most eccentric of all the *grandes dames* of English social history. In the twenty years between her purchase of the manor and her death at the age of eighty-five in 1744 she had Sir Theodore's house demolished and another built in its place. Not liking this new home she built a second vast mansion and had her first creation demolished. From the Duchess of Marlborough this palatial mansion, the lineal descendant of the medieval manor house, passed to the Spencers through her grandson, John Spencer.

Only forty years after the death of the Duchess (in 1785) the house was destroyed by fire. By then the park had been landscaped afresh by 'Capability' Brown and Henry Holland was engaged to design a new house. That house, too, though it escaped the perils of fire and the equally powerful danger of being replaced by another house to suit the whim of a new owner, has left no trace, though it was not until 1949 that it had fallen so far into disrepair that it had to be demolished. Now only the very attractive landscape designed by Lancelot Brown, with its graceful lake centre-piece, remains to remind the visitor of historic Wimbledon House.

Holland House in Kensington is slightly earlier in date than its fellow Jacobean mansions, such as Charlton. It was built to the design of John Thorpe in 1607, but only a fragment remains of the house, which was the social centre of the most talented Whig coterie of the eighteenth and early nineteenth centuries, as described by that equally talented historian and commentator, Lord Macaulay, when the third Baron Holland, kinsman of Charles James Fox, occupied it. The central and west wings of the house were gutted by incendiary bombs during the Second World War, and though the exterior of the east wing has been rebuilt, no effort has been made to restore the interior. This has been converted into dormitories as part of the King George VI Memorial Youth Hostel, one of five hostels which were proposed in 1959 by Queen Elizabeth II as a fitting memorial to her father. It is one of the saddest casualties of the war.

Swakeleys at Ickenham is another truly Jacobean mansion which forms part of Greater London's heritage. The estate on which the house was built was bought in 1629 by Sir Edmund Wright, sometime Lord Mayor of London, and is thus another important link between London and the countryside forged in the first half of the seventeenth century. When Pepys visited it in 1665 he described how the new owner, Sir Robert Vyner, who had purchased it from the Wright family, 'took us up and down with great respect; it is a place not very modern in the garden or house and some things to excess'. However, Pepys did concede that it was the most 'uniform' house he had ever seen.

That is the impression which it conveys to a visitor who sees it today for the first time. The carved screen which Pepys admired, too, is still in the great hall, but many alterations were made to the interior in the eighteenth and nineteenth centuries. However, the matching façades are virtually unchanged since the seventeenth century and the house, together with the lawns sloping to the lake, formed by widening a stream, make up one of the most impressive scenes of past elegance in the whole of Greater London. It remained in private ownership throughout most of the nineteenth century; more recently it has followed Holland House in the service of youth as a sports club-house. and there is a public walk by the lake.

Kew 'Palace' was also built in the first half of the seventeenth century. Before its purchase by George III it was known as the Dutch House, a singularly apt description, for it was built between 1630 and 1632 by Samuel Fortrey, a Flemish merchant whose wealth was derived from trade in the Low Countries as much as in the City, and who stipulated a style of architecture which originated in Holland and which is exemplified in a number of houses in East Anglia, as well as at Kew. Here, too, as at Charlton and Ham, the interest of the house is increased by the beauty of the seventeenth-century ceilings and other details of design.

The second half of the seventeenth century was less notably a period of mansion building than the first half. Certainly if one excludes the Lauderdale reconstruction of Ham House, singularly little has survived. Boston Manor, Chiswick, and Hall Place, Bexley, are two of the best examples but both were built on the site of earlier houses.

The manor of Boston was granted to the Prior of St Helen's, Bishopsgate, but there is no record of a house on the site until the land had reverted to the Crown after the Dissolution. One of the residents in the Tudor mansion was Robert, Earl of Leicester, to whom it was presented by Queen Elizabeth in 1572. It is likely that parts of this Tudor house were incorporated in a rebuilding carried out between 1620 and 1625, when the house assumed very much its present shape. In 1670, however, it was bought by a commoner, James Clitherow, who again carried out extensive alterations and whose descendants continued to live in the house until 1918. A few years later it was purchased by the local council. Its porch and some of the window moulding rank with the finest examples of seventeenth-century decorative architecture.

Bexley's Hall Place presents architecturally a much more confused appearance. As at Boston, the basis of the house is Tudor, but in the case of Hall Place instead of the Tudor house being enlarged and re-modelled, as at Boston and many other places, seventeenth-century improvement took the form of building a vast new wing in the Renaissance style. This was completed about 1660 and accords remarkably well with the adjoining Gothic wing. Only at Hampton Court is there an equally successful juxtaposition of the classical and medieval styles. Like Boston Manor, Hall Place was purchased between the two wars by the local council. The topiary garden is an unusually successful essay in this form of landscaping, which became popular towards the end of the sixteenth century.

If the second half of the seventeenth century is relatively poor in country mansions, the first half of the eighteenth century is singularly rich. Kneller Hall and Carshalton House are two distinguished mansions built during the first decade. Kneller Hall, Twickenham, was built for Sir Godfrey Kneller, officially designated State painter in three reigns, those of Charles II, William and Mary, and George I, a man with as much artistic influence at court as Holbein had in Tudor times. By a happy coincidence his house perpetuates the cultural tradition as the headquarters establishment of the Royal Military School of Music. By less happy design it has been so altered in the two and a half centuries of its life that it no longer does real justice either to the Queen Anne style or to the tradition of English country house building.

Carshalton House, completed in 1710 within a year of Kneller Hall, is in a very different category. Far less palatial but far more typical of its times, it is a four-square red brick house still surrounded by well-wooded parklands and little changed (except for the addition of a west wing) in its transition from the home of a London financier to the Convent School of St Philomena. An interesting link between Carshalton House and Wimbledon House is that Carshalton, like Wimbledon, was the home of a director of the South Sea Company, Sir John Fellowes. Sir John suffered precisely the same fate as Sir Theodore Janssen. When the Bubble burst he was forced to sell to satisfy Parliament's demand for restitution. To complete the parallel, just as Sir Theodore continued to live in Wimbledon, doubtless deeply disturbed by the Duchess of Marlborough's contempt for his handiwork, so Sir John Fellowes continued to live in Carshalton, happily without suffering the chagrin of seeing the house demolished in which he had taken so much pride.

Many fine houses were built near the river in the eighteenth century. Some of these were semi-town houses, as at Richmond, or if not town houses at least resembling town houses in that they had no parkland setting, though most had elaborate gardens. The Thames valley

between Richmond and Teddington was the most popular district for
new building. In Chapter 8 the numerous eighteenth-century houses
which made Twickenham the most classical town in the London
district have been mentioned, but on the other bank also there was
considerable building activity between Ham House and Richmond
Bridge. Sudbrooke Park, now the club-house of the Richmond Golf
Club, was built between 1720 and 1725, its first resident John, second
Duke of Argyll, who died here in 1743. It is still a lovely example of
Georgian architecture, famous for the panelled great hall.

Chiswick House, lower downstream, is much better known and just
as interesting. The early eighteenth-century building set in an uncommonly fine park which attracts thousands of visitors every year
was not the first house on the site. There are records of a Chiswick
House from the beginning of the seventeenth century but little is
known of it except the names of some of its owners. Towards the end
of the century it came into the hands of the Earls of Burlington. The
third Earl built what we know as Chiswick House between 1730 and
1736 to accommodate his art collection. He had travelled extensively in
Italy and admired the work of Palladio, after whose style this museum
was modelled. The Jacobean house, incidentally, was maintained as a
family residence and was linked to the art gallery by a covered walk.
The parkland was landscaped afresh at the same time in the classical
style.

In the eighteenth century the estate passed to the Dukes of Devonshire by marriage. The fifth Duke demolished the main part of the
Jacobean house and added wings to the art gallery, remodelling the
interior so that it could be used as a residence. Since it was purchased
by the local authority in 1929 much work has been done under the
auspices of the Ministry of Works to restore it to its original form as
conceived by the third Earl of Burlington.

Leyton and Walthamstow, on the fringes of the then still excellent
hunting country of the Forest of Essex, were almost as popular for
country houses as the riverside meadows. Inevitably the majority have
disappeared but one of the earliest, the Forest House in Leyton, is still
in existence. This was built about 1710 and can be found today by
determined visitors in the grounds of Whipps Cross Hospital. To be
more precise, the hospital was built in the grounds of Forest House.

The nearby Forest School in Walthamstow is another eighteenth-
century mansion much altered, while in the same district Walthamstow
House, dating from 1772 and enlarged by Sir Robert Wigram, a
merchant of the East India Company, a few years later, has become St
Mary's Orphanage School. It is a pleasant though unconfirmed tradition
that the cannon which serve as bollards at the entrance were once
mounted on one of Sir Robert's ships.

Highams, built in 1768, has become a girls' school. The Water House,
with its small but picturesque park, was built in 1762 on the site of an

earlier house. It became the home of William Morris and is now the William Morris Art Gallery. The moat which gave it its name is still clearly marked.

By the latter part of the eighteenth century Hampstead and Highgate had become rather too popular for many country estates to be laid out in their vicinity. They had become, in fact, extensions of the fashionable West End, with scores of large houses surrounded by well-tended gardens sheltering not only London business men but poets and artists and men of letters (as so many of Hampstead's smaller houses do today).

Kenwood House is the only one of this period which stands out as an exception to the general rule. It is a mansion in its own park landscaped with all the subtlety of eighteenth-century landscape gardeners. The central block represents a rather earlier house which Lord Mansfield, the Lord Chancellor, had purchased and in 1767 engaged Robert Adam to remodel and enlarge. The exterior is plain but harmonious. The interior is typical of Adam's work at its best and still almost exactly as Adam designed it, especially the library, which is regarded as one of the finest rooms of the period. The elaborate entrance on the north side is also Adam's work.

Country house development was taking place at this time in many districts to the north, south and west of London, and indeed to a lesser extent to the east of London also. No reliable estimate has been made of the number of late eighteenth-century country houses occupied by still active or retired London business men in the Greater London area. There must have been more than a hundred, though in some of these the 'park', an essential part of the fashionable country house, was little more than an oversize lawn and garden.

To the south, Beckenham Place is typical of the more grandiose establishments; to the north, Trent Park, fashioned out of what had been Enfield Chace; to the east, Langtons at Hornchurch; to the south-west, Morden Park (Morden Hall, probably on the site of the medieval manor house, is more ancient in origin than Morden Park). The two great houses of Sidcup also are typical, though neither in the eighteenth century would have ranked as exceptionally opulent. Sidcup then was not really a village but a tiny hamlet in open country with not even a church of its own until 1841: 'a small street with an inn' according to a contemporary writer in 1830. So Sidcup Place, which was built in 1743, and Sidcup manor house, built about fifty years later, were genuinely country houses, however difficult this is to imagine when Sidcup has become a flourishing town and both the great houses are in municipal ownership. The same is true of Lamorbey Park, built about 1750, though there the still ample parkland and the wooded course of the river near by combine to give an air of greater rural seclusion.

The former episcopal palace of Bromley was one of the finest of late eighteenth-century mansions. It has been kept in perfect order since it passed out of the hands of the Bishops of Rochester to a lay family in

1845, and has never been altered or added to enough to rob it of its eighteenth-century character. It was the last of a succession of houses on the site which had been built for the bishops. In 1184, in the time of Bishop Gilbert de Glanvill, a new house replaced an earlier one, and again in the sixteenth century, when it became the principal residence of the bishops. We know the appearance of this palace in the mid eighteenth century from an engraving which shows it to have been a substantial residence, mainly Tudor or Elizabethan, but with Jacobean additions. The most surprising thing about it is its great size and elaboration. It gives a good idea of the circumstances in which the hierarchy of the Church lived, after the Reformation as much as before.

By 1752 this mansion, like its predecessors, had fallen into disrepair. Horace Walpole, who visited it on 5 August of that year, described it as 'a paltry parsonage, with nothing but two panes of glass purloined from Islip's Chapel in Westminster Abbey'. But then Walpole was not only acid in his comments but highly critical of traditional institutions. However, Bishop Thomas must have agreed with the spirit of Walpole's thought, for when it was decided to rebuild a new home he had the old palace pulled down to its very foundations and had the present mansion built wholly in the contemporary style, a model of what a large country house in that enlightened age of English architecture should be. At the same time the small park was landscaped in the eighteenth-century style, so that the whole estate took on a new look. The only major addition which has been made since then is the colonnade on the south side of the mansion.

In the first decades of the nineteenth century there were signs of change. A few great mansions like Gunnersbury House were built or rebuilt, but mostly the accent was on smaller houses pleasantly situated in modest parklands. Now the scramble began for suitable sites within easy reach of the City in country which was still undeveloped and where existing farmland could be turned easily into the tree-studded parks which, however small, remained the hallmark of a 'gentleman's seat'. Camberwell and its now more famous progeny Dulwich, and Finchley and Mill Hill were among the districts most in demand. Brockwell Park and Clissold Park are two of the most tasteful and illustrative of this new style of country house building. Both stand on hills dominating the surrounding parkland. Both are relatively small and convenient, and but for the cost of keeping them in repair might be occupied as private houses today. Both, in fact, when they were in danger of destruction, were taken into the protection of the London County Council.

Although so many of the 'capital seats', as Victorians always called them, built in the eighteenth or early nineteenth century, have disappeared completely, in a few cases something of real interest has been preserved, either of the Georgian house or of an earlier manor house on the site of which it was built. Well Hall in Eltham is one of the most interesting of these. The existence of the manor is recorded at the beginning of the twelfth century. The names of many of the families through whose hands it passed are known, but few had much significance until 1525, when William Roper, the then lord of the manor, who was also Sheriff of Kent, married Margaret, the daughter of Sir Thomas More, and most probably built a completely new manor house for his bride.

Sir Thomas More became Lord High Chancellor in 1529 and when staying at the Lord Chancellor's Lodging by Eltham Palace was a frequent visitor at Well Hall. He was executed for refusing to take the Oath of Supremacy in 1535, but his death did not have much effect on the reputation of his son-in-law or of Margaret, who was regarded as one of the most beautiful and charitable of all the ladies who graced Eltham.

The Ropers were held in great esteem in north-west Kent for nearly two hundred years more, and when Eltham Palace ceased to be a royal home Well Hall ranked after Greenwich in this part of Kent. The famous painting of the More family by Holbein hung in the great hall until 1731. Early in the eighteenth century the Roper family sold the estate to Sir Gregory Page, who in 1733 demolished the Tudor mansion and erected a new palatial residence. This was a handsome and conventional house of the period. It was sold later to a Mr Arnold, who was watchmaker to George III. Mr Arnold built wings to accommodate his craftsmen on one side of the house and for the workshops on the other.

This house continued in private occupation until 1922, when one would have thought it might have been saved. But no, it was demolished because the expense of repair, as so often, was judged to be too great and only the grounds were saved by the Woolwich Borough Council, which purchased them in 1930. Nothing survives of the buildings except a large barn which bears the date 1568. It has been beautifully repaired and the original fine timbers of the roof restored.

The story of Beddington, which has a history as long as that of Well Hall and even more distinguished, makes a fitting epilogue to this chapter. It was the ancestral home of the Carews for five hundred years from 1349. The medieval manor house was rebuilt in the Tudor style about 1500, and was transformed into one of the largest and best appointed Tudor mansions of Surrey. Henry VIII was a visitor on more than one occasion, coming, it is said, with Anne Boleyn, who was related to the Carews, in 1531. Eight years later Sir Nicholas Carew was beheaded and the estate escheated to the Crown. On at least one occasion in 1541 the King held a council there. Sir Nicholas's son, Sir Francis, regained possession in the reign of Edward VI.

Additions were made to the Tudor house in later centuries but it remained in essentials the sixteenth-century mansion in which Sir Francis had entertained Queen Elizabeth. Its death knell was sounded in

1866, when the house and part of the park were sold for the use of the
Female Orphan Asylum, which had previously been in Lambeth. The
Tudor mansion virtually disappeared in an orgy of Victorian building
but the great hall was preserved as the centre-piece of the new
buildings.

A similarity between Beddington and Well Hall is that at both some
of the ancient outbuildings have survived the transition. At Beddington
the brick-built dovecot (colombarium), which replaced the original
Tudor one early in the eighteenth century, is a most unusual link with
the days of magnificence. There were nine hundred nests in this dovecot, and its normal population was two thousand to three thousand
birds, figures which give some idea of the truly wholesale scale on
which country mansions were run.

Church of St Alfege, Greenwich. This church is a medieval foundation but was rebuilt by Hawksmoor between 1712 and 1714 in the typical rectangular box style of the period with ornate tower and spire. Henry VIII, who was born in nearby Greenwich Palace, was baptized in the medieval church which preceded Hawksmoor's building. During the Second World War the fabric was damaged, it was thought beyond repair, by enemy bombardment but has been completely restored.

St Anne's Church, Limehouse (*right*). This is another Hawksmoor church, even more elaborate than St Alfege, Greenwich, and rather earlier in date. It was completed in 1712 and was one of the several London churches of which Hawksmoor was the nominal architect, though working in close collaboration with Sir John Vanbrugh, an association which began with the design of Blenheim Palace. All the towers of Hawksmoor's churches show imagination and novelty in design. This is one of the most remarkable, illustrating how novelty could be imposed on a classical theme without vulgarity and without undermining the essential classicism of the design.

[33]

Fitzroy Square (*left*). One of the triumphs of Robert Adam, built 1790–5.

Portland Place (*right*), today one of London's finest and broadest streets, was built in the last quarter of the eighteenth century to the design of James Adam. **Bedford Square** (*bottom*), another typical urban development dating from the end of the eighteenth century. It is in the Adam style but is believed to have been designed by a surveyor employed by the Russell family, who developed the estate.

e Paragon, Blackheath (*left*), built about 1800. **Holly Place, Hampstead** (*right*), with the sign the Holly Bush Inn. **The Riverside below Chelsea Bridge** (*below*), with buildings spanning the eteenth and twentieth centuries. **Isleworth Quay** (*bottom*), with the London Apprentice and Georgian houses side by side with more modern ones.

posite, from left to right: **Georgian Shop Fronts,
illery Lane; Sion Road, Twickenham; The
lleried Yard of the George Inn, Southwark;
e Wesley Chapel, 1777, and Statue, City Road;
vickenham Waterside from the Surrey Bank.**
s page: **Horse Guards, Whitehall** (*above*). This
e architectural composition, seen here from St
nes's Park looking across Horse Guards Parade,
s designed by William Kent and completed in
53. **St Martin-in-the-Fields** (*right*). This church
the north-east corner of Trafalgar Square is one
the finest designed by James Gibbs and was
npleted in 1726. **St Mary's Church, Lewisham**
ow). A good classical porch redeems the rather
in façade of this typical Georgian church built
ween 1770 and 1780.

In Pinner Churchyard. This unconventional monument is often known as the 'coffin above ground'. It is the most extraordinary of the hundreds of ostentatious tombs dating from the nineteenth century in the churchyards of Greater London. It commemorates a local farmer who died in 1809 and it is twenty feet high. The protrusions, one of which is shown, resemble a coffin but, of course, there is no coffin at this level and the design is wholly eccentric. In this same churchyard there is a grave-board marking the burial-place of a local resident said to have been 118 years old at the time of his death in 1775.

An early Eighteenth-century Country Church. The Duke of Chandos financed the building of this, the parish church of St Lawrence, Little Stanmore, in 1715, on the site of a medieval church of which the sixteenth-century west tower (in the background) was retained. The nave is at once a tribute to the genius of the architect, John James, and to the wealth of the Duke, who commissioned a church far larger than was needed for the small congregation of the times. The organ on which Handel played when he was the Duke's Master of Music is still used at services.

[38]

Richmond's Waterside. Richmond began to grow as a place of fashionable residence in the early years of George III's reign. The King himself was a frequent visitor. But at that time the principal development was on the hill near the entrance to Richmond Park. Later residences, many of them impressive, were built along the riverside almost as far as Petersham. This view from the bridge shows a group of these later houses between the junction of the bridge and Hill Street towards the Castle Hotel, a famous nineteenth-century resort.

Richmond Green. A few hundred yards from the busy main streets, Richmond Green retains much of the atmosphere of a village green, with the remains of Henry VII's Palace on one side, a number of Queen Anne and Georgian houses, and elaborate residences of the nineteenth century.

A Southwark Backwater. This imposing classical doorway is the entrance to the office of the Provost of Southwark Cathedral. It is in St Thomas's Street next door to a former church, now the chapter house of the Cathedral, built on the site of the original St Thomas's Hospital.

An Eighteenth-century Watchman's House (*below*). This small red-brick building survives in Oxford Street, which has been almost entirely rebuilt during the last sixty years. It was the house of the watchman who guarded the privacy of Stratford Place, built between 1770 and 1780

Trafalgar Square. Occupying part of the site of the former Royal Mews, Trafalgar Square was laid out between 1829 and 1841 and named after the battle of 1805. St Martin-in-the-Fields, pictured in the background, preceded the laying out of the square by more than a hundred years and remains the most striking feature of the architectural landscape.

10. The End of an Epoch

THE clouds that marred the closing years of the eighteenth century cast their shadow equally over the beginning of the nineteenth. Progress in any direction—towards the improvement of urban amenities, towards expanding the housing programme for the growing population, towards artistic expression of any kind—was negligible until the second Peace of Paris was concluded in 1815. For a few years before then optimists had believed that victory was assured and a number of schemes were started, though their completion in general was deferred until the years of peace and expected plenty. Only one phase of life in the Greater London area continued to thrive and expand during the years of trial. That phase was agriculture. The town and village communities around London had the utmost pressure brought upon them to increase their production of food for the people of London and to maintain their crops of hay to feed London's vast population of horses.

Many Acts were passed enclosing commons and wasteland so as to increase productivity but, as will be shown in the next chapter, the full fruits of the enclosures did not come to maturity until well into the reign of Queen Victoria, and then the harvest was all too often more houses rather than more acres for cultivation. However, apart from the commons and the traditional wasteland, it is probably true that by 1815 the land around London was as intensively worked as it has ever been before or since. In the absence of modern scientific aids to agriculture, however, it could not produce as much food per acre as similar land in the twentieth century. Prices were high and the farmers of Mitcham and Twickenham, of Tottenham and Dagenham, and every town and village one cares to mention within a day's ride of London, had their share of the profits. Their added prosperity is not reflected in appreciable new building, for the simple reason that men and materials were scarce, but when the wars were over the perimeter towns and village settlements were ready to forge ahead with as much vigour as the cities of London and Westminster.

Development, however slow and halting, did not come to a complete halt in the first fifteen years of the century. After all, the war itself was interrupted by short periods of uneasy peace, or at least inactivity. Here and there in the West End a few new houses were built and some that were destroyed by fire were replaced. This applied equally to a few buildings which were considered to have national importance. Theatres always have a peculiar value for morale in times of war, and when Drury Lane and Covent Garden were both burnt to the ground within a year of each other in 1808–9 immediate plans were made to replace them. Robert Smirke was commissioned to rebuild Covent Garden, Benjamin Wyatt Drury Lane. Smirke proved the speedier by far, for the new Covent Garden was producing plays just a year after the fire had destroyed it. (This theatre, too, was destroyed by fire in 1856 and the present façade is by E. M. Barry.) Benjamin Wyatt's Drury Lane, however, remains substantially as he designed it apart from the addition a few years later of the portico and the colonnade on the north side (internally the theatre has been completely remodelled).

In the City, too, the construction of one great and important building was continued, though with many pauses, through the war years. The Bank of England by Sir John Soane was that brilliant but enigmatic architect's greatest triumph. It had been started before the outbreak of war and was not completed until 1833, but the greater part of the building was carried out between 1780 and 1820. A small part of Soane's work, including the blind outer wall, or screen, has been preserved in the twentieth-century reconstruction, but it has lost its sense of size allied with style which contemporary prints show it to have possessed to an extraordinary degree. The new Royal Mint, by Smirke, was also completed in 1812. Smirke's building forms the nucleus of the present Mint. Though the architect might not recognize it in its present form, unlike Soane's masterpiece its character has not changed in spite of enlargement and major alteration.

The only other building of real note belonging to the war years was also by Sir John Soane, the mausoleum and art gallery at Dulwich, with which he was able to press on because the funds for building had been provided by a bequest made in 1811. The work was completed three years later, a tribute to the ingenuity as well as the determination of Sir John. An art gallery is not the best medium in which to express an architectural conception because of the limitation on the lighting necessary so as not to damage old pictures, but most critics of his own time as well as of the present century have praised the composition, a functional one perhaps rather than an aesthetic one, but singularly lacking in the fussiness of Sir John Soane's own house in Lincoln's Inn Fields and of many of the buildings for which he was responsible after the peace. The blindness of the walls invites an unlikely comparison between the Dulwich Gallery and the Bank of England. They are clearly by the same hand; indeed, there is something distinctive about Sir John Soane's work apparent in every one of his buildings, including his later churches.

The optimists who had made their plans before the actual peace were rewarded by being the first to have new houses and new services to offer in the early flush of Britain's renewed prosperity after 1815. Most of the fine houses under construction in Mecklenburgh Square were occupied on the very day the workmen moved out. Finsbury Circus, which was laid out on the site of the second Bedlam building, a former lunatic asylum, was equally successful. The even more optimistic

Southwark Bridge, 1819.

groups of financiers who obtained parliamentary approval before the Peace of Paris for building toll bridges at Vauxhall and Waterloo were rewarded with a vastly increased traffic as soon as the bridges were completed, Vauxhall in 1816, Rennie's Waterloo a year later. Both were fine engineering works, both bridges of beauty as well as utility, which Londoners came to love, regretting the necessity, as time passed, of supplanting them by more modern and wider structures. One bridge by Rennie, however, which has survived is the Serpentine bridge in Hyde Park, opened in 1828.

With Rennie's Southwark bridge, opened in 1819, the first suspension bridge at Hammersmith in 1827, and the new London Bridge in 1831 (also by Rennie, and retaining in its widened form some of the grace of the original), the links between the Middlesex and Surrey banks of the river were adequate for all practical purposes and remained so for the greater part of the nineteenth century. The roads on the Surrey side formed a network linked with the new bridges and remain with few exceptions the chief arteries of traffic in the twentieth century. Thus the way was shown to convert hundreds of acres into new housing where

New London Bridge, 1831.

before there had been only green fields or marshland. Building had taken place at the end of the previous century only along a few roads laid out after the opening of Westminster bridge. Brixton Hill and the Nelson Square area of Southwark were being developed before the reign of Queen Victoria began, though sadly many of the early nineteenth-century houses became dilapidated and were demolished to make way for much less graceful buildings at the end of the nineteenth and beginning of the twentieth centuries.

Another project which had been continued through the difficult years was the provision of new docks for the multitude of ships sailing up the river to London. This was an absolutely essential development,

since mooring facilities in the Pool of London had become vastly over-
strained. As commerce increased from decade to decade it became less
and less practical to handle the ships' cargoes in the streets of London
town. A start, as we have seen, had already been made in the eighteenth
century. This culminated in the opening of the West India Docks in
1802 and the first of the London Docks three years later. The separation
of the dockland area from the old City wharves was an important milestone in London's progress. The position of these docks and of the
later docks constructed to supplement them also determined the
position of the major working-class suburbs downriver. A number of
old houses at Wapping Pier Head and the adjoining Wilkes Street area
of Stepney survive to illustrate the beginnings of what became one of
the most overcrowded districts of London.

The completion of the Grand Junction Canal from the midlands
through Uxbridge to the Thames at Brentford was the prelude to the
growth of the latter as a river port and ultimately an industrial town
during the nineteenth century. The branch from Uxbridge to Paddington and the Regent's Canal were in operation by the third decade of
the century and, had it not been for the development of the railways,
might have played a vital role in the distribution of imported goods to
the north-western parts of Greater London as well as providing an easy
means of transporting the agricultural surplus of Middlesex direct to the
growing suburbs such as Paddington and Islington.

All these things, important as they were, proved a mere bagatelle
compared with the grandiose schemes for public and private building
which followed the Peace of Paris. The public buildings were designed
mainly to beautify the cities of London and Westminster and to supply
the people of London with amenities conforming with the spirit of the
nineteenth century. They are seen in better perspective if they are considered separately from the advance of bricks and mortar across the
open fields on the verges of London. The fact that many of these public
and quasi-public buildings are still in use helps to give a fuller apprecia-
tion of those wonderful years of endeavour, 1815 to 1837. They may not
all be of great architectural merit but they are all on the grand scale.

The new City Custom House, presenting a magnificent frontage to
the river not dissimilar from Somerset House, was one of the first.
Decimus Burton was the designer of the screen and Pimlico Arch
which were built as the entrance to Hyde Park in 1828, three years
after the tollgate had been removed. Both the screen and the arch
are still with us but Burton's grand composition has been obliterated.
To ease traffic congestion the arch was removed in 1888 from its
place as part of the screen-arch composition to a position at the top
of Constitution Hill and is now isolated on an island. What were
intended as two integrated parts of a single whole have glared at each
other for many decades across the inhospitable expanse of the Hyde
Park Corner traffic circus.

The building which now houses the Imperial War Museum, Lambeth Road, was part of the Bethlem Hospital, which took the place of the one in Finsbury (Bedlam). The present building is only the central block of the nineteenth-century asylum (which had a further move to Surrey in 1930). It was begun in 1812, completed in 1815, its portico and dome added by Sydney Smirke in 1846. The Orphan Asylum at Hackney completed in 1823 was another vast project which covered many acres with handsome classical buildings. One of these has survived as the Congress Hall of the Salvation Army. In the City the Fishmongers' Hall, opened in 1833, was one of the most attractive of

Hyde Park Tollgate, 1825.

the many company buildings designed in the period. The National Gallery, by William Wilkins, was opened in 1838, University College by the same architect ten years later. The British Museum was begun by Robert Smirke in 1823.

The Duke of York's Column in Waterloo Place was a striking new landmark added to the London scene in 1833. As an illustration of the club and institutional building which was taking place at the same time as all these great works, the Athenaeum is one of the most striking, though there are others in the Pall Mall district and northward towards Piccadilly which have survived in part the ravages of time and men.

Pall Mall as it took shape between 1820 and 1830 was an unmistakable emblem of the new wealth and the new leisure, and incidentally of a new way of life, in which men of wealth, and, as time went by, men of commerce, could meet together outside their homes in an atmosphere of uncommonly sober bonhomie. English club life has never been understood by continental people, who regarded it as an overt admission of

English perversion, but for the whole of the nineteenth century and into the twentieth century it represented a highly respectable and flourishing part of the life of the metropolis.

The King's Opera House was reconstructed between 1815 and 1820. Only a part of the arcades which surrounded it has survived as a reminder of this famous place of fashionable entertainment in the Royal Opera Arcade. In 1964 the latter was restored with expert care to its original appearance.

The days of palatial town houses were virtually over, but Wyatt was responsible for at least two between 1825 and 1830 which could hold their heads high in comparison with any mansions of the seventeenth or eighteenth century. One was Lancaster House (at first known as York House, later as Stafford House), which was built for the Duke of York, and Apsley House, built for Lord Apsley by the Adam brothers, 1771–8, and enlarged on the orders of the Duke of Wellington in 1828.

In the general expansion of London a new trend became obvious before the accession of Queen Victoria. That was the tendency for the West End and the districts to the west of London to become the only areas in which wealthier people sought a home, while speculative building to the east of London became more meagre, more strictly utilitarian. Stepney and Hackney never regained the atmosphere of solid and wealthy respectability which they had enjoyed since the Great Fire.

There was an abundance of new building, however, in every direction, while Georgian villages, such as Hampstead, expanded further. Apart from the new estates developed as part of Nash's great town-planning scheme, described in this Chapter, a most significant expansion was in what we call Belgravia. Eaton Square, a garden village in its own right, and Belgrave Square had both taken shape before 1830. In the following decades fine new houses spread out in every direction until Hans Town was swamped. New building ran riot, too, for the first time in Paddington, where Sussex Gardens, Sussex Square and Gloucester Square vied with each other in early nineteenth-century elegance. This was a very different elegance from that of the preceding century, based partly on stucco façades which were carefully tooled to imitate stone. The plain brick-built house was rapidly disappearing from the urban scene and, although there were many wall coverings with which individual builders experimented, stucco, which first appeared about 1790, was always the most popular.

The remaining part of the Bedford estate was largely built over, too, by 1837. Bedford House (formerly Southampton House), which had been the corner-stone of the Georgian Bloomsbury Square, had been demolished and Russell Square begun before the peace. Tavistock Square was laid out in 1820, Woburn Square in 1828, all bearing names associated with the Dukes of Bedford. Woburn Walk, with its interesting shop fronts, now restored, was completed about 1822.

Belgrave Square, 1828.

The bricks and stucco did not stop there. They crossed the New Road until much of modern St Pancras and St Marylebone was swallowed by them. Gloucester Place and Bryanston Square were completed by 1820. Dorset Square, Montagu Square and Euston Square soon followed. Harley Street was built up to its junction with the New Road; so was Gower Street. The Finsbury-Islington district filled out, but one estate, that managed by the New River Company, including Myddelton Square and Claremont Square, was designed very much on the lines of the earlier Georgian estates as a neighbourhood unit, self-contained and remote from the main arteries of commerce, with its own shops and its church. St Mark's in Myddelton Square, completed in 1827, in a rather decadent Gothic style, was one of the earliest examples of the Gothic revival which was destined to sweep the country in Victorian times. There were signs, too, of a Gothic revival in Islington's Lonsdale Square (1840) and in the quaint dwelling-places of Nichols Square in Shoreditch. But the most significant development to the east of London was that centred on Derbyshire Street in Bethnal Green, where a new kind of small house estate was built, principally as homes for the weavers who lived and worked in the neighbourhood. Many other rows of cottages for working men and their families soon followed in the eastern and northern inner suburbs.

In one way this expansion in the decades following 1815 differed dramatically from that of the previous century. Whereas throughout the Georgian period, once the impetus of the Act of Queen Anne had spent itself, few churches were built, now there was a positive spate of church-building, good, bad and indifferent. Many reasons contributed to this result. The lack of churches had been aggravated during the war years when building new ones was not a practical proposition. The proprietary chapels which had been financed in many places by subscription and maintained solely from pew rents had become inadequate for most of the districts they served. The upsurge in religious interest was illustrated by the growth of nonconformity.

To the government of the time it seemed that nonconformity was allied in some way with agitation for political reform. The nonconformist chapels were resorted to increasingly by what the nineteenth-century elect referred to as 'the people'. It was believed that if more attractive surroundings could be provided for Church of England worshippers the progress of the nonconformist movement might be halted. In 1818 the events of Queen Anne's reign were repeated but this time on a much more ambitious scale. An Act was passed to provide one million pounds for new church-building, and six years later another Act made a further half-million pounds available. These were big figures in relation to the cost of a nonconformist chapel, which was rarely more than a few thousand pounds and sometimes much less. The commissioners appointed under the Act made a fine start, but after the passage of the Reform Bill in 1832 interest waned, the willingness of the Government to subsidize church-building from taxes grew less, and later churches built under the Act were mean and unworthy of a prosperous nation.

The four churches completed between 1822 and 1825 in the parish of Lambeth represent the finest achievements under the Act. These are St John's, Waterloo Road, St Luke's, Norwood, St Mark's, Kennington, and St Matthew's, Brixton. They are often known collectively as the Waterloo churches and there is a weird but persistent legend that they form a memorial to the victory of Waterloo. The legend has not the slightest substance, except that without the victory of Waterloo the Treaty of Paris might never have been signed and the Act of 1818 never passed.

They were all handsome churches externally, rather like Greek temples, with good classical towers, far-seen landmarks designed to impress and fulfilling their intention in this respect well enough. If the interiors were not so well conceived as the external façade there was at least plenty of room for all who desired to worship in them, and they were good halls for preaching. However, all the churches built for the Ecclesiastical Commissioners were economically planned. Even these four did not attain the architectural distinction of some in the more prosperous suburbs where a new church was built by public subscription and the best architects were employed irrespective of costs. Thus Sir John Soane was the architect of Holy Trinity, Marylebone Road (1825). He was also the architect of the much less successful St Peter's, Walworth. Sir Robert Smirke was highly successful with St Mary's, Wyndham Place, with St James's, West Hackney, and with St Anne's, Wandsworth, which were all three opened in 1824. Thomas Hardwick was the architect of St Marylebone parish church (1817), three times as costly a building as any of the Waterloo churches, and his son Philip of Christ Church, St Marylebone (1822).

The Inwoods excelled themselves in St Pancras New Church (1822), one of the most memorable churches of the period, with a façade which is a mixture of the styles of several Greek temples (the younger Inwood had just returned from a trip to Greece) and mimicking the Erechtheum with its caryatides. Its similarity in other respects to St Martin-in-the Fields has often been noted. The Inwoods were also responsible for a number of other fine churches, including St Peter's, Regent Square (1822), and All Saints, Camden Town (1824). St George's, Well Way, Camberwell, is another highly successful 'Greek' church, built about the same time by the architect Bedford, a much less well-known architect than the others but one who showed great resource and some original ideas in his classical designs.

The churches of the Gothic revival cannot be overlooked, although many would say the least said about them the soonest mended. Few either in this period or in the subsequent Victorian expression of the same ideal recaptured wholly the spirit of the Middle Ages, yet few added anything to the medieval tradition or developed it into a truly nineteenth-century style. The Gothic churches were strictly imitative; it is perhaps not too harsh a criticism to say that their architects did not understand the principles of Gothic building either as well as the medieval master masons or as well as the classicists understood designs based on Greek or Roman models, or conforming with the Renaissance tradition handed down from the time of Inigo Jones and Sir Christopher Wren. St Luke's, Chelsea (1824), by James Savage, is one of the best known. But those designed by Barry are more characteristic, especially the three which were all completed in 1826 in the single parish of Islington (what a feat of organization of men and materials that must have involved)—Holy Trinity, Cloudesley Square, St John's, Holloway Road, and St Paul's, Essex Road.

Every period can be regarded as a transitional one, if only because the present is for ever merging with the future, as the present has evolved from the past. But few periods in English history so clearly mark a transition between one way of thought and another, between one way of life and a different one, as the nine years when Prince George was Regent, and the following ten years when he had become George IV. In art and architecture the Regency in this wider interpretation of the word is a clear-cut bridge between the Georgian and the Early Victorian.

In social life, too, it was the turning point between the aristocratic traditions of the reigns of the first three Georges and the democratic tradition which has its roots in the splendour and vulgarity of Victorian times. Among the men who contributed to the legacy of the years 1815 to 1830 the figure of John Nash towers over all others, not in the literal sense that he was a big man either in stature or perception, but in the sense that he typifies this period of transition more than any other single architect or, for that matter, any artist or man of letters.

Nash bequeathed a legacy of building, some of which is still with us —some of the best, one would say, after studying contemporary drawings. His work has a character, and a very positive one, of its own. Moreover it reflects the peculiar character of the age to a remarkable extent. Many of the buildings conceived by Nash are on the grand scale, as befits the work of the most famous architect of a country victorious in war and flourishing beyond expectation. But some are meagre and trivial, equally befitting the architect of a nation which had not learnt to conserve its wealth.

Nash's plans were often landscaped without thought of cost, outdoing in their own context the magnificence of the Elizabethan new wealthy or of the patriotic fervour of Sir John Vanbrugh. Critics may say, as they have often done, that the stucco which was the favourite wall covering adopted by Nash and his Regency contemporaries is a white mantle concealing manifold imperfections, the symbol of buildings more likely to fall down than those of medieval builders who had none of the accumulated experience or technical assistance of Regency builders. They may see in such a sham a reflection of the state of society in which the wealthy could happily have the world ransacked to provide delicacies for their enjoyment, while the poor not only of Ireland but of England itself could die of starvation by the thousand after a poor harvest. They may see a parallel, too, with the sham turrets and battlements of Victorian castles, in a world in which the appearance seldom corresponded with the reality and in which more perhaps than at any other time half of the people did not know how the other half lived. But that is only a part of the story. There was plenty of good solid workmanship, as much truth as deception. The Nash legacy is an apt epilogue to the tale of early nineteenth-century endeavour.

The background of the architect is important. For from this background were derived inevitably the qualities which made Nash at once the most favoured architect of his time and the one best able to interpret the spirit of the age. We remember him chiefly by his 'Regency' work, but in fact the commissions which he executed for the Prince Regent were the last of his life and the consummation of a career which had been by no means always successful and had been as varied in its commercial rewards as had the fortunes of England.

Nash was born of drab parents in a drab street of Lambeth in 1752. His father was a millwright who died when John was a child. Ultimately the child was decently educated and joined the staff of a well-known architect, Sir Robert Taylor. Probably his education was paid for by his uncle, a calico printer who had achieved more worldly success than his father.

For the first twenty-five years of his life there was nothing to distinguish John Nash from thousands of his contemporaries, but it was an age of adventure, when initiative was at a premium and the heroes of the time were the navigators who were taking British ships to every corner of the inhabited world, and the traders who, often at the risk of their lives, were opening out fresh markets for Britain. It was an age, in effect, when speculation was regarded as a virtue. The greater the risk, the more glittering the reward, the more honour was given to the speculator—when he was successful.

So it is not surprising to find the young Nash in his twenty-fifth year, in the midst of the political turmoil of the American war, engaged in speculation far beyond his means, rebuilding two large houses in London's Bloomsbury Square as well as a number of smaller ones with a view to reselling them at a profit. He failed and was adjudged bankrupt in 1783.

The interest of this escapade is twofold. It gives a clear idea of Nash's character, reflected in the bold, imaginative and rather slapdash architectural adventures of his later years and, more important, it shows the beginning of the young man's creative ability in the large stucco-fronted house which still stands at the corner of Bloomsbury Square and Great Russell Street, very little altered during the intervening century and a half.

There has been much criticism of the Bloomsbury Square house, but the general effect is good, and highly imaginative for such an inexperienced young man. It is significant that it looks back beyond the brothers Adam to the great Inigo Jones, rather than forward to any new interpretation of the classical style. It shows rebellion without eccentricity, and, above all, a fine feeling for design, which is what distinguished Nash as a Regency architect more than any preoccupation with inessential detail or ornament.

This, then, was a private disaster, which might have quenched the spirit of a lesser man in the eighteenth century—bankrupt, without funds and with little influence. Not so Nash. In 1783, the year of the Treaty of Versailles, when England had been compelled to swallow the national pride and acknowledge the independence of the United States and had patched up an honourable peace with France, Nash made his home with some relations of his mother's in Carmarthen. He remained in what then seemed a distant outpost of Britain for the next twelve years.

The ability to impress himself on influential people was one of the

most interesting facets of Nash's character from a young man to the
end of his career. From those modest beginnings he became the companion of men of birth and wealth, just as later he was to become a
favourite of the Prince Regent.

The years that followed showed a diversification of interest. Nash
was no longer a young man but young enough to be considered *avant-
garde*. His reputation spread. By the beginning of the Regency he was
never short of a commission and had finally achieved the financial
stability he had tried so disastrously to achieve thirty years before. He
established himself as one of the leading designers of country houses in
Britain. His work could be seen from Cornwall to the Home Counties,
from Sussex to Lancashire, and in Ireland too.

If Nash is remembered chiefly today, as inevitably he must be, by the
classical façades of the Regent's Park terraces, it is worth bearing in
mind that he showed a considerable aptitude for design in the Gothic
style, building castellated houses which looked forward with remarkable penetration to the stockbrokers' mansions of later times and to the
baronial Gothic of Deeside. Unhappily it is a costly business to keep
these old houses in repair and all too few have been thought worthy of
preservation unless, like the Regent's Park terraces, they have special
associations and powerful advocates to plead for them.

We can discount many of the accusations hurled against 'Prinny', the
Prince Regent, by contemporaries who were envious of him. But it is
fair to say that in health and in sickness, as an active young man and as a
rather decrepit elderly one, he used his better than average intelligence
chiefly to extract the greatest possible degree of pleasure from living.
He showed inventiveness of a high order in devising new ways of pursuing his goal. In his own way Nash did much the same with lesser
resources but with an equal flair. But Nash's aim was not ordinary self-
gratification so much as the expression of his artistic personality, to
which everything else in his life was subordinated. As Prinny was
representative of his age in the mannered ways of his Court, so was
Nash in the insolent grace of his mock castles or in the rather prim
vistas of his classical mansions.

Nash was appointed architect to the Commissioners of Woods and
Forests in 1806, but the idea for development of the farmland to the
north of Portland Place known as Marylebone Park goes back to at
least 1790. A prize of £1,000 was offered in 1793 for the best plan;
thirteen years later Nash was given the award. It was 1812 before a
coherent plan was made, and 1813 before Treasury approval was
received for work to begin. The complete scheme, involving the
development of the park, the building of its surrounding terraces and
the construction of a road to link the park with Carlton House, was not
finished until 1825.

The most outstanding feature of the Regent's Park scheme was that
it presupposed a self-contained community complete with a church and

a palace for a king. In its amplitude it differed from all previous town-planning schemes, and for that matter all future ones until the days of Letchworth and Welwyn Garden Cities a century later.

Many features of Nash's scheme were not carried out. The royal palace was never built, the 'country seats', within the landscape of the park itself, remained uncompleted, but the plan for the surrounding terraces and the link with Portland Place was carried out almost exactly as the architect intended. The real difficulty was money. Again and again the scheme looked as though it would founder through lack of capital. Yet it was a money-making scheme, for there was no lack of people who welcomed the idea of moving from the centre of London into the 'country', while the building of Regent Street was a major piece of land development which ultimately reaped enormous profits.

Most cunningly the line proposed by Nash and the one actually used cut through the western boundary of Soho and effectively divided the poor tenements and crowded narrow streets of what was then a most unsavoury district from the ample and spacious layout of the West End. The proximity of Regent Street to this area of wealth and fashion gave additional value to the buildings erected along it. Any land development company of today would have backed Nash's scheme without hesitation and would have ensured that it was completed within a few years to the profit of its shareholders. Unfortunately the pockets of the Commission were not so well filled as those of a twentieth-century real estate company. Whenever there was a shortage of money work stopped, while the ambitious plan to build a great new palace for the King on the site of Carlton House, which had been his London home for some time, was abandoned. The Duke of York's Steps with Carlton House Terrace, part of a revised Nash plan, was substituted as Regent Street's terminal point. So Nash retained the idea of a processional way. The Mall is seen as the logical continuation of the 'street'.

One of the most brilliant improvisations in the scheme often escapes notice. Having decided to use the existing line of Portland Place and determined the course of Regent Street itself, the Commission was left with the problem of linking the two. First a straight or slightly curving link was proposed but then, as now, the acquisition of land often presented greater problems than expected, if only because the landlords saw a golden opportunity to obtain an inflated price for their holding. In the end the straight link was abandoned and the present devious course adopted. The brilliance of the conception lies in the building of All Souls, Langham Place, which so effectively closes the architectural vista at the north end of Regent Street. All that can be seen by a traveller going up Regent Street is the steeple and portico. The latter escaped when a bomb destroyed almost the whole of the interior of the church during the Second World War. Although the church, as re-dedicated in April 1951, is to all intents a new church, the portico and most of the steeple belong to Nash's church, which was built elegantly in Bath stone.

Nash himself found contemporary criticism of All Souls galling. The Corinthian columns of the steeple were the features which most irritated nineteenth-century critics. The conical fluted steeple itself is certainly unique and with the portico makes just the right composition as a landmark terminus for Regent Street. One suspects that the architect was very proud of his idea and the complete break-away from tradition which it represented, but it took more than a century of reflection before it was grudgingly accepted. The people of the time just could not see Nash as a designer of churches. Perhaps his image was too closely associated with country houses.

Though one sympathizes with him in the case of All Souls, even a century of reflection has not greatly changed the estimate of his only other essay in London church building, St Mary's, Haggerston, a hybrid creation in the Gothic style with a tall bare tower crowned with a lantern flanked by small many-sided towers capped by stone domes. St Mary's suffered a harsher fate than All Souls, for it was completely destroyed by enemy action on 16 October 1940, and no effort has been made to rebuild it.

There may still be two opinions about All Souls, Langham Place, but remarkably few could be found today to criticize Carlton House Terrace, which was designed as part of a more ambitious scheme, including a corresponding terrace on the south side of the Mall. Although not hallowed by antiquity (it dates only from 1827) the terrace has so enshrined itself in public esteem that any suggestion to demolish it is greeted with a chorus of dismay. That surely is the true test of the people's affectionate regard, not only for Nash the architect, but for the spacious age which he represented.

Then there is Cumberland Terrace, one of the most magnificent of all Nash's conceptions. In plan it consists of five blocks divided by decorative arches and an ornate central façade consisting of a pediment supported on ten Ionic columns. What remains is an architectural landscape which compels attention. One regrets the Victorian fourth storey which has been added to one of the blocks, one may regret to a lesser degree that the sculptures which decorate the pediment (executed by J. G. Bubb) are rather trivial. One may even feel that the decorative arch is a strange conceit in this context. Even so, there is something positive and impressive about the whole thing which defies serious criticism. It is Nash *par excellence*, and Regency *par excellence*, or rather post-Regency, for the terrace was not completed until 1826.

Chester Terrace, built a year or two earlier, has the distinction of being the longest of Nash's unbroken terraces. Its houses are smaller, its ornament shows more contrivance, and there is much less to be said for the arches at right angles to the terrace than there is for the corresponding arches in Cumberland Terrace. However, it bears the stamp of the master. So does the earlier work of York Terrace and the still earlier Park Crescent, which was the first part of the development scheme to be completed, in the year of the retreat from Moscow, 1812, a major achievement by any standards when the resources of the country were diverted to the manufacture of armaments and the upkeep of an army. Park Crescent was designed as part of a circus but it is perhaps as well that the circus was never completed, because as it stands the composition is just right and a reiteration of the terrace style in a complete circus would surely have been overwhelming.

Park Village West was the last of Nash's essays in domestic architecture. This was designed as the urban equivalent of the rural 'Blaise Village', an elegant group of small private houses near Bristol. Two or three of them which have survived without major alteration are examples of Nash's domestic work at its best.

Nash and the Georgian monarchy declined together. The last great work which the architect was commissioned to undertake was the rebuilding of Buckingham House as a royal palace. Nash's plan was submitted in 1825. The new palace with its dome and turrets was to be as startling as the Royal Pavilion of Brighton in a more solemn, more English style. The scheme might have proved a success. Unhappily it did not. A parliamentary inquiry was ordered into what was regarded as a national disaster. The influence of the now moribund King counted for nothing. In 1830, the year of the King's death, after long deliberations by a select committee, Nash was dismissed from his office. It was left for another architect to redesign the front of the palace in a more conservative style (though a good deal of Nash's plan survives in the back of the palace facing the private gardens, which few people see).

The fore-building, constructed of costly Italian marble, was taken down in 1847 and re-erected at the western end of Oxford Street, where it stands today derelict on an island site, known to every citizen of London and to every visitor as the Marble Arch, a fitting tribute perhaps to Nash's genius and the misguided enthusiasm of George IV.

The story has an apt epilogue. The world of George IV died with him. Nash in his seventies, out of office, out of sympathy with the changing social pattern, retired to his castellated mansion at East Cowes and spent the last years of his life in the sumptuous Regency surroundings which he loved, wealthy and pampered, and it is said in good health and spirits. He died only two years before Queen Victoria came to the throne.

11. In Quest of Pleasure, 1660–1900

THE pleasures of the past have a fascination in retrospect which transcends in imagination those of the present. That is true of every period of history, of every nation, but there is something especially diverting about the pleasures pursued by Londoners from the Restoration down to the beginning of the twentieth century. They reflect the changing social pattern in a peculiarly vivid way. Before the seventeenth century pleasure was the prerogative of the wealthy, as a century earlier it had been the prerogative of the landed gentry. The common man was fully occupied in earning a living and in tilling his patch of ground if he was lucky enough to have one, and in being his own handyman to an extent almost unbelievable at the present time. The highlights of his year were the May Day festivities, the harvest home and the annual fair.

During the sixteenth and seventeenth centuries a middle class emerged with enough leisure to think seriously of enjoying themselves and with enough spare money to be able to pay for their pleasures. It was some time before the same could be said of the ordinary working man, who then, as now, made up the greater part of the population. By the end of the nineteenth century the social pattern was not so different from what it is today except in degree. The pleasures of the past had become the pleasures of the present, no longer designed for the enjoyment of the few but rather for the diversion of the whole people.

During the whole of this period two quite separate but closely related threads are woven to form various patterns in the fabric of life. These are the pleasure garden and the spa, often fulfilling virtually the same purpose yet maintaining their separate identity well into the nineteenth century. In their old age these two gave birth to the music-hall. This developed into the variety theatre, which ultimately took its place, however shamefacedly, beside the legitimate theatre. The latter had bravely maintained itself since the reign of Queen Elizabeth

against fearful odds which, as we have already seen, included government restriction as well as competition from more obviously popular
forms of entertainment.

If one thinks of the early part of the seventeenth century, when the
drama had developed into a fully fledged form of art under royal
patronage, as one of the golden ages of the theatre one cannot be
contradicted, but if one imagines that crossing London Bridge to the
south bank theatres was the common man's idea of an evening's entertainment, one is in a fool's paradise. The Puritan members of the Corporation of London regarded theatres as the haunts of vagabonds and
prostitutes. Doubtless the presence of cultured people at the theatre
attracted some of the latter in search of custom, some of the former in
the hope of an evening made profitable by the stealing of a purse. But
the pleasures available to working folk were very different. Dicing,
gambling and drinking were, according to an Elizabethan author, the
only diversions which the men ordinarily enjoyed as active participants.
Bear-baiting, cock-fighting and the harrying of ducks by spaniels
(whence the inn name Dog and Duck) were the elevating spectator
sports of the time. The place of women was in the house.

The middle class were little better off unless they had reached the
point at which they shared in the pleasures of the 'upper' class or were
invited to the dancing and decorous revelry which took place in the
town houses of the nobility. Early in the seventeenth century, as
travelling about London and its environs became gradually safer, as
London itself grew larger, the demand for some form of open-air
activity became apparent. Speculators saw the possibilities and were
quick to respond to the demand almost before it existed.

Open-air activities had been accepted as a part of French life for
many generations. Charles II's long sojourn on the Continent and the
fact that his mother was French may well have influenced his ideas and,
through him, those of many of his subjects. A contributory factor was
that there was scarcely anything outside the home that a woman could
do with propriety in the seventeenth century except to accompany her
husband on a country walk. After the Restoration the doors of the
theatres were soon thrown open to women, but they were always
debarred from coffee-houses and from the taverns to which it was
customary for men to resort for their entertainment when the day's
work was done.

This was the background against which pleasure gardens, where the
growing number of middle-class people could go for a walk and
refreshment in the open air, became established. In a sense Charles I
initiated the movement when he permitted bowling greens to be laid
out in part of the gardens of the Palace of Whitehall. Some years before
the Civil War this part of the gardens had become, if not a public resort,
at least an area of royal property in which a good many members of the
public were tolerated.

After the Restoration the Whitehall experiment was not repeated but commercial gardens became popular, among them the New Spring Gardens on the south bank of the river laid out in part of the park belonging to the house known as Fox Hall (Vauxhall). These New Spring Gardens were the forerunners of the enormously popular Vauxhall Gardens. They were open to the public on payment of a fee within a few months of the Restoration. There was another competitive establishment known as the Old Spring Gardens.

Pepys was as enthusiastic a visitor to the pleasure gardens as he was to the fields of the open country. 'On 29th May, 1662, with my wife and the two maids to Fox Hall, where had not been for a great while. To the Old Spring Gardens and there walked long. Thence to the new one, where I never was before, which much exceeds the other, and here we walked and gathered abundance of roses. And so to an ordinary house and here we had cakes and powdered beef and ale. And so home again by water with much pleasure.' There we have a perfect picture of a day's outing for a middle-class family on a fine May day of 1662. Apart from the location and the powdered beef, one might read 1962 for 1662. The very first mention of the New Spring Gardens is in Evelyn's diary entry for 2 July 1661.

Vauxhall was destined to become the most popular, the most lavishly extravagant and the most respected place of popular entertainment in Greater London. It was never a spa but first and foremost a garden laid out with pleasant walks and most of the then available flowers and shrubs. It was decorated with statues and set pieces, and had extensive accommodation for the service of meals. One could dine in gaily decorated alcoves in the gardens, as in the dining-room of the house which adjoined them. Throughout the century the principal attractions were the excitement of taking a trip 'across the river', the pleasure of walking in the gardens on a summer afternoon, or in the evenings when they were lighted by fifty thousand lamps, and the service of refreshments for all the family. When other attractions were added it was because the first flush of the gardens' popularity had waned. The firework displays were famous, some of the finest orchestras in the land were engaged to play, and dancing was organized as at almost all the other pleasure gardens and spas. In a sense democracy was born in the gardens.

Throughout the eighteenth century the carriage trade was the basis of the gardens' prosperity. On fine evenings long traffic blocks occurred in Kennington Lane and at the approaches to London Bridge. The proprietors of the gardens organized guards, hundreds of them, to keep the road from Southwark free of robbers, for crime increased throughout most of the century. But thousands of Londoners made the trip across the river by water. The ferry fare was modest and so was the price of admission. When the famous Jonathan Tyers became the proprietor in 1752 he invoked the help of Hogarth, who presented his

picture of Henry VIII and Anne Boleyn to decorate the Rotunda and
carried out many original decorations in the pavilions. It could be said
with truth:

> Vauxhall is the pleasantest place upon earth
> From the banks of the Thames to the Tiber,
> For one who is fond of most innocent pleasure
> Or one who is a perfect imbiber.

Fancy dress balls were extremely popular. It is interesting to notice
that a newspaper report on a masquarade in 1758 said that the most
'capital' figure was a lady in the character of Eve in a suit of flesh-
coloured silk with an apron of fig leaves. The most famous London
characters frequented the gardens, including a number of royalty. In
Rowlandson's drawing depicting the gardens in 1785 the group includes the Prince of Wales with his good friend Perdita Robinson,
Oliver Goldsmith with Mrs Thrale, Dr Johnson with his inseparable
companion James Boswell, and a number of high-ranking Service men
with their ladies (some of whom, incidentally, were their wives).
Vauxhall was nothing if not respectable!

The fame of Vauxhall began to decline at the beginning of the nineteenth century. The entertainments became more proletarian. People of
quality, as nineteenth-century writers insisted on calling them, no
longer formed the majority of the patrons who came to the firework
displays or enjoyed the sideshows. However, the concerts continued to
be well attended—and above all, the dances, which lasted throughout
the night.

> The people will dance by the light of the moon,
> And keep up the ball the next day at noon;
> The peer and the peasant, the lord and the loon,
> The haughty grandee and the low picaroon.
>   (Quoted by W. S. Scott, *Green Retreats*.)

The entertainers could not compete with the many alternative ways
of seeking pleasure in the middle of the nineteenth century. The
gardens no longer paid their way and closed their doors for the last
time on 28 July 1859—199 years after they had been opened.

By the time the gardens closed many bridges spanned the river
instead of the single crossing, London Bridge, which had to suffice for
visitors in the heyday of the gardens. It was no doubt because of the
vast number of people who came to the Vauxhall Gardens that Lambeth
became a centre of popular entertainment.

The original Vauxhall establishment was like a sun surrounded by
numerous satellites. None of them was as successful. Few survived
more than a generation or two. Most catered for a less responsible kind
of patron than Vauxhall. Three gardens were within a quarter of a mile
and twelve or more competed for trade between Vauxhall and London
Bridge.

Marble Hall was one of the most successful. It was opened in 1740 and demolished in 1813 to make way for the road approach to Vauxhall Bridge. Lambeth Wells had a life of more than fifty years, from 1696 to 1755, when its licence was discontinued because of its unsavoury reputation and the numerous brawls which took place there. When it opened it advertised the combined pleasures of purging waters and music from midday until seven o'clock in the morning. As time went on the purging waters became less popular, the music and dancing the chief attractions of the spa.

Many of the other gardens were suppressed because of their evil reputation, especially those like the Temples of Apollo and Flora, which stood close together and opened in the last decades of the eighteenth century. The proprietor of the Temple of Flora was actually given a prison sentence in 1796 for keeping a disorderly house. It might be said without too much exaggeration that the Lambeth 'temples' were the forerunners of the less reputable Soho strip-tease joints of the twentieth century.

The gardens which came closest to competing with Vauxhall were Cupid's (or Cuper's). These were situated by the river on or near the site of the Festival Hall, and were opened before the end of the seventeenth century, reaching their greatest fame when the Prince of Wales, accompanied by the Princess, attended the firework displays on more than one occasion in 1745. A renewal of the licence for music and dancing was refused in 1752.

Ranelagh was another famous resort, the only one to achieve real fame on the north bank of the river. The gardens were laid out on a site which includes that on which the Chelsea Flower Show is held. In the latter part of the eighteenth century Ranelagh vied with Vauxhall in its appeal to people of fashion, and in the next century competed with success for popular patronage with music, dancing, fireworks and other occasional entertainments. The 'Rotunda' was the centre of Ranelagh's social life but dancing by the river's bank was a special attraction. The gardens closed their gates never to reopen in 1804 and Vauxhall was left in undisputed command of the river banks from Chelsea and Battersea to the City.

Islington and Finsbury, which in the eighteenth century boasted some of London's best-known spas, achieved fame as London's 'green retreat' much earlier. Islington was remarkably late in development considering how close it was to the City of London; even at the end of the eighteenth century it could be described as a village standing isolated in open fields. An attempt had been made at enclosure of the open fields in the sixteenth century, but the local people apparently filled the ditches which had been dug to mark out the enclosures and, according to Holinshed, were ultimately confirmed in their action. As Lord Macaulay said centuries later, 'Islington was an island of solitude and poets loved to contrast its silence and repose with the din and turmoil of the monster London', no doubt recalling Cowley: 'Methinks I see the monster London laugh at me.' 'The fields about Islington', says William Howitt in *The Northern Heights of London*, 'have been from the earliest times a favourite resort of the Londoners for open-air exercise and sport.' Stow says that the fields to the north of London were 'commodious for the citizens therein to walk, shoot and otherwise to refresh their dull spirits in the sweet and wholesome air'.

That is the background of the claim made by the City of London to Finsbury Fields between Shoreditch and Islington for practice with the longbow. As early as 1365 Edward III had issued a proclamation requiring citizens to practise with bows and arrows on leisure occasions rather than waste their time playing handball or watching cock-fighting. There are numerous other examples of royal exhortations to improve the standard of archery among the people at large. In the reign of Henry VIII the City Artillery Company was formed under the protection of a royal patent granting immunity to anyone shooting at an accustomed mark who happened to wound or kill a passer-by. It is recorded that in 1682 Charles II attended a grand meeting of the Finsbury archers and bestowed on the most skilful the titles of Duke of Shoreditch and Marquis of Islington—titles which had fallen into abeyance during the Commonwealth. Samuel Pepys in his entry for 12 May 1667 says: 'I walked over the fields to Kingsland and back again; a walk, I think, I have not taken these twenty years; but puts me in mind of my boy's time when I . . . used to shoot with my bow and arrows in these fields. A very pretty place it is.'

The fame of Tunbridge Wells was like a bright light showing the way for some to wealth, for others to gaiety. The seventeenth-century success of the wells, with royal patronage setting the stamp of respectability on its ordered festivities, captured the imagination of Londoners. It is difficult to know precisely why this should have been so. Perhaps Tunbridge Wells seemed almost on London's doorstep, but in fact in the eighteenth century it was a considerable journey away, although it was at least a place which could be reached in a day once stagecoach services were established. Whatever the reason, the literature of the eighteenth and early nineteenth centuries contains repeated comparisons between the numerous 'spas' of the Greater London area and Tunbridge Wells. The spa in question might be no more than a well with facilities for 'taking the waters' and (in modern terms) a combined restaurant, lounge and dance hall attached, but the comparison was always with Tunbridge Wells rather than with Bath or any of the continental resorts such as Spa.

If one says that 'taking the waters' was only a minor part of the entertainment, one is probably understating the matter. The therapeutic value, real or imaginary, of the various springs provided only a threadbare excuse for a day's outing, or a week's stay in the country in congenial surroundings. It is difficult to re-create the atmosphere of these places, because few of them are well documented. They were, out-wardly at least, highly respectable even in the sternest Victorian sense of the word. But to the Victorians themselves the spas of the previous century seemed in retrospect a mixture of Gomorrah and Rome in the time of Nero, and many of the writers from whom our knowledge of them, such as it is, is derived belong to the Victorian tradition.

The Islington Spa, which to be in the fashion was advertised as the new Tunbridge Wells, was one of the earliest. By 1700 it was adver-tising music for dancing all day every Monday and Thursday during the summer. Princess Amelia visited it in 1733 to drink the waters on the advice of a physician. By 1776, however, it had fallen on bad times. Though the proprietor, a Mr Holland, advertised that the number of his 'patients' was scarcely to be credited he became bankrupt soon afterwards and the heyday of Islington Spa was over, though the gardens remained open for a time and people still visited them to drink the waters for the sum of sixpence. Spa Green covers most of its site.

Bagnigge Wells was more successful for a time. It was on or near the site of a house once lived in by Nell Gwyn, a circumstance which encouraged the proprietor to call his resort the Royal Bagnigge Wells. It was open for drinking the water and the usual entertainment from 1760 until 1813, when the proprietor was adjudged bankrupt and the fittings were sold. These fittings included two hundred 'tables for drinking', which gives some idea of the number of people who could be expected there on a fine Sunday.

Bagnigge Wells and many other less celebrated places of entertain-ment were in the valley of the Fleet River, which Stow calls 'the river of wells' and which flowed out of the Highgate ponds and Hampstead ponds, taking a south-easterly course to St Pancras, and then on to Newgate and into the Thames at Blackfriars. (It still flows in a sewer under New Bridge Street.) Bagnigge Wells were situated between Newgate and St Pancras.

Sadler's Wells, of which more later, was an unusually successful establishment. Cold Bath in Cold Bath Square was one of the most remarkable. It was fed by a spring discovered in 1697, when the owner of the land built a small bathhouse and advertised cures for every conceivable ailment at what was considered the high price of two shillings a time. Patients who were too feeble to take the bath without assistance were lowered into it seated on a chair suspended from the ceiling for a charge of an extra sixpence. The cold bath was short-lived but there is no evidence that any patients were killed by the shock of the cold water!

The London Spa was one of the earliest opened in Finsbury. A spring was found conveniently in the garden of an inn known as the Fountain in 1685. Though the spa survived for the better part of a century, it was better known for the strength of its ale than for the excellence of its waters.

Bermondsey Spa, competing with the more numerous and more fashionable resorts of Lambeth, was a late arrival on the scene. The 'spring' (most probably like the springs of many south bank spas derived from the draining of the marshes) was 'discovered' in 1770. Pleasure gardens and pavilions were laid out in the vicinity and for a time the spa was popular, well known for its fine music, its firework displays, and (an odd addendum) for the exhibitions of paintings by the respected proprietor, Thomas Keyse. Soon after the turn of the century takings fell and a quick profit by disposing of the land for industrial and residential development was accepted with alacrity. This was a factor, incidentally, which precipitated the closure of many other spas and gardens.

Scarcely anything is known of some of the London spas. Probably many existed of which there is no record at all. The Pancras Spa, for instance, would be almost unrecorded were it not for a handbill dated 1697 which has been preserved and shows it to have been one of the earlier and more 'honest' spas, its appeal to the health-seeking rather than the pleasure-loving Londoner. 'At Edward Martin's at the Hornes at Pancras is that most excellent water, highly approved of by the most eminent physicians and found by long experience to be a powerful antidote against rising of the vapours, also against stone and gravel. It likewise cleanses the body, purifies and sweetens the blood, and is a general sovereign help to nature. I shall open on Whitson Monday, the 24th of May, 1697, and there will be likewise dancing every Tuesday and Thursday of the same season at the place aforesaid. The poor drink the waters gratis.'

The wells of Hampstead were among the best-known resorts. It was, according to one authority, celebrated in the early part of the eighteenth century as the meeting place of the wealthy and the idle. Houses of amusement and dissipation, it was further stated, started up on all sides and the papers 'teemed' with advertisements of concerts at the Long Rooms, revels at the wells, races on the heath, and private marriages at Sion Chapel. The last-mentioned item is substantiated by others. There was a chapel called Sion Chapel at which marriages were solemnized in a very informal manner but quite legally and only on the production of a marriage licence. Hampstead was by no means a Gretna Green.

Something of the atmosphere of the place is given in a comedy called *Hampstead Heath*, which was acted at Drury Lane Theatre in 1706. One of the characters says: 'We have city ladies that are over-dressed and no air, court ladies that are all air and no dress, and country dames with broad brown faces like a Stepney bun, besides an endless number of seamstresses whose clothes hang as loose about them as their reputations.'

The wells were in what is now Well Walk and the assembly room later became a chapel, a singularly inapposite transfer of use in the eyes of the Victorian residents of Hampstead (incidentally among the many famous residents of Well Walk in the early part of the nineteenth century were Constable the painter and Keats the poet). As Howitt wrote in 1869: 'Those who now see the Wells Tavern very seldom have any idea of the scenes that took place there at no very distant date.' Always there is innuendo, suggestion, never definite facts.

The spa started, no doubt, like so many of the others, in imitation of Tunbridge Wells, as a commercial venture at a time when physicians all over the country were recommending the drinking of chalybeate water. Howitt even asserts that through the recommendations of a group of physicians the wells became as celebrated and as much frequented as those of Tunbridge Wells (it is very doubtful whether that was ever so). However, it is true that from 1700 onwards the fame of the Hampstead waters was such that they were carried fresh from the spring every day and sold as far afield as Holborn Bars, Charing Cross and Temple Bar, while Mr Philips, an apothecary of Fleet Street under the sign of the Eagle and Child, not only sold the water in his shop at threepence a flask but delivered it from door to door at fourpence a flask, the flask being returnable.

That was in the first decades of the eighteenth century, yet by 1734 Hampstead doctors saw their steady revenue from fashionable patients diminishing. One of them, a Doctor Soame, wrote a book to revive the fame of the wells, giving instances of the cures effected by the waters, but to no avail. The happy days of 1700 to 1715, when advertisements were appearing in every issue of the *Tatler* and fashionable people were driving every day to Hampstead, were past. The advertisements do show, however, that the main attractions were a tavern, coffee-room and dancing-room, with bowling greens and the promise of good eating and drinking 'with a convenient coach house and very good stables for fine horses with good sustenance'. But there is nothing to suggest that, as Howitt has it, 'Hampstead speedily became as dissipated a watering place as any in the kingdom or any in Germany at the present moment' (1869).

There was music for dancing all day every Monday during the season. To cater for less wealthy visitors a stagecoach made the journey regularly to London and a 'chariot' could be hired from the wells at any time in the evening or morning. Even if dancing did continue into the small hours of the morning, as the advertisement suggests and as the story of Vauxhall confirms, far more people went to hear the recitals given by prominent musicians in the assembly rooms than to take part in the dances.

The greatest days in the Hampstead season were 1 to 4 August, when the fair was held in the Lower Flask Walk quite near the wells, and races were run on the Heath for considerable wagers. And there is some reason for thinking that the fair days did provoke a certain amount of disorder and a few brawls in which some of the fashionable people of London became involved. Certainly the reputation of the fair was bad, if only because it attracted, like many nineteenth- and twentieth-century fairs, a host of pickpockets and confidence men looking for easy game.

Apart from the spas there were in the eighteenth century a number of pleasure gardens in the suburban outskirts. None of them approached the splendour of Vauxhall or Ranelagh or made a tithe of the artistic or recreational contribution to social life that was achieved by Vauxhall. One of them, Belsize, shared in a kind of reflected glory for a time and showed emphatically that eighteenth-century Londoners were prepared to take their leisure in the fresh air, weather permitting, without the special excuse of drinking the waters and without the much publicized attractions of Vauxhall.

It is significant that Belsize never attracted to itself the abuse levelled at Hampstead Wells. The manor of Belsize had a long and honourable history. Prints of Belsize House show a distinguished mansion in a rather flamboyant adaptation of the classical style. One of its owners, Sir William Wade, had been a confidential emissary of Queen Elizabeth I to foreign sovereigns and was knighted by James I. He was Clerk of the Council for a time under Queen Elizabeth and councillor to James I— quite a remarkable achievement. After Sir William's death the house was occupied by his stepson, Lord Wotton. On the latter's death it was regarded as too dilapidated for immediate reoccupation and ceased to be a private residence. After being let for a time to subtenants, the house and gardens were opened as a place of amusement on 16 April 1720 with 'an uncommon solemnity of musick and dancing'. It was promised that from Easter Monday throughout the season the park would be thrown open at six o'clock in the morning until eight o'clock in the evening without charge, and that there would be music and dancing every day. There is a marked similarity between this advertisement for Belsize and an advertisement which would serve well to publicize the gardens of some ancestral home today. A handbill issued in connection with the opening says: 'The park and gardens have been wonderfully improved and filled with a variety of birds which compose a most melodious and delighting harmony. Persons inclined to walk and divert themselves may breakfast on tea or coffee as cheaply as in their own chambers.'

A difference between the advertisement of 1720 and one of the present day is that the Belsize handbill promised twelve stout fellows well armed to maintain a continuous patrol along the road from Belsize to London. Belsize became popular and twelve stout fellows proved insufficient for the purpose. Within a few years the number had been increased to thirty. In addition armed men were posted permanently at the gates of the park and the door of the house.

There was gaming in the house as well as dancing, but in spite of the casual statement of one writer that 'the immorality of the place was enormous' its chief appeal seems to have been the gardens and the

relaxation they afforded after the crowded, stuffy, evil-smelling atmosphere of the city and its nearer suburbs. On one special occasion more
than three hundred private coaches brought visitors for a deer hunt in
the park. The record says that the deer was duly killed before many of
the company after nearly three hours of continuous entertainment.

The custom of holding hunts as a spectacle in private parks during
the eighteenth century was a well-established one, and one which,
though it may offend twentieth-century susceptibilities, did not cause
the raising of a single eyebrow two hundred years ago. The only
criticism of Belsize which eighteenth-century people made was that
'women, whether maid, wife, or widow', took the opportunity of a
temporary escape from home to make assignations. The fact that they
were generally with their husbands or fathers (except for the widows)
seems to have escaped the notice of the critics.

There were, of course, in London during the eighteenth century what
Victorians called sinks of iniquity and places of entertainment which
were generally referred to as folly houses. One folly house, a large ship,
was permanently anchored in the Thames opposite Somerset House,
and several others lower downstream towards Blackwall. Even these
varied in the 'iniquity' which they purveyed, some specializing in
gambling which, after all, was commonplace in Georgian times and
was certainly not regarded as vicious, others being frankly brothels with
or without a thin veneer of respectability. But Belsize was not one of
these, nor was Ranelagh or Vauxhall.

Among the establishments deserving the name of pleasure gardens
(though not to be mentioned in the same breath as Vauxhall) which
competed for custom with the spas, the Pantheon in Finsbury was one
of the most elaborate. It was a teahouse on the site of an old inn, the
Ducking Pond House, with gardens attached and an organ installed
for musical entertainment. It only had a short life, the people of
London preferring the more robust entertainment of other establishments. By 1779 it had become, appropriately enough, the Spa Fields
Chapel.

One Finsbury place of amusement was at least unique in the attractions it offered. The Peerless Pool in Moorfields was originally a pond
fed by a spring. Known as Perillous Pond in the sixteenth century, later
as Parlous Pond, it was renamed when its commercial possibilities were
recognized in 1743. It was deepened, and grottoes and promenades
were built around it. So it became London's first outdoor swimming
pool. Another large pond fed by water drawn from the Peerless Pool
was stocked with fish for the use of visitors, who 'find their amusement
in angling' or, to quote another advertisement, 'admire the amusement
of angling'. The Peerless Pool had a long life. It was still attracting
visitors in the middle of the nineteenth century.

Hackney had its counter-attractions for London people in search of
an afternoon in the open air. Pepys went there with his wife on a fine

June day in 1664 and commented on the good refreshments, on the cream and the cherries, and the enjoyment of a game of shuffleboard. The most famous of Hackney gardens was the Mermaid, where there were bowling greens and shrub walks and ample refreshments served outdoors or in the neighbouring Mermaid Tavern. Well established before the end of the seventeenth century, the Mermaid was still flourishing in 1811, when balloon ascents were made from the gardens to attract even more people.

There were fewer pleasure gardens to the west of London, partly because this was an exclusively fashionable district and partly because available sites were farther from the city than Finsbury or Hackney and lacked the romantic air of resorts 'across the river'. The Marylebone Gardens were the most successful. Like Vauxhall, they were designed at first for the fashionable but later had a more mixed clientele. They were opened in the first half of the eighteenth century, their chief attractions the bowling greens and the tea gardens. They competed with Ranelagh and other gardens by giving firework displays and special concerts, as well as providing music for dancing. But, successful though they were, Marylebone Gardens soon ceased to attract the intelligentsia and the leisured classes, which were essential to continued solvency.

Eighteenth-century speculators saw every spring as a potential gold mine. If the spring water was discoloured by mineral deposits, so much the better. But it was sufficient if medical analysis showed it to contain 'salts'. A nasty taste was no drawback; perhaps it was an advantage, if only because people who had really come to the wells to enjoy themselves could reassure their own conscience with the displeasure of drinking the water, a displeasure which was followed in many places, as at Epsom, by a more acute physical discomfort. But then millions of people are still happy to endure the selfsame physical discomfort in the sacred cause of good health, obtaining their Epsom salts in a neat sealed packet with far less trouble (and also far less pleasure) than their ancestors did from the water containing similar salts.

The wells at Acton are seldom remembered in this context but they were uncommonly popular in their own time, even though to reach them from London involved a rather arduous ride. The Acton wells were 'rediscovered' in the reign of Queen Anne, though there are few references to their early history. However, by the early part of the eighteenth century an assembly room had been built. The spa was recommended by doctors, as we know from handbills which have been preserved. The spa achieved its greatest popularity during the reign of George III. The water was said with relish to be 'more powerfully cathartic than any other in the kingdom of the same quality except that of Cheltenham', with the added inducement that the quantity of salts in each pound weight of the Acton water was forty-four grains. It must have been a powerful draught which attracted not only permanent residents to East Acton and Friar's Place, which adjoined the hamlet of East Acton, but thousands of visitors for the day from London.

Brewer, writing in the early years of the nineteenth century, when the fame of Acton Wells had waned, divides the visitors after the manner of his time into those 'allured by the hope of remedy' and those 'tempted by the love of dissipation'. 'Both classes', he says, 'have long since abandoned the spot. The assembly house was many years back converted into a private dwelling and is now occupied as a boarding school of a very respectable character.' Now even the school has disappeared as have all traces of the assembly rooms. But the wells were still popular in 1771, when an advertisement announced the opening of a new season 'by the request of several physicians and by the encouragement of several of the nobility and gentry'. The wells were to be opened every Monday, Wednesday and Friday from Lady Day to Michaelmas, with a family subscription of a guinea covering the use of the 'new room' and consumption of the water, to be enjoyed on the spot or to be taken home. The advertisement added: 'The public-house adjoining the wells, with good stabling, is now open, with proper accommodation and on timely notice dinners are provided.'

Though Acton Wells did not survive the eighteenth century, they provided an interesting nineteenth-century postscript. In 1870 a 'people's garden' was laid out on Old Oak Common, adjoining the site of the wells: what remained of the wells house by then having been adapted as an outbuilding of a farmhouse by the side of the Great Western railway track. The people's garden was taken over by the German Club of London, which was said to have 'transformed it into a veritable summer *Biergarten* with the biggest dancing platform in this country, where German is chiefly spoken'. That was an oddly appropriate postscript to the Wells if only because if we discount the absurd nineteenth-century version of the profligacy of spa life, a genuine similarity of purpose is discernible between the eighteenth-century English spa and the nineteenth-century German *Biergarten*.

Pepys and Evelyn were untiring takers of the waters. Many of the spas on the fringes of Greater London might have been forgotten but for their diaries. The Barnet Physic Well, for instance, was often visited by Pepys. Fuller, writing about the same time as Pepys visited them, states that the number of cures achieved by drinking the waters was so great that there was hope that the waters would make good the whole loss of life in the Battle of Barnet. The well came to light again during the present century when the land was being excavated for a housing estate. An analysis was made of the water, which proved to be genuine mineral water, though only slightly saline in character.

Evelyn is the authority for Sydenham Wells, which he visited in 1675 on his way back to London from Dulwich College. We have his word for it that the medicinal value of the waters of the spa was highly regarded and that many visitors from London were attracted during the summer.

Tottenham, though rather far afield for most Londoners in the seventeenth and eighteenth centuries, achieved a high reputation for its mineral springs. According to the *Ambulator* magazine, 'the people reported many strange cures performed at Bishop's Well'. The Tottenham springs were placed in the same category as those of Cheltenham in the treatment of rheumatic ailments.

When the spas, or the medicinal wells, or the physic wells, as they were variously called, were in vogue anyone who could 'find' water on his estate was sure of a credulous public if he cared to develop his treasure. An actual well which was the mecca of health-seeking pilgrims from London in the eighteenth century still exists in the Rookery Gardens of Streatham Common. The gardens surrounding this and other wells in Streatham attracted visitors from about 1660 until 1792, when the main source of water failed. Soon afterwards another well was 'discovered' near by and, combined with a tea garden, was operated on a commercial basis until the middle of the nineteenth century. An analysis of the Streatham waters published in 1750 recommends a dose of three cupfuls which, it says, is equivalent to nine cupfuls of Epsom water. Londoners bound for Streatham must have needed strong stomachs! One of the latest spas opened was in the Greater London borough of Croydon on Beulah Hill. There a saline spring became the centre of a development which included some spa buildings designed by Decimus Burton and opened to the public in 1831. Beulah Spa had a life of only twenty-seven years, but it might have survived longer had not the opening of the Crystal Palace in 1854 provided intolerable competition.

Apart from the formal entertainment of the spas and gardens, Londoners in the eighteenth century continued to enjoy a day in the country as much as they do in the twentieth century. The country to them, however, was no farther afield than Islington or Highbury in the north, or Chelsea in the west. Few crossed the river for such expeditions: London was still very consciously a town of the north bank and, as we have seen, crossing the river to Vauxhall Gardens was quite an adventure. Oliver Goldsmith has immortalized a trip to Islington, with hot rolls and butter at the White Conduit House after walking up the City Road and through the fields to Highbury Barn for midday dinner, followed by another walk in the fields before adjourning to the White Conduit House about six o'clock.

Writing in the *Connoisseur* in 1754, Bonnel Thornton says: 'An acquaintance lately laid before me an estimate of the consumption of bread and cheese, cakes and ale, in all the little towns near London every Sunday. It is incredible how many thousand buns are devoured in that one day at Chelsea and Paddington, and how much beer is sold at Islington and Mile End.' The picture he draws is of a mass exodus, the majority of people travelling in one-horse chaises, but many also travelling on foot, 'trudging patiently with a child in one arm while his beloved doxy leans on the other and waddles at his side, sweltering beneath the unusual weight of a hoop petticoat'. Thornton had no confidence in the country-loving character of the Londoners of his time. He says he cannot suppose that the country had any particular charms 'to most of our Cockneys. It serves only as an excuse for eating and drinking. They get out of town merely because they have nothing to do at home.'

Thornton and his *Connoisseur* readers were like the arty critics of every century. The country had no charm for them, so it could have none for anyone else! The whole history of London from the seventeenth century onwards shows that Londoners have taken any and every opportunity to escape from its crowded streets whenever the necessity to earn a living permitted them the luxury.

In the nineteenth century as in the eighteenth, there were a number of popular pleasure gardens, though generally they were less formal and less elaborate in their entertainment than in the previous century. They did best when they could draw for their patrons on a sizable local community and also on people making a day's excursion from London. At a time when the acme of holiday enjoyment was represented by a trip on the river, many riverside communities supplied suitable amenities to attract trade.

Erith was one of the places which made a brief though not very successful attempt to profit from the popularity of river trips. The waterside gardens are shown on the ordnance map of 1865 complete with pier and Pier Hotel. They covered a considerable area and had the usual bandstand and tea gardens. Most of their customers came by river from London, but when the North Kent railway line was opened many came also by train. Yet by 1893 the gardens had disappeared completely and in their place Anchor Bay Wharf, the property of a coal-distributing company, had replaced the pier, and railway wharves were being built on the site of the gardens.

The gardens of Erith and other places along the Kent coast were poor imitations of the famous Rosherville Gardens of Gravesend, which were as fashionable as Richmond Hill until the Sunday crowds frequenting them became too large and noisy for the world of fashion. The *Princess Alice*, which foundered after a collision between Erith and Woolwich on 3 September 1878, when seven hundred trippers were drowned and 'for several days the dead bodies were cast upon the muddy banks of the river at Erith', was returning to London from a trip to Gravesend. The disaster made such an impression on the Victorian world that the popularity of steamer trips down the river declined for several years and the riverside gardens never regained their popularity.

The spas were the direct forerunners of the music-halls, which became a settled part of London and provincial life in the second half of the nineteenth century. Sadler's Wells is the best-known example. When people went to it as a spa it was not as popular as the Hampstead Wells, or even the Bagnigge Wells, but as a musick house it became one of the most frequented of all places of entertainment.

The tradition of the musick houses derived directly from the Restoration, when the theatre, which had ceased to exist under the Puritan regime, was revived and branched out in many directions. Many of the early musick houses, such as Coleman's, described as near Lamb's Conduit, i.e. the present Theobald's Road area, won a highly unsavoury reputation and were suppressed. There is reason to suppose that many of them were virtually brothels, and it may well have been the greater respectability of the wells establishments, in spite of all that the nineteenth-century writers have to say about them, that made them so popular.

Sadler's Wells, which was identified with Miles's Musick House, was the exception which proved the rule, but in this case the musick house came first. The well was in a garden belonging to the musick house, which had been built by a Mr Sadler on the north side of the reservoir into which the New River flowed. The statement, whether true or invented, was made that before the Reformation many extraordinary cures had been achieved by drinking the water of the spring which on that account was called a holy well. It was even said that priests from the Priory of Clerkenwell had initiated ceremonies and had made people believe that the virtues of the water proceeded from their prayers.

Mr Sadler's contribution to the welfare of mankind was to dig in his garden and rediscover the well. Backing his well both ways as it were, he duly obtained the support of physicians for the value of the water, which was sold in bottles as well as being drunk at the well. By the beginning of the eighteenth century the musick house and the wells had been separated, the former doing good business under the name Miles's Musick House, the latter continuing to be known as Sadler's Wells.

There was a good deal of competition between the traditional coffee-houses of London and the musick houses. Plays were performed in the coffee-houses; one particular Islington establishment presented a comedy or revue, as we should call it, and changed its programme every week, which in Howitt's words: 'Presents a most awful and disgusting picture of coarse things, obscene and vile debauchery in language which could not be read now in any decent family.' But the precise nature of the vile debauchery remains a mystery, except that the weekly comedy did satirize someone who at Sadler's Wells for a wager of five guineas ate a live cock, feathers, entrails and all, with only oil and vinegar for sauce, and half a pint of brandy to wash it down.

Later came rope dancing, juggling, and gradually all the kinds of entertainment associated with nineteenth- and twentieth-century

Covent Garden Opera House. This, the rather flamboyant Bow Street façade of the present-day Opera House, was built to the design of E. M. Barry after the earlier theatre was destroyed by fire in 1856. Barry did, however, maintain the spirit of the Opera House as designed by Smirke in 1809. Smirke's theatre replaced an earlier one which was also burnt to the ground. Theatres in this part of London have had a most unhappy history, for Drury Lane Theatre, designed by Henry Holland and only opened in 1794, was also burnt down in 1809.

The Soane Museum. The central white façade is of the house which Sir John Soane built for himself in 1813 and in which he lived until his death in 1837. The house beyond it was also designed by Soane at an earlier date. Soane used it not only as a residence but as a musum for his remarkable collection of art and antiquity. He bequeathed the house and the collection for the use of 'amateurs and students' by an Act of Parliament of 1833, with the proviso that his collection should not be added to or altered. So the interior is unique in surviving intact and unrestored as a gentleman's residence at the beginning of the nineteenth century.

The Grand Union Canal at Uxbridge. The construction of what was originally the Grand Junction Canal and of the Uxbridge to Paddington Branch revolutionized the trade and development of Uxbridge. Linked by cheap means of transport with the markets of London and the coalfields of the Midlands, it had become a thriving industrial and commercial town in its own right well before the middle of the nineteenth century.

The Thames at Hammersmith. The canalizing of the upper reaches of the Thames brought a rapid increase in trade to riverside places on the tidal waterways above London during the nineteenth century. Hammersmith was one of the numerous places to develop quickly even before it became virtually a suburb of London. The commercial growth depressed the status of Hammersmith's Mall, which had been fashionable in the eighteenth century. The suspension bridge in the background was opened in 1887, replacing the earliest suspension bridge across the Thames built sixty years before.

Masterpieces of William Wilkins.
William Wilkins was one of the most successful of the classical designers of the first part of the nineteenth century, more academic in his treatment of classical motifs than Smirke but freer in his interpretation than Smirke. As the architect of Downing College, Cambridge, he won a major national reputation. So it is not surprising that his designs both for the National Gallery (*right*) and University College (*below*) were accepted in competition with several other well-known architects. The portico is the centre-piece of both designs, the similarity of which is obvious in these two photographs. The central domes represent an effort to make the designs more interesting, although Victorian critics were almost unanimous in condemning them. University College was the earlier of the two buildings and was completed in 1827, while the National Gallery was not finished until 1838.

Myddelton Square, Finsbury. Named after the pioneer of
the New River, Sir Hugh Myddelton, Myddelton Square is of
twofold interest, first, as one of the earliest estates to be laid
out for residential purposes after the Battle of Waterloo, and,
second, as the projection into the nineteenth century of the
'little town' principle which originated in the squares of
Bloomsbury and the West End. Each 'little town' was a
self-contained unit with fine residences for the wealthy and
the noble, smaller ones for the middle class, a church and a
nearby market or shopping street. It is an added point of
interest that Myddelton Square is still owned by the New
River Company, the direct successor of the company of
which the earliest shareholders were Sir Hugh Myddelton and
King James I (a far more prosperous concern, incidentally,
than it ever was in the seventeenth and eighteenth centuries).
The church of St Mark, the centre-piece of the square, a good
example of the early Gothic revival in church building, was
completed in 1837.

[44]

...ton Square, Westminster. The
...elopment of Belgravia in the angle
...ween Hyde Park and the gardens
...Buckingham Palace, reaching as
...west as Sloane Square, took place
...ween 1825 and 1840. Eaton
...are—not really a square but an
...ngated rectangle with fine gardens
...ning from end to end—was begun
...the Cubitt Brothers in 1827.

...Matthew's Church, Brixton. One
...the four churches traditionally
...own as the Waterloo Churches,
...hough they had no connection
...ept a temporal one with the Battle
...Waterloo, it was built between
...22 and 1824. The architect was
...F. Porden, who was cramped in
...design by the limitations of cost
...posed by the Church Building Act
...1818.

All Souls, Langham Place. This church is an integral part of John Nash's overall plan for the construction of a new highway from Regent's Park to Carlton House. Its position is due to the fact that the line of the new Regent Street and of Portland Place could not be aligned, the church being a feature to make a virtue out of necessity. The semicircular portico is unique and one of the happiest inspirations of Nash, who designed the church for the Church Commissioners.

[46]

lassical Pattern at the junction of New Cavendish Street and Portland Place.

egency Design. The imposing entrance to Chester Terrace by John Nash.

Chislehurst Common. This is the traditional centre of a village which has now become a dormitory suburb. The ancient church of St Nicholas on the farther side of the green is of Norman foundation, but was largely rebuilt in the fifteenth century. The still clearly visible circular depression in the common is the cockpit, a centre of Chislehurst entertainment until cock-fighting was made illegal in 1834. The annual Whitsun Fair, however, which by tradition was held around the cockpit, continued until 1862.

A Link with Shakespeare. In a back street of Southwark this tablet let into the wall marks the approximate position of the Globe Theatre, in which Shakespeare enjoyed so many of his triumphs. The relief clearly shows the theatre itself, most of Southwark, and the Borough High Street leading to Old London Bridge and the City on the farther bank of the river.

music-halls. However, whatever the quality of the audience, the musick houses long survived the popularity of the wells themselves, and Sadler's Wells, as the musick house was by then known, was rebuilt completely in 1765, the old wooden building that had seen service for nearly a hundred years being replaced by an up-to-date brick-built auditorium. In this theatre seats had backs with shelves so that the audience could drink in comfort during the performance, glasses with short stems being supplied. The whole of the interior was redesigned in 1778 and among the performers great names like Grimaldi began to appear in the bills. Mr Siddons, husband of a more celebrated wife, was one of a syndicate who bought it for further development near the end of the century, while early in the nineteenth century Sadler's Wells broke new ground by giving a water entertainment, the water being drawn from the New River into a basin which took the place of the stage. In this reservoir ships sailed and sea monsters sported!

If the musick house attached to the eighteenth-century spas was the true progenitor of the Victorian music-hall, the public appetite for sing-songs, for music, and for interesting and exciting acts compelled many of the taverns on the outskirts of London to follow the example of the spas. Some establishments ceased to be primarily taverns and became music-halls, later once more changing their names and becoming variety theatres. To choose one typical example from many, the Metropolitan in the Edgware Road, which was finally demolished in 1963 but in its heyday was one of the most famous of all music-halls, started its long history as the White Lion. This ancient inn was rebuilt in 1836, when the population of Paddington was just beginning its meteoric rise. Singing was the chief entertainment offered, but in 1852 a concert-room was added in which one could enjoy liquid refreshment and at the same time watch acts on the stage. So the White Lion became the Metropolitan Music Hall. Unlike the pleasure gardens of the eighteenth century, it catered for the mass of the people, making no appeal to the gentry. It was known not inaptly as the 'Gentleman's Gentleman's Theatre'.

Some of the great names of the English theatre first appeared in the bills of this kind of hall, names such as those of Marie Lloyd and Talbot O'Farrell. It was only in the last years of the nineteenth century that the Metropolitan became the Palace of Variety as the modern idea of a variety theatre was born.

A great number of music-halls developed on this pattern in London and its suburbs, from the lordly Alhambra, the Oxford and the Tivoli, to suburban theatres such as the Hackney Empire, the very names of which have been forgotten by the vast majority of people, and the buildings of which have long since been demolished. Some had a surprisingly short life. Deacon's Music Hall in Finsbury, for instance, opened in 1860 and ended its career in 1891, when the land on which it was built was required for the construction of Rosebery Avenue.

o

For the people of inner London Islington remained a great centre of entertainment, just as it had been since the Restoration. Highbury Barn was a famous rendezvous in the middle of the nineteenth century. Collins's Music Hall by Islington Green originated, like the Metropolitan, in the singing-room of an inn, the Lansdowne Tavern. Like the Metropolitan, it was extremely successful in the last decades of the nineteenth century, but its popularity waned after the First World War. Finally, like the Metropolitan, it continued in active service as a place of entertainment until recent years. Incidentally Gracie Fields was one of the famous people who appeared on its stage—in 1915.

Shoreditch, which proudly boasts that it was the first district near London to have a theatre (Burbage's 'The Theater' was probably built in the sixteenth century outside the City boundaries to avoid the City's ban on drama), maintained in the nineteenth century its tradition of entertainment with several song-rooms and music-halls. So did St Pancras, with the Alexandra and the Camden, which was previously known as the Euston Theatre of Varieties.

Almost every inner London suburb had its music-hall, most of them several. Many of the growing towns on the outskirts were by then large enough to support theatres of their own. The opening of the Richmond Theatre in 1899 with a performance of *As You Like It* was a token of the increasing interest in serious drama among a substantial number of people—substantial enough to support a serious theatre, however precariously, in a community small by comparison with the crowded inner suburbs of London.

By then the pleasure garden was a memory of the past, the spa ideal confined to famous places such as Bath and Tunbridge Wells, Harrogate and Baden Baden. The reasons for the complete change in fashion were many. The railways had brought the opportunity to thousands of people to expand their horizons. A day in the country could now be an expedition to the sea or to the hills of Surrey or Buckinghamshire. Spectator sports were beginning to attract a large following. Although the phenomenon of hundreds of thousands of Londoners spending their Saturday afternoons watching Association football and other sports belongs rather to the twentieth century than to the nineteenth, people were beginning to be more interested in watching others' sporting achievements than in making their own entertainment.

As so often in social history, the wheel of change has turned full circle. Hundreds of clubs and a few inns not only in London but in all the large industrial towns of England present entertainments today with singing and dancing very similar to the sing-songs and the diversions of the music-hall attached to the eighteenth-century spa or tavern. The Londoner has not lost his love of a formal garden. Thousands admire the flowerbeds of London and suburban parks, where hundreds once admired the artistry of the gardens of Ranelagh. And thousands, too, make a journey by car or train to spend the afternoon in the grounds of one of the country mansions which throw their gardens open on a few days in the year. To draw the parallel one stage closer, betting was the chief inducement for people to attend the cockpits in the sixteenth and seventeenth centuries. It is equally the chief inducement which attracts people today to watch greyhounds pursuing a mechanical hare.

12. Railways Change the Picture

THE young Princess Victoria was at Kensington Palace on 20 June 1837 when the death of William IV threw on her the responsibility of sovereignty. Little had happened by then to warn her or any other observer that in the course of fifty years a complete social revolution would take place, bloodless but nevertheless effective. The omens were good for the country's continuing prosperity, as indeed they had been without a break for a hundred and fifty years except when wars threatened the economy, or, less often, the nation's independence. But there was little to suggest that during Queen Victoria's reign, a period of peace unbroken except for the Crimean War and the Indian Mutiny, and at its end the South African War, there would be such an upsurge in endeavour that the country would become indisputably the wealthiest in the world, dependent not only on its own efforts as the workshop of the world, but deriving enormous additional wealth from its world-wide empire.

These momentous events are reflected with marked precision in the history of Greater London and its development into one of the world's largest and certainly the world's wealthiest community, in which by the end of the century, although poverty had not been outlawed, all the appearances were of well-being and graceful living. By 1837 the Industrial Revolution had disrupted the even tenor of life in the north country. The mills of Lancashire were turning fast. People in their thousands and tens of thousands had deserted the countryside for the bright lights and gin palaces of the towns, where they lived in un-believable squalor, if only because they bore down on the towns like a flood which could not be dammed. The rate of building new homes could not be raised high enough to provide adequate accommodation for them even when they had the means to pay for it.

The north country had already felt the devastating effects of slumps. Those who had migrated knew by now that starvation was an ever-present threat more imminent than in the countryside. But the horrors of recurrent booms and slumps had not yet hit London. The Industrial Revolution in the widest sense of its meaning had made little impact.

Machinery was taking the place of human hands, new industries were being started in many of the small towns round London, and undeniably an unwanted influx of workers from foreign countries and from the more distant countryside made unemployment acute in some districts. But that was all.

London was the commercial centre of the country, and of the world, rather than its industrial centre. A large and growing middle class as well as an aristocracy of wealth and a few remaining noble families maintained the prestige of the fashionable suburbs. London could be proud, too, of its magnificent heritage of Renaissance and Georgian architecture and could shut its eyes to the self-contained slum areas in which the poor and the sick and the shiftless were crowded together ten or twenty to a room.

Prosperous business men still drove into town in their carriages, their coachmen fighting their way with ever-increasing difficulty through the traffic blocks of the City and its approaches. The clerks and the less prosperous were also moving out of London into the nearer suburbs, travelling by coach or on foot. Better accommodation was available for them, but many could not take advantage of it because rents were often higher than they could afford.

Just when the position was becoming intolerable, when it seemed as though the middle class itself might be submerged in conditions approaching the slums of the poorest, the building of the railways changed the picture out of all recognition. It took time for people to realize that a real and lasting change had taken place, to appreciate that with the railways capable of carrying thousands of people from London into the countryside in a matter of half an hour or less, the clerk was in as good a position as his employer to live the kind of life which for so long had been the latter's prerogative—working in town, living in the country, and enjoying the best of both worlds. That is really the whole story of the incredible expansion of Greater London which took place in the second half of the century.

The speculative builder once more came into his own, but he was catering for a very different class of customer from the speculators of the seventeenth and eighteenth centuries. The building budget must be adjusted to suit the needs of the new suburbanites: costs would not allow the fees of a well-known architect, so mass production must be the order of the day. And so we find rows on rows of houses built in long terraces, or for the slightly more prosperous, in semi-detached units, all identical except in the smallest details, few with any pretensions to solid building or excellence of design but all immeasurably better than two rooms in the crowded districts surrounding the City and Westminster, which was all that could be obtained for the rent that the clerk or craftsman could pay.

The employers held their ground for a time in their Georgian residences, but as the network of railways became more complete (incidentally the services were almost as fast as those of today) many decided to move farther out of town, preferring a seat in a first-class compartment to a slow and nerve-racking journey in their own carriage and pair. It was a quicker journey for them, and in the long run a cheaper one. Ten minutes more in the train would allow them to leapfrog over the new middle-class suburbs and build houses for themselves in areas to which their employees had not yet penetrated.

Unhappily by this time, towards the end of the nineteenth century, Victorian builders had destroyed the canons of design so laboriously built up in architecture during the last two hundred and fifty years and had found nothing as yet to replace them. The late Victorian mansions of a Sydenham or a Chislehurst are sumptuous enough but florid and rather characterless, eccentric sometimes, with a garnish of towers and pinnacles derived from goodness knows what inspiration, or else a sombre pile, typical of the 'stockbroker's solid', in a heavy style derived indirectly from the classical and sometimes, to be fair, aping classical motifs with considerable skill. In default of a new idiom, the Georgian revival was already in sight.

As emblems of the wealth of the times and of the respectability of Victorians, a number of new churches were built to grace the more prosperous suburbs. A bill introduced by Sir Robert Peel in 1843 made it possible for new parishes to be formed without a special Act of Parliament. The bill was well timed and presaged a return to something distantly related to the outlook of pre-Reformation days, when a man's greatest pride was to make his contribution to the enrichment of his church or to endow a chantry chapel to the greater glory of God. Every parish found its benefactors, its lists of willing subscribers, and in every new parish (literally hundreds of them in Greater London) a new church was built, nine out of ten of them distinguished by a tower and lofty spire rising high above the rooftops of the nearby villas.

The nonconforming churches were equally active in building but often their benefactors were not so wealthy. The free churches' modest and sometimes crude efforts to provide themselves with places of worship were often and occasionally justifiably referred to with scorn by members of the established churches as tin tabernacles.

The picture is certainly not one of unrelieved gloom, even from an aesthetic point of view. Most people today regret that such vast areas of excellent agricultural country were covered in a rash of bricks and mortar. Some few Victorians deplored it and made vain efforts to stem the outward flow. But it was a problem for which even the highly self-conscious town and country planners of the twentieth century have not found an answer. How much less could the Victorians be expected to do so. One cannot even blame the speculative builders on the meaner estates. They had a market to cater for. They supplied the goods. By no means all of them found this a way to quick riches, for competition was severe and the pockets of their tenants limited.

There was much of excellence, too, in Victorian architecture. A few of the Gothic churches such as St Mary's, Stoke Newington, show real imagination. A few, but alas only a very few, of the town halls and other public buildings are excellent in design as in purpose. It is unfair to judge a great era by reference to the Albert Hall and the Albert Memorial, which were regarded by contemporary critics as the quintessence of beauty and elegance. Inexpensive villas (and these were numerically by far the largest part of Victorian building) do not present the easiest of architectural problems. The twentieth century has not done so very much better than the nineteenth, and in some cases perhaps not so well.

The reign started very well, showing no break with the building tradition of the past thirty years. Even the smaller houses, of which so many survive along the Mile End Road, Bow Road and Commercial Road, and around Albert Square and Arbour Street, are in impeccable taste. On the other side of the river Southwark's Trinity House Estate (Trinity Square and Merrick Square) were begun as early as 1822, but many of the houses in the vicinity were built after 1837 and here the visible difference between the two periods of building is negligible. The statue in the centre of Trinity Square, incidentally, was brought from the north front of Westminster Hall in 1822 when the hall was being refurbished. It is certainly the oldest statue in London and presumably dates from the end of the fourteenth century when the hall was re-modelled by Richard II. Nothing is known of the figure portrayed, though many believe it is King Alfred.

To the west of London, too, there is no fault to be found in the development of Pimlico by the Cubitts, who were also responsible for laying out much of early Victorian Clapham and Cubitt Town in the Isle of Dogs, a most unusual working-class estate many years ahead of its time designed for the people who worked in the West India Docks (which make the Isle of Dogs an island in fact as well as in name).

All this work was nearing completion by the time of the Great Exhibition in 1851. The westward spread of London to Bayswater and Notting Hill had started by then, though it was almost the end of the reign before every open space was filled with houses. George Wyatt's Princes Square in the Chalk Farm area and Wood's Lancaster Gate are both products of the eighteen-fifties. Both are highly commendable efforts to retain some of the best features of the Regency style and yet give a distinct Victorian flavour, while Bedford Park, which was begun in 1876, positively looks forward to the garden suburbs of the twentieth century.

There is, of course, another side to the coin, though most of it has been erased and leaves no regrets. The cottages of Victorian times were not built to last and they have not lasted. The majority of those within six miles of Charing Cross were damaged, if not destroyed, by aerial bombardment. Few were worth rebuilding, while many had already been cleared to make way for more modern dwelling-places or offices before the outbreak of war. However, anybody who walks through the little streets of Paddington or Islington today will still come across groups of mid or late nineteenth-century small houses which have escaped destruction either in war or peace and are certainly not good advertisements for the building style or methods of the unknown architects of the time or for the good taste of the speculators.

Islington is especially illustrative. It is the only district in London in which it is possible to trace the changes in mood and purpose which distinguish almost every decade from 1820 to the end of the century. The admirable composition of the New River Company's Myddelton Square on the Finsbury boundary has been mentioned in Chapter 10. A little farther north Canonbury Square and Cloudesley Square, with Barry's Holy Trinity in imitation of King's College Chapel, Cambridge, also date from the latter part of the Regency period. Lonsdale Square, an unusual example of the Tudor Gothic revival, and Gibson Square, are early Victorian, about 1840 to 1845, Arundel Square was laid out between 1850 and 1860 and Union Square in 1860. The heterogeneous assortment of roads still farther north is a product in the main of the period 1860 to 1900.

It is easy to see the changes when each period is set against the next in so small a space, and to observe the gradual degradation of the Georgian style, the loss of the self-contained community spirit of Myddelton Square, the increasing shabbiness of architecture as the century progressed, the absence of any really ample dwelling-places towards its end, the dullness which succeeded the graciousness without elaboration of the earlier sequences, the lack of originality which mars the later work. When it is recalled that in 1801 the population of Islington was 10,000, in 1901, 335,000 (more, in fact, than its population today), it can be appreciated that in this area of a few square miles there is a microcosm of the whole development of Greater London over a century.

Contemporary commentators note the change not only in architecture but in the quality of the population. At the beginning of the century Canonbury is described as a place of elegant houses and spacious villas, the dwelling-places of prosperous City men and merchants. In 1864 there are far more 'clerks, printers, watchmakers, butchers, brick-makers, schoolmistresses, washerwomen and dressmakers'. (One wonders what a schoolmistress would say just a hundred years later to be listed alongside a washerwoman.) By the end of the century the bulk of the population was frankly working class. The 'elegant houses' had been deserted by the 'wealthy merchants' and were beginning to deteriorate if not into slums at least into rather overcrowded tenements. It was no longer necessary for people to collect near the Angel at the sound of a handbell to march under protection to the City as it had been a century before. There were horse buses by

1850 and electric trams by the eighteen-eighties, giving direct services to King's Cross as well as to the City. By 1896 Islington became the third London district to have its streets lighted by electricity in order to lessen the danger of walking abroad at night. A hundred years after the last of the highwaymen had been executed there was still a chance of being attacked in a dark corner and being robbed.

The revolution was even more obvious in a place like West Ham, which felt the impact of industrial development far more than the nearer suburbs. By the end of the century it had become an industrial town in its own right and a very important one at that. Amazingly in 1837 West Ham was still largely rural. Stratford High Street and its environs were the most thickly peopled areas. Then with the coming of the railways, railway works and shipbuilding yards were opened. Large-scale manufacturing appeared by the eighteen-fifties. Inevitably the demand created the supply. Thousands of people flocked in from the country in search of work and were accommodated in mushroom settlements, many of them built on marshland. The Vestry, one main purpose of which was to look after the poor, was quite unable to cope with this great new influx or with the poverty arising from unemployment, which arose partly from an over supply of labour, partly from periodic falling off of industrial activity.

An inquiry presided over by Alfred Dickens, the brother of the novelist, uncovered a terrible picture of numberless people living many to a room with no sanitation, little or no drainage, no paved roads, no amenities of any kind. It took fifty years and a complete change in the local government of the outer suburbs in general, and West Ham in particular, to strike at the roots of the evil. The increase of population during the century from 2,500 in 1801 to 267,000 in 1901 (compared with 157,000 in 1961 when West Ham still appeared over- rather than under-populated) and a mushroom growth of more than 130 major factories within the area during the century tell their own story.

The growth figures of Islington and West Ham are exceptional, but even Hammersmith, a relatively quiet residential suburb on the privileged west side of London, grew from less than 25,000 in mid century, when it was a suburb of Fulham, to more than 150,000 at the century's end.

As Greater London spread abroad in every direction, the population of the City shrank. During the reign of Victoria almost the whole of it was rebuilt, the vast majority of the seventeenth-century and eighteenth-century merchants' houses giving place to warehouses and offices and enlarged company halls. In retrospect it seems a tragedy that so much fine architecture should have been thrown to waste without a thought, without indeed a word except the constant cry of progress and improvement. But most of the fine houses had been abandoned by their wealthy owners, and many alleys and squares of unsavoury and insignificant houses were demolished at the same time. Now that the clerk and the craftsman had followed their masters into the country to sleep, London was depopulated and space could be found for the commercial improvements and for the new office buildings which were badly needed. Many of the new warehouses and offices were unbeautiful. The determined searcher after truth can still find a few left among the towering blocks of post-war reconstruction, but only a few. Like the mean residential streets of the inner suburbs, they were built, served their brief purpose, and then fell, either to a demand for better utilization of the space they occupied or to the bombs of German aircraft.

By 1900 the population of the City was less than a quarter of what it was when Queen Victoria came to the throne, less than a tenth of what it had been before the Great Fire (in 1901 it was 26,000 compared with 120,000 in 1801, and fell still further by 1939 to 9,000). Yet just outside the City boundaries 129,000 were crowded together in the less than one and a half square miles of Shoreditch by 1861. After that there was a decline, but only a slow one until the next century (the comparable figure in 1961 was 40,000, a number which could only be accommodated in present-day standards of comfort by the replacement of old and dilapidated houses with multi-storeyed blocks of flats).

The combination of low wages and high rents produced appalling conditions in Shoreditch, which was described as one of the worst slums in the whole of the Greater London area in the last quarter of the century. Hoxton, only 150 years before a suburb of fashion, was the most unsavoury part of it.

Thr new Royal Exchange was one of the finest buildings, made possible by the metamorphosis of London from a mixed residental, commercial and industrial area to one devoted wholly to commerce. It was symptomatic of the times that Bartholomew Fair, which had long outgrown its usefulness, was brought to an inglorious end in 1840. Yet Smithfield remained the nation's greatest cattle market and the only one in London until 1855, when the live cattle market was removed to Islington. Smithfield, however, showed the conservatism so common, not only in London but in provincial towns, and is today, however improbably, the chief meat market in the London area. Its only rival in Greater London has been Southall, where a market charter was granted in 1698, and the cattle market in comparatively recent times was second in importance only to Smithfield.

It was regarded as a token of progress that a fruit and vegetable market with the active assistance of the then Duke of Bedford replaced in 1833 the piazzas and fine residences of Inigo Jones's Covent Garden. It was a matter of congratulation that this market should have been so successful that additions to it were called for at frequent intervals during the rest of the century.

It was equally a sign of the expanding economy that London's docks, as they were in 1837, proved inadequate for their purposes. To the East and West India Docks were added the Victoria Dock in 1855, the Millwall

Dock in 1868, the South-West India Dock in 1870 and the Royal Albert Dock in 1880. On the south bank of the river the Surrey Commercial Docks centred on Rotherhithe were taking their share of traffic.

St Paul's School was one casualty of the rebuilding of the City. It had remained in St Paul's churchyard from the time of its foundation by Dean Colet but in 1884 was removed to the still open fields by Hammersmith to find its home in one of the least admirable of major late Victorian buildings, a Gothic monster in red brick designed by Waterhouse. And now in the sixth decade of the twentieth century, when the bricks and mortar have closed in on the Victorian school and an arterial road threatens its playing fields, plans have been made to remove it once more to a green oasis on the other side of the river near Hammersmith bridge. Less than twenty years earlier Dulwich College had split the stays of its former home and was removed in 1866 to another red brick Gothic monster by Charles Barry, comparable with St Paul's. Old boys seldom fail to argue about the relative merits of their respective school buildings. Boys from both schools find it easy to be uncomplimentary about each other's Alma Mater.

In Westminster the school, which dates from the break-up of the medieval abbey, stood its ground, but everything else in Westminster, as in the City, was changing. Fire destroyed almost the whole of the Palace of Westminster except the great hall in 1834. Sixteen years later a new Palace had been completed, with a vivid irregular skyline, an impressive and in many ways a worthy home for the Mother of Parliaments. The building was the combined work of Sir Charles Barry and of Pugin, who was a leader of the Gothic revival. The result is a composition reminiscent of Tudor Gothic with classical undertones, due no doubt to Barry's classical training and his greater facility with the forms of the Renaissance.

Trafalgar Square was completed, great new government offices appeared on both sides of Whitehall, and the Mall became a fine processional way leading to the renovated and re-fronted Buckingham Palace.

The Great Exhibition, the brain-child of the Prince Consort, was a tremendous success. Its glass buildings were later removed to Sydenham and renamed the Crystal Palace, while the profit derived from the exhibition was used to start a national centre of culture in South Kensington, where the South Kensington Museum was completed in 1857. Ths collections were later split up as they outgrew the buildings, and in 1899 the foundation stone was laid for the renamed Victoria and Albert Museum.

So much is written about the bad state of the roads in the eighteenth century and the improvement effected by the passing of innumerable Turnpike Acts that it is often forgotten that the nineteenth century also was a period of major road improvement, especially in the London area. Traffic problems were possibly greater before the motor-car had been invented than they have ever been since. Contemporary prints of the city streets in the nineteenth century show a congestion far greater than would be tolerated by any modern Minister of Transport. Many improvement schemes, such as the construction of Holborn Viaduct, eased but did not remove the problem.

In the first half of the century the planners were concerned even more to assist the passage of traffic approaching and leaving London, especially where the main roads passed through growing villages or had to surmount some natural hazard. Highgate Hill was one such obstacle. The scheme proposed, and in the end carried through to a successful conclusion, involved the engineering of one of the earliest by-pass roads. Inevitably the project was costly and subject to many delays.

Highgate presented two difficulties. It lay astride the main road to the north and was rapidly growing from a hamlet into a small town with a good deal of traffic of its own which sometimes created a major obstacle to through traffic. London was still, as it had been from the early Middle Ages, the commercial centre of the country, in spite of the rapid growth of midland industrial towns such as Birmingham (a village in the eighteenth century). It was also still the most important port. As the population and, therefore, the productivity of the country as a whole increased, so the amount of traffic, bound to and from London, increased. A great deal of this used the North Road. At the beginning of the nineteenth century, apart from the difficulty presented by Highgate itself, Highgate Hill was regarded as dangerous for heavily loaded wagons, especially as it proved impossible to maintain a good surface on the steeply inclined roadway. As it was illegal to use a team of more than five horses many loads failed to negotiate the gradient and many wagons became out of control, with resultant damage and loss of life.

Accordingly in 1809 a scheme was projected to divert through traffic from the hill by building a tunnel 375 yards long, 24 feet wide and 18 feet high through the hill itself. The scheme was proposed by Robert Vazie, a gentleman who, apart from this revolutionary suggestion, made little mark on the history of Greater London. The scheme was received with some ridicule, but by the time the great Rennie and the ubiquitous John Nash had worked on it a modified scheme was evolved. The idea of a tunnel was retained but its length was reduced to about 250 yards and cuttings were to replace the tunnel for the remainder of the distance.

The Highgate Archway Company was formed in 1810, with authority by Act of Parliament to raise a total of £60,000 and to levy perpetual tolls not exceeding sixpence for every horse or other beast drawing a carriage on the new road. Work began and more than a hundred yards of the tunnel had been excavated. The operations attracted a great number of sightseers and scores of enthusiastic geologists, who stocked their collections with a variety of fossils until that momentous day, 15 April 1812, when the tunnel fell in with a crash, which it was said could be heard at Kentish Town. The subsidence brought down Hornsey Lane, which became impassable for carriages.

The traders, especially the publicans, of Highgate were jubilant. They had visualized their business being sadly diminished when London-bound traffic ceased to flow through their village. They had always heaped scorn on the project. Now they were fully justified by events and they tried to discourage any further attempt by distributing pamphlets to their customers. Some of these pamphlets contained surprisingly good satire. The following is an extract from one of them: 'The Highgate Archway having fallen in, it is intended to remove the whole of the hill entire by a mechanical slide, including the chapel and bowling ground. It is intended to remove it into the valley behind Ken Wood where the seven ponds now are, thereby forming a junction with Hampstead and inviting the approach of the two hamlets in a more social manner. On the spot where Highgate now stands it is intended to form a large lake of salt water and to supply the said lake with sea water from the Essex coast by means of earthen pipes, iron pipes being injurious to sprats. It is intended to stock the said lake with all kinds of sea fish except sharks, there being plenty of land sharks to be had in the neighbourhood, to supply the metropolis with live sea-water fish at reduced prices. It is intended to have 100 bathing machines to accommodate the metropolis with sea bathing and to erect a large building on the north side of the lake, which building is intended for insane surveyors and attorneys who have lately infested the neighbourhood of Highgate and annoyed the peaceful inhabitants . . .' and so on.

However, nothing halted the march of progress. The Highgate Archway Company was still in existence, even if its tunnel had fallen in, and John Nash was very much alive to give further advice. So another Act was passed, in 1812, enabling the company to raise a further £70,000 to build an open road on the line of the intended tunnel. This road passed under an arch which carried Hornsey Lane. The preliminary work was carried out with dispatch. Even then there were more difficulties to be overcome. The deep cutting proved difficult to drain and water frequently rushed down the roadway after heavy rain, carrying away the top surface. The road was more or less permanently under repair at least until 1829, when another great engineer, Telford, was responsible for redesigning the drainage and for laying the road in a thick bed of cement.

This plan proved successful. But there was a sad aftermath. Telford's work had been done by Government loan under the Act for improving the mail road between London and Holyhead and the company owed the Government far more than it could ever hope to pay. Moreover the dues or tolls decreased in value as more and more traffic was diverted to the railway. No dividends were paid to the shareholders, who had subscribed in all more than £100,000, while the company's debt to the Government was settled by an agreement to cease to levy tolls in 1876.

The road was thrown open to the public on 30 April 1876 and its upkeep became chargeable to the parishes of Islington and Hornsey. By then the shares of the original company were worthless. But there was an odd postscript to be written. The company remained in existence and had the pleasure of seeing the value of the surplus land which they had bought for the road but which had not been used rise with the general increase in the value of Highgate property. Ultimately the directors were able to sell the land for building purposes at a price which enabled the shareholders to be repaid a substantial part of their original subscriptions. By then, 1887, few if any of the original share-holders were alive but their heirs at least enjoyed a windfall from their courageous investment.

One other postscript to be written to the construction of the 'High-gate by-pass' is that the number of suicides who threw themselves off the bridge was so great that in 1885 the stone parapet was removed and iron railings seven feet high substituted. A contemporary writer says 'this no doubt effects the object in view but has certainly not improved the appearance of the bridge'. He need not have worried. The stone bridge was replaced before the turn of the century by the steel archway which is still standing. Twentieth-century records show that it is not proof against the temptation of suicide, nor is it particularly beautiful, but it does at least give the same view to people walking along Hornsey Lane as that enjoyed by Hans Christian Andersen who, when driving over the archway by night saw, in his own words, 'the great world metropolis mapped out in fire below me'.

In London itself there was still room for improvement and better roads were demanded to facilitate trade. In 1847 New Oxford Street was cut through the rookery of St Giles, and a little later a number of sub-sidiary roads including Endell Street linked the new highway with Long Acre and Covent Garden. This was the beginning of slum clearance with a vengeance. St Giles, which had become an Irish colony, had as bad a reputation as any slum area on the fringes of London, worse even than Hoxton at one time. Driving a new road through an area like this entailed demolition and that in turn entailed rebuilding and rehousing.

Progress was not quite so orderly as it is today. Probably more actual suffering was caused by the change but the net result was the same. The trouble was the lack of a central government for Greater London. The care of the poor and a number of other local government functions were carried out with varying success by the parish vestries, but boards for major works were generally set up by Act of Parliament. In the eighteen-fifties there were hundreds of these boards, which showed remarkably little knowledge of each other's activities. The result was a long-overdue effort at centralization with the establishment of the

Metropolitan Board of Works in 1855. When this had outworn its use-fulness the London County Council was created in 1888 and twelve years later the metropolitan boroughs, which remained unchanged until 1965, became the principal units of local government within the sphere of the London County Council.

The Metropolitan Board of Works, which of course had no control over the City, achieved a great deal in the areas under its jurisdiction. It had, for instance, to face the problem of St Giles, only the surface of which had been scratched by the construction of New Oxford Street. In 1850 a report described the area as 'rows of crumbling houses flanked by courts and alleys, in the very densest part of which the wretchedness of London takes shelter, squalid children, haggard men in rags, many speaking Irish, women without shoes or stockings, decayed vegetables strewing the pavements. In one house a hundred persons have been known to sleep on a single night'. A determined effort was made to replan the whole area. By 1887 Shaftesbury Avenue and Charing Cross Road had both taken shape.

By then, too, the river banks had been built up, mainly between 1865 and 1875, and new roads made available from Blackfriars bridge to Westminster bridge, and on the other bank from Lambeth to Vauxhall. The Albert bridge was opened in 1873. With the completion of Holborn Viaduct and Queen Victoria Street, which gave direct access to the City from Blackfriars bridge, central London began to assume a far more modern appearance. Holborn Viaduct was opened by Queen Victoria in 1869, on the same day as the new and wider bridge at Black-friars. It was ironic that three years later the Government was being widely attacked in the press for its failure to deal with the traffic blocks in the City and Westminster. On the Surrey side of the river the Metro-politan Board of Works was just as active and was instrumental in the creation of Southwark Street in 1864, part of the direct route from London Bridge to Westminster bridge. This virtually completed the main road system of the south bank up to a distance of two miles from the bridge approaches.

There were many casualties directly attributable to the 'improve-ment' schemes apart from the old houses lost in the rebuilding of the City. Northumberland House, which was pulled down to make way for Northumberland Avenue in 1874, a development made necessary by the reclamation of the Embankment, was one of the most notable of these. It was virtually the last of the palatial mansions left along the course of the Strand, the town house of the Dukes of Northumberland. Its passing caused many expressions of public regret, even though most people recognized that it could not possibly have been saved. Frag-ments of it have survived in Greater London, however—the wrought-iron gates of Syon House, for instance, and surprisingly a stone gate-way which has been re-erected a hundred yards from the parish church of St Mary, Stratford-le-Bow. It was purchased by the owner of a house which stood on the site of what is now a recreation ground as an ornament for the gardens.

The Blackwall Tunnel, linking Poplar with Greenwich, was another great work to facilitate transport carried out in the last years of the century. It was opened in 1897 and was an immediate and permanent success, a credit to its engineers and to the foresight of its builders. It is equally a tribute to the strength of City finances that the cost of building Tower bridge, opened in 1894, was met wholly by the City of London without subsidy.

The bringing of the railway terminals within walking distance of the business centres of the new London involved much difficult planning and determination. It also aroused a great deal of unreasonable opposition. The first terminus approaching inner London was the London Bridge end of the London and Greenwich line in 1836. Euston was opened in 1838, Cannon Street in 1866, Liverpool Street and Holborn Viaduct in 1874. The Victoria and Hungerford railway bridges were opened in 1862 and 1864 respectively, marking a most important stage in the railway story because they brought the lines from the south to Victoria and Charing Cross. It was the first step in the development of these areas as secondary business centres.

Many who worked in the City, however, spent almost as much time on the horse-bus from these West End terminals as they did in the train from the outer suburbs to London (and very often more). That was an inevitable drawback to living in some of the newly developed suburban estates, until the underground railways resolved the problem. It is interesting to note that the first terminal station of the London and Southampton Railway was at Nine Elms, where the entrance still stands guard over the goods yard, and similarly that the terminal of the South Eastern Railway was at the Bricklayers' Arms for a few years. The lot of the earlier 'commuter' was certainly a difficult one. The daily influx of people by railway, apart from those actually working in London, made traffic congestion worse, and it was specifically to relieve this that the idea of an underground railway was proposed.

Opposition to this was even fiercer than to the idea of main line terminals to the inner zone. (The Duke of Wellington had protested in vain that one day a train might pull up in the centre of London carrying a whole French army without anybody knowing that they had landed.) However, nothing could halt the flood of 'invaders' from the countryside and from the provinces and nothing, it seemed, could mitigate the consequent overcrowding of the London streets. Hence the brilliant idea of a City man, Charles Pearson, who suggested schemes to connect the northern termini by a network of underground railways and was prepared to find the financial backing to make it possible. Inevitably press and Parliament united in condemning the scheme. No building, it was said, would be safe if holes were dug under the town. In prospect, Pearson's brain-child was called the 'sewer railway' and the heavy

artillery of the Established Church was added to the batteries opposed
to the scheme, with the thought that burrowing beneath the feet of
God-fearing citizens must be contrary to the will of God.

After nearly fifteen years of public argument Parliament authorized
the formation of the North Metropolitan Railway Company in 1853.
But work did not begin until 1860 because finance was lacking, and it
was 1862 before Mr Gladstone and other members of the Government

AWKWARD

Railway Porter: 'Now then, sir! By your leave!'

made a trial trip from Paddington to Farringdon Street. In the following year the line was officially opened, only a few months after its
originator, Charles Pearson, had died. Like so many schemes which had
been pilloried for years, this one proved a great success from the
beginning and there was little opposition from any important source
when the time came to construct the deeper underground railways.

The effect of the new means of communication with the outer
suburbs in terms of bricks and mortar has already been noted briefly.
Its incidence, however, was far from uniform. Most of the development of the mid century was almost accidental. It occurred chiefly at
places through which railway lines happened to pass. When, for
instance, the North Kent line to Gravesend was opened in 1849
following closely the banks of the Thames, new building began within
three or four years at most of the towns or villages where there were

P

Rushey Green, Kent, in 1771. It was on the North Kent railway route and like many such places was changed from a rural village to a London suburb by the arrival of the railways.

stations as, for instance, at Erith. But it was very much a matter of the railway coming first and suburban development following in its wake.

The first step towards expansion was sometimes the building of a railway hotel (the Wheatley Arms at Erith was opened just one year after the station) and most often by the speculative building of a row of villas at the station approach. These were given names which may have sounded romantic to the ears of people just becoming accustomed to the idea of a railway age, but have proved so repugnant to their descendants that they have often been changed in redevelopment schemes—names such as Railway Cottages, Railway Terrace and Railway Villas. More grandiose names, such as Station Parade, were usually of later origin.

A corollary of the principle 'a station makes a suburb' was that the expansion of some otherwise highly favourable places such as Bromley was delayed for many years when a station on one of the through lines did not happen to be conveniently near the town or village. When new lines were built and suitable stations were opened expansion tended to take place in the immediate vicinity of the stations irrespective of the traditional centre of the town. The Bexleyheath line, built to connect the North Kent line with the Dartford Loop, greatly facilitated the suburban development of the area. Bexley Heath was originally an actual heath, part of the undulating countryside which included Black-heath, based on the sands and gravels of the ridge of which Shooter's Hill is one of the highest points. Towards the end of the nineteenth century communities much farther from London than Bexley Heath had grown into extensive suburbs just because they happened to be served by a railway. Development schemes for the as yet unpopulated plateau swiftly followed the plan for a railway line, the name of the locality was changed from Bexley Heath to Bexleyheath, and a new suburb was born.

The Bexleyheath line, which was opened in 1895, was thus one of the first of the truly suburban railways. The only loss was that Bexley Heath, which after enclosure in 1814 became a famous fruit-growing area, was lost for ever to agriculture. The only reminder of the orchards was the inclusion of two apples in the armorial bearings of the Bexley Borough Council (and incidentally 'an oak tree proper' in the arms and 'heather proper' in the crest as reminders of the heaths and wood-lands).

A similar sequence of events occurred in every part of Greater London. Once there were facilities to live outside the crowded central area and work inside it, the movement was for ever outwards and still farther outwards. There has really been no pause in the expansion from the middle of the nineteenth century to the present day. The covering of bricks and mortar, and in recent years concrete, is like a mass of viscous fluid, bubbling up from a well in the centre and spreading out on all sides, destroying every minor obstacle in its course and reluctantly flowing round major obstacles, dashing forward at great speed where it finds a line of low resistance, and then spreading out again where there is more to check its flow. Even when the reservoir at the centre of this mass is nearly empty it still spreads out, carried forward by its own momentum.

Many readers of this book will have in mind some near-contemporary development in their own locality by which whole rural vistas have disappeared in a time so short that it seems only yesterday that cows were grazing where there is nothing to be seen now but roads and villas and trim gardens. If so, they are likely to be living more than twelve miles from the centre of London. But identical changes were taking place a hundred years ago before the eyes of people who lived only three or four miles from the West End or the City.

Consider the people of Hampstead, for instance. Happy they must have been in the early part of the nineteenth century, the fear of foot-pads and highwaymen removed, the roads well policed, and travelling in daylight safe enough. How rural they must have felt when they drove down Haverstock Hill past the wall of Belsize Park, with its mature trees and green vistas, on their way to the City or West End. This was the estate that Pepys visited in 1668 on 17 July to confer with the Attorney-General 'and after a little talk went and saw the Lord Wotton's house, Belsize, and garden, which is wonderfully fine, the best indeed and the most noble that I ever saw for orange and lemon trees'. Now read what one Londoner, William Howitt, had to say in 1869. 'The lane which passed Belsize House from St John's Wood to Haverstock Hill might still be called a rural lane in 1852, but St John's

Wood was crowding up to it. When I returned from Australia two years afterwards house, park and all were gone and a town stood in their place, still called Belsize Park, it is true, but a park of streets and human dwellings. The old elm tree avenue leading from this ancient site to Haverstock Hill is the only thing now denoting its ancient whereabouts.' And, as most people who live in the district or visit it will know, even the elm tree avenue has gone. For most people Belsize Park is the name of a tube station.

The extension of the Metropolitan line to Harrow virtually created Willesden as a suburb. The latter had a population of 750 in 1851, and grew steadily to 16,000 in 1871. Then in thirty years it multiplied itself seven times, reaching 115,000 in 1901. The same is true of Hendon, where the railway arrived in 1868. In 1871 the population was a mere 7,000 but by the end of the century it was a large and flourishing town which had more than doubled its population.

Walthamstow and Wood Green are two other typical examples. Walthamstow, protected as it was by the Lea and the marshes, was extraordinarily slow to develop. Its population of 3,000 at the beginning of the century had only risen to 5,000 by 1851. The opening of Lea Bridge station in 1840 made some difference but it was not until the Chingford line was driven right through the parish between 1870 and 1873 that the gentle flow became a torrent. From 11,000 in 1871 the population rose to 97,000 in 1901, doubling itself in each decade.

Wood Green was a mere hamlet of Tottenham with a population of about 100 at the beginning of the nineteenth century and did not even have a chapel of its own until 1844. The railway station was built in 1859 and the population grew from less than 3,000 in that year to almost 50,000 by 1911. The building of the railway was also an important factor in the decision to create an entertainment centre for the people of North London to give the same service as the Crystal Palace did for the people of South London. Alexandra Palace (Ally Pally, as many Londoners refer to it affectionately) was opened in 1873. Two weeks later it had been razed to the ground by fire. After only two years a new palace had been completed and a racecourse laid out in the park. In time this, London's own racecourse, became even more popular than the palace.

Some towns were as suspicious of the railways as London, most notably Kingston-upon-Thames, which was an important coaching centre in the first decades of the nineteenth century, and one of the most flourishing market towns in Surrey. When the London–Southampton Railway was proposed the local council positively refused to allow it to enter the town. It won its battle. The railway was driven through the Kingston Hill cutting and the main station in the district was Surbiton. That was in 1838. Kingston did not acquire a station within reach of its centre for a further twenty-five years. By that time Surbiton with a population of 10,000 had grown from a village into a town, numerically as important as Kingston.

Suburban expansion during the latter decades of the nineteenth century frequently followed an Enclosure Act earlier in the century. The most fruitful type of Enclosure Act was that introduced for the purposes of enclosing common land which had been allowed to go largely to waste. Whereas these 'open spaces' would have been remarkably welcome to the people of the twentieth century, they were a distinct embarrassment in the early part of the nineteenth century, if only because, apart from hindering outward growth, they provided cover for footpads and increased the risk of highway robbery.

In this respect Bromley Common was near enough to London to be a possible rebuke to the metropolis as well as to the parish of Bromley. It did not have such a bad reputation at the beginning of the nineteenth century as a hundred and fifty years before, when John Evelyn, travelling through it on 11 June 1652, was robbed by two cut-throats and was lucky to escape with his life—and that on the main road only a mile or two from Bromley parish church. The bad state of the road made it easier for highwaymen to intercept carriages crossing the common. As late as 1755 the main coach road to Tunbridge Wells was no more than a track which a disinterested resident marked out with white painted posts, partly to prevent the drivers of vehicles from losing their way and wandering from the turnpike on to the common, which was described as 'not only dreary but affording every facility for the commission of robberies'.

The commoners made little use of it, even though they guarded their rights jealously, while many residents deplored not only the facilities offered to robbers by the existence of such conveniently situated lurking places, but also the waste of what was clearly potentially good land, whether for agriculture or building. There had been a partial Enclosure Act in 1764. This, however, applied only to a small part of the area and proved rather unsuccessful. When William Cobbett passed through on his way to Sevenoaks in the first days of January 1822, he said: 'Here there is a common, part of which has been enclosed and thrown out again, or rather the fences carried away.' It was not until 1821 that a general Enclosure Act was introduced, and it was 1826 before the Commissioners' awards had been made and transferred to a map (which incidentally is preserved in Bromley parish church).

The new roads laid out over the common land were an outline sketch from which the map of twentieth-century Bromley Common could be drawn. Ditches were dug and drains laid, and parts of the old common were sold to defray the expenses of improvement. In particular, landowners whose premises fronted the common were encouraged to purchase adjoining land. Although residential development was not the purpose of the Enclosure Act, it was the inevitable consequence of it. Landlords who acquired the old common lands found that there was a ready market for new houses built on them. The speed with which development took place is illustrated by the fact that by 1839 a new church, Holy Trinity, was required to cater for the spiritual needs of the new population. By 1886 yet another church, St Luke's, was founded, Holy Trinity having proved quite inadequate by this time to accommodate its parishioners and a temporary church built of iron having served as an overflow place of worship.

At the end of the century almost the whole frontage of the old turnpike road was occupied by a succession of mostly rather elaborate houses. The turnpike road itself had become a wide thoroughfare and every vestige of the common had disappeared. The coming of the railway to Bromley South enhanced the value of the houses and of the land on which they stood. A number of residential roads led to east and west from the main road, and partly, no doubt, because Bromley Common had been a slightly fashionable place in which to build one's house, the name became used rather loosely to describe the whole district to the south of the station as far as the municipal boundary when the borough was incorporated in 1903.

'Perhaps few places can show such extraordinary development and extensive topographical changes during the Victorian era as Ealing,' said Edith Jackson in 1898. Certainly the transformation of Ealing from a country parish into a crowded suburb is typical of the inevitable progression of events that changed the character of many communities which had so far escaped the effects of London's growth.

The change can be measured here, as in many other suburban areas, not only by the bare figures of increasing population but by the multiplication of residential facilities, particularly of the churches. In 1800 there was only one church, the medieval parish church of St Mary, which was rebuilt between 1735 and 1740 and converted into a 'Georgian monstrosity', according to a Victorian commentator. It was rebuilt again to accommodate a larger number of worshippers in 1866 and was transmogrified, according to an enthusiastic reporter, from a Georgian horror into a Constantinopolitan basilica. The basilica still stands, a rare example of this species.

Before the rebuilding of St Mary's, daughter churches had been founded as the parish churches of new parishes. Ealing people were very proud of Christ Church, which was built to the design of Sir Gilbert Scott in 1852, of St John's, which was completed in 1870, of St Stephen's, completed six years later, of St Matthew's, opened for worship in 1884, and of St Peter's, 1891. The last of the nineteenth-century churches was St Saviour's, completed in 1898. But that was not the end of church building by any means. Ealing received its royal charter in 1901 and within six years three more churches, All Saints', St James's and St Paul's, Northfields, had been added to the list.

With such a wealth of churches, quite apart from the comparable number of places of worship belonging to denominations other than the Church of England, it is perhaps not surprising that a census carried out by the *Daily News* in 1904 showed that Ealing had the best record of any town in the London district for attendance at divine service.

Love of fresh air followed very close after godliness and cleanliness in the list of Victorian virtues. The progression of the respectable middle-class suburbs can be measured with equal precision by one amenity other than churches, that of open spaces and parks, often at ten times the price that it would have been possible to purchase them only a few years before the decision to do so was taken. This involved an unceasing struggle in local councils between those landowners who desired to reap the biggest possible harvest from their land and those established rentiers who argued that amenities such as parks not only were beneficial for the people living in the neighbourhood but kept up the rateable value of the surrounding properties.

That was the background of the successful struggle to retain as open spaces the few areas of common land which were still unenclosed in the last decades of the nineteenth century. Ealing Common was one of these surviving areas. Its preservation was a major triumph. Then in 1901 the parklands now known as Walpole Park were purchased and formed a green belt preventing development from the Broadway outwards, while the former Pitzhanger Manor House, which had been reconstructed by Sir John Soane, became the public library. These Victorian beginnings were improved upon by twentieth-century municipal planners. In Ealing since the turn of the century Pitshanger Park, Gunnersbury Park (in conjunction with neighbouring local authorities) and Horsenden Park have all been secured for public enjoyment.

The sudden increase in the rate of development of communities such as Ealing during the nineteenth century inevitably brought with it a major change in the social life of the community. A village cannot change into a large town within a hundred years and retain its character as a village, however desperately it endeavours to do so. A Dulwich can by the exercise of discipline and control retain in its centre the appearance of a village or, as so many have done with rather less trouble, retain a few of the old houses. But more than that cannot be done, however enlightened the local government, however carefully planned development may be.

If the nineteenth-century story of Ealing provides a commentary on some of the changes inherent in development as a suburb, and the great efforts made by church and civic leaders to keep pace with changing circumstances, Beckenham, which has a superficially similar history of development, illustrates more precisely the detail of the changes in local life and local administration which affected one and all of the Victorian suburbs. Beckenham has special interest too, because it embodies the residential traditions of three centuries, the eighteenth, nineteenth and twentieth, in the outer areas of Greater London, and because it still is, as it has always been, a prosperous place, created and maintained for people of substance, through the age of carriages to that of the railways and the motor-car.

These three methods of transport have determined the life of Beckenham in their respective ages, first as the week-end home of city magnates, then as the dormitory suburb of managers and executives, protected from the threat of social decline chiefly by the price of land and the cost of renting or buying houses built on it. Beckenham's near neighbour, West Wickham, which was incorporated in the borough of Beckenham, carried on the story where Beckenham's story was nearly complete, by providing the land for further development in the middle decades of the twentieth century, when there was virtually no land left in Beckenham to develop.

In 1821 the population of Beckenham was 1,180 and when the census was taken there were only fifteen houses in course of construction. About half of the families living there depended on agriculture, directly or indirectly. A few were engaged in local trading and handicrafts, but about one-third of the breadwinners of the village won their bread elsewhere, either in Croydon or in London itself: Beckenham had begun its history as a suburb of the metropolis. But it was still a country village. Some of its estates were occupied by families which had held them for centuries, but some few mansions had been built during the eighteenth century for foreigners—foreigners, that is, to Beckenham, mostly people whose fortunes were made in London and who had retired to the seclusion of the country to live.

The eighteenth-century description, quoted in a modern guide, is probably not far from the truth. 'To the citizen and the courtier such a spot must be an invitation to repose from the bustling scenes of the capital, for Beckenham has long been distinguished as the retirement of opulent merchants and persons of fashion.' The writer was an enthusiast without doubt. He says, 'The circumjacent country is nowhere offensively level nor incommodiously high, but beautifully varied by alternating elevations and depressions interspersed with magnificent seats.' No one could have put it better! Most of the seats were still intact in 1821, though a good many of them had been altered almost out of recognition to conform to the classical fashion of the day. Some of them were very handsome, like Beckenham Place, Beckenham Lodge, Elmer Lodge, the Clock House, Kelsey Park, Eden Park and Kent House. There were very pleasant Georgian farmhouses too, such as Stone Farm and Elm Farm, and a fine rectory with a handsome portico and Regency ironwork.

Altogether it must have looked a very Georgian village at the turn of the century. Some of the estates had a long history behind them, especially Kelsey Park, which is recorded in the reign of Henry III. Others were comparatively new, including what must have seemed a really magnificent edifice at the time, Beckenham Place, which was built about 1773 by the Cator family, who had been lords of the manor of Beckenham for many generations and had lived until then in the old manor house facing the church.

So little has survived of that eighteenth-century elegance that it is hard to re-create even in the imagination a true picture of Beckenham as it was then. The Georgian pattern survived virtually intact for the first thirty or forty years of the nineteenth century. But now most of those 'magnificent seats' have been pulled down and their estates covered in roads and the villas of the late nineteenth and twentieth centuries. The Clock House and Kent House are remembered as the names of railway stations. But by happy chances both of the Cator family homes have been preserved and are in useful employment, the old manor house by the church first as a council house and now as a public hall, and Beckenham Place as a golf house in the centre of what became a London County Council open space, while the park of Kelsey, with its lakes, waterfalls and mature trees, has also become a public open space.

The trend of Beckenham's growth is remarkably similar to that of Ealing. From the thousand-odd population in 1821 the figure increased to 6,700 in 1871 and 26,000 in 1901, while during the century the single old parish church had been joined by seven others belonging to the Church of England alone. One can trace the same preoccupation with providing open spaces when it was almost too late to do so, but not quite too late, since by 1964 when Beckenham was still a borough in the county of Kent with an area of just under 6,000 acres, there were 270 acres of public open space and a further 300 acres of open land with full public access.

Those are the bare bones which make up the skeleton of corporate growth. The known detail serves to fill in the flesh and blood. The picture which results, though it is of Beckenham, might just as well be of any other of the outer suburbs. The first great event in the story of suburban Beckenham was the election in 1839 of a Beckenham man, Alderman Samuel Wilson, as Lord Mayor of London. It was an event which finally confirmed Beckenham in its position as the home of the wealthy and powerful, and Beckenham people were wonderfully impressed as they saw the Lord Mayor's coach leaving his home at Village Place almost every day to carry him to some civic function.

Another event in the same year was almost equally significant. The 'Railway Road Company' was assessed for church rate at £9 a year. The record is clear on that but it is less certain which railway was concerned. Probably it was the London to Croydon Railway, which was opened in June of 1839 and passed through a far-flung corner of Beckenham parish. But there was no station in Beckenham and the immediate significance was lost on the people except for the windfall to the Vestry funds. Although the Brighton Railway also was assessed for church rate in 1848, it was not until 1857 that the railway came into Beckenham proper with the opening of Beckenham Junction station. This was for a time the terminus of the Mid Kent Railway. Only a year later the London, Chatham and Dover Railway and the Crystal Palace line brought every part of the parish within easy reach of the iron road. That was the beginning of more rapid change, though even then, well into the second half of the nineteenth century, the local people saw it as a convenience to themselves and did not visualize in the least the flood of new residents which would engulf their village life in the following fifty years.

In 1857 the total length of the roads in the old parish was eight and a half miles. Today it is more than fifty miles. Three years before, in 1854, the very first street lighting had been installed by the Crystal Palace District Gas Company by invitation of the Vestry—three lamps, one at the rectory gate, one by the village lock-up and one at the entrance to Beckenham Lodge. It must have been an exciting time, what with the glare of the three street lamps, and the monstrous new skyline formed by the Crystal Palace.

It was a bad time for agriculture and there were a number of unemployed. So in one way the work provided by re-erecting the Crystal Palace was a godsend but in another a distinct embarrassment, for two hundred navvies who were not local men sought accommodation in the parish, and proved quite a problem. However, the rector of the time and his wife took them in hand, persuaded many of them to go to church, and requisitioned a barn for meetings at which they doubtless increased their knowledge of the scriptures. In time Beckenham took the Crystal Palace to its heart and went to enjoy its gardens and the wonderful views they commanded over the Kentish countryside, as well as to share in the entertainment provided by its captive animals. It was a sad day in 1886 when the glass palace was seriously damaged in a conflagration which could be seen from Bromley to Croydon. But the Crystal Palace was rebuilt, only to blaze again and this time to be destroyed in 1936. It had provided at least one more memorable occasion, in 1900, when Charlie tore up the garden fences and destroyed the flower beds of hundreds of bright new suburban villas before he was caught on Hayes Common. Charlie was an elephant who had escaped from the Crystal Palace zoo.

Long before then Beckenham was preoccupied with the pains of too rapid growth. In 1869 the Vestry found it impossible to keep 'so thickly filled a churchyard in order by hand' and the churchwardens were wisely authorized to admit sheep to help keep the grass tidy. In 1872 the Vestry was rudely robbed of its authority when local self-government was revolutionized by the Public Health Act. For a time the Bromley rural central authority was responsible for most of the functions of the Vestry. This satisfied no one and the parochial committee threw in its hand in frustration. Fortunately the ratepayers were soon numerous enough to allow Beckenham to qualify as a local government district. In consequence the parochial committee of the Bromley central authority became in 1878 the local government board. Things were run with far less acrimony, if not with greater efficiency, by this board, until by the Local Government Act of 1894 Beckenham became an urban district and the board changed its name once more and became an urban district council.

And so with much church building and still more house building the century drew to its close, but many interesting things were happening in Beckenham while local government was being rationalized. A public hall was built in 1883, a year in which the bounds were beaten for the last time in the century. The pound, with the cage and the stocks, were removed in the cause of road improvement. The old trees in Church Hill were cut down when a new police station was being built, and the handsome porch of the old manor house was demolished so that the road could be widened. The church house in the High Street was completed in 1893, just after the opening of the recreation ground had been celebrated by a public demonstration and procession.

The old regime was merged in the new, but the old community spirit was dead. That is something which not only appears in retrospect but was recognized by the people who lived through these years of change. When Beckenham became an urban district in 1894 it was hoped that there would be a keener interest in local affairs. Far from it. Robert Borrowman, whose book *Beckenham Past and Present* was published in 1910, wrote rather sadly: 'The inhabitants in recent years have changed more rapidly than in the earlier days. We doubt whether there is the same keen interest in the election of the members to the district council as there used to be in the days of the Vestry.' However, the urban district council pressed forward, and in a comfortable age of affluence added amenity to amenity. Public baths were proposed in 1894 (though the scheme was deferred until the Clock House had been demolished, when its place was taken by the baths and by the technical institute). More trees were felled to facilitate road widening and the traditional Lovers' Lane became a main highway. To celebrate Queen Victoria's diamond jubilee a wing was added to the cottage hospital and a new recreation ground was opened. And to bring the future borough right up to date, electric lighting came to Beckenham in the first year of the twentieth century.

The stories of Ealing and Beckenham are typical of nineteenth-century communities in Greater London, but a few of the small towns on the outer fringe changed little, or were fortunate enough, like Woolwich, to have a history in their own right irrespective of the outward spread of London. In 1837 Woolwich was described as a watering-place and a fashionable resort, but its prosperity was linked with its naval yards and they were proud days when Queen Victoria launched the *Trafalgar* in 1841 and the *Royal Albert* in 1854. By 1869 the shipbuilding yards were closed because the wooden walls of England had become iron ones, and Woolwich could not compete with Clydeside and Tyneside. But by the end of the century it had become one of the most important military towns in the country, the headquarters of the Royal Artillery and the site of the Royal Military Academy until the latter was transferred to Sandhurst.

Chislehurst proudly claimed the name Imperial Chislehurst, because the French royal family lived at Camden Place from 1870 to 1881. Before then, in 1834, cock-fighting had been prohibited in the traditional cockpit on the common. It was one of the last places round London where the sport always drew a good audience. Many large Victorian mansions were built in the surrounding countryside and vying with them in architectural exuberance was the water tower erected in 1860, which still stands, its arch spanning the main road.

Many villages, however, remained wholly rural. Orpington was famous for its market gardens. Chelsfield and most of the Cray villages were equally occupied with working the land. So were most of the villages of farther Middlesex, especially in the low-lying land towards the Thames and the Brent. There was still mixed farming in many districts but the accent was more and more on supplying the most immediate needs of London people. Hay and corn could be imported from farther afield but fresh fruit and vegetables commanded such a ready market and gave relatively such a good return to the farmer that before the end of the century they became the crops of most farmers' choice.

Even Harrow grew only very slowly until the twentieth century. Ruislip was scarcely touched because it was remote from the early railway line. Enfield, too, another place famous for its orchards, expanded little until the last decades—remaining a passable imitation of the sylvan retreat in which Charles Lamb made his home in the early part of the century to escape from his over-solicitous friends in London. In the Enfield and Tottenham area, too, the Enclosure Acts relating to Enfield Chace did in the end result in hundreds more acres being cultivated, though it was many years before the crops began to be gathered. Because Enfield Chace is part of the green belt it has escaped suburban development in the twentieth century. The story of its enclosure and the nineteenth-century apportioning makes a fitting epilogue to a chapter so deeply preoccupied with the harvest of brick and stone.

Though royal parties, as mentioned in Chapter 4, frequently hunted in the Forest of Middlesex no king ever claimed extensive 'rights'. Several statutes confirmed the right of freemen of the City of London to hunt at will in the forest. One part of it, however, known as Enfield Chace (always spelt thus in contemporary documents), was always regarded as royal in every sense of the term. The manor of Enfield, which included most of the Chace, was part of the property of the Duchy of Lancaster from 1399, and therefore a royal manor. In 1483 the manor, including the Chace, was given by Richard III to Stafford, Duke of

Buckingham, but when the latter was beheaded for high treason it reverted to the Crown and was presented by Edward VI to Princess Elizabeth, later Elizabeth I. For a century it was the favourite centre for royal hunting parties, Queen Elizabeth often residing at Elsynge Hall.

When James VI of Scotland became James I of England, one of his first acts was to exchange the manor of Hatfield for Theobald's Park with the Cecils (whose residence is still Hatfield House). The sole purpose of the exchange was to enable the King to develop Theobald's Park into a hunting lodge on the very fringe of the Chace. In the following reign the lodges were built and bailiffs appointed.

Oliver Cromwell was perhaps the first to see that something more could be made of the Chace than use as a sporting reserve. It was seized, of course, in common with all royal land, and at one time eight of the captains who had served in the Commonwealth forces were established on estates in the Chace. But the new landholders were far from popular, the immemorial rights of the commoners were said to be infringed, and there were riots in Enfield and Edmonton, with the result that a company of soldiers was drafted into the area to keep order. There were scuffles between the Commonwealth army and the citizens and at least some of the people of Enfield lost their lives. It is evident that the eight captains achieved little progress in making the land productive. A survey carried out during Cromwell's regime showed that the Chace covered almost eight thousand acres, of which about three thousand acres were attributable to the commoners and most of the remainder to the Duchy of Lancaster. The area of unenclosed land seems to have been very much the same when the estates returned into royal possession with the accession of Charles II.

John Evelyn in his diary gives the most vivid picture of what the Chace was like in the seventeenth century. Writing in 1676, he says: 'That which I most wondered at was that in the compass of 25 miles yet within 14 of London there is not a house, barn, church or building beside the three lodges.' He was staying at the time in West Lodge, which was demolished in 1832. The other two were known as South Lodge and East Lodge. All three were built for the bailiffs, whose principal duty it was to inhibit commoners from infringing the royal rights. A clue to the extent of the Chace is that the South Gate gave its name to the twentieth-century town of Southgate, which was previously known as South Street, while Arnos Grove was originally Arno's Grove, a house on the edge of the Chace which was described as a 'residence which is to be numbered among the villas which ornament this large hamlet', i.e. South Street.

That description was penned in the early years of the present century. By then the miracle that scarcely anyone thought possible had been achieved. Most of the undergrowth had been cleared, most of the old trees felled, and the bulk of the Chace was enclosed and productive. It had been divided, as a first stage, between 1777 and 1779 after agreement had been reached between all the parties concerned. The royal estate received 3,218 acres, the parish of Enfield 1,732, that of Edmonton 1,231, that of South Mimms 1,026, that of Hadley 240. The remainder was divided between the tithe owners and a small number of residents on the fringes of the area who had already been permitted to enclose their estates.

The division of the bulk of the land, apart from the royal estate, between the parishes concerned left the onus of deciding commoners' rights fairly and squarely on the shoulders of the parish councils. Most of it remained wasteland, used only for occasional pasture until the end of the century. Of Enfield's share only 200 acres were being cultivated by 1801.

With the country at war and food becoming scarce, another Enclosure Act was passed in 1803 which changed the picture. The Act relating to the enclosure of the Edmonton allotment shows clearly how comprehensively the enclosure commissioners were briefed, and goes a long way towards explaining the success which attended their efforts. The following are extracts from the actual documents:

Allotment of the Residue

That after the making of the said several allotments hereinbefore directed, and before or after such sale or sales as hereinafter mentioned, the said Commissioners shall set out and allot all the then residue of the said common or allotment of Enfield Chace, and the said open and common fields, common marshes, and waste lands in the Parish of Edmonton aforesaid, unto and among the several persons, bodies politic and corporate, who shall be entitled to any estate, property or interest therein, according to their respective rights and interests, in such quantities, shares, and proportions, as by the said Commissioners shall be adjudged and declared to be a compensation and satisfaction for their several and respective rights of common and other rights or interests; and in the making of such allotments, the said Commissioners are to have regard as well to the quantity as to the quality and situation of the land to be allotted to each party; and the allotments to be made to any parties having homesteads or inclosed lands adjoining to the lands and grounds hereby intended to be divided and inclosed, shall be laid as near to such homesteads or inclosed lands, or some of them, as the said Commissioners shall deem to be consistent with general convenience.

Respecting the Allotments to Houses

That in the making of such allotments, the said Commissioners shall consider all houses, messuages, tenements, and cottages, which have been erected and built and used as dwelling houses twenty-five years and upwards, as entitled to right of common, and shall allot unto and amongst the owners of all such houses, messuages, tenements, and cottages such part or proportion of the said lands and grounds hereby intended to be divided and inclosed as in their judgment shall be fair and reasonable; and that no other dwelling house, messuage, tenement, or cottage, which shall have been since erected or built, shall be entitled to any share or allotment of the said lands and grounds hereby intended to be inclosed, save and except such messuages, tenements, or dwelling houses as have been erected within the aforesaid space or time of twenty-five years upon the sites of other messuages, tenements or dwelling houses, which had been erected and built before the time aforesaid.

Clearly this final enclosure was very much in keeping with the spirit of the allotment of twenty years earlier, when it was laid down that the land 'shall be vested in the churchwardens of the parish in trust for the sole benefit of the owners and proprietors of freehold and copyhold land within the said parish entitled to a right of common or other rights within the Chace according to their estates and interests therein'. The chief difference in the nineteenth-century proceedings was that the brief of the commissioners was to finalize the matter so that wasteland could be made productive with the least possible delay. The special allotments referred to in the extract given above included in the case of Edmonton approximately one-sixteenth to the King as lord of the manor, a similar acreage to the Dean and Chapter of St Paul's Cathedral as patrons of the Edmonton church, a small acreage to Trinity College, Cambridge, in respect of their manorial rights, and a small allotment to the vicars of Edmonton. It was also laid down that as much of the residue was to be sold as was necessary to defray the expenses of the survey, allotment and road-building, and also expenses in defending any legal actions brought by commoners who desired to appeal against the decision of the commissioners.

Sir Walter Scott had Camlet Moat in mind when he wrote an impression of the Chace country: 'The sun was high upon the glades of Enfield and the deer with which it abounds were seen sporting in picturesque groups among the ancient oaks of the forest' (*The Fortunes of Nigel*). By this time the deer were domesticated and the wooded area was small. In fact the part of the Chace which he saw had been enclosed for some time. Two hundred acres from the royal manor were granted to Sir Richard Jebb the physician, in the reign of George III, as the nucleus of Trent Park, which was subsequently increased to a thousand acres and included Camlet Moat, a legendary hiding-place of Dick Turpin though associated with the most famous of highwaymen by no positive evidence. Trent Park is still very much a part of the Chace scene.

Between the division of the Chace and the Enclosure Acts most of the area was cleared of its ancient trees, which records show fetched a poor price except for the oak. The reason why cultivation did not take place before the end of the century was said to be the poverty of the soil, but although the Chace does not have a particularly rich soil suitable for intensive arable cultivation, its subsequent history has shown that it is adequate for good pasture and for more intensive husbandry on a limited scale. The necessary work of drainage was carried out after the final enclosure, when a vigorous policy of manuring with marl, fortunately found in abundance in the neighbourhood, was instituted and found highly successful. The change from waste to agricultural land pleased almost everyone but not always for the obvious reason. Edward Ford, writing in 1873, says the neighbourhood had lost much of its picturesque attraction, but a sylvan wild of this extent situated in the vicinity of the metropolis was a dangerous source of mischief. It is difficult to know at what this typical Victorian author was hinting, but if the moral benefit was in his view great the agricultural benefit was unquestionable.

Today, when almost the whole of the original Chace has been converted into pasture land and ploughed fields, there is still one fragment within the boundaries of Enfield in which visitors can recapture something of the atmosphere of the Chace. White Webbs Park has kept alive the spirit and to some extent the appearance of the forest, even though its glades and lawns are artificially contrived rather than natural features of the Chace before it was enclosed.

The Albert Memorial. Situated on the Kensington Road side of Kensington Gardens near Queen's Gate, the Albert Memorial is a conspicuous landmark to travellers on the way from Knightsbridge to Kensington. It was designed as a national memorial to the Prince Consort by Sir Gilbert Scott, and Queen Victoria took a keen interest in all the stages of its construction. It was completed in 1872 and typifies the most bizarre phase of Victorian building, though when unveiled it was greeted with rapturous admiration. No expense was spared in building it. The steps are of granite, partly from County Down, Northern Ireland, partly from Kirkcudbrightshire, Scotland, while the granite for the lower steps on the south side was brought from Penrhyn in Cornwall. The terminal blocks are capped with pink granite from Mull. The intricate work of the spire is in gilded and enamelled metal, the top of the cross is 180 feet high. The statue of the Prince, wearing the insignia of the Order of the Garter and apparently reading the catalogue of the Great Exhibition of 1851, is entirely dwarfed by the magnificence of the superstructure. The frieze surrounding the base is the feature of greatest artistic merit. At the corners of the frieze there are groups of figures representing commerce, agriculture, engineering and manufacturing, the quadruple foundation on which Victorian prosperity was based.

uary of the Albert Memorial. At the four ners of the monument between the upper and er flights of steps there are stone blocks, each porting a group of sculptured figures in marble resenting the four continents—Europe, Asia, ica and America. The quality of the kmanship is generally considered to be far erior to that of the design, as shown in this, the st striking of the four groups, representing Africa.

Blackfriars Bridge. J. Cubitt was the architect of this, one of the most handsome of nineteenth-century London bridges. It was completed in 1869 to replace the bridge which had been opened just a century earlier.

The Angel, Islington. The Angel, once a famous hostelry and later a restaurant, is on the site of a galleried coaching inn demolished in 1819 (*see* page 128).

Lonsdale Square. One of the few estate-planning experiments in the Tudor Gothic style, Lonsdale Square was built between 1840 and 1842

Pancras Station. St Pancras station was opened in 1868, the hotel five years later. The architect was Sir Gilbert Scott and it is said that the design adopted had been submitted earlier for a block of government offices! It is probably the finest monument to the Victorian Gothic style of secular building in Great Britain, certainly in London. The towers are more than 250 feet high and the hotel was confidently and accurately described at the time of its opening as the finest in the world. The station and hotel replaced a notorious slum in which more than three thousand dwelling-places were demolished.

Building Panorama, 1837–1914. The period between the accession of Queen Victoria and the outbreak of the First World War was one of extremely rapid expansion throughout the Greater London area, and an era of experiment in building styles which were greatly admired by contemporary critics but find much less favour today, though all are agreed on the excellence of individual buildings. It was a period in which the Gothic style was used generally for churches, a debased classical style for public buildings and a singularly florid version of the traditional vernacular style derived from Georgian originals for the more modest dwelling-places. The New Palace of Westminster (*above*) was a notable exception to the general rule of adapting classical forms to public buildings. It was specifically designed in a style of Tudor Gothic and was carried out most effectively by Sir Charles Barry and the doyen of the Gothic revival, A. W. Pugin. The greater part of the building took place between 1840 and 1850. The complete revolution in vernacular building before the end of the nineteenth century is illustrated by the early Victorian houses in Commercial Road (*opposite, top*) and the corresponding row of villas in Walthamstow, which are dated 1898 (*opposite, middle*). The early Victorian style of Commercial Road is a rather conservative adaptation of Regency style (note that the house on the extreme right is being demolished, a fate which probably awaits the majority of these pleasant houses). The Walthamstow villas illustrate the full flowering of Victorian terrace building in a tradition which was carried to even greater lengths during the first years of the twentieth century. The years immediately preceding the First World War also witnessed the first signs of original design (as opposed to strictly classical or strictly Gothic) in public buildings. Many of these first efforts to establish a twentieth-century style were unsuccessful. Lambeth Town Hall, Brixton (*opposite, bottom*), is a fair example of the work of this period. It was completed in 1908.

Greater London's Canals. The construction of the canals in and around London facilitated the rapidly expanding commerce not only of the City and its immediate environs but of many towns on the outer perimeter during the first half of the nineteenth century. Though some of the canals no longer contribute to solving the problems of transport, their banks have added to Greater London's amenities. The Grand Union Canal near Harefield (*left*) makes a pleasant rural scene only a few miles from the busy streets of Uxbridge. The Hertford Union Canal, or as it is sometimes known, the Sir George Duckett Canal (*below*) is a popular hunting ground for fishermen from Bethnal Green and Poplar.

London's Dockland. The West India Docks were opened in 1802. Today they are connected with the Millwall Dock and are among the most up to date in Britain, as witness the banks of massive new-style cranes.

Carshalton (*below*). This peaceful rural scene shows the largest of the series of ponds from which emerges the River Wandle, with the medieval Carshalton church in the background.

Paddington Lido (*bottom*). The basin which marks the junction of the Regent Canal with the Paddington branch of the Grand Union Canal has been transformed into an attractive green-fringed lake. It is the starting-place of pleasure trips by canal boat to the Zoo in Regent's Park.

[55]

Green Oasis in the Isle of Dogs. The Isle of Dogs is a singularly little-known part of East London, to most people a symbol of nineteenth- and twentieth-century industrial expansion. Yet this area, which is enclosed by a wide loop of the Thames and contains the West India Docks and the Millwall Dock, is a planned development, with Cubitt Town, a large residential centre, at its southern end. Here the Island Garden, with its striking statue representing Diana, gives one of the finest views across the Thames to Greenwich. In this photograph the gigantic power-station on the Greenwich bank accentuates the beauty of the garden.

Riverside Industry. Upstream from Teddington, where the canalized part of the river begins, Kingston upon Thames has become one of the most flourishing commercial towns within the Greater London area. Here pleasure boats are moored in the foreground, with barges at the quay of a timber yard in the centre, and behind the railway bridge the stacks of the modern power-station. The photograph was taken from the bridge linking Kingston with Hampton Wick.

13. The Pattern of Industry

It is often said that early industrial development was inhibited in the Greater London area because of the proximity of London. That sounds uncommonly strange at a time when parts of that area have become an industrial complex and the industries of the City are virtually extinct. Nevertheless, it is as true as any generalization can be. The craft and farmhouse industries which were an important part of the economy of Britain as a whole before the Industrial Revolution were never highly developed in the Home Counties, certainly not to the same extent as in many parts of southern England, as for instance, in the Cotswolds or East Anglia. Most of the industrial activities mentioned in the records of Greater London are local in importance, apart, of course, from the famous industries which originated in the districts immediately adjoining the City, including Southwark and Shoreditch. No independent community in what is now Greater London showed any sign until the nineteenth century of growing into an industrial centre in its own right.

When one says that there was little industrial activity, however, one is excluding agriculture, the most important of all industries and one which was greatly assisted in its development by proximity to London, which provided a market for surplus products of every kind and description. Farming for profit as opposed to farming for subsistence cannot be said to have originated in the Home Counties. That is a distinction which belongs rather to the midland shires and East Anglia. But it is accurate to say that farming for profit became the general rule in Greater London long before it did in most parts of England.

By no means all the countryside within a twelve-mile radius of the City was suitable for intensive agriculture. The extensive heathlands of the northern heights and the sandy country which extends in an arc from Wimbledon to Blackheath and Bexleyheath were quite unsuitable. The persistence throughout the Middle Ages of areas of wasteland such as Hounslow Heath is additional evidence that the use that could be made of the land was limited until modern scientific agriculture had got into its stride.

Kent has been famous for its orchards from Tudor times to the present day. The Thames Valley is traditionally pasture land, much of which above the flood plain of the river proved ideal for the dairy herds which were increasingly profitable when the value of milk as an article of diet had come to be recognized, and especially from the beginning of the nineteenth century.

Paradoxically Middlesex, which in the Middle Ages was a land famous for its hunting country, became the most important agricultural centre of the Home Counties. At the time of the Domesday Survey, when the primeval forest land had not been cleared completely, some Middlesex manors, especially Harrow, were unusually productive. John Norden, the cartographer, writing in 1593 on the western marches of the county, was positively entranced by the fertility of the area from Heston to Harrow and Ealing: 'The soil is excellent, fat and fertile and full of profit. It yields corn and grain not only in abundance but most excellent good wheat. The vision of this especial corn seems to extend from Heston to Harrow on the Hill. It may be noted also how nature has exalted Harrow on the Hill, which seems to make ostentation of its situation. Towards the time of harvest a man may behold the fields round about with such comfortable abundance that the husbandman who waits for the fruits of his labour cannot but clap his hands for joy to see this vale so to laugh and sing.' Elizabethan writers are not noted for their exuberance or for their enthusiasm for the pleasures of nature. The Middlesex scene must have been very 'especial' to arouse Norden to such lyrical praise.

Two centuries passed and the story is very much the same, but told in the measured prose of a Board of Agriculture report of 1790. 'The whole county may be considered as a sort of demesne to the metropolis, being covered with six valleys, intersected with innumerable roads and laid out in gardens and enclosures of all sorts for its convenience and support.' From Kensington to Hounslow 'it is one great garden for the supply of London'. The only blot on this pastoral horizon was the continued existence of unenclosed waste and common. 'It is hardly to be credited', said a report of 1793, 'so near to the Metropolis, yet certain it is that there are still many common fields in the country', and two years later, 'to the reproach of the inhabitants and the utter astonishment of foreigners, many thousand acres within a few miles of the metropolis are as little improved by the labour of man as if they belonged to the Cherokees'.

That gives an idea of how one section of informed opinion regarded Hounslow Heath and Finchley Common, Uxbridge Moor and Ruislip Common, towards the end of the eighteenth century. It is a clue to the speed with which enclosure of the commons took place in the first three decades of the nineteenth century, until the wheel turned full circle, and by 1845 Parliament was passing Acts restricting the freedom to enclose wasteland within fifteen miles of the metropolis because of the public outcry at the enclosure of land used for fresh air and exercise. It is really amazing that informed opinion should show such a complete volte-face in fifty years. It was not so much, of course, a change of opinion as a conflict of interests between the small but vocal land-owning class and the ever growing number of people who looked on the land not as farming country but as a source of pleasure to themselves.

The picture was much the same in Essex as in Middlesex, except that orchards never became so well established. The forest country, of which Epping Forest is a present reminder, covered more of the land before the nineteenth century than it did of Middlesex or Surrey within the Greater London area. Otherwise the pattern was similar, with the accent on dairy farming but with more cornfields than market gardens.

A major setback to this thriving agricultural industry occurred in the nineteenth century. The Home Counties and the London district did not escape the depression which overtook the whole country after the repeal of the Corn Laws in 1846. But by then the London suburbs were beginning to stretch out long tentacles into the countryside and an increasing acreage was being lost to agriculture.

Nevertheless the hungry forties were a cruel time for many of the people of Greater London, who had grown accustomed to a relatively high standard of living. It was all the more difficult to bear because of the boom in agriculture which had coincided with the Napoleonic wars, when every possible effort had been made at central and local government level to persuade farmers to grow more food. In many places the very character of agriculture had been changed. Considerable capital had been sunk in making land more productive, and normally profitable crops sacrificed to plant those which were necessary to sustain the country in the years of crisis.

In the eighteen-forties and eighteen-fifties, when the expansion of London was approaching its peak, when the railways had already begun to carry Londoners to homes on the outer fringe, when coach services were remarkably well organized, making it possible to travel by road from the suburbs of London every day, some places within twelve miles of Charing Cross actually showed a decrease in population. That was a token of the gravity of the crisis which faced agriculturists in even such a specially favoured district as the Home Counties. The crisis precipi-tated what was destined to be the final change of farming emphasis in Greater London, a change-over from arable land to pasture land and market gardens by farmers who had maintained the traditional staple crops on their land or had changed over to them during the Napo-leonic wars. Little more corn was grown in the Home Counties after 1850 except crops to serve as animal feeding stuff so as to obviate the necessity of buying expensive hay or substitutes for it to feed stock during the winter months.

The demand for milk was increasing. From 1850 large dairy farms competed with housing for the land available. Islington was especially well known for its dairy herds and dairy produce until nearly the end of the nineteenth century. Even in the twentieth century places such as Harrow, Beckenham and Sidcup had their large and profitable herds. Inevitably until there was a genuine network of motor roads milk distribution had to be partly on a local basis, even though the railways played a part. The dairy farmer's object was to supply his own suburb and export to central London whatever surplus was left over. It is not surprising that milk was regarded as a luxury in many of the poorer eastern districts of London, even though the reclaimed marshes of Dagenham and Rainham provided ideal pasturage for cows.

This major change was the last in a series which had begun when the farms in what are now London suburbs began to exploit the possibilities of selling their produce for profit to the people of nearby London. That happened very early, although it must be remembered that in the Middle Ages hundreds of the people of London had their plot of land to cultivate outside the city walls. Self-sufficiency was the ideal of London as well as of every other town. Two factors combined to prevent the ideal from being realized for long after the twelfth century. One was the rapid growth of the population, the other the wastage of agricultural land for necessary building outside the walls. Directly these processes had upset the balance there was a golden opportunity for the commercial farmer. Hay for the horses of London and corn for its people were the first requisites, and these continued to be the staple crops for hundreds of years. As transport improved, however, particularly as country roads became passable at all seasons of the year, these commodities could be imported from farther afield and there was a gradual change-over from hay and corn to market garden produce, fresh fruit and vegetables, for which there was an ever-increasing demand.

The canals and then the railways, and finally the roads, made all and every difference to food distribution. The Grand Junction Canal made it possible to bring the agricultural produce of the midlands to the very doorstep of London. The railways and the roads in their several ways brought fresh fruit and vegetables to the London markets, so that they could be consumed the day after they were gathered a hundred miles away. Just as the railways and the roads have created the sprawling metropolis by providing facilities for transport between people's homes and their places of work, so they have made possible the supply of food for the many millions of people who live in this vast built-up area. The rapidly increasing trade done in Covent Garden Market since its inception in the nineteenth century is not only a token of the large number of people requiring its products but of the smaller area within Greater London available for production and, therefore, of the smaller quantity of fruit and vegetables grown locally in the suburbs.

The fact that agriculture was virtually the only important industry of

Greater London until the latter part of the eighteenth century made it inevitable that the most important towns outside London (and its immediate suburbs such as Westminster, Southwark and Finsbury) should be the market towns. And very flourishing these towns were throughout the later Middle Ages and into modern times. Some of the fifteenth- and sixteenth-century markets are continued in the present century. Romford market and Kingston market, to name two almost at random, still attract vast crowds of shoppers, some of them eager to find a bargain but most of them following tradition without any special thought of economy. It is scarcely an exaggeration to say that the markets of the towns in the outer zone of Greater London are super-markets offering almost every conceivable kind of merchandise for sale, with the accent still on market garden produce, though little of it is locally grown. When the traditional market in the open air has been abandoned, the covered market may be a poor substitute for lovers of tradition but in practice it is just as popular, its character not changed in the slightest by its transference from the market square to the market hall.

The greatest development of local industry in the eighteenth century took place in the communities near the banks of the Thames and its navigable tributaries. One has to think of the Thames and its tributaries not only as means of transport but as the only available source of power to drive the machinery of corn-mills and every other industrial operation. The windmill was important throughout the country but it was always the poor relation of the water-mill, and this was especially true in the eighteenth century. A great deal of labour was expended on the excavation and maintenance of mill-streams, and in at least one instance, in the parish of Isleworth, the existing river, the Bourne, which proved inadequate to drive the requisite number of mill-wheels, was relieved by the 'building' of a new river from the Crane across Hounslow Heath. That considerable feat of river engineering was completed in the sixteenth century. The mills worked by the new river were still operating three hundred years later, though by then steam-engines had been installed. Thus the Isleworth manor mill, which became known as Kidd's mill, was not demolished until 1941. In the nineteenth century it was reputed to be one of the largest flour-mills in the country.

The new river, known as the Duke's river because it was a project financed by the Dukes of Northumberland, served mills of many other kinds in the seventeenth and eighteenth centuries. There was a well-known copper-mill and a paper-mill in existence by 1607. Later in the same century there was a powder-mill which provided some of the needs of the Commonwealth army. The warlike traditions of this part of the Thames valley were continued by the nineteenth-century Bedfont gunpowder-mills on the River Crane.

This important centre of early industry reached its peak of development about 1769, when the Isleworth calico-mills were opened. This venture did not last far into the following century.

Before the Industrial Revolution reaction to local industries being established was not always favourable. For instance, fears were frequently expressed that the gunpowder from the mills of Isleworth, which was loaded into barges, might cause an explosion, a recurring theme in the relations between the village people, the lessees of the mills and the lord of the manor. There are records of a proposal to erect a limekiln on the banks of the Thames between Brentford and Twickenham as early as the seventeenth century, but the proposal was abandoned, apparently because a petition was presented to the lord of the manor by the local people on the ground that the place was too fair for so foul an employment, a quite remarkable sentiment in the practical politics of the seventeenth century.

If the Thames provided the power for more of Greater London's mills than all its tributaries together (a statement which is probably true), several of the tributary streams were put to extremely good use. The mills along their banks were just as important to the communities which grew up by the Lea, the Brent and other tributaries. South of the Thames many mills were worked by the Cray, the Ravensbourne and the Wandle. It is only ten miles from the head of the Wandle to its mouth. It may well be true, as one historian has said, that it had a more extensive commerce than is known in the same compass of any stream in the kingdom. The Domesday Survey shows that in the eleventh century there were thirteen corn-mills in the valley. By the beginning of the nineteenth century there were nearly forty mills manufacturing a wide variety of products, though even then the majority were still flour-mills.

Wandsworth owes its industrial importance to the Wandle. Calico bleaching was a famous industry of early origin, to which printing was added before the end of the eighteenth century, when a single mill employed more than two hundred people. The mills which manufactured dyestuffs were noted in the sixteenth century and continued in operation into the nineteenth. There was an iron-mill where cannon were manufactured on a large scale, and the mill was famous for its mechanical hammer, which weighed six hundred pounds. When steam-power was replacing water-power some of the mills continued obstinately to use the traditional source of power. A few were converted to steam-power, their giant water-wheels coming finally to rest and rusting away, but the majority were left untenanted when their owners built new premises to house the newfangled machines. A few became private residences. In all the circumstances it is remarkable that so many have survived, a few of them magnificent examples of eighteenth-century architecture.

Enfield is another important town in the Greater London area which owes its early industrial fame to the neighbouring river's water-mills. In 1653 emissaries of the Long Parliament negotiated for the use of a group of mills on the banks of the Lea near Enfield to make gunpowder.

This powder-mill was the direct forerunner of the nineteenth-century small arms factory known by 1823 as the Royal Armoury Mills, which produced the world-famous Lee-Enfield rifle a century later.

The few windmills which can be seen today are without exception badly mutilated. Repair has robbed them of their original character. But they are genuine enough and some, well restored like Arkley Mill and Upminster Mill and (essentially members of any company of London mills if only because of their strange position) the mill on Wimbledon Common, and that still more improbable one re-equipped with sails in 1964 at the back of Brixton's Blenheim Gardens.

Apart from milling, brewing and brick-making were the staple industries of English communities. Brewing goes back into the Middle Ages. There were brewhouses in the vicinity of almost every sizable community before Tudor times, like the one at Brentford bridge, which was well established in the reign of Henry VII. Brickworks are a more recent feature of the countryside, since the use of bricks in building was not reintroduced much before the end of the fifteenth century (they had been widely used more than a thousand years before in Roman Britain).

Once established, however, brick-making as an industry made rapid strides. All over the Greater London area it was found more economic to build the great number of new houses required in the seventeenth and eighteenth centuries in brick rather than in the traditional materials of timber and stone. No doubt the poverty of south-east England in natural building material induced Sir Christoper Wren to encourage the opening of new and enlarged quarries in the Isle of Portland to supply the material for St Paul's Cathedral. The ever-increasing demand for bricks brought great prosperity to some communities which had rich deposits of brick earth in their vicinity. In the Erith and Crayford districts the scars of the brickfields are a present reminder of the industry, but until brick-making became a rationalized industry centred in Bedfordshire and a few other especially favoured localities in the nineteenth century, small brickfields were worked in almost every part of the Greater London area. One of the first instances positively recorded of brick-making was at Syon Abbey, where the Abbess contracted with a tenant for the supply of 12,000 bricks a year, some of which were used in erecting the conventual buildings of the Abbey. The Syon Abbey brickfield was the forerunner of several others in the district, especially in the neighbourhood of Heston, where the unemployment of brick-workers during the winter months was a local problem as late as 1834 and where brick-making continued until the beginning of the twentieth century.

Londoners have been fishermen at every period. When supplying London with an adequate and regular supply of food was a major preoccupation, fish caught from boats plying from the wharves of the City made a substantial contribution to its food supply. Billingsgate, for instance, has traditions as a fish market or reception centre going back at least to the eleventh century. From the time that the land north of the Thames belonged to the kingdom of the East Saxons and that south of the river to the kingdom of Kent fishing was carried on as an essential prerequisite to a well-fed life by the people of the communities which were established along both banks of the river, including Bermondsey, Greenwich, Crayford and Dartford on the south bank, Dagenham and Barking on the north. The presence of extensive marshland, much of it undrained, acted as a barrier between many of the settlements of south Essex and the river, but Barking was a fishing port from the earliest times and contributed more than any other place to the supply of fish for the London market.

In the seventeenth century, when the Thames was famous for its salmon, Barking was reputed to be one of Britain's greatest fishing ports. When Daniel Defoe was 'viewing the sea coast of this county [Essex]' he travelled from Stratford to Barking, which he described as 'a large market town chiefly inhabited by fishermen whose smacks ride in the Thames, from whence their fish is sent to London to the market at Billingsgate by small boats'.

This was an important industry, on which the prosperity of Barking largely depended. There was clearly a market for fish greater than could be supplied by the fishing grounds of the Thames itself. The problem was to catch the fish and bring the cargo back fresh enough to be sold. About 1800 a Barking vessel sailed for the first time with a hold full of water into which the fish were thrown as soon as they were hauled aboard and kept alive until the ship returned to port. This was regarded as a great innovation at the time.

The first major step towards transforming the local fishing into a national industry was the use of ice for the preservation of the fish. This enabled fishing vessels to be away from port for a week and return with their catch in better condition than those working without ice after two days. Ice is a much more durable commodity than most people imagine. The Barking firm which pioneered the new kind of fishing realized this and incidentally created a new agricultural industry in the surrounding parishes. Many of the low-lying fields in what had previously been undrained marshland were flooded regularly in the season of autumn rains. Others were flooded artificially when the harvest had been cut, or when cattle grazing in them had had to be withdrawn to drier pastures. At the first sharp frost of winter the local farmers collected the ice which had formed on the flooded fields, stacked it in carts, and drove into Barking to sell it to the fishing firm, which stored it in specially insulated ice-houses so that, unbelievable as it sounds, it lasted throughout the following summer. Contemporary accounts tell how at times of heavy frost there was an unbroken queue of carts waiting to deliver ice, reaching from the wharves through the whole of the town into the countryside. Nature was helped by opening the sluice-gates controlling the river above the town so that the marshes were flooded at the first high tide. The average price of ice was about six shillings a cart-load, but much better prices were obtained when winter came late and every extra pound was valuable to the fisheries.

Another means adopted to speed delivery was to send carrier cutters to the place where the trawler fleets were fishing and transfer the fish from the trawlers to the cutters by small boats. At its largest the Short Blue Fleet of Barking numbered 220 vessels. No other fishing fleet is recorded in the early nineteenth century with more than a hundred vessels. The carrier cutters of Barking were surprisingly fast vessels. In the early summer they abandoned their activities with the fishing fleet to make a voyage to Spain to bring back the first Spanish fruit to England. As the first fruit fetched a high price in the London market, this early summer trip became a race, the captain of the winning boat being given a handsome present by the owners. The race continued every year until steam superseded sail.

Steam fishing boats and the railways combined to sound the death knell of Barking and other smaller towns along the Thames as fishing ports. It became cheaper and more convenient to land the fish at coastal ports and send them to London by rail in ice-boxes. The Barking fleet was transferred to Yarmouth. In 1899 the fishing port of Barking ceased to exist.

Fishing was for long a staple occupation of the people of the settlements upstream from London and in the valley of the Lea. Twickenham, Kingston and Teddington all had important fisheries, but these tended to die out when transport made the supply of sea food a practical proposition. The value of freshwater fish was discounted for many generations until it recovered part of its popularity in the present century.

Brentford was one of the fishing centres upstream which had more than local importance. In 1800 at least a hundred families were supported by fishing, but soon afterwards there was a decline. The first record of the fishing industry in Brentford is a grant in 1313 by the Bishop of London to his cook for maintaining the weir. It is probably no exaggeration to say that fishing for profit rather than subsistence lasted here for five hundred years.

Teddington, in addition to its fisheries, enjoyed more than its share of industry from Tudor times to the nineteenth century. Its association with linen-bleaching lasted for the whole of the latter half of the eighteenth century. When this industry declined its place was taken by wax-bleaching and candle-making. A commentator writing in 1831 says that the area under wax in the summer approached four acres and that 200,000 pounds of wax were bleached annually. This appears to have been the largest establishment of its kind in England and prospered for nearly a century.

Inevitably boat-building was an activity of many settlements by the banks of the Thames from early times, but no local industry approached the importance of that of Barking in the construction of estuary and deep-sea fishing boats. Elsewhere boat-yards before the nineteenth century were small and in terms of labour employed unimportant, only coming into their own with the popularity of fishing as a hobby in the nineteenth century and the vast increase in pleasure boating at places such as Richmond and Twickenham.

Though devoid of minerals, the London Basin is rich in deposits of sand and gravel. Many of the district's longest established commercial operations are concerned with the extractive industries associated with them. The Woolwich beds, which are the main feature of the geology of the area to the south-east of London, are a mixture of clays, sands and gravels, all three of which have served many useful purposes during the last three or four hundred years. Downriver towards Crayford and Erith the chalk of the downs is near the surface. During the nineteenth century sand and gravel were being extracted there in vast quantities, as they still are, while the chalk quarries which had been in use from the Middle Ages were still being used to provide material for the Thames wall.

The extensive use of flint in medieval church building is an indication of how long and how intensively the chalk has been quarried. Even the Chislehurst caves, to which all kinds of romantic stories had been attached, turn out to be chalk workings of great age and extent, though surprisingly little is known of them. So far as the 'quarrying' of gravel and the like from the neighbourhood of the Thames is concerned, all who know the river meadows on the Surrey bank between Richmond and Kingston have seen for themselves the devastating effect on the landscape which these activities can produce. They have seen, too, the considerable and not unsuccessful efforts which have been made to restore the landscape. In the early years of the present century the scars on the face of the land near Ham were comparable, though on a small scale, with those caused by open-cast coal-mining in the midlands, and did not heal so readily.

The Colne valley was developed in much the same way after the opening of the Grand Junction Canal; its natural resources, hitherto barely tapped, proved the foundation of its nineteenth-century prosperity, and indirectly enabled it to make the tremendous strides which it took during the next 150 years, to become a highly industrialized part of Greater London.

The geological formation of the district, which is unusual, gives a clue to this early development. To the south of Uxbridge the subsoil is brick earth overlying deposits of sand and gravel. To the north there are also large deposits of gravel near the flood plain of the river. Beyond the gravel deposits and the clay which forms the subsoil of the rest of the valley the chalk which forms the bedrock of the Chiltern

Hills come very near the surface. As soon as canal transport was available a number of sand and gravel pits were opened. These have supplied the raw material for the manufacture of various concrete products. The high silica content of the flints in the gravel deposits make possible the manufacture of the well-known Uxbridge flint bricks, while the chalk has been used in many local industries, such as the production of distemper and agricultural lime.

An interesting postscript has been written to this economically valuable use of local raw materials. The scarred landscape, with large unsightly areas of pits half filled with water, did not trouble the people of the early part of the nineteenth century, but as the population increased and there arose a greater awareness of natural beauty, the existence of such scars became a matter of disquiet. The Uxbridge Urban District Council, and after it the Borough Council, solved this local problem remarkably well. It acquired a number of these areas of lagoon or dry-bed pits, utilized them for controlled tipping of refuse, and subsequently restored the land either for recreational or agricultural purposes. Once the worst of the scars had been removed in this way, the council imposed conditions on companies engaged in the mineral working to ensure adequate after-treatment of the land by the companies concerned.

So far as general manufacturing industry is concerned, the City of London was the principal centre until the growth of its commercial activities forced industry beyond its walls. Even then industry lingered on into the Victorian era and is still as firmly established as ever in the districts which lie immediately to the east of the City. In many cases Dutch, Flemish and Italian craftsmen laid the foundations of industries which were successful for several centuries. In Tudor times pottery and glass were two of the City's specialities, but everything for the home, from pins to furniture, was made in the City workshops.

In the seventeenth century there are numerous references to London knives, which were regarded as the best in the world. By then, too, the reputation of London leather work had spread far beyond the confines of Britain. Even during the commercial expansion of the eighteenth century clothes, furniture and tableware were all being made in London, while just outside the City boundary Spitalfields was famous for its silk, Shoreditch for its furniture. Chelsea china had a brief but glorious career. Battersea enamels reached a surprisingly high standard, Fulham was noted for its stoneware and Lambeth, like Chelsea, for its china. By then, however, the bulk of London's industries had found their way across the bridge into Southwark, which became the City's workshop.

The outward spread of industrial activity was made necessary by the multiplication of wholly commercial premises in the City and by the increasing population, which made production essential on a larger scale than was possible in the City's craft factories. It was given additional impetus by the increased facilities for delivery consequent on the revolutions in transport in the nineteenth and twentieth centuries.

Until the nineteenth century goods transport (except for local hauls) meant transport by water. The improved roads of the eighteenth century were a great help in bringing goods needed by Londoners to the metropolis, but cattle were still driven into town by drovers to supply meat. Generally it remained cheaper and easier to bring goods by water, whether from abroad or from other parts of England. The capacity of the workshops of London and Southwark was not great enough to supply the whole of the Greater London area by the beginning of the nineteenth century, and the enlargement of the London docks, to which reference has been made in Chapter 12, was made necessary by this development. A high proportion of the trade passed through the London docks but many riverside towns had their own wharves. This is still true.

Few would think of Erith as a port, yet 10,000-ton ships still use it and are accommodated at a pier which was completed in 1957 and fitted out with all the latest machinery, including eight-ton electric cranes. Coal is the main import and it is handled with the help of modern coal-discharging plant. A great number of vessels also use Anchor Bay Wharf, with regular sailings in cargo to Holland, Belgium and Sweden. Erith is an important link in the vast system of the Port of London.

It is hard to realize in these well-ordered days of the twentieth century, when the vagaries of the Thames as a highway of commerce have been overcome, that the position was very different less than a century ago. In 1812 a ship canal, prospectively named the Royal Clarence Canal, was seriously considered to link Woolwich Arsenal with the Erith reach, the reason for the plan being that the river was so shallow that it would not float ships drawing eighteen feet of water except at spring tides. Even in 1885 John Harris, a knowledgeable author, commenting on the twenty-foot earthen banks along the river from Greenwich to the Isle of Grain, could say in all seriousness: 'Without this grand bulwark the maritime commerce of London (such as it is in the present day) would be destroyed', and that quite apart from the 'many miles of rich fertile land which would be lost'. The correlation between the river walls and navigation appears now faintly ridiculous, but it is at least true that it was by no means easy to maintain a navigable channel right up to the City of London.

The River Lea was an artery of commerce, second only to the Thames before the Grand Junction Canal was built. It provided a direct link between the towns and villages of east Middlesex and Hertfordshire and the Port of London. It was always regarded as important at parliamentary level. In the sixteenth century steps were taken to make it navigable as far as Ware, and in 1580 great resentment was expressed by Enfield carriers at their consequent loss of trade.

The City of London claimed navigation rights from time immemorial. When a Lea Navigation Commission was appointed in the reign of Henry V it was laid down that 'in all commissions touching the water of Lea the Mayor should be a member'. Every right carries corresponding obligations, and it was by virtue of their navigation rights that the City of London was required by Parliament to make the river navigable to Ware in 1751.

The New Cut was completed in 1789, not without further disturbance caused by the Enfield and Edmonton carriers and the commoners who feared that the river would inundate the land on which they held commoners' rights. Matters reached such a pitch that the Commission of Sewers was charged specifically with the duty of dealing with sabotage and preventing further acts of violence. However, the New Cut was a great success and became known as the River Lea Navigation or Barge River. It made a large contribution to trade between the City of London and the northern marches of Greater London during the nineteenth century. Smeaton (of lighthouse fame) was one of the engineers engaged in surveying the land in 1768 for the work which shortened the course for barges by seven miles between Ware and London. In 1803 Rennie, the designer of London bridge and the finest of Waterloo bridges, was commissioned to report on the possibility of flooding the lower part of the Lea Valley by the building of dams as a defence against invasion.

In retrospect the scheme appears a curiously ill-conceived one, especially now that so much of the lower valley has been built over, but it was no stranger than many of the emergency measures considered at the height of the panic caused by Napoleon's continental victories. By then the Lea Navigation was being used intensively for the carriage of goods, especially timber and agricultural products from the fertile countryside through which it flowed, a countryside that once the market gardening industry had come into existence had a major exportable surplus.

The building of the canals and the canalization of existing rivers altered the picture completely. The Grand Junction Canal, like the Lea Navigation, made a real contribution to London's supply problem, reaching Paddington and Brentford before 1806. The two branches to Paddington and to Brentford were closely linked economically, and for a few decades dominated the goods transport of this part of Middlesex. The Paddington branch had a regular passenger service in the eighteen-twenties, plying between the Paddington terminus and Uxbridge, with a stop at Greenford Green, but it was only a summer service. It afforded a pleasant way of spending a day for the people of Paddington (and of London too), but was never a commercial service competing with the stagecoaches.

The canalization of the Thames above Teddington was as important as the building of the Grand Junction Canal, while the Regent Canal and the several canals linking the dock areas with the populous districts on both sides of the Thames completed a network which, but for the development of the railways, might have been extended still farther. Canals held their own through the early decades of the railway age, and today still play a part in the complex system of industrial transport.

The canals, the railways and the roads combined to make possible the cataclysm in industry and commerce which took place during the nineteenth century. A phenomenon quite separate and distinct from the industrial growth of a West Ham affected Greater London. Industry began to take root in all the communities within the complex. Hackney became famous for its silk factory, which employed seven hundred people. Enfield developed a flourishing textile industry. Small factories producing furniture and household goods, shoes and clothing, were established in many of the larger towns. Long-established industries like the paper-making industry of the Cray valley, centred on St Mary Cray, increased their production and adopted new machinery. Timber brought by ship to the Port of London and carried upstream by barges was off-loaded at riverside wharves such as Kingston, where there were usually sawmills nearby producing wood for making furniture and a host of other purposes.

The nineteenth century, however, was only a foretaste of what the twentieth century had in store. As motor road transport made communication by land still easier, industry was attracted to the new roads on the outskirts of London, to the Great West Road and the Kingston by-pass. In the twenty years between the two world wars Greater London became far more industrial than anyone would have thought possible at the turn of the century. Industrial development centred on Dagenham along the Essex bank of the Thames, and the opening of trading estates such as that of Park Royal posed new transport problems.

Many have commented on the waste of time and effort involved in so many people travelling daily into central London in the morning and home again in the evening. It has almost escaped notice that central London is not the only 'metropolis'. The Middlesex borough of Acton, which included part of the Park Royal estate, had a resident population of 65,000 in 1961, comprising 22,000 private households. Yet there was in that year a daily influx of 50,000. There appears to be no real solution of the problem. A remedy would only have been found if Greater London had been planned a hundred years ago. The manufacturing companies, many of which have moved to the London area from the north country, are reaping the benefits of operation in close proximity to what is incomparably the biggest market in the world. Any major change now presents insuperable obstacles.

14. Royal Green to Green Belt

HENRY VIII started it all when he confirmed the right of the people of London to practise archery in Finsbury Fields. The idea of the common people having a right to land for sport or recreation was born. Subsequent attempts to enclose Finsbury Fields were vigorously and for long successfully resisted. By custom, too, the fen or moor to the north of the City walls was set aside for the pleasure of Londoners. It doubtless achieved this distinction because before it was drained it was wholly unsuitable for agriculture. After it had been drained it continued by the right conferred by custom to be regarded as a place where Londoners could walk on a summer's evening in sight of the protection of the walls. By the beginning of the seventeenth century it had been planted with trees and laid out with paths crossing it, so that it looked, one imagines, very like a modern recreation ground.

There were other 'fields' set aside by custom for the use of Londoners when their work was done. The confirmation by James I of the citizens' rights in Lincoln's Inn Fields was noted in Chapter 6. The trees that were planted when the fields were laid out as gardens are still looking very beautiful, though some of them unhappily are beginning to decay.

The word 'custom' has been used more than once in these first paragraphs. Custom was really the only ground of claim which the citizen had to the use of green fields. That is not surprising. English law is based on customary practice. Even in the twentieth century in order to establish a public right of way it is necessary to prove that its use as such has been customary 'within living memory'.

London gained its green in the following centuries chiefly by establishing a customary right or privilege. It was all quite haphazard and there was certainly no coherent plan at any time until the nineteenth century to provide open spaces for the enjoyment of the people. However, except in the residential areas which sprang from nothing after the Industrial Revolution, London is an uncommonly green city—not, that is, the City itself but the area from the City westward to the fashionable West End and to what were the outer suburbs until the nineteenth century—Knightsbridge and Kensington.

The Earl of Southampton who obtained a licence to develop his Bloomsbury estate during the Commonwealth set a precedent which was followed by the speculators of the seventeenth and eighteenth, and even the nineteenth centuries in the well-to-do suburbs. Southampton House was, as we have seen, the centre-piece of an urban landscape which included a large central square and garden. Bloomsbury Square is still a garden. So are many other squares in Bloomsbury, Mayfair, St Marylebone, Belgravia, Pimlico, Westminster, Kensington, Chelsea, and northward to Finsbury and Islington (with a few also in south and east London).

These seventeenth-, eighteenth- and early nineteenth-century square gardens are still a most important and attractive feature of the London scene, but many have an aesthetic rather than a practical value for the man in the street. Originally access to them was gained by keys supplied only to residents in the square. That is still true of many in the West End and Pimlico, and even in Kensington. Some of the gardens, however, are open to the public, including Russell Square, Soho Square and Leicester Square.

The royal parks make up a high proportion of London's green beauty. All started, as their name implies, as royal demesnes. All are now administered for the benefit of the public, though the royal family has its own small but charming park or garden protected by high walls at the rear of Buckingham Palace. This is a sylvan scene observed by few except those invited to royal garden parties and those who work on the top floors of Portland House.

Charles I set the example of 'customary access' when he thought it would be a good idea to mix with his subjects in the gardens of Whitehall Palace. Very soon specific invitations became unnecessary and the bowling green of Whitehall was treated in spirit, if not in name, as a public meeting place.

Hyde Park is historically the oldest of the royal parks. The manor of Hyde was a royal manor granted by the sovereign to the monks of Westminster and valued by them because it gave them a supply of fresh water derived from the River Westbourne which flowed through it, and from a spring at the Westminster end of what is now the Serpentine. When the Abbey of Westminster was dissolved the manor reverted to the Crown but in 1637 King Charles I, perhaps the greatest friend that Londoners have ever had, made it freely available to the people as a place of recreation. And so it has remained ever since.

The other royal friend of Londoners in this context was Queen Caroline, wife of George II, who had Kensington Gardens laid out and was responsible for the improvement of other royal demesnes, such as St James's Park and the Green Park. During her lifetime Kensington Gardens remained a royal pleasaunce. The Doge of Genoa sent her tortoises and she herself was responsible for introducing red squirrels. Foxes and deer were hunted in the gardens. But soon the royal family felt an obligation to share the gardens with their people and permission was given for the public to be admitted on Sundays (excluding only sailors, soldiers and servants in livery). These exceptions caused deep resentment, which was aired in the daily press. As 'fashionable' people went for their Sunday morning stroll in the gardens they were barracked by large numbers of liveried servants and by members of the services. Nevertheless a precedent had been set and it was not long before the gardens were open to all, whether they were in uniform or not.

St James's Park, with its extension Green Park, was part of the land bought by Henry VIII from Eton College. Only a small portion of that land was laid out as a park, but there was a farm in St James's Fields which Charles II enclosed with a brick wall, frequently broken down by the citizens of Westminster. Although privileged people were admitted, the struggle between the Crown and the people over St James's Park continued longer than in the case of other royal parks. By 1749 the wall was so completely breached that it became impossible to limit the number of people entering. However, repairs were carried out at frequent intervals.

When Boswell came to London in 1762 St James's Park was still nominally open only to those who had received royal permission to enjoy it. The gates were locked at 10 p.m., but six thousand five hundred keys had been issued and many of these had been duplicated. The duplicates were in the possession of hundreds of prostitutes and of large numbers of men requiring their services. It is not surprising that the royal parks won an unenviable reputation towards the end of the eighteenth century, a reputation which incidentally survived into the twentieth century, when they were freely open to all.

Regent's Park, laid out by Nash in 1812, was thrown open to the public in 1838, with no nonsense about keys or, as the people of the time called it, favouritism. That finally set the seal on the popular enjoyment of the royal parks. The full and unrestricted enjoyment of these beautiful though man-made landscapes within a few minutes' drive of the centre of London has been accepted as an inalienable right ever since.

The royal parks of central London are only a small part of the 'royal green'. Richmond Park, the Home Park of Hampton Court Palace, and Bushy Park formed a green belt reaching from Kingston Vale through Kingston into what is still country long before any government department had thought of the magic name 'green belt'.

Richmond Park originated as an enclosure of more than two thousand acres made by Charles I in 1637. The King stocked the park with fallow and red deer, of which there are still considerable herds. Bushy Park and the Home Park formed part of the gigantic landscape garden of Hampton Court Palace laid out by Sir Christopher Wren, his assistants and his successors. Although the Long Water of the Home

R

Park is wholly artificial, the corresponding water feature of Richmond Park, the Pen Ponds, was created out of disused clay pits—the pits from which it is said that clay for making the bricks of the park wall was obtained.

Public access to Bushy Park and Richmond Park was not secured without a struggle. When Charles I enclosed Richmond Park complaints were made that an immemorial right of way had been obstructed. In practice the right of way was maintained, access to the park being by means of step-ladders. For more than a century this makeshift arrangement proved satisfactory. Few people in any case used the right of way, and anyone who wished to use the park for clandestine assignments was able to do so. Then in 1751 Princess Amelia, George III's aunt, was granted the office of Ranger of Richmond Park. That was a fatal move so far as the royal family was concerned. The admirable Princess Amelia was the embodiment of all the qualities which are usually ascribed to Mrs Grundy. She ordered the gate-keepers to remove the step-ladders and stated that she regarded it as shocking that ordinary people should be allowed access, for whatever purpose. The reply of the people of the adjoining towns and villages was to break down the walls at various points, but these were rebuilt at the Ranger's expense. A legal action was brought against the Princess without avail, but in 1758 an action by a Richmond brewer against one of the gate-keepers for refusing access to a right of way was successful. Admission to Richmond Park has never been queried since then.

It was much the same in the case of Bushy Park. Apart from the Grand Avenue, a triumphal way leading to the palace, the park had been enclosed as a hunting preserve but little hunting was done, and in practice the people of the surrounding communities had more or less free access. In this case it was a shoemaker of Hampton Wick who asserted the public rights, a craftsman by the name of Tim Bennett. He brought an action against the then Ranger, Lord Halifax, but the action was never taken to court. Lord Halifax gave way and 'customary access' was once more vindicated. There was a right of way, too, through the Home Park. The whole park became 'public' when Hampton Court was no longer used as a royal residence.

The agitation about access to the royal parks was slight compared with that which led to the preservation of Greater London's heaths and commons.

Hampstead Heath is the most country-like of the open spaces within a few miles of the centre of London. To the uninitiated it seems as though, as a modern guide-book says, 'it is in its picturesque natural state'. It is, of course, 'natural' compared with the contrived artificiality of a Regent's Park or a Hyde Park. But the descriptions of writers who knew it a hundred years ago show how much it has changed in appearance, as well as in the use that is made of it.

The Heath as we know it only came into existence in 1871, when

240 acres became vested as a public open space. Additions were made to it as opportunity offered. Like Epping Forest, it is a permanent monument to the enthusiasm and single-mindedness of the many people whose efforts have contributed over a long period to ensure a 'green belt' on the very threshold of London. Though Ken Wood is fenced to protect wild life, unlike the Heath which is unfenced and always open, it forms an integral part of the Heath for the tens of thousands of Londoners who enjoy their week-end walks across it. The wood was purchased with grants made by the London County Council and the neighbouring local authorities in 1924, while the Kenwood House estate was bequeathed to the nation by Lord Iveagh in 1927.

It is fascinating to read what informed people thought about the Heath in 1869, just two years before the first part became public (though even then it was customary to use it as an open space for fresh air and exercise). William Howitt, writing in that year, deplores the changes which had overtaken it in his own lifetime. He says: 'It is greatly diminished from what it once was and greatly defaced with the destruction of trees, the uprooting of its luxurious furze and broom, and the carting away of its heathery surface for gravel and sand.'

At the beginning of the nineteenth century the catalogue of plants on the Heath included lily of the valley, the bilberry and wild raspberry in abundance. As Howitt says: 'How terribly must the surface of the Heath have been ravaged and deteriorated within the last fifty years,' and goes on 'only by the jealous care of its inhabitants has it been saved from the process of enclosure which has swallowed so many of the open spaces around the metropolis so vitally essential to the health of its inhabitants'.

The difficulties which had to be overcome in order to ensure preservation were identical with those facing the planners of today. 'It is not to be wondered at that the lords of the manors, tempted by the enormous value which such open expanses have acquired as building land, should have exercised all their power and influence to appropriate them.' How many times has the same thing been said since London's outer 'green belt' was dedicated between the two world wars. Hampstead led the way in checking the monetary ambitions of the landowners. Local people, holding commoners' rights, started litigation, claiming rights as valid as those of the lord of the manor. These rights were upheld in the courts. The lord of the manor of Wimbledon resolved the problem by vesting the common in public trustees, but it was not quite so easy at Hampstead, where there was a great deal of feeling against the lord of the manor, Sir Thomas Wilson who, Howitt says, writing in Wilson's own lifetime, had made numerous attempts to beguile Parliament into sanctioning his desire for enclosure. It was only when the courts upheld the commoners' rights as being as valid as those of the lord not only at Wimbledon and Hampstead, but at Berkhamsted and elsewhere, that people began to realize that they really had the power to prevent the enjoyment of the commons being taken from them.

The success of the campaign to maintain the commons as open spaces turned on a maxim of common law, that the unrestricted enjoyment of property over a long period of years conferred a right to its continued enjoyment. This was construed more and more often as meaning that if the public had enjoyed the use of open land for an unspecified period their right to continue doing so could not be challenged and that, therefore, enclosure could not take place without the consent of the people of the neighbouring communities, even if the lord of the manor had the consent or even the support of the actual freeholders, copyholders and commoners. In the case of Hampstead it meant that none of the Heath could be enclosed without the consent of the people of Hampstead and Highgate. This constituted only a meagre assurance though it was a long step in the right direction. The difficulty was that the people of neighbouring communities were represented normally by their local councils, the members of which more often than not included the lord of the manor. Often through apathy enclosure took place, and Hampstead Heath could not be said to be saved until it was actually vested in the representatives of the public.

An Act of 1866 barred the enclosure of common land within fourteen miles of Charing Cross. That was a real milestone in the story of London Green, even though, like hundreds of other Acts regulating enclosure from the time of Elizabeth I, it has not always been observed. However, as a contemporary commentator reported with glee: 'It proved a serious obstacle to the inflated demands of Sir Thomas Wilson of around a million pounds for Hampstead Heath as advance on the building land value of the Heath to the Metropolitan Board of Works.' Even then it needed a prolonged inquiry in Chancery to ascertain Sir Thomas's real rights. The inquiry 'resulted in a fresh formal confirmation of the solid and inalienable claims of the public over all lands where they have for more than 30 years established a user'.

These public rights did not prove in practice to be as solid as the nineteenth-century planners hoped, but undoubtedly the Act of 1866 and the weight of public opinion prevented a great deal of speculation which might well have resulted in the disappearance of Hampstead Heath, and many others of London's present-day open spaces, as Bromley Common had ceased to exist only fifty years earlier.

Historical references to Hampstead Heath are unusually numerous because it was so near London and was skirted by the road to the north, as Hounslow Heath was skirted by the road to the west. Roger of Wendover, quoted by Matthew Paris, is the authority for saying that packs of wolves ranged over it in the thirteenth century, when it was considered too dangerous to cross at night. When the four-legged wolves were exterminated two-legged ones took their place and proved just as difficult to control. From the fourteenth century until, amazingly, the early part of the nineteenth century the Heath was the happy hunting ground of highwaymen and armed robbers of every kind, who preyed with remarkable success on travellers to and from the metropolis. It is easy to understand how brigands survived before there was an organized police force. Many of them were soldiers discharged after some warlike expedition. Later they were drawn from the slums of London, where there were plenty of people who preferred the risk of death by execution to the slow death of starvation.

It is more surprising, however, to find armed robbers still operating less than ten miles from Charing Cross in the nineteenth century. The *Gentleman's Magazine* for July 1803 recounts how a Mr and Mrs Orrell were driving in their chaise over Golders Green on their way to Hendon when they were stopped by a highwayman, who produced a pistol and demanded their money. Mr Orrell was obviously a tough man. While the highwayman held his pistol to his wife's head he jumped out of the chaise and disarmed the highwayman, who galloped off towards Hampstead. The highwayman was equally imperturbable. Foiled of this quarry he stopped the Hampstead stagecoach at Red Lion Hill and robbed its six passengers of more than £40, and then, in the words of the *Gentleman's Magazine*, 'although there were several persons passing at the time he rode coolly off'.

Most people who live near the Heath or visit it regularly know the Vale of Health and the discreet hostelry which provides a much-needed refreshment after a brisk walk from Highgate or Kenwood. What a palaver there was when it was built in the middle of the nineteenth century. It was seen as 'a monster public-house with a lofty tower and flag to attract the attention of strollers on Hampstead Heath, as a Tower of Babel in that formerly quiet spot, the Vale of Health'. It was said that it was reasonable for refreshment to be available for the numerous visitors who came to the Heath on Sundays and public holidays but that 'gin palaces on a Titan scale' should not be licensed where people resort for fresh air so 'converting the bosom of nature into a hot-bed of demoralization'. One commentator wrote that he could hear from his garden 'the continuous hubbub of the returning pleasure-seekers stretching all the way from the Heath itself to the bottom of Haverstock Hill, demonstrating the worst effects of the liquors which they had imbibed for the benefit of the excise duties and the damage of individual health'.

The 'demoralization' of the Vale of Health paled into insignificance when put against the contemplation of the fairs which had been held on Hampstead Heath for centuries before then and which were prohibited early in the nineteenth century because they 'drew so much dissolute company and produced such scenes of riot and gambling'. It is a comforting thought that the tradition of the Hampstead Heath fair is not entirely dead. The number of people thronging the fairground on a twentieth-century bank holiday would stagger the chroniclers of the Victorian age. And incidentally residents still complain that many of the visitors go home the worse for drink and 'make it impossible to enjoy the heath on a bank holiday'.

Primrose Hill rises sedately between Regent's Park and the heights of Hampstead like an advance guard of the Heath. It is in geological fact a foothill of London's northern heights and because it stands out to the south of them commands views over the Thames to the Surrey hills almost as extensive as those from the Heath itself. No one knows the origin of the name, though a Primrose Lane is recorded at least two hundred years ago and the district was well known for its wealth of primroses when all this part of London consisted of open fields. An early name of the hill is Barrow Hill and there was a nearby Barrow Farm. This led early antiquaries to speculate on whether a battle had been fought on the slopes of the hill and the dead interred on the spot under a mound of earth. If the name really referred to a barrow (and there is not the slightest trace of one today or any record of one having existed), it would be more likely to have been a Roman burial mound like the Bartlow Hills or the Dane John in Canterbury. Whatever the origin of the name, Primrose Hill was a very welcome addition to London Green because it makes it possible to walk from Portland Place to the Victorian terraces of Belsize Park without leaving the green except to cross one main road.

Hounslow Heath was never countryside to which residents resorted for fresh air and recreation as they did to Hampstead Heath. Without undue exaggeration it might be described as a perpetual nuisance and embarrassment to the people of Middlesex and to travellers bound for the west country. One reason for its neglect was that there was no town adjacent to it with enough inhabitants to make full use of it. Hounslow did not become a sizable town until the nineteenth century, while the vast expanse of the heath, together with its reputation of being the lurking place of highwaymen, were effective in keeping people away from it.

The original heath was roughly co-extensive with the area in which the subsoil is what is known as Taplow gravel. It was productive only of poor grassland rather than of the interesting and distinctive scenery of Hampstead Heath or even of Epping Forest. In the Middle Ages it may have covered as much as ten thousand acres but a good deal of enclosure took place between 1100 and 1500, including Hanworth Park about 1495. In the reign of Henry VIII it was surveyed and estimated still to cover between four thousand and five thousand acres, penetrating into the area of cultivated fields round Twickenham, Teddington, Feltham and Isleworth. In 1545 an Act was passed to enclose the whole heath, dividing it among the surrounding parishes, the manorial rights in most of which were held by the Crown.

This grandiose example of attempted Tudor enclosure, which if successful might well have added greatly to the revenues of the sovereign through an increase in the value of the manors, was as complete a failure as most of the other Tudor 'developments' of heathland and waste. All that was done—and even this was not completed for a hundred years or more after the Act was passed—was to establish parish or manorial boundary lines across the heath. The boundaries were of no practical significance. In the middle of the eighteenth century the heath still reached from Hampton church to Heath Row (that is, near the present London Airport).

It was one of the favourite hunting grounds of James I, who used parts of it to preserve game and seems to have treated it as an extension of the royal parks round Hampton Court Palace. It is significant that in 1629 the law was invoked to prohibit hunting except by royal licence, but soon after the heath fell out of favour as hunting country and assumed a rather strange military role. It was, of course, suitable for military reviews because it was relatively free of woodland and conveniently near to London. A number of reviews were held there during the seventeenth century. Then James II established a permanent camp, and this was maintained in succeeding reigns. A market was established in Hounslow expressly for the provisioning of the camp, or barracks as they became in 1793, when detachments of cavalry were quartered there, and were followed by infantry in the nineteenth century. Ultimately the camp became the nucleus of the headquarters of Eastern Command.

Several Enclosure Acts were passed between 1800 and 1820, and by 1830 almost all the heath was under cultivation except the area reserved for the military and about 150 acres which are still called Hounslow Heath. Even this is War Office property, though not used for many years for military purposes. Thus what might have been one of modern London's finest open spaces was whittled away because of the apathy of the people who might have benefited from it. Unsung and unlamented parts of it still fall within the twentieth-century 'green belt'. That can only be small consolation for its loss as permanent common land.

Wimbledon Common and Putney Heath, though ultimately saved, had a similarly chequered history before they became open spaces for the enjoyment of the people. Together they are more than a thousand acres in extent, making with the adjoining Richmond Park a 'lung' which belies its urban surroundings. Yet access to Wimbledon Common was restricted until 1864, when Earl Spencer was lord of the manor and found increasing pressure being brought on him to extend the commoners' rights. (These included the right to pasture cattle and pigs and to a limited extent to cut wood and take away gravel.) Nineteenth-century Wimbledon residents had little wish to cart away further gravel but, like the people of Hampstead, they were determined to translate these rights into something appropriate to the nineteenth century. Lord Spencer acknowledged the great changes which had occurred in recent years as a result of the growth of a 'suburban population in the neighbourhood and the grave responsibility which this put upon him as lord of the manor'.

The upshot was a private bill presented to Parliament proposing the sale of part of the common to provide funds to maintain the remainder, the appointment of trustees to supervise the common as an enclosed public park and the maintenance of the windmill site as a place where the lord of the manor could build himself a home. This bill provoked an outburst which Lord Spencer cannot have anticipated. The people of Putney joined with those of Wimbledon in opposing the idea that a part of the common land could be sold by the lord of the manor and with equal zest the idea of enclosing part of the common as a public park.

The battle was waged for six years, but in 1870 Lord Spencer abandoned the struggle, though not without profit to himself. He agreed to the conveyance of all his rights as lord of the manor over Wimbledon Common and Putney Heath to public trustees but claimed an annual payment equivalent to the income which he had derived from the common during the previous ten years.

A bill was presented to the House of Commons in 1871 and this duly became law. By this the whole area is administered by eight conservators, of whom five are elected by the local ratepayers and the other three appointed by the Home Secretary, the Minister of Works (and his assigns) and, most remarkably, the Minister of War. The payment to Lord Spencer and his descendants was agreed at £1,200 annually, raised from a special rate on houses situated within three-quarters of a mile of Wimbledon Common and Putney Heath, a rate, incidentally, which decreased according to the distance of the houses from the common. Tradition dies hard. The rate is still levied.

During the last half of the nineteenth century and the first decades of the present century London Green was augmented by a number of parks and public recreation grounds. The methods by which this end was achieved are implicit in the subject-matter of previous chapters but the way in which the problem was faced, often too late, is exemplified by the case of Bromley.

Bromley was, as we have seen, a small market town which became one of the most populous dormitory towns of Greater London within the space of fifty years. Its traditional place for recreation was the part of Bromley Common which immediately adjoined the lower end of the high street. This had been enclosed by the time the need for a 'lung' was recognized and was largely covered with villas. There was, however, in the centre of the town adjoining the White Hart Hotel a field which, by grace of the lord of the manor when the manor was held by the see of Rochester and afterwards, had been set aside for public recreation. Among the many ways in which it had served Bromley was as an early ground of the Bromley cricket club. However, the town had no title to the land and it was entirely due to the generosity of the then lord of the manor, a Mr Coles Child, that it was vested in the care of the local council. Mr Child chose the occasion of Queen Victoria's diamond jubilee in 1897 to present the land to the town on condition that it should be converted into a public garden.

There had also been great concern in Bromley about the fate of Martin's Hill, a local viewpoint commanding a magnificent vista of the valley of the Ravensbourne. The view from its summit reminded people that they were really living in the country in spite of the increasingly urban appearance of their neighbourhood. It was a perfect site for building and but for the organized agitation of the townspeople would almost certainly have been covered in bricks and mortar by the eighteen-seventies.

Rumours that it was being sold for building purposes provoked a campaign in the local newspaper, in which it was claimed that it was a 'blessed piece of land'. The point was made that although the freehold of the land was part of a manorial estate, there had been public usage of it from time immemorial. The argument did not in this case win the day, partly perhaps because a leasehold of the land had been sold by the lord of the manor to others. Accordingly a project was launched to purchase it for the town. Public subscription was inadequate to meet the price put on it by the proprietors and the scheme lapsed, although as a result of the outcry the land was not at the time sold for building purposes. Then in 1878 it was again put on the market. This time the local council acted with courage and purchased the land. Nine years later Queen Victoria's jubilee was made the pretext to purchase adjoining land, so that in the end the town had a fine park, which is even more useful now than it was at the turn of the century.

Many, but by no means all, the open spaces acquired for public use during the latter part of the nineteenth century were private parks or land designated as recreation grounds. Sydenham Wells Park, for instance, was a disused brickfield which it needed the prescience of the local council to visualize as the attractive open space it is today. The 120 acres of Finsbury Park were thrown open to the public in 1869 after a long tussle between conflicting interests. Battersea Park was opened in 1859, but this also represented the result of protracted endeavour. It will be a surprise to most people who enjoy its green lawns (quite apart from the area devoted to the Festival Gardens) to learn that it was built up with the help of debris from excavations for the St Katharine Dock.

During the early part of the twentieth century local authorities continued the good work that had been begun in the nineteenth, helped by the London County Council and the Corporation of the City of London. The latter body threw off its conservative mantle and played a major part in securing open spaces for the enjoyment of Londoners. So far as the local authorities were concerned the policy of providing open spaces was assisted to a material extent by the setting aside in 1935 of £2,000,000 from county funds for grants towards the cost of securing open spaces. The success of this scheme, which was promoted by Mr Herbert Morrison, was proved by the fact that within two years thirty thousand acres had been the subject of preservation orders, many landowners being compensated for refraining from the temptation to sell their property for building development. Quite apart from this vast acreage, the London County Council in the last years of its life maintained more than 6,500 acres of parks and open spaces which involved the capital expenditure of more than £3,000,000.

One of the ways in which local authorities catered for the needs of their ratepayers was by securing access to land outside their boundaries. An interesting example of such acquisitions was that by the Southwark Borough Council of Belair in Dulwich (in the Metropolitan Borough of Camberwell). It was planned primarily for hundreds of children, who were brought by bus to Belair from the crowded streets of Southwark for a day in the fresh air every week. The plan provoked some resentment among Dulwich people, who regarded the water meadows of Belair as their own heritage. But the scheme was a success, made easier in this case by the incorporation of Southwark and Camberwell in the new Greater London Borough No. 8 (Southwark).

The City of London was most active in the years immediately preceding the Local Government Act of 1888, which designated the new County of London and established the London County Council as the planning authority for the whole area. West Ham Park at Forest Gate was secured to Londoners by the efforts of the Corporation in 1873. In 1878 it acquired six thousand acres of the medieval Forest of Waltham, known today as Epping Forest. Seventy acres of Highgate Wood and the Queen's Park, Kilburn, were taken over in the next year and West Wickham Common in Kent in 1892. In 1880 it purchased Burnham Beeches, three years later the Coulsdon Commons. In addition Spring Park Wood was given to the Corporation in 1924.

Purchase by local authorities and gifts by landowners account for the principal open spaces in Greater London, but some areas have been secured by private subscription. One of the most interesting and beautiful of the latter kind of open space is Petts Wood, covering eighty-eight acres of thickly wooded land, which was acquired in 1927 as a memorial to William Willett, who is buried in Chislehurst churchyard and is best known as the inventor of summer time (in the sense that he set in motion the train of legislation which ended in the Summer Time Act of 1916).

The story of London Green is inevitably almost complete, because little land is left which can be acquired for recreational purposes. Its future lies not so much in making additions to it as in preserving what exists against pressure from whatever direction. Every acre of the old County of London is accounted for, but there are still a few hundred acres in the new Greater London which retain their agricultural tradition and have been converted neither into building estates nor into public parks.

These form an essential part of what is now known as the green belt, a phrase on the lips of every planner of the new London, though its precise implications are often overlooked. The Ministry of Town and Country Planning evokes Queen Elizabeth I as the originator of the green belt idea. Certainly in 1580 Good Queen Bess made a proclamation forbidding new building on any site within three miles of the City gates. In 1657 the Commonwealth Parliament was responsible for an Act requiring new houses within ten miles of London to be surrounded by at least four acres of open land. Needless to say, both these regulations were neglected and ultimately forgotten.

The idea was not revived until 1927, when the Greater London Regional Planning Committee was established. The purpose of this committee was to envisage methods of securing for London an outer belt of agricultural land to prevent further indiscriminate development. The result of this committee's deliberations was the Green Belt Act of 1938, when the work of the London County Council was recognized and grants were made available to the councils of the Home Counties towards the cost of acquiring land for inclusion in the 'green girdle'.

The net result of the Green Belt Act of 1938 and of the previous efforts of the London County Council is the dedication of nearly forty thousand acres, to which additions are still being made. Since the Second World War the Town and Country Planning Act of 1947, by laying it down that no land can be developed without permission, made it easier for local authorities to maintain a green belt simply by refusing permission for development. This Act allowed for compensation to be paid by the Government, thereby placing the financial responsibility for the maintenance of a green belt on central rather than local funds. Greater London's green belt came into real and one hopes permanent existence with the approval in 1959 of the official development plans for all the Home Counties.

Although the character of London's green belt, determined as it is by previous development, is principally that of a buffer against endless expansion and of a green interval between the outer fringe of Greater London and its satellite towns, some parts of it actually fall within the new Greater London. Hainault Forest is part of the green belt; so is the still green country to the east of Dagenham and south of Hornchurch as far as Rainham. In what was once Kent there is the greater part of the valley of the River Cray, with the Chislehurst Commons, the commons of Hayes and Keston, and the rolling country which extends in an almost unbroken belt from Biggin Hill to the valley of the Darent and includes unspoilt villages such as Downe, Cudham and Chelsfield. In what was Surrey there are the commons to the south of Croydon and a small acreage of agricultural country near Sutton. What was Middlesex contains many pleasant vistas, the heritage, it is hoped, of Londoners hundreds of years hence. Some of the most unspoilt countryside is in the Greater London Borough of Hillingdon to the north and west of Harrow, round Stanmore and Northwood, and from Mill Hill towards Barnet and Enfield Chace.

It is a heritage of which any city might be proud, the culmination of hundreds of years of endeavour by leaders of local and central government and by private individuals.

15. The Motoring Age

DISPASSIONATE assessment of the twentieth century is out of the question. It is theoretically possible to be dispassionate in judgment on half of it but in practice it is so difficult as to be almost impossible. Looking back over the centuries that went before one can see the upward curve of progress; with equal facility one can pick out periods of ten or twenty years in which social and economic development appear to go into reverse and far longer periods when the impetus which drives people towards their goal appears to have died, when stagnation replaces progress and human misery steals the limelight of history.

Historians of the future will doubtless be able to define the real motifs of the twentieth century and will be able to give due weight to events and trends of fashion which bulk far too large in contemporary criticism. The people of the twelfth and thirteenth centuries at every level of society were calling for a return to the times of Good King Edward. It was customary for the Norman kings of England when pacifying their disgruntled subjects to promise them a return to the laws and customs of the said Good King Edward. But would the people really have liked to put the clock back to the first half of the eleventh century? They might have chosen to do so, but they must have been grievously disappointed if they had had their wish.

So it is today. Many people now not so young recall life as they knew it in their youth with endless nostalgia, 'Ah, those were the days.' They are aided and abetted in their hopeless longing for a return to the past by the voice of the Press. But they see the past through rose-coloured glasses, the dark smears blotted out by a trick of memory, the greatest service of which to mankind is to enable it to forget.

The history of Greater London in the twentieth century points this moral, if moral it is, as well as any facet of life, better than most. Greater London is one of the largest and most populous 'conurbations' in the world, the City of London still, as for a thousand years, the centre of Britain's economic life, Westminster still Royal Westminster, the West End still the arbiter of fashion, the standard of living in the hundreds of square miles which make up Greater London higher than in many parts of the country. But we are still not satisfied. If we cannot go back to imagined glories we must go forward towards the happiness which appears just round the corner.

Could it be otherwise in a period in which so much change has taken place not only in London, not only in Britain, but in the world? The nineteenth century was a time in which the full impact of the Industrial Revolution was felt. The twentieth century has been a time in which the inevitable though scarcely foreseeable results of that revolution have permeated into the home of every citizen, with the result that a social revolution, complete and irrevocable, has taken place. Class distinction has worn thin. The craftsman of today may be the millionaire of to-morrow, accepted into the once iron-bound circle of the aristocracy of birth.

The ordinary citizen's horizon has extended decade by decade. The railways began the story but their effect was negligible compared with that of the motor-car. Passive entertainment in the home is the prerogative of everyone every hour of the day. The modest breadwinner in his suburban home has as much right to a say in the government of the country as the noble lord in his Mayfair penthouse. Everything is writ large. And all this in a land fit for heroes, a working democracy committed to progressive ideals.

These are factors which have influenced the development of London since the turn of the century and which indirectly have determined its shape, its building styles, its distribution of population, its very existence as a living organism. Inevitably the accent in building has been on providing homes for the working people, who for the first time have not only deserved but demanded a home for every family. That has involved an acceleration of the outward spread already apparent in the nineteenth century. It does not matter whether one calls it slum clearance or municipal rehousing. It comes to the same thing and it is the principal factor which has determined the speed of Greater London's expansion, limited only by the labour and materials available.

The popularization of the motor-car as a means of family transport is the other factor which has contributed most to the expansion. The family motor-car can itself be regarded as an emblem of the social revolution, comparable with the greater influence which women have had indirectly in planning since they proved their worth as citizens in the crisis of the First World War. It is certainly women's influence which has had most effect on the design of the modern home, which occupies a disproportionate surface area compared with the homes available for people of comparable income a hundred and fifty years ago.

The century to date divides itself into three periods, each of which has witnessed a particular phase of Greater London's history. The first of the three consists of the fourteen years which preceded the outbreak of the First World War. It has been called a transitional phase by many commentators, comparable with the period of the Regency. It does indeed represent a transitional period in that it divides Victorian London from the very different London of the nineteen-twenties and thirties. But it is scarcely justifiable to stress its transitional character. Every age is transitional, in that it follows from one way of life and leads to another. The first fourteen years of the twentieth century were no more transitional than the years which immediately followed the Second World War. It is more accurate to say that the First World War marked a real break in tradition and that the beginning of the century looked back to Victorian times far more than it looked forward to the present day. Expansion continued. Estates continued to be developed, transport improved. There was a natural increase in population and a further influx of invaders from the countryside and provincial towns. There was much talk of decline compared with the reign of Queen Victoria.

The second period spans the twenty-one years between the two wars. That is a period which was different from any other in the story of London. It was, in effect, the story of unplanned expansion on a scale undreamt of before—and largely unplanned expansion which because of the motor-car and the motor-bus could take place in any direction and did not need to follow the lines of the railway network. It was a time of speculation run riot, of rocketing land values, but one in which at least hundreds of thousands of families found decent homes which their ancestors had never had, a period which was probably an essential forerunner of the years of progress which followed the end of the Second World War. Gradually planned development, universally acknowledged to be necessary, took the place of unplanned and uncontrolled expansion. Whether the planning is good or bad makes no difference to the basic fact that the need for it has been recognized and the machinery for enforcing it exists.

The City, the very hub of Greater London, though divorced from its government, was, as ever, conservative until the aerial bombardment of the Second World War made conservatism in this case meaningless. The inner zone, already overcrowded, is adjusting itself to changing conditions, giving itself a face-lift but not changing in essentials; the outer zone, which still has many gaps to fill, is busy in attempting to cope with the overflow from the inner zone, and is adventurously treading the few paths which have not so far been trodden.

The City of London has been largely rebuilt. By the beginning of the twentieth century it was prepared to rest on its laurels economically as well as architecturally. The first fourteen years of the twentieth century were mainly years of consolidation, of great businesses strengthening their foundations rather than of new enterprises breaking fresh ground. Queen Victoria Street and Ludgate Hill looked very much the same in 1913 as they did in 1900. Many of the businesses occupying their

Victorian premises were the same. Here and there roads were widened, office buildings enlarged, and occasionally rebuilt. But generally change was slow from year to year. Even after the First World War the picture did not vary much. Some businesses needed to expand and, finding lateral expansion impossible, became converts to vertical expansion in the American style. By 1939 an ever-increasing number of Victorian and Edwardian buildings were being replaced by modern blocks, many of them using the new building materials, steel and concrete, which had revolutionized the urban scene in American and many continental cities. But in London there was no sudden transition, but rather the conservative use of new methods, new designs and new materials as the exigencies of commerce dictated. The *Daily Express* building in an ultra-modern style of architecture caused much the same reaction as the Countess of Shrewsbury's Hardwick Hall ('more glass than wall') in the reign of the first Elizabeth. Eyebrows were discreetly raised and learned critics drew depressing pictures of London in a hundred years' time. Today the monstrous glasshouse fits well into the contemporary scene. So much for the gloomy forecasts based on a failure to appreciate the logical development of the use of new materials.

The inner zone comprising the West End and the majority of metropolitan boroughs showed a very different reaction to the changing times. In some districts stupendous efforts were made to clear the remaining slums. Modernizing for modernizing's sake was the order of the day. A large area of slum property was cleared and modern buildings put in the place of the slum tenements when Kingsway was built in the first years of the century. This represented the final stage of a plan which had begun nearly a hundred years before. The last vestiges of the rookery centred on St Giles were swept away. New homes brought new self-respect. It is a tribute to the foresight of these pioneers of rebuilding London that hundreds of the flats built in the area cleared are still serviceable homes for the descendants of their first tenants.

Northumberland House was one of the last of the palatial mansions between the City and Westminster to be demolished, but there were still a number of great houses farther west. A few of them have survived to this day—houses such as Derby House, Londonderry House and Hertford House. But many passed from the London scene between the wars. In Park Lane, Dorchester House, one of the finest of them all, gave way to the Dorchester Hotel in 1931, and Grosvenor House, the town house of the Dukes of Westminster, gave way four years earlier to a hotel of the same name. Both of the hotels were described as ugly buildings, both are now pointed out with pride by Londoners and admired by visitors.

Regent Street was given a completely new look and in this case the final disappearance of the Nash buildings, mutilated though they had been long before, was not only recorded with regret at the time but is still remarked upon with some lack of enthusiasm. That is partly

London Green. The numerous squares and hundreds of acres of parkland in the heart of London's West End form a vital part of its beauty. Pedestrians are attracted to Berkeley Square (*above*), with its lovely pattern of mature trees, to greet the early spring sunshine before the leaves are on the trees. In summer thousands of office workers flock to the shaded walks and lanes of Green Park (*below*). Berkeley Square, the Buckley Square of Thackeray's *Ballads*, was laid out in the latter part of the eighteenth century, the plane trees planted in 1789.

Gilding the Lily. The natural beauty of many of London's parks and gardens has been formalized, especially in the nineteenth century, and even in the present century the temptation to improve on nature has not always been resisted. Modern statuary is a feature of Battersea Park (*above*), where a visitor is emulating the sun worship of the statue. The Serpentine in Hyde Park, known as the Long Water where it traverses Kensington Gardens, was created by widening the course of the River Westbourne and building a dam at its eastern end. It was inspired by Queen Caroline, wife of George II. The Italian Gardens (*below*) were added at the head of the Long Water in the nineteenth century, the Prince Consort being credited with the design of the pavilion, left centre. Queen Anne's Alcove in the background, however, was part of the eighteenth-century layout of the gardens and is credited to William Kent.

Richmond's Terrace Gardens.
These gardens were originally part of the Richmond estate of The Dukes of Buccleugh. They were purchased in 1886 by the Richmond Vestry, laid out more or less in their present form, and opened to the public in the following year. They are justly famous for the views of the Thames, visible in the background of this picture. Many of the trees which beautified the Buccleugh estate have been retained and a number of flowering trees and formal flower beds have been added. The stone basin in the foreground was formerly a large ornamental fountain. The nude statue, after being in position for some years, was removed by order of the local council on the ground that it offended decency.

The Northern Heights.
Hampstead Heath, together with the adjoining Ken Wood and Parliament Hill Fields, is one of Greater London's largest and most beautiful open spaces. The greater part of the heath land has been allowed to remain in its natural state. The eastern part of the common land, which includes the artificial Highgate Ponds, a favourite place for sailing miniature yachts, falls within the former metropolitan borough of St Pancras, and until the formation of the Greater London Council was administered by the London County Council. The largest pond is pictured, with the typical group of Sunday morning sightseers interested in the launching of a yacht.

In Waterlow Park. This attractive example of landscape gardening, with many exotic trees and a large artificial pond, is situated on high ground between Highgate Village and Parliament Hill Fields. The park includes Lauderdale House, much restored and recently damaged by fire, in the time of Charles II the home of the first Duke of Lauderdale, who according to tradition made it available for the use of Nell Gwyn.

In Bushy Park. This royal park, formerly part of the estate of Hampton Court Palace, is best known perhaps for the triple row of chestnuts, now long past their prime, which mark the carriageway from the Teddington end to a point opposite the Lion Gate of Hampton Court, a major part of the landscape planning scheme carried out under the direction of Sir Christopher Wren. The herds of deer which graze over it, like the corresponding herds in Richmond Park, are another traditional feature.

[60]

Rivers of Greater London. The Wandle and the Ravensbourne, flowing northward into the Thames from the low hills which form the southern rim of the Thames basin, both retain several attractive reaches. The Wandle (*above*), which rises near Carshalton and empties itself into the Thames at Wandsworth, is here seen as a widening stream flowing through the parklands of Beddington. The Ravensbourne is fed by a spring traditionally known as Caesar's Well (*below*), the water from which flows into the Keston Ponds. The river emerges from the lower end of the Ponds and flows round the hill on which Bromley is built, continuing to the Thames at Deptford.

Twentieth-century Homes.
Many architectural styles have
made their bow since the turn of
the century, but the current trend
in home-building on the massive
scale is towards the steel-framed
structure with ample window
space designed for flats. The block
of flats in Lyte Street, E.2 (*top*), is
an excellent example of this
tendency carried out with restraint
and a due regard for utility. The
tree-lined green and the balconies
are interesting features. The
houses in Coulsdon (*centre*) make
a complete contrast. They are an
uninspired version of the Tudor
style which was especially popular
between the two wars and came
to be known, not inappropriately,
as 'by-pass Tudor' because of its
frequency on estates bordering the
new by-pass roads. But what
ingenuity went into their
construction! Connoisseurs will
notice with admiration the Tudor
brick arch of the garage and the
artfully contrived bent beams
above it. The typical corner of the
Becontree estate at Dagenham
(*bottom*) is equally illustrative of
the 'little box' type of villa in
this vast L.C.C. housing estate,
also built between the two world
wars.

A Modern Town Hall. One of the most graceful of public buildings erected during the nineteen-thirties in a distinctive modern style, Hornsey Town Hall was built in 1935 to the design of R. H. Uren.

Ribbon Development. The most unfortunate feature of planning, or rather lack of it, since 1920 has been the tendency for ribbon development along new by-pass or trunk roads. Here, immediately adjoining the Kingston by-pass, are houses, shops and factories. This self-defeatist policy has been resisted more strongly at Government level since the end of the Second World War.

Endeavour House, Hendon. Endeavour House represents the very latest trends in architecture and in industrial development. It was built by the Hendon Borough Council primarily to give factory and office accommodation to light industries formerly established in areas of the borough redeveloped as housing estates. There is room for seventeen moderate-sized firms in the one building. The design takes the principle of more glass than wall to the point of no return.

New Building in the City. In an effort to reduce car-parking problems in the City of London, the six-level covered car park shown below has been built by the banks of the Thames. The dome of St Paul's Cathedral can be seen in the background, still bravely holding its head above the office buildings, which many feared when the reconstruction of bombed London began would overshadow it.

[64]

because the redesigned Regent Street, opulent in appearance though it is, is a hotch-potch of disharmonious styles, clearly put together without the oversight of a master designer such as Nash. The Quadrant was rebuilt in 1926, remaining recognizably in a style based on that of Nash, doubtless a counterblast to the Tudor mansion of the Liberty store, completed in 1924. The discerning will find many styles represented, each block nudging its neighbour in impatient competition.

The effect was not always so unhappy as in Regent Street. The river front contains a variety of styles, the buildings spanning two centuries, but there is something magnificent in each of the three chief components, Somerset House, the Savoy Hotel and Shell-Mex House—each is admirable in its own way. Few would wish to change this grand vista (and when change comes, as it inevitably will, many will call for its preservation). The addition of the ultra-modern government offices between Westminster bridge and Hungerford bridge has added to the disparity of architecture, but here again the new building takes its place as of right, a fine composition in its own style, adding to rather than subtracting from the aesthetic value of the whole river frontage. Shell-Mex House was one of the first London buildings to show so clearly the influence of American architects, Bush House, between the Aldwych and the Strand, built in the nineteen-twenties, was another. Appropriately the archway which forms its entrance from the north has above it a sculptured group by Malvina Hoffman which symbolizes the cultural links between Great Britain and the United States.

Nothing could be more English than County Hall on the other side of the river. Though classical in design, it is certainly not scholarly, as some critics have described it, in the sense of being purely imitative. It shows little of the pedantic maintenance of conventional but unsuitable forms which mar many nineteenth- and early twentieth-century buildings.

The Roman Catholic Cathedral of Westminster, destined for long to be a landmark in the new London, though more adventurous, fits less harmoniously into its surroundings. Its architect, John Bentley, attempted to adapt Byzantine forms to the English climate, translating them freely in terms of brick and stone. It was impossible. The Cathedral looks today rather like a stranger in a strange land, surrounded on every side by earlier buildings and by the new glass and concrete structures which are gradually taking the place of the old buildings of brick and stone.

Everywhere in the West End the story was the same—new vistas in Oxford Street, new shops in Bond Street. Here and there imaginative new blocks arose in the twentieth-century style. The Freemasons' Hall in Great Queen Street, Unilever House (1932), a mixture of the old and the new, the giant new office blocks of Millbank (in harmony with the rebuilt Lambeth bridge, which was opened in 1932) and, above all, the Senate House of the University of London (1933–7)—these were

s

more than architectural triumphs. The last set Bloomsbury firmly on a pedestal as the cultural centre of Greater London and did something to repair one of London's greatest deficiencies.

It was not until 1836 that a charter was granted to the University of London. Even then the University was not more than an examining body for academic degrees, and it was 1900 before it had been converted fully into a teaching university. The chief milestone in its transition was the incorporation of University College and King's College into the new University. But the building of the Senate House (which contains the University Library) and the adjoining blocks marked the first real attempt to give unity to the University. Even now much of the University's instruction is given at institutions separated geographically and administratively from Bloomsbury.

The clearance of the slums of inner London and the multiplication of larger commercial premises spelt one certain thing for a number of the metropolitan boroughs—depopulation. The City, as we have seen, was being depopulated steadily from the seventeenth century onwards. The inner boroughs were equally affected. Southwark, for instance, had a steady decline from the turn of the century until 1931, when the population was 172,000. This fell in twenty years to 97,000. Many saw in this the effect of wartime bombardment and the consequent dispersal of the population. Between 1951 and 1961, however, the number of residents fell still further, to 86,000, and is still decreasing at the rate of about a thousand a year.

The population of Hackney, a little farther from the centre, was 219,000 in 1901 and still rising. It reached a peak of 223,000 in 1911, held it during the next ten years, but fell away by 1951 to 171,000 and in 1961 to 165,000. In the ten years between 1951 and 1961 Battersea lost 11,000, Bermondsey 9,000, Bethnal Green 11,000, Deptford 7,000, Fulham 10,000, Hammersmith 9,000, Islington 7,000 and Westminster 14,000, the biggest loss of all. Among the metropolitan boroughs Stoke Newington is the only one which maintained a more or less constant population.

As rehousing continues, many of these areas will show a further decrease in the number of residents. In the old County of London only the outer boroughs were increasing their population, and those only slowly. Kensington, for instance, showed an increase of about 3,000 between 1951 and 1961, Hampstead one of 4,000, but even these have probably reached something near their zenith. What a contrast these figures show in the way of living when they are compared with the corresponding figures for private dwellings, which increased between 1951 and 1961 in Southwark, for instance, by 2,000, in Hackney by nearly 3,000, and in prosperous Kensington by 11,000 or more than 25 per cent, and in Stoke Newington by 5,000, or nearly 50 per cent.

The obvious question which arises from this statistical survey of some of the metropolitan boroughs is: 'Where do the people go?' The equally obvious answer is 'Into the areas of Greater London farther from the centre.' The expansion of population in some of these outer areas has been quite as dramatic as the contraction in the inner areas. The area of Malden and Coombe, for instance, increased from a population of 6,000 in 1901 to 46,000 in 1961. Between 1921 and 1961 Hendon increased from 58,000 to 150,000; Bexley from 21,000 in 1921 to 90,000 in 1961; Sutton and Cheam from 45,000 in 1931 to 78,000 thirty years later. Many districts showed similar increases.

The bare figures give an idea of the changes that took place. The reality was often more striking than imagination can depict. Many square miles of farming country disappeared under roads and houses in an incredibly short space of time, especially between 1921 and 1938, when the apparently insatiable demand for accommodation had not yet been satisfied. Later many rows of new houses began to display notices 'For Sale' or, less frequently, 'To Let'.

Then came the cataclysm of the Second World War and a new demand which all the years of building since its end has not satisfied. The style of building which, after all, is the determining factor in the appearance of Greater London varied in sympathy, as it were, with conditions in the period 1900 to 1914 and of 1919 to 1939 and again in the years since 1945. In the first period there was little to distinguish the rows of villas from those of the preceding century. Many people thoughtlessly, but understandably, fail to differentiate between the Victorian and the Edwardian, consigning both with equal vigour to the scrap-heap. It is certainly true that some of the less elegant terraces of suburban London which are described as Victorian are in sober fact Edwardian.

In public building the battle between the giants of the Gothic Revival and the protagonists of the Classical Revival was still being waged endlessly. If size is a sign of excellence, some of the town halls and other public buildings of the beginning of the century must be excellent indeed. They are exemplified by East Ham's town hall, which was completed just before the turn of the century. It makes a striking contrast with the regular lines of neighbouring Dagenham's civic centre, the first part of which was opened shortly before the outbreak of the Second World War. There is a more modern annex to the East Ham town hall and to many others, which have proved inadequate for increasing civic business, but Lewisham is one of very few places where one could see with a single sweep of the eye the municipal styles of three generations: the Gothic of the original Victorian town hall, opened in 1875; the quite typical 1932 extension; and the contemporary office annex in a very forward-looking style of architecture. By the time this last addition was in progress of construction it was time, according to the council, to rebuild the original town hall.

Since the Second World War most new dwelling-places have been designed for people of moderate means, but that was not so universally

true in the period before the First World War. Two experiments in
suburban planning carried out during the first few years of the century
were highly successful. One is the Hampstead Garden Suburb, which
represents the dream come true of Dame Henrietta Barnett. With the
help of Sir Edwin Lutyens and other distinguished architects she
devised a town planning scheme which it would be difficult to better.
It was strongly reminiscent of the earliest London squares, with its
green surrounded by houses in a Renaissance style of architecture and
its own places of worship on the green. The first stones were laid in
1907 and the planned population of 14,000 was reached soon after the
end of the First World War.

The Woodcote Estate in Purley was being developed about the same
time. This was frankly a wealthy man's estate, each house built to a
different plan, each with its own large garden—large enough to include
a tennis court while leaving ample space for horticulture. The architectural ideas of the purchasers contributed in some cases to the design
of the house. The result inevitably is a strange mixture of styles but not
always a displeasing one.

The Woodcote Estate provides a link between the last decade of the
nineteenth century and the first decade of this century. Its 'village
green' has become a memorial dedicated to the use of the public in
memory of the residents of Coulsdon and Purley who sacrificed their
lives in the two wars. The adjoining Promenade de Verdun is more
especially a monument to the allied casualties at the Battle of Verdun
in the First World War. It is flanked by Lombardy poplars which have
grown in a mixture of French and English soil. Ten tons of earth were
brought from Armentières.

Dagenham is the between-wars complement of the garden suburb
and of Woodcote, a production-line development designed for people
whose work lay mainly on the production lines of modern factories. It
was and still is unique in the sheer size of its conception. It was a
project which threatened abysmal failure but has become outstandingly
successful. Dagenham, or rather the Becontree housing estate, to give
it the name by which the project was designated, was conceived under
the Act of 1919, which in effect permitted the London County Council
to purchase land outside the boundaries of the county for rehousing.
The plan was for an estate of 90,000 to 100,000 inhabitants governed by
a single local authority. Things did not quite work out like that. Three
thousand acres of land were bought, most of it in Dagenham but some
in Ilford and Barking. Consequently three local authorities had
responsibilities for various parts of it. Moreover for various administrative reasons building was most uneven, with three thousand houses
completed in some years, less than a thousand in others. Delays
occurred in supplying essential services. Transport took a long time to
organize, and the strain put on the area, the population of which before
1919 had been less than 10,000, by the influx of such a large number

of people proved severe. Full employment was also difficult to achieve.

By the middle thirties Dagenham had passed the stage of first teething troubles. By then there were great new industries expanding rapidly and providing employment. The people, mostly from East London, had settled into their new surroundings not, as one might have thought, adapting their character to their surroundings but rather re-establishing the community life of East London on this unlikely site.

This is the largest housing estate in the world, its 90,000 people accommodated almost exclusively in red-brick two-storey houses with no central community centre, no central shopping facilities. What distinguishes it from the new towns and most of the estates planned since 1939 is that it was designed as a working-class community. The unfriendliness and stress which occur in many new communities are absent. As Peter Willmott says in *The Evolution of a Community*: 'People see their fellows not as adversaries but as allies in a general advance.' Perhaps Dagenham has something to teach the planners of the sixties and seventies.

Private enterprise building resulted in an equal change in the face of the countryside, an equal or greater wastage of agricultural land, following generally in the wake of the roads and the tube extensions. Morden and Cockfosters are classical examples of the latter. The suburban development near the Great West Road, and the Kingston by-pass, are good examples of the former.

A marked difference between this middle-class housing and the Becontree estate was that it lacked the uniformity of the latter. Although it occupies a vast acreage in all it was normally carried out in smaller parcels. In places the trees of the countryside were retained and a real effort made to preserve a rural aspect, though not often with much success. Many of the cherry and apple trees which grace suburban Kent were once the trees of orchards, and there is more than a trace of surviving woodland in parts of suburban Surrey.

The architecture of the new middle-class housing estates was conservative and undistinguished except for an outburst of what became known sarcastically as by-pass Tudor. To be fair, the Tudor style was no more prevalent along the by-passes than on some of the new estates far from any main road. In Old Coulsdon the Tudor style predominates to a remarkable degree, complete with Tudor arches spanning the built-in garages and twisted black timber beams interspersed among the bricks of the façade. Ye Olde Tudor Inn completes the picture of 'Merrie England'.

One feature common to all the new estates, whether built by municipal effort or private enterprise, was that every home had its garden. Even in the motoring age gardening took and still takes pride of place among the household's summer occupations. In the wealthier districts the jobbing gardener came into his own but always as the assistant to the master of the house. There is no need to underline the fact obvious since the seventeenth century that every Englishman loves a garden. Now it is his privilege to possess one of his own.

As Greater London expanded, pressure on accommodation near the centre did not decrease. It became a choice between a home with a garden in the outer suburbs and a flat in a new block with the advantage of proximity to central London. Dolphin Square in Pimlico with a population comparable with that of many small towns was an outstanding achievement. It boasted proudly of being the largest block of flats in Europe.

If the twentieth century is regarded primarily as one in which the four corners of the earth have been brought closer together, the construction of London Airport, a truly international one, within the limits of the new Greater London takes on a new significance. Heath Row until 1939 was a hamlet in the urban district of Yiewsley and West Drayton. The first stage towards making it London Airport was its wartime choice as a site near London capable of handling military transport aircraft. Work began in 1944 on clearing the agricultural land in an area of more than four square miles and demolishing the buildings which stood on it. Before the airfield was ready the war was over.

But for the accident of war Greater London might not have had its modern airport so soon. The first civil aeroplane used the field in June 1946. The airport's development has been as remarkable as that of any other feature of the Greater London scene. In its first full year of operation it handled less than 100,000 passengers. In recent years the number has been climbing towards ten million. The number of aircraft landings and take-offs has increased from 2,000 to more than 150,000 in the same period. London Airport can substantiate two remarkable claims, first that it is the busiest airport in Europe, second that more international passengers pass through it than through any other airport in the world.

16. Epilogue

During the last seventy years London has expanded more than it did in two thousand years before. Most of this recent expansion has been haphazard. Whatever planning there may have been has been chaotic. The 'monster' has become out of control and nothing now, it seems, can bring it under control again.

The London County Council was constituted in 1888. Eleven years later the metropolitan boroughs were delineated. The London County Council remained the central administrative body for more than sixty years after that, while the boundaries of the county were not altered. But nothing stopped London's outward spread, which absorbed the whole of Middlesex and parts of Buckinghamshire, Essex, Kent, Surrey and Hertfordshire. Throughout the whole of this period the City of London remained independent of the County of London, as it still is of the Greater London Council, with its own police force and its own government headed by the Lord Mayor. But that makes little difference. The City of London remains the centre of what was formerly the County of London and now has become the area administered by the Greater London Council. It is part of an integrated whole, however massive, still the commercial and financial centre of the new Greater London.

An ever-increasing number of buildings were built near the centre to accommodate the staffs of companies which regarded office accommodation in central London as a status symbol, especially after the devastation caused by aerial bombardment in the Second World War. Arterial roads assisted the development of suburbs as the car began to usurp the functions of the railway. The First World War made little impact. Few buildings were destroyed and the shape of London did not alter. After the war a wave of speculative building engulfed many green fields and much of the farmland within a radius of twenty miles of the City centre. Had it not been for the slump in the thirties this outward spread might have proved fatal to the last of the farmlands within this area.

Since the Second World War development companies and local authorities have ensured that every available acre of land within that

radius has been put to use, many of them buying up old houses as far
afield as Croydon and Chingford merely for the purpose of pulling
them down and building blocks of flats in their place. It is a sad story,
but perhaps a necessary one. London, in effect, broke its bounds
between the beginning of the twentieth century and the present day. It
has paid the inevitable price. It no longer exists as a town, only as a
conurbation.

'Live in Metroland' was the catch-phrase of the Metropolitan
Railway, and a very effective one. 'Metroland' extended as far as
Aylesbury. Walthamstow and Kentish Town became areas of tenements. It was only the determination of the Government, assisted by
the London County Council, to establish a green belt which slowed the
uncontrolled expansion of London.

A new London has emerged but it is a London of steel and concrete
and glass, of towers rising high above the level of the houses, of office
blocks and blocks of flats far, far different from anything that has gone
before. These may be well designed—some of them certainly are—but
none of them are in the tradition of the London which most of us
know and have come to love, whether in the City or in the inner
suburbs such as Battersea or Chelsea, or even in the outer suburbs such
as Croydon. To many observers of the London scene the new 'sky-
scrapers' appear as interlopers, however well designed, however well
the architects may have interpreted their instructions.

The City will certainly continue to be the commercial and financial
centre of the Commonwealth, as long as the latter term means anything,
and Westminster will continue to be the seat of government. The City
was virtually destroyed in the war of 1939–45. The delay in its rebuilding was due mainly to other priorities, principally the need to provide
dwelling-places not only for the people of London but for millions of
others in Britain as a whole. The target of up to 300,000 new houses a
year for the country as a whole set by post-war governments demanded
in the years immediately following the end of the war the fullest use of
Britain's resources. The building of offices and public buildings had to
wait until the housing programme was well under way. Twenty years
after the end of the war many plans for redevelopment which had been
approved were still incomplete.

In October 1964 the first of the 'chief planners' for Greater London
was appointed: Mr Bernard Collins, who previously had been Secretary
of the Commission for the New Towns. That was a step in the right
direction. Clearly Greater London needs a central planning authority.
On his appointment Mr Collins committed himself to the opinion that
decisions about expansion in the green belt area should be more 'firmly
entrenched' than others, and added that there must be a quantitative
plan for London which included finding out how many people could
work in a particular area and could be brought to it by rail or road
without ruining it. Few would disagree with him.

Yet it is difficult to take planning seriously, whether the planning is in the hands of a government ministry or a local authority. There is perhaps no validity in the philosophy of history, so called, but at least when events repeat themselves so often one has some reason for supposing that the sequence of events will once more occur.

During the last two hundred years the expansion of London encroached on the immediate environs of the City and Westminster before running riot in the outer suburbs. It has flowed round the inner parks and swallowed all the communities within the old County of London, so that a continuous development has linked Stratford with Hammersmith, Hampstead with Clapham. Then expansion surged on again down the corridors of the main roads and railway lines into the countryside of the new Greater London until it was brought up against the rampart of the green belt, which is an artificial creation of the twentieth century designed solely to hold in the monstrous flood. At every point round the vast perimeter the flood has reached the edge of the green belt. Already trickles have seeped through the weak points down the roads and railway lines to the farther side of the belt.

An artificial barrier like the green belt can be demolished as easily as it can be created. There is no more difficulty in encroaching on the woods and fields of the belt than in slicing off a section of Hyde Park to build a road. Whatever is done is done against the background of economic necessity or convenience. But so far the green belt has stood firm, buffeted a little, suffering a few slight encroachments, but still easily recognizable for what it is.

Meanwhile, as the flood has engulfed hundreds of square miles of country the reservoir which feeds it is almost empty. The population of the City of London has fallen decade by decade, or rather the night population has fallen. It is now a place in which to work, not in which to sleep. Blocks of flats erected in it since the Second World War for people who work in it are regarded as something of an oddity. The population of Westminster has tended to decline, too, in spite of the building of vast new blocks of flats. Pressure is exerted no longer from the centre but from points along the zone which once represented the perimeter of the flood. To move from the City to Islington was tantamount to moving into the country two hundred years ago. With Islington engulfed, people moved on over the northern heights to Finchley, and from Finchley they moved on to Barnet, ever outwards, always seeking a sight of green fields, a breath of country air, or to be more precise, a home in the kind of surroundings in which it was possible to cultivate a garden at their back door and take a Sunday walk in the country.

One thing which is certain is that the new Greater London with its thirty-two boroughs and the City of London is an administrative entity far more realistic than the County of London and likely to provide the local government of eight million people or more for the next fifty

years. As the new boroughs are greater in population than the metropolitan boroughs of yesteryear or the local government areas outside
the County of London, they will individually have more authority. The
Greater London Council is, in effect, a planning council, a co-ordinating
body which is expected to delegate more of its powers to the constituent boroughs than the London County Council did to the metropolitan boroughs. The following is a complete list of the new boroughs,
with a note of the areas which they cover and a rough estimate of their
populations based on the 1961 census.

No.		*Population*
1.	Westminster, including the City of Westminster and the metropolitan boroughs of Paddington and St Mary-lebone	269,000
2.	Camden, including the metropolitan boroughs of Hampstead, Holborn and St Pancras	246,000
3.	Islington, including the metropolitan boroughs of Finsbury and Islington	262,000
4.	Hackney, including the metropolitan boroughs of Hackney, Shoreditch and Stoke Newington	257,000
5.	Tower Hamlets, including the metropolitan boroughs of Bethnal Green, Poplar and Stepney	205,000
6.	Greenwich, including the metropolitan boroughs of Greenwich and Woolwich, except the part of Woolwich which was situated north of the Thames	230,000
7.	Lewisham, including the metropolitan boroughs of Deptford and Lewisham	290,000
8.	Southwark, including the metropolitan boroughs of Bermondsey, Camberwell and Southwark	313,000
9.	Lambeth, including the whole of the metropolitan borough of Lambeth and part of the metropolitan borough of Wandsworth	341,000
10.	Wandsworth, including the metropolitan borough of Battersea and the parts of the metropolitan borough of Wandsworth not included in Lambeth	335,000
11.	Hammersmith, including the metropolitan boroughs of Fulham and Hammersmith	222,000
12.	The Royal Borough of Kensington and Chelsea, includ-ing, as its name so aptly suggests, the metropolitan boroughs of Kensington and Chelsea	218,000
13.	Waltham Forest, including the metropolitan boroughs of Chingford, Leyton and Walthamstow	248,000
14.	Redbridge, including the municipal boroughs of Ilford, Wanstead and Woodford, part of the municipal borough of Dagenham, and part of the urban district of Chigwell	249,000

No.   *Population*

15. Havering, including the municipal borough of Romford
    and the urban district of Hornchurch   .   .   .   243,000
16. Barking, including the greater part of the municipal
    borough of Barking bounded by Barking Creek, and
    the greater part of the municipal borough of Dagen-
    ham (except for the small area included in No. 14)   .   179,000
17. Newham, including the county boroughs of East Ham
    and West Ham, a fragment of the old metropolitan
    borough of Woolwich north of the Thames, and a
    fragment of the old municipal borough of Barking
    west of Barking Creek   265,000
18. Bexley, including the municipal boroughs of Bexley and
    Erith, the urban district of Crayford and that part of
    the urban district of Chislehurst and Sidcup which
    lies north of A 20   210,000
19. Bromley, including the municipal boroughs of Becken-
    ham and Bromley, the urban districts of Orpington
    and Penge, and part of the urban district of Chisle-
    hurst and Sidcup south of A 20   294,000
20. Croydon, including the county borough of Croydon
    and the urban district of Coulsdon and Purley .   .   327,000
21. Sutton, including the municipal boroughs of Beddington
    and Wallington, and of Sutton and Cheam, and the
    urban district of Carshalton   169,000
22. Merton, including the municipal boroughs of Mitcham
    and Wimbledon, and the urban district of Merton and
    Morden   189,000
23. Kingston upon Thames, including the municipal
    boroughs of Kingston-upon-Thames, Malden and
    Coombe, and Surbiton   146,000
24. Richmond upon Thames, including the municipal
    boroughs of Barnes, Richmond and Twickenham   .   182,000
25. Hounslow, including the municipal boroughs of Brent-
    ford and Chiswick, and of Heston and Isleworth, and
    the urban district of Feltham   209,000
26. Hillingdon, including the municipal borough of Ux-
    bridge and the urban dictricts of Hayes and Harling-
    ton, of Ruislip-Northwood, and of Yiewsley and West
    Drayton   228,000
27. Ealing, including the municipal boroughs of Acton,
    Ealing and Southall   300,000
28. Brent, including the municipal boroughs of Wembley
    and Willesden   296,000
29. Harrow, comprising the old municipal borough of
    Harrow   209,000

No.   *Population*

30. Barnet, including the municipal boroughs of Finchley
   and Hendon, and the urban districts of Barnet, East
   Barnet and Friern Barnet   318,000
31. Haringey, including the municipal boroughs of
   Hornsey, Tottenham and Wood Green   .   .   .   259,000
32. Enfield, including the municipal boroughs of Enfield,
   Edmonton and Southgate   274,000

It is anybody's guess how these new and strange boroughs (with apologies to Harrow) will design the Greater London of the future. There is unending conflict—conflict between those who desire to preserve the London of yesteryear and those whose only interest is to develop a new London without thought of the historic heritage, between those who believe that the old roads should be retained and those who see only the need to improve the flow of traffic. 'Traffic-crazy planners' is a phrase which one has seen more than once but it certainly represents a school of thought which would prefer to sacrifice the legacy of the past to the convenience of the future. As Wentworth Day wrote so trenchantly in December of 1963 about Hampton Wick, which is threatened by a new bridge across the Thames involving the demolition of a number of historic houses: 'All the clanking monstrous machinery of the developer, that hydra-headed Moloch, is waiting to rumble in, plough up, batter down and bully its way through houses, gardens and beauty.'

Harsh words, perhaps, but with the ring of truth in them. The London of only thirty years ago is disappearing so fast in the cause of 'improvement' that one is bound to wonder whether the past must be sacrificed entirely to the present and whether the sacrifice always brings the benefits which it is expected to do. Certainly the vast increase in the number of motor-cars has slowed down traffic not only in the City and the West End but in all parts of Greater London to an alarming extent.

The efforts to find a solution are by no means always effective. London has a far greater problem to solve than Chicago with its vast downtown car parks and its shopping and commercial centres within relatively easy reach of them. That is because Greater London is not one town but the combination of many, each with its own business and shopping centres, a far more complex growth than any other in Europe or America.

Grandiose schemes have been announced in recent years by many local authorities. One can only assume that most of these will be carried out by the councils of the new Greater London boroughs. Some, like the motorway on stilts linking London Airport with the Kensington area, are already realities; others, like the £5,000,000 redevelopment scheme for St Mary Cray, have already started. The motorway M 1 will certainly find its way into Greater London by one route or another. The construction of a motorway along the railway line by Blackheath is not yet a reality but there is at least a probability that what the committee representing fifteen local organizations described as 'a belt of noise and fumes thrown across an area of high amenity' will become a reality before many years have passed.

The Hyde Park Corner-Marble Arch road improvement scheme has already been completed and has indeed improved the traffic flow in this part of London, although some motorists maintain that it has caused a greater build-up of traffic and consequent delay on the approach roads. The cost has been the loss of a small part of Hyde Park and of the Cumberland Screen which formerly graced the Marble Arch entrance to Hyde Park. The Cumberland Screen is not necessarily a great loss to London. It dates only from 1910 and London soot had already caused grave damage to its fabric. Perhaps it is fortunate to have found a home (at a cost of £1,055) outside a Lancashire textile factory. But its removal is symptomatic of the ruthless way in which local and central authorities have interpreted the need to modernize London.

Uxbridge has announced a redevelopment scheme for the whole of the central area of the town involving multi-level circulation of pedestrians and wheeled traffic, with complete segregation of the two as the final part of the scheme, which, it is expected, may take twenty years to complete. That is not an isolated example of the growing tendency to segregate pedestrians from motor traffic in the shopping centres of the constituent towns of Greater London. The idea has already been adopted in the planning of some of the New Towns outside London and is an integral part of Romford's plan for preserving its market-place as a zone reserved wholly for shoppers on foot, with a ring road and abundant parking spaces on the perimeter.

Sutton has an equally magnificent scheme for the redevelopment of the town centre, a far more acceptable one than most because no historic buildings are involved. This scheme also will take twenty years to complete and involves the provision of parking space for 8,000 cars, traffic-free shopping precincts, and new office blocks for firms which see the advantages of moving out of central London.

Even today a few open spaces not dedicated as public parks or commons are available in Greater London. One of them is the now disused Croydon Airport. Here again the scheme is idealistic, providing housing for more than 5,000 people on about 115 acres, with segregation of pedestrians and motor traffic, leaving more than 250 acres free for the provision of public open spaces and playing fields. This community would be virtually a New Town, with four schools and three churches as well as shops, a library and other public amenities. The only snag to this development is the proposal to build a new motorway, M 23, across the airport. Here again the conflict between the many needs of the great city is apparent.

In the inner areas, in the West End, in Westminster and in the City, similar conflicts are even more apparent. The rebuilding of the City is far from complete but the skyline has changed out of all recognition since 1945. That is not surprising, since of the forty-seven churches which remained within the City boundaries at the outbreak of war, twenty were completely destroyed or damaged beyond repair, as were eighteen of the thirty-six livery halls. The Guildhall has been rebuilt, many new fine blocks of offices have appeared, one of the finest of them Bucklersbury House. Many medieval churches, such as St Giles, Cripplegate, have been restored or rebuilt, as have a number of the Wren churches. The Coal Exchange was one of many buildings sacrificed to road widening, but the iron dragons above the portico were transferred, presumably as a memorial to the past, to mark the boundary of the City of London on the Victoria Embankment.

The Wren church of St Mary Aldermanbury has been another casualty but that has been re-erected on the campus of Fulton University in the U.S.A., where it must contrast strangely with the modern university buildings. On the other hand, the watch house of St Sepulchre Without Newgate, Holborn, has been rebuilt in perfect conformity with the building of 1791, the purpose of which was to check the activities of body-snatchers.

In the West End many schemes have been proposed to remodel Piccadilly Circus to resolve what Professor Colin Buchanan describes as 'the humiliating agony of the Circus'. Ultimately, of course, Piccadilly Circus and the surrounding streets will be rebuilt at an astronomical cost, but there is no certainty yet what form the new Circus will take. Nor is there any certainty whether the overdeck plan for Victoria station, that is to say, a roof to be built over Victoria station which would provide an assembly point for travellers by rail, coach and air, will mature within a reasonable time.

Covent Garden Market will certainly be removed from its present site, perhaps to Nine Elms, and that will make possible the complete replacement of the area first planned by the Russell family with the help of Inigo Jones. The area includes Great Queen Street, which still retains a number of Georgian houses. One hopes that some of these will be spared in the redevelopment scheme.

One important scheme which has made good headway is the provision of a riverside promenade on the South Bank of the Thames between Blackfriars bridge and Waterloo bridge. Land has already been reclaimed here and the river wall is being extended. An hotel and shopping area will be built on a site which includes about $3\frac{1}{4}$ acres.

These are only a few typical examples of the changes which will alter the face of Greater London. A recent curb on further development and an outstanding example of the conflict between the three keystones of planning—provision of more accommodation, the avoidance of such concentration of employment in one area that travel to the place of employment becomes impossible, and the need of dispersal in the scheme of national defence—was evidenced by the announcement in the House of Commons by the Labour Government in November of 1964 that from the time of the announcement there would be a standstill on new office projects in London and that permits from the Board of Trade would in future be necessary both for new building and for the change of use of buildings within a radius of forty miles from Charing Cross.

This was nothing new. It will be interesting to observe during the next twenty or thirty years how effective the bill will be, how soon it will be forgotten.

The conflict of planners in recent years is exemplified by the opposition of the London County Council in 1963 to the proposal of British Railways to redevelop the Euston Road aspect of Euston station by building several blocks of offices. Here the conflict is clear. The supposition is that the offices when built would be let and the revenue would have accrued to British Railways, which in the final event is subsidized by the taxpayer. So, in however minute a degree, the new office blocks which the London County Council had the power to forbid would have put money directly into the pocket of the taxpayer. The position of the Council was equally clear. It had agreed after consultation with the Ministry of Town and Country Planning to limit the provision of additional office space in the central area so as to prevent further road congestion and this, it might be argued, relieved the taxpayer of expense, namely that of providing new or wider roads to accommodate the additional traffic which might be expected to result from building more blocks of offices on this particular site.

The many pleas at government level which have been made for dispersal of population are only an echo of the declared policy of governments for five hundred years. Today we are told that London must sprawl no wider because it makes such a good target for nuclear bombs. A similar consideration determined policy between the two world wars, the only difference being that then the fear was of aerial bombardment rather than attack by guided missiles.

The benefits of removing industry from London to Northumberland or Lancashire, to Clydeside, or even across the North Channel to Northern Ireland, are widely advertised to industrialists but few respond to the invitation. Still the drift goes on, the drift from country to town, as fewer are required to work the land, and from Wales and Scotland and the north of England to the area of the metropolis. Nothing, positively nothing, restrains the movement. There is much talk, even more writing, but little action.

If the past is any guide to the future the growth will continue. The only difference which the railway and the motor-car have made is to allow a greater outward spread and so make it possible for people to live in the country and work in the town. The preservation of a green belt may be a sacred trust but already some of the towns beyond the green belt have become virtually suburbs of London, and the Greater London of today still does not embrace the whole of the vast area which looks to London as its place of work.

Queen Elizabeth I was as alarmed at the 140,000 people who sheltered within the walls of London as twentieth-century ministers have been at the eight million who provide a target for nuclear explosions. In 1580 the Queen issued from Nonesuch Palace a proclamation which called attention to the danger of a growing London exposed to risk from plague owing to overcrowding and want of food through difficulty of distribution. She expressly forbade the building of any further houses within the City walls or within three miles of any of its gates. The proclamation also laid it down that only one family should live in a house, calling on the City Corporation to disperse any surplus population. What a farce it was! The opportunity was taken to expel some beggars from the streets of London but that was all. Long before the Queen's death the order was utterly forgotten, or forgotten at least by the Corporation of London, though not by King James I, who gave orders for all the houses which had been erected contrary to Queen Elizabeth's proclamation to be demolished.

King James seems to have felt even more strongly about the problem than Queen Elizabeth. In 1617, and again in 1624, he gave instructions for all noblemen who did not have business in the City to go to their country homes and remain there until they were recalled to Parliament, and then to leave their wives and children in the country. His example was followed by his successors and there was a similar Order in Council of Charles II in 1674. Before then Cromwell was responsible for an Act fining anyone who had erected a house without land attached the then enormous sum of £100.

The visitations of the plague probably did more than any royal edicts to discourage people from living in the capital, but once the plague had ceased it was soon forgotten. By the end of the seventeenth century the population of London and its suburbs was approaching half a million, by the beginning of the nineteenth century a million (the census of 1801 showed the actual population of London, Westminster, Southwark and adjacent areas to be 864,845). Today the population of Greater London is more than eight million.

When will they ever learn?

Books about Greater London

No SINGLE book which I have found deals with the area of the new Greater London as a whole, or with any area approximate to it. The volumes of the Victoria County Histories where available are fine source books but, unfortunately, too technical in the main to interest the general reader. This is equally true of the original series and of the volumes currently being published. More than fifty years in some cases separates the publication of volumes dealing with the same county. So Volume 2 of the *Victoria History of the County of Middlesex* was published in 1911, Volume 3 in 1962. All, however, are works of genuine scholarship, well presented for historians, however much they vary in style and approach.

Books dealing with individual parishes or local government areas, by contrast, are legion. The nineteenth century was the golden age of local topography. Many are excellent, almost all are interesting. The following is a long but far from complete list in which I have marked with an asterisk those books (including some modern ones) which I have found most informative. Most of those listed are long out of print but copies of almost all are in the appropriate local libraries.

Numbers in square brackets refer to the new Greater London boroughs
in the map on p. xvi

ANDERSON, J. C.: *Short Chronicle concerning the Parish of Croydon*, 1883 [20]
* BAKER, W. K.: *Acton, Middlesex*, 1912 [27]
BARRATT, T. J.: *The Annals of Hampstead*, 3 vols., 1912 [2]
BARTLETT, W. A.: *The History and Antiquities of the Parish of Wimbledon*, 1865 [22]
BEARER, A.: *Memories of Old Chelsea*, 1892 [12]
BEDFORD, G., and RICHES, T. H.: *History of Uxbridge*, 1818 [26]
BENTHAM, T.: *History of Beddington*, 1923 [21]
BESANT, W.: *East London*, 1903
BIGGERS, J. R.: *Finchley and its Neighbourhood* [30]

* BLANCH, W. H.: *Ye Parish of Camerwell*, 1877 [8]
  BOGER, C. C.: *Southwark and its Story*, 1881 [8]
* BORROWMAN, R.: *Beckenham, Past and Present*, 1910 [19]
  BOSWELL, J.: *The London Journal, 1762–1763*, Heinemann, 1950
  BOWERS, R. W.: *Sketches of Southwark Old and New* [8]
  BRAYBROOKE, N.: *London Green*, Gollancz, 1959
  BRETT-JAMES, N. G.: *The Story of Hendon Manor and Parish*, 1931 [30]
  BURNETT, R. G., and TATTERSALL, E. W.: *London Lives On*, Phoenix House, 1948
  CARTER, E.: *The Future of London*, 1962
  CHANCELLOR, E. B.: *History and Antiquities of Richmond*, 1894 [24]
  CHAPMAN, A.: *Handbook of Kingston*, 1877 [23]
  CHIBNALL, M.: *English Lands of the Abbey of Bec*, 1951
  CHINGFORD COUNTY HIGH SCHOOL MEMBERS: *Chingford*, 1959 [13]
  CLAPHAM, A. W.: *Lesnes Abbey*, 1915
  CLUNN, H. P.: *The Face of London*, Phoenix House, rev. ed. 1951
  COHEN-PORTHEIM, P.: *The Spirit of London*, 1935
  COPLEY, G. J.: *An Archaeology of South-East England*, Phoenix House, 1958
  COULL, THOMAS: *History and Traditions of Islington*, 1861 [3]; *History and Traditions of St. Pancras*, 1861 [2]
  COX, THOMAS: *Magna Britannica*, 1721
  CUNDALL, H. M.: *Bygone Richmond*, 1925 [24]
  DAVIS, T.: *The Architecture of John Nash*, Studio Books, 1960
  DE SALIS, RACHEL: *Hillingdon through Eleven Centuries*, 1926 [26]
  DENYER, C. H.: *St Pancras through the Ages*, 1935 [2]
  DEWS, N.: *History of Deptford*, 1884 [7]
* DRUETT, W. W.: *Harrow through the Ages*, 1956 [29]
* DU BOULAY, F. R. H.: *Medieval Bexley*, Bexley Public Library, 1961 [18]
  DUNCAN, L. L.: *History of the Borough of Lewisham*, 1908 [7]
  DYOS, H. J.: *Victorian Suburb: A study of the growth of Camberwell*, Leicester University Press, 1961 [8]
  ELLIS, H. M.: *Bygone Wimbledon and Merton*, 1906 [22]
* ELSLEY, H. W. R.: *Wembley through the Ages*, Wembley News, 1953 [28]
  EVANS, E. T.: *The History and Topography of the Parish of Hendon*, 1890 [30]
  EVELYN, J.: *The Diary of John Evelyn*, Oxford University Press, 1950
  EYRE, MONTGOMERY: *Saint John's Wood*, 1913 [1]
  FAULKNER, THOMAS: *The History and Antiquities of Brentford, Ealing and Chiswick*, 1845 [25, 27]; *Chelsea and its Environs*, 2 vols., 1829 [12]; *The History and Antiquities of Kensington*, 1820 [12]
  FISK, F.: *History of the Parish of Edmonton*, 1914 [32]
  FRY, K.: *History of the Parishes of East and West Ham*, 1888 [17]
* GAUNT, W.: *Chelsea*, Batsford, 1954 [12]

GODFREY, W. H.: *A History of Architecture in and around London*, Phoenix House, rev. ed. 1962

GREGORY, R. C.: *Story of Royal Eltham* [6]

HARRIS, J.: *The Parish of Erith in Ancient and Modern Times* [18]

HASTED, E.: *History and Topographical Survey of Kent*, Vol. I, 1797

HIGHAM, F.: *Southwark Story*, Hodder & Stoughton, 1955 [8]

* HORSBURGH, E. L. S.: *Bromley, Kent*, 1929 [19]

* HOWITT, WILLIAM: *The Northern Heights of London*, 1869

HUNTER, A.: *History of London and its Environs*, 1811

JACKSON, EDITH: *Annals of Ealing*, 1898 [27]

JOWETT, E. M.: *An Illustrated History of Merton and Morden*, Merton and Morden Committee, 1951 [22]

KENDRICK, T. D., and HAWKES, C. F. C.: *Archaeology in England and Wales 1914–1931*, 1932

LLOYD, J. H.: *History of Highgate*, 1888 [2]

* LOFTUS, E. A., and CHETTLE, H. F.: *A History of Barking Abbey*, Wilson & Whitworth, 1954 [16]

* LYSONS, D.: *The Environs of London*, 5 vols., 1792–1800

MACQUEEN-POPE, W.: *Goodbye Piccadilly*, Michael Joseph, 1960 [1]

MARSHALL, C. J.: *A History of the Old Villages of Sutton and Cheam*, 1936 [21]

MIDDLETON, J.: *View of the Agriculture of Middlesex*, 1798

MILLS, T.: *History of the Parish of Hayes*, 1874 [26]

MITCHELL, R. J., and LEYS, M. D. R.: *A History of London Life*, Longmans, Green, 1958

MURRAY, J. F.: *A Picturesque Tour of the River Thames*, 1865

* NELSON, J.: *The History, Topography and Antiquities of the Parish of St Mary, Islington*, 1811 [3]

O'LEARY, J. G.: *The Book of Dagenham*, Dagenham Borough Council, 1949 [6]

PEARSON, M. S.: *The Parish of Rotherhithe*, 1912 [8]

PEPYS, S.: *The Diary*, Everyman's Library edition, 1906

PERFECT, C. T.: *Ye Olde Village of Hornchurch*, 1917 [15]

PHILIP, G. W.: *History and Antiquities of the Parish of Bermondsey*, 1841 [8]

PINKS, W. S.: *The History of Clerkenwell*, 1865 [2]

POTTER, S.: *The Story of Willesden*, 1926 [28]

PRICKETT, F.: *History and Antiquities of Highgate*, 1842 [2]

RAMSEY, S.: *Historic Battersea*, 1913 [10]

RESKER, R. R.: *The History and Development of Purley*, 1916 [20]

* ROBBINS, MICHAEL: *Middlesex*, Collins, 1953

ROBINS, W.: *Paddington: Past and Present*, 1853 [1]

ROBINSON, W.: *The History and Antiquities of Edmonton*, 1819 [32]; *The History and Antiquities of the Parish of Hackney*, 1843 [4]; *The History and Antiquities of the Parish of Stoke Newington*, 1820 [4]; *History of Tottenham*, 1840 [31]

270

ROUMIEU, J. J.: *Ruislip*, 1875 [25]

SCOTT, W. S.: *Green Retreats*, 1955

SHAWCROSS, J. P.: *A History of Dagenham*, 1908 [6]

SMITH, H. L.: *History of East London*, 1939

SMITH, J. T.: *A Topographical and Historical Account of St Marylebone*, 1833 [1]

SMITH, R. P.: *A History of Sutton*, 1960 [21]

STOKES, A.: *East Ham: From Village to County Borough*, 1933 [17]

STOW, J.: *A Survey of London and Westminster*, 1598

STROUD, D.: *The Architecture of Sir John Soane*, Studio Books, 1961

* SUMMERSON, JOHN: *Georgian London*, Pleiades Books, 1945

TASKER, C.: *The History of Ilford*, 1900 [14]

TERRY, G.: *Memories of Old Romford*, 1888 [15]

TRENCH, F. C.: *The Story of Orpington from Olden Times to the Present Day*, 1897 [19]

* TUFFS, J. C.: *The Story of Wanstead and Woodford*, 1962 [14]

* VULLIAMY, C. E.: *The Archaeology of Middlesex and London*, 1940

WALFORD, E.: *Greater London*, 1890–5

WATSON, I. L.: *A History of West Wickham, Kent*, P. M. E. Erwood Ltd, 1959 [19]

WEBSTER, A. D.: *The Regent's Park and Primrose Hill*, 1911

WILLIAMS, GWYN A.: *Medieval London: from Commune to Capital*, Athlone Press, 1963

WILLIAMS, J.: *Historical Notes on Wallington*, 1867 [21]

WRIGHT, JESSIE D.: *London's Old Buildings*, 1936

WROTH, W. and A. E.: *The London Pleasure Gardens of the Eighteenth Century*, 1896.

Index

N.B. Bold figures indicate page number of plate, and asterisks illustrations in the text